PARTS OF A WORLD

PARTS OF A WORLD

W·A·L·L·A·C·E S·T·E·V·E·N·S REMEMBERED

An oral biography

BY *PETER BRAZEAU*

RANDOM HOUSE · NEW YORK

Portions of chapters 1–5 and 8 have been published, in slightly different form, as: "Poet in
a Grey Business Suit: Glimpses of Stevens at the Office," *The Wallace Stevens Journal*,
Spring 1977; "Wallace Stevens on the Podium: The Poet as Public Man of Letters," *The
Wallace Stevens Journal*, Fall/Winter 1977; " 'A Collect of Philosophy': The Difficulty of
Finding What Would Suffice" and "A Trip in a Balloon: A Sketch of Stevens' Later Years
in New York," in *Wallace Stevens: A Celebration*, ed. Frank Doggett and Robert Buttel
(Princeton: Princeton University Press, 1980); " 'My Dear Old Boy': The Wallace Stevens-
Arthur Powell Friendship," *Antaeus*, Winter 1980; and " 'Hepped on Family Ties': Wal-
lace Stevens in the 1940s," in *The Motive for Metaphor: Essays on Modern Poetry in Honor
of Samuel French Morse*, ed. Francis Blessington and Guy Rotella (Boston: Northeastern
University Press, 1983).

Grateful acknowledgment is made to the following for permission to reprint previously
published material:
Alfred A. Knopf, Inc., and Faber and Faber Ltd: Excerpts from *Letters of Wallace Stevens*,
selected and edited by Holly Stevens, Copyright © 1966 by Holly Stevens; *Opus Posthumous:
Poems, Plays, Prose by Wallace Stevens*, edited by Samuel French Morse, Copyright © 1957
by Elsie Stevens and Holly Stevens; *The Necessary Angel*, by Wallace Stevens, Copyright
1951 by Wallace Stevens; and *The Collected Poems of Wallace Stevens*, Copyright © 1954
by Wallace Stevens.
Alfred A. Knopf, Inc.: Excerpt from *Souvenirs and Prophecies: The Young Wallace Stevens*,
by Holly Stevens. Copyright © 1966, 1976 by Holly Stevens.
Faber and Faber Ltd: Excerpt from uncollected material by T. S. Eliot from
Trinity Review, 1954.
New Directions: Excerpt from "Late for Summer Weather," from *Collected Earlier Poems
of William Carlos Williams*, by William Carlos Williams, Copyright 1938 by New Directions
Publishing Corporation; reprinted by permission. Previously unpublished material by William
Carlos Williams, Copyright © 1983 by William Eric Williams and Paul H. Williams,
used by permission of New Directions Publishing Corporation, agents.
Oxford University Press, Inc.: "At the Canoe Club," from *Collected Poems 1930–1976*, by
Richard Eberhart. Copyright © Richard Eberhart 1960, 1976.
Princeton University Press: Excerpts from *Wallace Stevens: A Celebration*, by Frank Doggett
and Robert Buttel, eds. Copyright © 1980 by Princeton University Press.

Library of Congress Cataloging in Publication Data
Brazeau, Peter.
Parts of a world, Wallace Stevens remembered.
Includes index.
1. Stevens, Wallace, 1879–1955—Interviews.
2. Poets, American—20th century—Interviews.
I. Stevens, Wallace, 1879–1955. II. Title.
PS3537.T4753Z616 1983   811'.52 [B]   82–40133
ISBN 0-394-52734-8

To JIM HARRISON,
for his wise counsel and encouragement

Preface

In 1975, some twenty years after Wallace Stevens' death, I began interviewing everyone I could find who had known him, with the aim of preserving a record of the personality, habits, attitudes, sayings and doings of one of our greatest poets, as recalled by his contemporaries. Stevens moved to Hartford from New York in 1916, at the age of thirty-six. Since virtually everyone he knew prior to this is no longer living, *Parts of a World* focuses primarily on his years in Connecticut, where Stevens spent more than half his life and wrote most of his poetry. I am most grateful to the more than 150 writers, scholars, business associates, neighbors, friends and members of Stevens' family who shared their memories of him with me during our tape-recorded interviews, for their contributions are the heart and soul of this book. I regret that I was unable to quote from all of them in the pages that follow. Those quoted are listed in the interview log at the end of the volume.

The excerpts from the tape-recorded interviews that I have used in this book are taken verbatim from the transcripts. If a topic recurred at various points in the interview, however, I have edited the remarks to form a continuous sequence. I have also substituted a proper name for a pronoun when necessary to avoid ambiguity, employing the form of the name most frequently used by the interviewee when referring to an individual.

I am grateful to the staff at the following institutions for assistance in my research into Stevens' papers and his milieu: Historical Society of Berks County (Pennsylvania); College of Insurance Library (New York); Dartmouth College, Baker Memorial Library; Faber and Faber Ltd.; Hartford Insurance Group, especially William Alberti, Edith Foster and Raymond H. Deck; Henry E. Huntington Library; Alfred A. Knopf, Inc., especially William Koshland; Mount Holyoke College, Williston Memorial Library, especially Elaine Trehub; New York Public Library, Berg Collection; St. Joseph College (West Hartford, Connecticut), Pope Pius XII Library; Southern Illinois University, Morris Library; Trinity College (Hartford, Connecticut), Watkinson Library; University of Chicago, John Regenstein Library; University of Dublin, Trinity College Library; University of Manchester, John Rylands Library; University of Massachusetts at Amherst Library, especially Benton Hatch; University of Miami Library; Yale University, Beinecke Rare Book and Manuscript Library.

For fellowships and grants that aided me in researching and writing this biography, I am indebted to the American Council of Learned Societies; the Henry E. Huntington Library; the Ingram Merrill Foundation; the National Endowment for the Humanities; the Edward C. and Ann T. Roberts Foundation; and the St. Joseph College Faculty Development Fund.

Finally, a special word of thanks is due to a few individuals whose wise encouragement made all the difference: Richard Eberhart, Jonathan Galassi, J. Ronald Harrison, Frederick Morgan, Samuel French Morse and Holly Stevens, who, though she declined to participate in a taped interview, patiently answered innumerable questions over the years.

Contents

Wallace Stevens: A Chronology

1879	Born October 2 in Reading, Pennsylvania, to Garrett Barcalow Stevens, a lawyer, and Margaretha Catharine Zeller Stevens, a former schoolteacher; the second of five children.
1886	Elsie Viola Kachel, Stevens' future wife, born on June 5 in Reading.
1892–1897	Takes classical curriculum at Reading Boys' High School, after attending Lutheran grammar schools in Reading and in Brooklyn, New York.
1897–1900	Attends Harvard College as a special student; contributes poetry and prose to undergraduate magazines, including the *Harvard Advocate,* of which he is president.
1900–1901	Moves to New York, where he works as a reporter on the New York *Tribune* and as an assistant editor at *World's Work,* a monthly magazine.
1901–1903	Attends New York Law School, graduating on June 10, 1903.
1903–1904	Works as a law clerk in the office of New York attorney W. G. Peckham, where he had clerked during his last year in law school.
1904	Admitted to the New York Bar on June 29. Meets Elsie Kachel on summer trip to Reading. Begins short-lived law partnership with Lyman Ward, who

had been a special student with Stevens at Harvard, in New York in the fall.

1905–1907   Drifts in and out of three New York law firms: Eugene A. Philbin, Eaton and Lewis, and Eustis and Foster.

1908   Joins New York branch of American Bonding Company of Baltimore, his first insurance firm, on January 13; by the following year is made assistant manager and resident assistant secretary of the New York office.
Writes "A Book of Verses," a collection of poems for Elsie Kachel's twenty-second birthday.
Engaged to Elsie Kachel during Christmas visit to Reading.

1909   Writes "The Little June Book," a collection of poems for Elsie Kachel's twenty-third birthday.
Marries Elsie Kachel on September 21 in Reading, after which the couple live in New York at 441 West Twenty-first Street until their move to Hartford, Connecticut, in 1916.

1911   Stevens' father dies on July 14 in Reading.

1912   Stevens' mother dies on July 16 in Reading.

1913   Named law officer at the New York office of Fidelity and Deposit Company of Maryland, which had bought American Bonding Company in January.

1914   Hired as resident vice-president at New York office of Equitable Surety Company of St. Louis in February; remains there after firm merges with New England Casualty Company of Boston on July 1, 1915, to become New England Equitable Insurance Company.
"Carnet de Voyage," a set of eight poems, appears in the September issue of *The Trend*, the first verse of Stevens' to be published since his Harvard lyrics.

1916   After New England Equitable Insurance Company abolishes his position in February, joins home office staff of Hartford Accident and Indemnity Company on March 15; moves permanently to Connecticut in May.
"Three Travelers Watch a Sunrise" wins $100 prize offered by Players' Producing Company of Chicago in May.

1919   Mary Katharine Stevens, his youngest sister, dies on May 21 in France.

1920   *Poetry* magazine's Helen Haire Levinson Prize, awarded to "Pecksniffiana," announced in November.

1923   *Harmonium* published by Alfred A. Knopf on September 7; reissued with additional poems on July 24, 1931.

1924 Holly Bright Stevens born on August 10 in Hartford.

1932 Moves in the fall to 118 Westerly Terrace, the one home owned by the Stevenses.

1934 Named a vice-president of Hartford Accident and Indemnity Company on February 15.

1935 *Ideas of Order* issued in a limited edition by the Alcestis Press on August 12.

1936 *The Nation's* Poetry Prize, awarded to "The Men That Are Falling," announced in October.
Ideas of Order published by Alfred A. Knopf on October 19.
Owl's Clover issued in a limited edition by the Alcestis Press on November 5.
Reads "The Irrational Element in Poetry" at Harvard University on December 8.

1937 *The Man with the Blue Guitar* published by Alfred A. Knopf on October 4.
Garrett Barcalow Stevens, Jr., his older brother, dies on November 3 in Cleveland, Ohio.

1940 John Bergen Stevens, his last surviving brother, dies on July 9 in Philadelphia, Pennsylvania.

1941 Reads "The Noble Rider and the Sound of Words" at Princeton University on May 8.

1942 *Parts of a World* published by Alfred A. Knopf on September 8. *Notes toward a Supreme Fiction* issued in a limited edition by the Cummington Press on October 13.

1943 Elizabeth Stevens MacFarland, his last surviving sister, dies on February 19 in Philadelphia, Pennsylvania.
Reads "The Figure of the Youth as Virile Poet" at Mount Holyoke College on August 11.

1944 Holly Stevens marries John Martin Hanchak on August 5 in Pleasant Valley, New York.

1945 *Esthétique du Mal* issued in a limited edition by the Cummington Press on November 6.

1946 Inducted into National Institute of Arts and Letters on May 17.

1947 Reads "Three Academic Pieces" at Harvard University on February 11; the lecture is issued in a limited edition by the Cummington Press on December 8.
Transport to Summer published by Alfred A. Knopf on March 20.
Peter Reed Hanchak, his grandson, born on April 26.

Receives an honorary Doctor of Letters degree at Wesleyan University on June 15.

1948 Reads "Effects of Analogy" at Yale University on March 18 and at Mount Holyoke College on April 2.
"A Primitive Like an Orb" issued as a Prospero pamphlet on June 17.
Reads "Imagination as Value" at Columbia University on September 10.

1949 Reads "An Ordinary Evening in New Haven" at the sesquicentennial celebration of the Connecticut Academy of Arts and Sciences on November 4 in New Haven.

1950 Awarded Bollingen Prize in Poetry for 1949 on March 27.
The Auroras of Autumn published by Alfred A. Knopf on September 11.

1951 Reads "The Relations between Poetry and Painting" at the Museum of Modern Art on January 15.
Receives Gold Medal of the Poetry Society of America on January 24 in New York.
Receives National Book Award in Poetry for 1950 on March 6 in New York.
Accepts an honorary Doctor of Letters degree at Bard College on March 30.
Reads "Two or Three Ideas" at Mount Holyoke College on April 28.
Receives an honorary Doctor of Letters degree at Harvard University on June 21.
Holly Stevens granted divorce from John Hanchak on September 25.
The Necessary Angel: Essays on Reality and the Imagination published by Alfred A. Knopf on November 12.
Reads "A Collect of Philosophy" at the University of Chicago on November 16 and at City College of New York on November 26.

1952 Receives an honorary Doctor of Letters degree at Mount Holyoke College on June 2 and at Columbia University on June 5.

1953 *Selected Poems* published by Faber and Faber Ltd. in London on February 6.

1954 *Mattino Domenicale*, selected poems translated by Renato Poggioli, published by Giulio Einaudi Editore in January.
The Collected Poems of Wallace Stevens published by Alfred A. Knopf on October 1.
Reads "The Whole Man: Perspectives, Horizons" at the Metropolitan Museum of Art on October 21.

1955 Receives National Book Award in Poetry for 1954 on January 25 in New York.
Operation in Hartford on April 26 reveals incurable cancer of the stomach.
Awarded Pulitzer Prize in Poetry on May 2.
Receives an honorary Doctor of Humanities degree at Hartt College of Music (Hartford) on June 9 and an honorary Doctor of Letters degree at Yale University on June 13.
Dies on August 2 at St. Francis Hospital, Hartford.

1963 Elsie Stevens dies on February 19 in Hartford.

P·A·R·T I

THE INSURANCE MAN

CHAPTER ONE

At the Hartford

· I ·

IN NEW YORK

During the winter of 1916, Wallace Stevens was suddenly out of a job. On February 8, the New England Equitable Insurance Company unexpectedly announced from its home office in Boston that the firm was all but going out of business.[1] By the end of the month, it would no longer offer most types of insurance, including the lines Stevens was handling at its New York branch at 55 Liberty Street, a few blocks from Wall Street. As a lawyer in the bond department, the thirty-six-year-old Stevens specialized in both fidelity bonds, which guaranteed employees' honesty, and the more sizable surety bonds, which guaranteed a contractor's satisfactory completion of, say, a sewer line or a road paving. As of March 1, however, New England Equitable would no longer offer such bonds, or liability, or workmen's compensation, the three lines of insurance that produced most of its two million dollars a year in business.

Rumors that the company was in some trouble had been circulating during the past weeks, especially after its president had been replaced in a mid-December coup by some members of the board of directors.[2] Nevertheless, the staff at the New York office seem to have been caught off guard when they learned that most of their jobs were being eliminated at month's end in a last-ditch effort to save the company. Stevens had good reason to be as stunned as any of his colleagues when he was told that even his department was being liquidated, since bonds accounted for half of the new company's business. New England Equitable, which had been formed only the previous

July by a merger of Boston's New England Casualty Company and the Equitable Surety Company of St. Louis, had begun 1916 as one of the largest bonding companies in America.[3] Stevens had been vice-president of the Equitable's New York branch when the companies merged in the summer of 1915; he had stayed on with the new firm, knowing that its bond division was not without problems. Not long before the merger, New England Casualty had reported extremely high bond-claim losses; the new company had also inherited a number of high-risk bonds.[4] Nonetheless, reports out of Boston at the start of 1916 hardly suggested to men in the field like Stevens that their line would be liquidated before the winter was out. Year-end reports showed that the company had almost a million dollars in bond premiums for 1915, while the $345,000 it had paid out in claims was only slightly higher than the industry average.[5]

As Stevens and his colleagues in the field would later learn, however, reports from the home office that winter had been misleading about the underlying health of New England Equitable. The announcement that a supposedly healthy company was going out of business less than a year after it had been organized soon triggered an investigation of home-office records by the insurance departments of Massachusetts and Missouri, which revealed that the company had misrepresented its financial stability. The $200,000 surplus it had reported on hand at the beginning of the year was a fiction; more importantly, half of the million-dollar capital that was on the books had, in fact, been impaired.[6] As a true picture of New England Equitable's precarious financial condition began to emerge, it became clear how badly the company had been mismanaged at the top. The inept former president had "reposed absolute confidence in individuals and was fleeced to the queen's taste," as one analyst explained, by the incompetence of "some of the lemons he shouldered as aides at the home office and as heads of important agencies...."[7]

Stevens and his colleagues at the New York branch had received little if any advance notice that their jobs were being eliminated before hearing Tuesday morning's announcement out of Boston. Trying desperately to stay alive, the home office had been carrying on secret negotiations with the Aetna Accident and Liability Company of Hartford, which had sufficient reserves to take over most of the policies and thus leave New England Equitable solvent enough to continue on a greatly reduced scale, keeping only its $150,000 line of industrial accident insurance. During these secret negotiations, which had been concluded only the previous afternoon, the New York office had apparently been kept in the dark about plans to scale back the company's operation. Only a week earlier, the manager of that branch had hired an individual away from another company to head a department that the home office now announced would be liquidated before the month was out.[8]

Though he was out of a job, Wallace Stevens was not without well-placed friends in insurance to whom he could turn, among them James L. D. Kearney, who headed the bond department of an expanding Connecticut corporation, the Hartford Accident and Indemnity Company. Stevens telephoned Kearney to tell him he was looking for a new position. "Come to Hartford," Kearney replied, "and I'll put you to work."[9] The words had a familiar ring, for Kearney had been Stevens' boss soon after he had started working in the insurance business eight years earlier. A young lawyer from

Maryland, Kearney had been named one of the two vice-presidents in charge of the New York branch of the American Bonding Company some months after Stevens had begun his career as an insurance man there in the winter of 1908.[10] American Bonding's Manhattan headquarters was a seventh-floor office at 84 William Street, located within those few blocks between Wall Street and Broadway where Stevens had drifted in and out of three private law firms in the three and a half years since being admitted to the New York Bar in 1904 and forming a short-lived partnership with another young attorney, Lyman Ward.

Stevens' first years as a lawyer had been lackluster indeed. Not long before he was hired by the American Bonding Company of Baltimore, he had been out of work for some three months, after having been let go by the prominent firm of Eaton and Lewis, whose clients included Marconi and Edison. During the frustrating months that followed, as he looked for yet another position in the late summer and fall of 1907, Stevens finally decided, at twenty-eight, not to try any longer for a career in a Manhattan law firm. At these firms he had developed a background in surety law, and he now began to look into a job with one of the surety companies in New York. After working briefly in his last private law firm, Eustis and Foster, while his new plans simmered, Stevens was lucky enough to be hired by the New York branch of the American Bonding Company on January 13, 1908, becoming assistant manager there within a year.[11]

It was a singularly good place to apprentice in the insurance business, Stevens learned, due in no small part to the connections to be made there with promising young lawyers like James Kearney. So new were bonding companies in the United States at the turn of the century that American Bonding, though a scant fourteen years old, had been one of the pioneers and was now among the four largest such insurance firms in the country.[12] It was developing a reputation, as well, as the West Point of the industry. Its young executives, such as Kearney, who had built his reputation out of the rubble of the San Francisco earthquake by settling claims there brilliantly for the company, were much sought after by newer firms moving into this burgeoning but risky field.

Stevens soon recognized the value of this network of young American Bonding alumni who, after they had graduated to more responsible positions elsewhere, could be counted on to help along friends made at their alma mater when they knew of an opening. In the summer of 1911, an attractive position opened up that Stevens hoped to get, as surety manager of a large New York insurance agency, Whilden and Hancock.[13] Stevens felt he had served his apprenticeship as an insurance executive during three and a half years at American Bonding and hoped to get this new post, in part, through the influence of two of the friends he had made there, James Kearney and Heber Stryker, a young insurance man who had gone on from American Bonding to become president of the Surety Association of America. Stevens was disappointed when his friends chose to help Stryker's assistant, J. Collins Lee, instead. For reasons that are now unclear, this genial Southerner would also prove to be an adversary throughout much of Stevens' later career in Hartford; in fact, the poet once suggested that his failure to be named an officer of the Hartford Accident and Indemnity Company until he was fifty-four was due to Lee's obstruction there. That summer of 1911, however,

Stevens had worried that Lee would be chosen ahead of him because of loyalty that Kearney and Stryker felt toward a friend they had known since their hometown days working together at American Bonding's main office in Baltimore. While Stevens was in a low humor when he found that he had indeed been passed over in favor of Lee, still he cheered himself and his wife with the thought that he was next in line.[14]

He was overly optimistic. The year 1911 ended on a frustrating note when Kearney, who had been hired away from American Bonding that summer to organize the New York branch of the newly formed Equitable Surety Company of St. Louis, by-passed Stevens and selected their mutual friend at American Bonding, Edward B. Southworth, Jr., as his assistant. Indeed, Stevens served a longer apprenticeship than did most of the young friends he had made after he joined American Bonding in 1908; he was one of the last to be given a leg up by these friends after they had gone on to more influential positions in the industry. Stevens was still at American Bonding in January 1913 when it merged with the Fidelity and Deposit Company of Maryland, and he remained there for still another year as law officer in New York for the latter company.[15] The break Stevens had trusted would happen soon that summer of 1911 did not come, in fact, until the winter of 1914. When the opportunity finally arose, however, it did so as he had thought, thanks to well-placed friends. In February 1914, as Kearney was leaving Equitable Surety for a better job and Southworth was named to succeed him as manager of its New York office, Stevens was tapped to fill Southworth's former position as resident vice-president and second in charge of Equitable's New York branch.[16] Ironically, the break that Stevens had waited for so long turned out, only two years later, to be a bad break indeed.

"Come to Hartford, and I'll put you to work," Kearney said when he heard the news that winter of 1916. As it turned out, Kearney was in the midst of expanding his small surety staff as the Hartford Accident and Indemnity Company, which had been in existence less than three years, sought to establish itself in the bond business. Since its organization in August 1913, the company had concentrated on building up other lucrative types of casualty insurance, such as its automobile line, now that there were a million cars on the road. At the beginning of 1916, however, the management decided to make its surety business a priority for the coming year. Kearney had been expanding his operation, appointing new agents and improving office facilities at various points around the country, when Stevens got in touch with him. By year's end the effort paid off, as the company nearly doubled its surety business. More premiums, of course, meant more claims, which increased almost sevenfold by the end of 1916. On March 15, Stevens joined the company, having been hired by Kearney to handle such claims and to oversee the legal affairs of the growing bond department.* After twelve years, Stevens had finally found his niche as a lawyer. Only death could retire him from the Hartford Accident and Indemnity Company thirty-nine years later.

---

*The Hartford Agent, March 1916, p. 347. On April 1, 1918, two years after Stevens was hired as a lawyer in the bond department, a separate fidelity and surety claims department was set up, which Stevens headed until 1955. (Wallace Stevens' "Employee's Record Card," HIG; Best's Insurance Reports: Casualty and Miscellaneous [New York: Alfred M. Best, 1919], p. 112.)

Events had moved so quickly that winter that it took Stevens and his wife, Elsie, the next two months to catch up with them. Not until May were they ready to leave behind their apartment at 441 West Twenty-first Street for Hartford's Highland Court Hotel. This Windsor Avenue "hotel for home lovers," as it liked to advertise itself, was their temporary residence until the end of June, when they moved into summer quarters close to the Kearneys' home in Farmington village, a ten-minute trolley ride from town.[17] "Farmington might be called the Barbizon of America,"[18] the American Impressionist Walter Griffin had exclaimed a few years earlier. It attracted artists from Boston and New York, and almost every day the white umbrellas that shielded them as they painted could be seen near the river, which ran through the center of town, and among the hills that circled Farmington. The Stevenses' first home in Connecticut was just off the village green, where the clapboard colonials of Farmington's Puritan founders and the elegant houses of the prosperous sea captains who lived there in the eighteenth and nineteenth centuries gave the well-to-do suburb its distinctive appearance. One of the best-preserved towns in Connecticut, it was a showplace for three hundred years of New England architecture. This sense of place is captured in Stevens' late poem "The River of Rivers in Connecticut," where "The steeple at Farmington / Stands glistening,"[19] an apt synecdoche for the classic New England appearance of the town.

While Stevens expected to like his summer stay in this picture-postcard version of New England, he had come to Hartford that spring with decidedly mixed emotions about settling there. On the one hand, he had clearly advanced his business career by moving to Hartford. For the first time he was not in a branch office handling regional claims but was an executive at the home office in charge of a nationwide operation. Stevens' mixed feelings about the move were not the result of any uneasiness that in joining yet another new insurance company he was running the risk of repeating his experience with the defunct New England Equitable. His move to the young Hartford Accident and Indemnity was insured, as it were, by one of the oldest and most stable companies on the American insurance scene, the Hartford Fire Insurance Company, founded in 1810. Types of insurance coverage had proliferated during the first decade of the twentieth century, when Stevens had begun working in the insurance industry. Because many states would not allow fire companies to offer other kinds of policies, Hartford Fire had set up its wholly-owned casualty company, Hartford Accident and Indemnity. Stevens' ambivalent feelings had nothing to do with joining the new Connecticut company; they had everything to do, however, with living in Hartford.

"I miss New-York abominably,"[20] Stevens lamented soon after he arrived in Hartford, three hours by train from the metropolitan life he was accustomed to: the first-rate museums, libraries and galleries, for example, that he had savored since settling in Manhattan sixteen years earlier. Recently, he had also become part of a loosely drawn literary circle there, about the time of his "awakening,"[21] as he later described the surge of creativity during his last years in New York that marked the start of his mature career as a poet. In 1914, Stevens had begun to publish poetry again for the first time since his undergraduate days at Harvard, making his debut with a sequence of eight lyrics, "Carnet de Voyage," in the September 1914 issue of *The Trend*. *The*

Trend was only one of the little poetry magazines in which Stevens' new work began to appear in the months that followed. By the time Stevens moved away to Connecticut a year and a half later, poems such as "Sunday Morning" and "Peter Quince at the Clavier" had quickly established his reputation as one of the most accomplished poets of the younger generation. Looking back on these *anni mirabiles* in New York, Stevens associated his "awakening" as a writer with his friendships there with young literati like Walter Arensberg, a fellow poet and a wealthy patron of the avant-garde. The Arensbergs' apartment at 33 West Sixty-seventh Street became the center of Stevens' first literary circle in New York once Arensberg had moved there from Cambridge in 1914. "When I got to New York [1900] I was not yet serious about poetry. . . . I wrote occasionally," Stevens once explained. "It was not until ten or fifteen years later when some friends of mine came down from Cambridge that I became interested again. After that, I began all over."22

Stevens and Arensberg had been friendly as undergraduates at Harvard in the late 1890s, where they were among the most active young men of letters on campus, chosen as members of prominent literary societies, as poets for class events, and as editors of campus journals. While Stevens headed the *Harvard Advocate*, it was in Arensberg's *Harvard Monthly* that the most famous of the score of poems Stevens published as an undergraduate appeared. Stevens' sonnet "Cathedrals are not built along the sea" had immediately elicited a poetic rebuttal from George Santayana, who was then a young member of the philosophy department and one of Stevens' mentors. As an undergraduate at Harvard, where he took most of his courses in languages and literature, Stevens impressed other literary eminences on the faculty as well, among them his English professor Barrett Wendell, who recommended Stevens as a young man of "marked literary aptitude"23 to his friend Oswald Villard, head of the New York *Evening Post*, when Stevens left Cambridge for Manhattan in June 1900. Unlike Arensberg, who was an English major, Stevens was not enrolled in a degree program and left Cambridge at the end of his junior year. (While Stevens' father was a successful lawyer in Reading, Pennsylvania, having three sons in college simultaneously was a strain on family finances, so that Stevens had enrolled at Harvard in 1897 as a special student.)* That June, as the wealthy Arensberg graduated and prepared to leave for Europe, Stevens headed for New York, where, after a few weeks of making the rounds of newspapers and publishing houses, he was hired as a reporter for the New York *Tribune*. Garrett Stevens had encouraged his son to try his hand at a practical literary career like journalism; later that winter, however, he was not sympathetic when his son spoke of resigning from the *Tribune* to devote himself exclusively to his own writing. Instead, his father urged him to take up the law, and in October 1901, after working briefly as

*According to Elsie Stevens, "Not having been prepared in High School for a college entrance, he [Stevens] became a special student at Harvard College, and in three years at Harvard, completed sixteen and one-half courses, and then left college." (Only sixteen courses were required in four years.) ("A Branch of the Bright Family" [1945], p. 24, HL.) Mrs. Stevens' explanation of her husband's special student status at Harvard, however, does not square with the fact that Stevens had graduated from high school having completed the classical program, which prepared students for college entrance.

an assistant editor of the *World's Work*, a magazine devoted to politics and practical affairs, Wallace Stevens rather reluctantly enrolled at New York Law School. Arensberg continued to follow his literary inclinations abroad, spending much of his time in Italy on his English translation of *The Divine Comedy*. [24]

While the two Harvard friends met again in New York during Arensberg's stint there as a reporter between 1905 and 1907, they began to see more of each other once Arensberg and his wife, Louise, settled in Manhattan in 1914, some months after the celebrated Armory Show had opened their eyes —and America's, generally—to modern art. During their next seven years in New York, the couple became avid collectors. Cubist and Dadaist acquisitions soon lined the spacious studio at West Sixty-seventh Street where the Arensbergs, who enjoyed entertaining, played host to an international circle of young poets and painters. Expatriate artists from Europe—among them Francis Picabia, Jean Crotti, and Albert Gleizes, who wrote the first book on Cubist theory—mingled at the Arensbergs with American literati like novelist and music critic Pitts Sanborn, reporter-poets Donald Evans and Allen Norton, and Wallace Stevens. Stevens continued to visit even after moving to Hartford, until a contretemps shortly before the Arensbergs moved to California in the early 1920s severed the long-standing friendship.*

As part of this New York circle, Stevens was in touch with the avant-garde on both sides of the Atlantic. When Marcel Duchamp, whose *Nude Descending a Staircase* had been the cause célèbre of the recent Armory Show, arrived from France in the summer of 1915, he headed straight for the Arensbergs' apartment, which he used as his studio in the months that followed. Before the summer was out, Stevens was among the favored few who had spent the evening with him, getting on so well that Duchamp invited him back to the Arensbergs' to see his latest work. "I made very little out of them," Stevens confided to his wife the next day. "But naturally, without sophistication in that direction, and with only a very rudimentary feeling about art, I expect

---

*In a November 10, 1954, letter to Weldon Kees, Stevens described the mishap that had breached his friendship with Arensberg. "Walter and I were good friends over a long period of years and I saw a lot of him and of his wife. I liked both of them. Walter Arensberg's apartment in New York was a kind of meeting place for a good many Frenchmen whose company he enjoyed. One day one of his very oldest friends spoke with some soreness to the effect that Walter was giving a lot of time to these Frenchmen and neglecting others. I had not myself noticed this. But I thought that I would do the man who had spoken to me a good turn and relieve his feelings by telling Walter what he had told me. . . . Walter froze up when I spoke to him and when he froze up, I froze up too. A little later Carl Van Vechten invited my wife and myself to come to dinner at some place on Bleecker Street. . . . When we went there to dinner there was no one there and after waiting ten minutes or so I told my wife that apparently this was a joke. I suggested to my wife that we forget all about it and go somewhere else. Just as we got up to go Walter Arensberg and his wife walked in. In other words, Carl Van Vechten was trying to engineer a reconciliation by way of embarrassing both Walter and myself. I don't remember anything that was said: nothing much, but my wife and I left the place almost immediately. I think that she spoke to both of them because she did not know what it was all about, whereas Walter and I remained on our high horses. I never saw him again." (*LWS*, p. 850.)

little of myself."[25] At the Arensbergs, where discussions went on until the early hours of the morning, Stevens could not but become more sophisticated in such matters. Indeed, as part of this circle, he began to learn firsthand what modern poets had in common with modern painters; his visits at the Arensbergs' New York apartment during the 1910s doubtlessly sowed seeds that bore fruit in his 1951 lecture, "The Relations between Poetry and Painting," at the Museum of Modern Art in New York.

"I miss New-York abominably," Stevens lamented a few weeks after he and his wife had left it behind in the late spring of 1916 to begin their life in "a typically American small town,"[26] as he later described Hartford. Indeed, Wallace Stevens was as forlorn at the prospect as Elsie Stevens was delighted by their recent move to the small state capital on the banks of the Connecticut River. Elsie Stevens had remained a small-town girl long after her marriage had brought her from Reading, Pennsylvania, to Manhattan in October 1909. She was uninterested in the advantages of metropolitan life that her husband savored.[27] She had little in common with his literary friends, not even their taste for his recent poetry, as she made clear the first evening she spent at the Arensberg salon in November 1915. As the guests gathered in front of the studio fireplace to hear some of Stevens' latest work, he prefaced his reading by remarking that his wife, who had hinted disapproval before he began, did not like the poems. " 'I like Mr. Stevens's things,' she said, 'when they are not affected; but he writes so much that is affected.' "[28] Hers was a minority opinion of one among the Arensberg circle, since almost all of the poems Stevens published during the first three years of his "awakening" appeared in the little magazines, such as *The Trend, Rogue* and *Others*, that were edited by admiring members of his New York set, who were a far more encouraging audience for the fledgling poet than his wife. Many in his circle would doubtlessly have agreed with Stevens' daughter, who, years later, decided that her mother was a woman of taste but little imagination.[29] Lonely and discontent during her years in New York, Elsie Stevens had continued to hope that someday she and her husband would move back to Pennsylvania. With a population of 145,000, Hartford was not a great deal larger than Reading, and she quickly began to feel at home.[30] "Mrs. Stevens, with murderous indifference, pretends that Hartford is sweet to her spirit,"[31] Stevens wrote in dismay to a writer-friend back in Greenwich Village soon after they settled in Connecticut.

· II ·

ON THE ROAD

At first, Stevens spent very little time in Hartford after he and his wife moved there in May. He saw a good deal more of Albany, New York, and St. Paul, Minnesota, as it turned out that his new job kept him constantly on the move that spring. Indeed, during his first three months with the company, Stevens the businessman traced a wearying three-thousand-mile triangle between New York, Florida and Minnesota. Not surprisingly, the first impressions the new bond-claims man made on his colleagues at the Hartford home office, such as the young underwriter Charles Beach, were fleeting ones.

Charles Beach

I didn't see much of Stevens. He was generally tucked away somewhere in connection with his work. He wasn't the kind of fellow, "Well, I'm Wallace Stevens!" He wasn't the blustery type. He just went quietly about his business and did what was necessary. It was passing on claims as they came through; they were important and could run into money.

You immediately had respect for him. He was such a big man physically that he impressed you, and you sort of stepped aside a little bit when he would come. He was a very charming man, very polished. And he conducted himself in such a way that would impress you.

[By the end of June 1916, Beach and the home office staff generally, had learned that their new claims attorney was also a promising young poet.] I heard about it while he was just starting in.[32] I think he had something published, and it got quite a bit of publicity. Frankly, it was a little over my head. As I remember, it was very interesting work, not just designed for the average person. [The home-office staff] was quite proud of the fact.

Stevens arrived at the Hartford office as something of a celebrity. The commonly held view that his co-workers did not know he was a poet until many years after he had come to Hartford is more myth than fact. The week after he and his wife arrived in town, Stevens won his first poetry prize. As often happened that spring, he was out of town on May 19 when a letter from Harriet Monroe, editor of *Poetry*, came to the Highland Court Hotel informing him that "Three Travelers Watch a Sunrise" had been selected from among some eighty one-act plays submitted for the hundred-dollar prize offered by Chicago's experimental Players' Producing Company. Stevens' verse play concerned three Chinese sages who sit atop Mount Penn trading aphorisms on life and art until the sunrise discloses a hanged man on a tree behind them and silences their aesthetic conversation. He agreed to make some revisions in the play, and the prize was his.[33] Elsie Stevens was excited enough that Friday morning to telephone her husband in Albany with the news, even though he would be back in Hartford that evening to spend the weekend.

What had sent Stevens to Albany a few weeks after he had joined Hartford Accident, was the necessity of establishing the Hartford Live Stock Insurance Company as a New York corporation.[34] Hartford Fire was setting up yet another subsidiary, this one offering animal insurance, and because the Connecticut legislature was out of session that spring, the company decided to incorporate in New York State, so Stevens spent much of May shuttling back and forth to the insurance commissioner's office in Albany to work out the legal details.[35]

In June, his primary job at the company, as the lawyer in charge of its bond claims, kept him away from his new home and in Minnesota for much of the month. Grain-storage bonds were a recurrent problem there for many years,[36] and it was already Stevens' second trip to St. Paul since he had joined the company less than three months ago. Before this bond man could return to Hartford, he faced the prospect of brief visits to Nebraska and Iowa on claims as well. "My cases oppress and depress me,"[37] he confided to his wife as his assignment in St. Paul was ending that June, and he understandably looked forward to their upcoming stay in Farmington over the summer as his first chance to settle down in Connecticut since taking his new job.

These first hectic months on the road were a foretaste of Stevens' first five years with the company. Until he hired his assistant, Ralph Mullen, in 1921, Stevens was often obliged to travel. "The work was mainly a fact-finding assignment," explains an assistant who later took over much of the travel, "and, based on the facts, determining and recommending what should be done. For example, it would be [the bond-claims man's job] to check the financial position of the contractor, his assets, how far the job had progressed, what it would cost to complete the job by getting out other bids, and whether we should finance the contract to completion. But when it came strictly to court work, that was farmed out."[38]

The appropriate initial view of Stevens as a Hartford businessman, then, is of Stevens outside Hartford. "It's just like being a bag-man as they call them in England," he once remarked to his wife, "traveling with a strange line, however, for I go around to patch up trouble or else to cause it."[39] The following accounts give a sense of Stevens as a businessman on the road: the types of cases he dealt with, from embezzlement to claims for the upkeep of mules, and the way he dealt with the people he met on these cases—fellow lawyers like Manning Heard or the company's field men like Robert DeVore or Coy Johnston.

Robert DeVore

I first met Mr. Stevens in Philadelphia in 1928. We had a contractor who we were bonding to the Board of Education, guaranteeing the performance of his contract. The fellow went broke, and we had to contact the home office to let them know we were in trouble with this man. Mr. Stevens got on the phone and told the manager that it was important enough that he felt he ought to come down to Philadelphia. I was a bond special agent, and I had had something to do with the execution of the bond. Mr. Stevens wanted to talk to me about the contractor and also wanted to see the lawyer representing the school board.

He wanted me to meet him at the station, take him to the attorney's office. I stood at the gate in the station, and when he came through I didn't have any trouble spotting him. Here was a fellow that matched the description the manager had given me: tall, austere, very dignified, an unusual-looking man. He said, "Let's get on our way. We want to go to the attorney's office and get into this thing right away. We don't want to waste any time." I said, "No, sir!"

Then he said, "The attorney's office is down on Chestnut Street, so on the way down what do you say we get some cinnamon buns." I said, "Cinnamon buns?" "Yes," he said, "I always, whenever I come to Philadelphia, buy these cinnamon buns at Lahr's." I thought, This is strange to do before we're going to an attorney's office. He ordered a dozen to send to Hartford. I thought, Oh, that is that. Then he wanted a dozen more; they put them in a bag, and we started off. And I thought, My gosh, I wonder where he's going to eat these things. Well, we got to the attorney's office, and we went through the introductions and into the conference room. There were about seven of us. He opened up his bag, put it in the middle of the table, and said, "Let's have a cinnamon bun." Everyone, trying to be polite, agreed with him, and we all reached in and got a handful of goo. And we started our conference.

Mr. Stevens acted with great authority and was rather final in his assertions. He didn't mince words. He would be quite direct in what he would do and what he wouldn't do. You just had the feeling that this fellow was different than the common herd. He came to conclusions promptly. That was the way he saw it, and that was the way he was going to stay with it. Not much debate that I remember. I doubt if the meeting lasted more than an hour.

[The electrical contractor] just ran out of money. He was a good contractor, and the result of this visit from Stevens was our agreeing to finance him through to the completion of the job. It was about a $100,000 job, and from that point I was named assignee for the benefit of creditors. I would receive the payments from the Board of Education on the work that was done; then I would pay off the laborers and the material furnishers. I reported to Mr. Stevens. He gave me a lot of leeway, and I was able to exercise my own judgment, which probably wasn't too mature because I was quite a young man. [In his letters] he wouldn't waste a lot of time with pleasantries, things that weren't to the point, so that you knew exactly what he had in mind and what he expected of you. When it was all over, I made my report to Wallace Stevens, and as a result of that he came to Philadelphia again and wondered if I would like to go to Yale to study law on the Hartford and get into the claims department. At the same time I received an invitation from the secretary of the company to go to Syracuse in the production end of the business. My decision was to accept the secretary's offer rather than Mr. Stevens'.

[Before being transferred, however, DeVore encountered Stevens at the home office at the Hartford's annual production conference between field men and management, a year-end ritual in Stevens' life at the office.] They were generally meetings to talk about the results of the year just passed, do long-range planning, and also receive some words of advice from top management. He would never speak. I think he would just insist on sitting there and not being put on any kind of assignment. He didn't want to get involved. I sat next to him. Sometime during the meeting I shifted in my seat, and he said, "You going to get up, Robert, and say something?" I said I hadn't planned to. He said, "Aw, get up and tell them what's what!" With that, I was sort of shoved out of my chair, and I had to think of something real fast. Subsequently I thought, I'm going to sit somewhere else; he's not going to do that to me again.

During the years, I had contact with Wallace Stevens on many situations involving bond claims. He was a fellow you always felt somewhat in awe of. You felt you were dealing with a superintellect. In the many exchanges we had over the years—letters—I always had the feeling that here was a man that could get right down to the nub of the matter. His letters were always sharp and to the point. But I always had the feeling that here was a man you just didn't get to know too well. He was always somewhat of a stranger, in the sense that most of the company men that I met I became very friendly with. We had many things we exchanged, personal things. But you didn't do that with Wallace Stevens. He was always aloof and pretty much his own man.

Manning Heard

I first met Mr. Stevens in Washington, D.C. [in 1932]. I just knew him by reputation because he was considered a quite capable surety-claims attorney, in addition to being a very accomplished American poet. The Hartford had bonded a contract for the construction of a very large diesel engine. The total amount of the bond was in excess of a million dollars, which in those days was a substantial sum. The engine would not live up to any of the specifications called for in the contract. So the government, through a Mr. Nicholson, refused to accept the imperfect engine and made a claim for the full amount of the bond. Now the Hartford had reinsured its liability, partly with the Union Indemnity Company, with which I was employed, and with several other companies. It being such a large bond, Mr. Stevens insisted that representatives of the other companies participate in all discussions leading to a settlement or a suit by the government.

We started these negotiations. Over in the corner there was a man with a little machine in front of him. Mr. Stevens said to Mr. Nicholson, "What is that thing?" It was, of course, a recording device. Mr. Nicholson told him. Mr. Stevens said immediately, "I won't say a word if anything I say is taken down." Then I said, "Neither will I." The other representatives said, "Neither will we." That's the way it started. [Negotiations] were carried on and off. We'd meet in Washington, get up to a point where we could go no further, then I would go back to New Orleans and Mr. Stevens would go back to Hartford.

Finally, between our visits, Mr. Stevens went on a diet. When I first met him, he was quite heavy, with a good-sized abdomen. He loved to eat. He was a tall man, about six foot two. He weighed at the time close to three hundred pounds. I went up to one of the meetings after he was on a diet; you wouldn't recognize him. He hadn't had his tailor adjust them and his clothes looked like a sock on a rooster. He looked awful. It affected his disposition the same way. Mr. Nicholson was a typical bureaucratic counsel, very meticulous, very sure that nothing he was going to say would be used against him. And he got to be, in many respects, rather exasperating. In one of the conversations—it was after Mr. Stevens was on a diet and he wasn't in too good a humor anyway—he called Mr. Nicholson a silly old fool. Mr. Nicholson got up and said, "I refuse to have any further conversation with this gentleman. As far as I'm concerned, as long as he participates, our conversations leading to a settlement of this case are closed." That created somewhat of a crisis. That also started a most peculiar and amusing arrangement. Stevens would stay in a Washington hotel [room overseeing the negotiations from across town], and we would meet with Mr. Nicholson. We ultimately agreed on a settlement, giving the government half a million dollars.

Mr. Stevens was not a good bargainer. He was too impatient. He was the type of individual who didn't relish a skirmish with a mentality that he considered a little bit lower than his.

Coy Johnston

Stevens had arranged a meeting in Charlotte, North Carolina, in connection with a case which involved two or three million dollars arising out of breaches of faith by an executor of a man who owned a number of cotton mills. The executor had used the funds and committed suicide. The case was of considerable concern. Stevens undertook to handle it through Daughtry in Atlanta [C. L. Daughtry was the Hartford's Southern claims manager.] Daughtry had employed a lawyer named Moran to deal with it. Stevens decided he had to personally meet Moran and journeyed to Charlotte, where Daughtry and I met him at the railroad station. We then adjourned to meet Moran. Stevens discussed the case with him; so did Daughtry. They both concluded afterward that Judge Moran was not the lawyer to handle that particular case, whereupon they cast about for another. I suggested Charles Hundley Grover, a very able lawyer. We went to the Law Building in Charlotte, and Stevens employed him. The case took about two or three years to handle.

Stevens' dealings with all these people was very cold, very distant. He seemed extremely detached. Grover invited Stevens, Daughtry and me to have dinner with him that evening. We were met by a colored chauffeur; he carried us to the Grovers' home. To some extent Stevens was just suffering the affair. Nothing about it greatly interested him, although he ate voraciously and had a couple of drinks. In the course of the meal, which was extremely formal—everybody was watching their p's and q's; I was absolutely silent; Stevens did very little talking—the waiter in his white jacket leaned down to Grover and whispered, "Boss, shall I give the old man a second helping of peas?" Stevens laughed—or smiled, anyway.

When I first met Stevens in Charlotte, Stevens expressed the thought that if we didn't find what we wanted in the way of a lawyer, namely, Grover, he would bring Fletcher into the case. [A. J. Fletcher was a prominent lawyer in Raleigh whom Stevens selected to represent the Hartford on cases in North Carolina, which he did for thirty years. At the time] Fletcher was working for Stevens on a rather substantial highway contract case. The case involved the default by a dirt contractor—that is, a contractor who'll excavate the soil and the landfill for a highway. The contractor had a lot of mules which were used with scoops to build this highway. There was a claim for upkeep of the mules, hay supplied the mules—that kind of thing. Stevens made a number of trips to Raleigh to see Fletcher in connection with that case. Fletcher and I many times would talk about Stevens. Fletcher was a lawyer's lawyer. He said that he admired Stevens: that his ability to reason logically and put a case into perspective was magnificent, that he didn't know anything in the practice of law he enjoyed more than dealing with Wallace Stevens. That he was foremost as a poet. [In the early 1930s] Fletcher read to me a number of verses from a book of poetry [Harmonium]. I even borrowed the book and went in Fletcher's law library and tried to read Stevens' poetry for an hour, to kill time. I remember particularly "Thirteen Ways of Looking at a Blackbird." I never could quite get it.

I met another man who was a friend of Stevens in Portland, James Powers. [At the time, Johnston was returning from Oregon to the home office and Powers] asked me to deliver a message to Stevens. Stevens was behind his desk; he had a few files on his desk, and he had his head buried in one. I made my statement, and Stevens said, "Is that all? You shouldn't have bothered yourself." In other words, get out of here! I had no further business dealings, and I made up my mind I would not have, in view of that little incident.

I saw him on several occasions after that. We threw a fortieth anniversary party for George Merrick, who was then a vice-president in charge of the New York department. It would have been 1950 or 1951. Paul Rutherford, president of the company, came down from Hartford; so did Wallace Stevens; so did Joseph Broucek, who was the comptroller, and Wilson Jainsen [a fellow vice-president]. And about ten of us from the New York department. We had a large room [at the Biltmore], a bar, plenty of whiskey. An accordion player played as we ate. Everybody seemed to get pretty liquored up as the evening wore on, and then the dancing began. All men. You never saw such a sight: Jainsen dancing with Wallace Stevens, swinging him around the room to a Polish polka. Wallace Stevens would throw up one foot as he would twirl. That's a side of Stevens nobody knew existed. The party started about four in the afternoon. Stevens disappeared at eleven o'clock; so did the whole Hartford crowd. Paul Rutherford didn't. He said, "That's just like my Hartford vice-presidents. They all have to go to bed." The party continued with the New York bunch through breakfast.

· III ·

ON EXECUTIVE ROW

Even during his first five years with the company, when Stevens was on the road and away from Hartford on claim matters some three months out of the year, Stevens the businessman was still most often the man at the office. When he joined the home office that spring of 1916, his quarters, like those of the rest of Hartford Accident's small staff, were on the third floor of Hartford Fire's four-story headquarters at 125 Trumbull Street, a block below the city square. The ornate Second Empire–style headquarters of the oldest insurance company in the city and its new subsidiary were suitably massed on a prominent corner of downtown Hartford, the insurance center of America. The city's insurance "companies were known for their fiscal conservatism, and their stability proved a boon during the Chicago Fire of 1871 and the San Francisco earthquake of 1906, when Hartford Fire and other local companies managed to pay all their claims and stay in business while many of their competitors were wiped out. By World War I, Hartford was the undisputed capital of the nation's insurance."[40]

Soon after Stevens joined its staff, the Hartford, like many other prospering insurance companies in town, began planning larger quarters. In November 1921, Stevens moved out of the downtown din to the company's new home office, built on a residential hill overlooking the city's compact downtown area. That year Stevens also hired an assistant, who took over most of the traveling, so that, except for his annual business-vacations to Florida each winter or an occasional trip on an important surety matter, Stevens' business life became what it remained for the next thirty-three years, a life at the office.

The essential portrait of Stevens the businessman, then, is of Stevens on executive row at 690 Asylum Avenue. The company's new home office, where Stevens spent most of his working hours during his Connecticut years, was located on the site of what had once been the Connecticut Asylum for the Education and Instruction of Deaf and Dumb Persons; it had given the name to the avenue that, in turn, gave Stevens his rather quirky Hartford address as a poet as well as a businessman, since he had all his mail sent to his Asylum Avenue office. The three-story building in which Stevens worked was designed in the Beaux-Arts tradition; adorned by six massive columns at its entrance and surmounted by a replica of the Pantheon's dome, the home office had the look of an insurance temple. Huge brass doors at the entrance opened into a large rotunda of cream marble, with the Hartford Accident and Indemnity wing to the right and the Hartford Fire offices to the left.

John Rogers, later a professor of black history at the University of Hartford, was manservant to Stevens and the few officers of the Hartford Accident and Indemnity during the 1920s and 1930s. He recalls the ambience in which Stevens worked on executive row and the men he worked with. As a lawyer with quarters in the law library opposite Stevens' office, Hale Anderson, Jr., had the view of Stevens at his desk that most employees saw as they passed along the first-floor corridor. Members of Stevens' small surety staff, however, had the insiders' view of Stevens' daily life at the office: his secretary, Marguerite Flynn; his mailboy, Richard Sunbury; his lawyer-assistants, John Ladish, Leslie Tucker and Clifford Burdge, Jr., recall what it was like to work under him over the years.

John Rogers

I was there to take care of the officers' needs. Sometimes I would be up with them till three or four in the morning. It was a fantastic experience for me because that group of officers that comprised the executive suite at that time was composed of four outstanding men. The [first general manager] was Norman Moray. He was a character. He came from Ontario. Apparently, Moray [first] got a job in the insurance business around New York City. Now, Moray was different from the rest of these fellows. He was aggressive; he would knock down a wall if it got in his way. But he was the right man to set up the new company. He was always a showman. There was never a day too hot for him to have his light-colored flannel clothes and his cane and his spats. And he had the most gaudy car, an old Stutz Bearcat. He was not college-educated, and he wasn't culturally on the same plane.

James L. D. Kearney was just the opposite: dressed quiet, sensitive, a beautiful person. He had a brain like a wizard. And not only a brain, but he had a fantastic classical and cultural outlook, and I owe a lot to that personally. I spent a lot of time with Kearney. Kearney and I used to go riding in the woods, slowly, on back roads. We'd see all kinds of growing things: he could give the Greek name and the Latin name. He had a fantastic knowledge of history and the arts. Kearney was the most literate man I've ever known. He held Stevens in very high regard. Kearney was a man who would appreciate a poet. Not too much [talk about Stevens' poetry by Kearney]. Kearney was a kind man; he was compatible with any human being unless that human being was arrogant. I used to watch this closely. The lowest woman, a charwoman, would come into Kearney's office to ask a favor. The moment she came in, Kearney would rise to his feet. He paid the same respect to the charwoman as he did anyone else.

Now the other part of this combination with Stevens was a Southerner, Joseph Collins Lee, who was the treasurer of the Society of the Lees of Virginia. Lee's line had come from Light-Horse Harry Lee, the Revolutionary War Lee. These guys were all classical scholars. Lee gave me his mother's books, and among his mother's books a fantastic Latin lexicon that a thousand fellows borrowed and reborrowed, some college professors. I often say that the ten years I spent there I couldn't have done better going to Yale, just being in the presence of these men and some of my experiences with them.*

All of them were [mentors]. Where I sat they had a law library and a general library. I had a lot of time, and I read a lot. When I read something legal and wanted to have something defined, I simply asked Stevens. They were the most accessible men in the world; there were no barriers. It was the most democratic situation I've ever seen. There was no employee who didn't have access to these fellows.

*The most distinguished scholar among Stevens' colleagues at the Hartford was Benjamin Lee Whorf, the pioneering linguist who worked at the home office as an engineer for Hartford Fire from 1919 until his death in 1941. The support that top management at the company gave to Whorf's linguistic studies suggests the respect for the life of the mind among Stevens' fellow executives. In 1930, for example, James Wyper, a vice-president at the home office, wrote to the company's agent in Mexico City that the Hartford had two purposes in sending Whorf on a trip to Mexico: to consult with the agent on company business and to continue his studies of the Maya and Aztec civilizations and languages on which he was an authority (letter to Manuel E. Levy, January 11, 1930, HIG).

Stevens was a very meticulous worker. He worked hard. He was the only man I'd ever seen do research the way he did it. I've seen Stevens with as many as thirty lawbooks at one time. He would get these books day after day: you'd see him with maybe twenty or thirty books, all place-marked, all around him, on a certain subject. He was a terrific man for legal research. [There were books] on the desk, on the chair. You'd have to bring in extra chairs to hold the books. Now this guy would roll his sleeves up; he was a worker. Lots of others leave to play golf; not Stevens. Stevens was right there, grinding. He was the grindingest guy they had there in executive row.

Stevens was a man who demanded discipline. In fact, to keep that type of machine going you have to have it. One of the things that's very important, that a man who wants discipline, if he displays that in his own action, I think it affects his subordinates. And he had good subordinates. Now Stevens was a no-nonsense guy when it was business.

I never see him make too much of luncheon, except that he would go with his subordinates. At first when he was there he would always be with his subordinates. And they used to hang around him like disciples around a master. No [this was not true of other department heads]; he was the only one. Now at three o'clock every afternoon he would do this: He'd buy imported tea; he'd invariably have this in the afternoon with some little tea wafers. None of the rest of the officers were drinking tea but Wallace in the afternoon. Offices in those days were not like they are now [with cooking facilities]. [In the basement, however] they had a little gas range. He'd go down and brew his tea every afternoon. Occasionally, he would [invite someone]. This was one of his daily habits.

Another interesting thing about Wallace, he always had a little humor. But the little humor was always intertwined with logic: he was conveying something. We were talking once about people. He said he noted that when he was a boy in Pennsylvania his mother used to hire servant girls. And he said, "I never saw any difference between the servant girls and the lady. But it's an interesting thing looking at human beings. They always seem so [much] more secure when they feel somebody else is under them."

I don't think he was too much of a social creature. But he had one social day, Christmas. My assistant was my brother-in-law, George Majors. And George would pick him up on Christmas morning. He'd make his social rounds and have a drink with his friends. Once in a while, we'd have a good company party, executive get-together. All the fellows up from New York or some from the Coast would come over on the Twentieth Century. They'd have a good drink-up at one of the country clubs that some of them were members of. Now Stevens was great at these parties. This is where the old

Harvard-Yale football-game levity would appear. He would sing there and get around. This is the other side of Wallace Stevens. He was as boyish as he could be in this situation. The Harvard-Yale game was always a big thing for him. To see Wallace Stevens with a red feather stuck in his hat was so different from the meticulous lawyer. That's a Harvard symbol. But anyway, he took on a little levity at this time.

Mrs. Stevens wasn't too socially inclined. It was interesting: Wallace was such a giant of a man, and she was just a little person. If she called or wanted something, his response was fantastic. It would always give you the impression of a big man [being very intimidated]. She was a very conservative person. She never dressed to any particular fashion; she had a mode of her own. He had a tailor. All his clothes were cut to one pattern, and all his suits were one color. Apart from his tuxedo, he always wore steel gray, invariably dark gray.

Stevens was a very interesting man when it came to spending his own money. I recall that one time RCA had put out a batch of records for children. And they were expensive. But the same records were very reasonable in England. He told me, "Now I want you to get this certificate okayed because they can't charge us duty on them [when he opted to import them] because they're manufactured in [America]." I never noted anybody else that was as astute in spending money, to trade this way. From time to time he gave us a check to cash. He always carried new, clean money. He used to give us a check to cash, and we'd look at that signature and shake our heads. We had a little nickname for him because anybody looking at his signature and trying to decipher it would invariably say it was signed by Mr. MUMMM.

Stevens had an attitude that was always self-confident. I recall a case of a large bond loss. A bond that we had posted had to do with a device [that was contracted for by the United States Navy]. In the testing, the thing did the very thing it was bonded against: it came back after being shot and mangled the government vehicle. It was one of the company's biggest losses. It was about half a million dollars. Stevens had gone down to head the case, and they had lost the case. At that time, Hartford Accident and Indemnity was a subsidiary of Hartford Fire, and the president of Hartford Fire was a whipper-snapper. Just coincidentally, the president of Hartford Fire was walking through the hall when Stevens came in the door. Abruptly, without hailing Stevens—this was Bissell's way, he was very abrasive—he said to Stevens, "How did we make out on the case?" Stevens answered him very abruptly, as acidly, back. "We lost the damned case!" And walked right by him to his office. There were very few guys would have done that. No one ever intimidated Wallace Stevens.

I found out when I was working for him that he was a poet. The man was exceptionally modest [about it]. I remember several times we discussed his poetry, but a lot of times we discussed his outlook on life. He would always talk like this: "Well, John, I'll tell you from my experience," or "When I was a boy, I saw this and concluded this." I think he gave me some poetry [to read] at one time. There were some references to Greek classics in that; that's what we were discussing. He said something to the effect, "You see, human nature doesn't change." He implied that he could have taken the same thing not from a classical point in time but from another situation. I often felt sorry that I didn't pay more attention to it at that time.

Hale Anderson, Jr.

We were billeted on the same floor. I was stuck away in the stacks and lawbooks [of the company's law library], and he had an office on the front hall. I cruised up and down the front hall, and we got to know each other. He was a rather aloof person, but he could be quite warm and jovial. We spent more time on trivia than we did on business. Once in a while he would casually wave across his office to a book that had come in from some part of the world. This was part of his character, to have enjoyable moments with people but to hold them at arm's length. Stevens was unique. Most executives, whenever they are free to do so, love to sit around and chat, relax, unwind, lollygag. Stevens was not that kind of person. He was not receptive. There were times when he'd dearly love to have someone come in and chat about something, usually not business. By and large, he did not have an invitation hanging on the door—quite the reverse. He was always, to most people who didn't understand him, formidably busy.

With a large bonding company, claims can remain open for many years while they are contested out in the field by practicing lawyers who are hired to try the case. The net result is a huge accumulation of files that have to be kept track of. And it was perhaps here that from a visual standpoint Stevens was quite remarkable. Every day a load of these files, several feet high in total, would be placed on his desk. They would be dragged out on diary. He would go through them, peruse his last notations, and decide whether something had to be done or whether to leave it to the people in the field to carry on. If something had to be done, he would dictate his correspondence. If not, for some period, he would simply throw the file on the floor and leave it to the clerk to pick up the accumulation at the end of the day. Suddenly the system changed. A box on wheels was left at his desk, and he threw them in the box. It was a big case, three feet by two by two. The story was that some pleasant little girl got thoroughly aggravated at crawling around on the floor picking up these files and called him down. The issue was drawn., so a box was provided instead.

His office was routine—routine for the front hall. I had one for some time. Roughly fifteen by sixteen, with a large window facing south, a door coming in from the north off the main corridor. It was no different than any other senior executive office. In Stevens' case, as you came through the door on the left, with plenty of room to turn around, there was a large, very expensive mahogany table on which he might have a shipping package of some kind. Never a file. There might be, to his great glee, a carton in stitched-up canvas, an order of tea that had finally gotten through from Ceylon. Or propped up against the wall, resting on the table, there might be a print. This was the repository on which he would place things that he had ordered, and they would stay there until he was ready to take them home. His desk was approximately eight or nine feet diagonally across from that table, facing it, so he could see what was on the table. There was room on his right for the rolling box. There would be a chair in front of his desk; on his left, there was a chair. Very few pictures on the wall.

He didn't keep family pictures. At the most he might stand up on the table across from his desk a print or a book that had come in from some part of the world, where he could glance at it from time to time. But you see, with the absolutely methodical pace at which he worked with this stack of files, he didn't have time for anything else. He just concentrated on what he was doing, unless he pushed everything aside and began to scribble some poetry. One could never tell whether he was writing poetry; I never peeked over his shoulder—not by any means. But there were times when he would just put everything aside and be working on some personal notes. He would quite frequently amble into the library, settle down with Webster's dictionary and amble out again, apparently having satisfied himself as to a word which he presumably wanted to use or not use. Then he would on occasion give Marguerite Flynn, his secretary, a note for her to type. And she would be the only person who could possibly decipher his handwriting. It was an up-and-down series of V's, for practical purposes. He would sit at his desk in the morning and just stay there. He was not one to get up and wander around and visit other people. Quite the contrary: someone needed to see him, they would come and see him if they could.

I do recall a long walk with him one evening after work, out Farmington Avenue, when I told him that I had gotten hands on some of his poetry and I was absolutely lost. Could or would he give me any clue or key that would enable me to understand his writing? We walked several paces, and then, with a combination chuckle and snort, he said, "Oh, forget it. You're much too literal-minded!" And that subject never came up again. This is something of which Mr. Stevens was capable; he could be very abrupt. I recall one or two files in which his criticism of someone out in the field was what I would almost call savage. He could be very hard; I don't mean *mean,* he was more Olympian than that. I recall one or two occasions when I had been involved doing some work for him on an extraordinarily complicated matter, and I'd heard nothing further about it. I was curious; after all, a lot of time and effort had gone into it. And one day I just stood in his doorway and asked if I could be of any further help, which was my way of asking how things were going. And I was summarily dismissed to the effect that there was nothing I could do to be of any help at all. But aside from an incident or two like that, he never hurt my feelings. Quite the contrary. It was a very relaxed, natural relationship between a senior and a junior.

On a few occasions he asked me to do some research for him. The basic concept of a surety bond is that a person who is responsible is guaranteed by another person that he will do his job. And the person for whom the work is being done can call upon the guarantor, the surety, if the work is not done. It still remains the job of the contracting party to perform his work. If he does not, then his surety can be called upon. But not having taken on full responsibility for all the details [in] the contract initially, the surety is going to make darned certain that every inch of the way the person wanting the work done has performed his side of the bargain. If he's been sloppy, if his specifications are bad, if he has failed to make payment in due course, if he's done any one of a number of things that any contracting party can do and do badly, then the surety is going to assert those defenses, because he sees himself moving into the position of the contractor. This is where it becomes arcane. This is where underwriters and claims people alike have to be very sharp-eyed and understand all the details of exactly what the contract was, who said what to whom, what defenses are available. All of the facts have to be dug out and disclosed. And where you're talking about the construction of a dam, a highway or a coliseum roof that collapses, an awful lot of expertise has to come into play. This is where he had his expertise and demanded it of those he was directing.

John Ladish

Ours was a small department. When I went there [1924], there was Mr. Stevens, Ralph Mullen, a secretary for each one of them, and a girl that did the bookkeeping. That was the extent of it. I was a mailboy and a runner. And one of the things that I remember having to do was every once in a while running down to the cigar store and buying three cigars for a dollar. And that was rather high at that time. But he smoked three cigars each day. Later on, he gave up smoking; I'd say probably fifteen years [before he died].

[At the time of Stevens' death in 1955] we must have had twenty in the department, including the secretaries. He didn't have what you'd call a receptionist. The secretaries were in another room; they just took care of his dictation. You didn't have to ask for an appointment. It was a high-ceilinged office. His desk was kitty-corner at one end near the window. I think he may have selected his own rug, an Oriental. The room had a closet, for his coat and hat; there was a sink.

He would have [his files] come out on his diary for review. But most generally correspondence came along, so they brought the file out at that time, and he brought himself up to date. In the morning the mailboy would open [the letters] and sort them, giving the fidelity to Mr. Mullen and the surety mail to Mr. Stevens. He didn't handle any fidelity. Mr. Stevens [took] charge of the surety claims. And that would include judicial bonds, court bonds, the contractor bonds and appeal bonds, too. He supervised and handled most of [the contract cases], the road paving and construction. Mr. Stevens kept those pretty much to himself. It requires a knowledge of a great many legal points and also a judgment as to whether a company should complete or get somebody to do it. They're usually for sizable amounts.

Mr. Stevens would come in about quarter to nine. Then he would look over the mail and give it back to the mailboy to get the files with the letters and put them on his desk. Then he reviewed them and would dictate on all of them. Some [days] he'd only use that one file, if it was a complex situation. And other times, why, it might be a dozen cases or more. When a claim first developed, he would get notice of it, and then it would be up to him to refer it to the man that he thought would handle it properly. If they ran into a situation where they required a little advice, why, they'd take it up with him. I don't recall that he ever did [take back a file].

Occasionally, I could see that he was making a lot of notes, and he wouldn't have a file there. So you would say that he probably was just jotting down something [related to his poetry] that came into his mind. He asked us occasionally to go to the State Library and look up certain words and their definitions, not only in the American dictionaries but the Oxford English and any others that he would tell us to check. These were just words that he wanted to fit into his poetry. I never talked at all about poetry because I was ignorant of it. I thought, What's the sense of causing myself embarrassment? I remember [*Harmonium*'s publication in the fall of 1923], but I didn't pay much attention to it because I didn't know him personally until I started working for him a few months later [when Ladish was transferred to Stevens' department]. The only [literary] thing that I recall coming up: Odell Shepard was one of the professors over at Trinity [College]; he was having Archibald MacLeish come up. He called Wallace Stevens on the phone and asked if he could bring Archibald out to Mr. Stevens and have a little session. Stevens said, "Well, I don't think you'd better. Tell him when he gets a reputation, I'll be glad to see him." That was when MacLeish was head of the Congressional Library. Sometimes that was his way of being humorous. But, after all, it cut quite a bit. That was probably one of the things that kept him where he was as far as the social end of it was concerned. They probably just didn't quite know whether he was being facetious or not.

Before he came to the office, a great many times he would walk—he wasn't too far from Elizabeth Park—and he'd walk through there just looking around, and get a thought, and write a poem about it. He needed the exercise; that's about all he did for exercising. He was a big man and always heavy. Shortly after I was there, he was attempting to get a life insurance policy from the Connecticut General. Mr. Stevens had applied, and they had him examined by a doctor and they found he had high blood pressure. So then they waited awhile and it had persisted, so they wouldn't write him. He said, "Oh, I'll forget about them. I'll set aside so much every month." And that's what he did over the years. 'Cause after all, when he died he wanted to have something left for his family.*

Mrs. Stevens was a very highly nervous person, particularly with [Holly, the Stevens' only child]. Afraid she would hurt herself with something. Pair of scissors might be on the table in the next room, and she'd run over and put them away. I got out there once or twice, on Farmington Avenue [the apartment where the Stevenses lived from 1924 to 1932] before they went to Westerly Terrace. It was only a six-room flat—a nice building, but if it was in another location it would be just a flat. [One] had to go upstairs. He didn't have his oil paintings at that time. He waited until he got into the big house,

*Stevens, who died intestate, left an estate appraised at $95,760.60. The major assets were: deposits in three area banks, $22,972.94; 315 shares of Hartford Fire Insurance Company stock, $54,810; U.S. Treasury bonds, $5,000; royalties from Alfred A. Knopf, Inc., for the period October 30, 1954, to August 2, 1955, $3,019.02; publisher's agreements with Alfred A. Knopf., Inc., based on anticipated royalties, $3,640; library, $3,563.95. It was a conservative estimate of the worth of Stevens' estate, since the value of unpublished literary papers and manuscripts, plus his correspondence, was set at $1,500; in 1975, his daughter sold this literary archive, plus most of Stevens' library, to the Huntington Library for $225,000. "Inventories, Administration Accounts and Commissioners' Reports" (Hartford: Probate Records), 1042: 51–53.

then he wrote to some agent in France and had him select different pictures and send them.*

Clifford Burdge, Jr.

It was intriguing. He was not in any way a typical corporate executive. In fact, I think he was miscast as a corporate executive: he was a brilliant man, but I don't think his main talents lay in supervising the work of others or in running a department of a company. He had difficulty relating to people; he was not oriented toward being able to see their problems. I got along beautifully because I'd gone to Harvard Law School, and he had gone to Harvard College for a while. He seemed to think that gave us something in common. He talked a little bit about [Harvard]. Of course he didn't graduate, and I think that bothered him considerably. His ability to relate to the average insurance employee was not great. Most of his subordinates had gotten accustomed to him; he'd been there for quite a long time.

He didn't exercise much close supervision. The department had the job of settling claims on surety bonds, and I was obviously very new at it, but he would send me out to Bangor, Maine, and Omaha, Nebraska, and Buffalo, New York, completely on my own to settle a case, giving me a company checkbook to write whatever check I decided to settle it. I never worked with him; very few people worked with him. He was sort of a loner. I worked for him in the sense that some contractor had gone bankrupt in Washington, D.C. He left a school unfinished and a church remodeling job unfinished, and I went to Washington for six weeks to get this thing cleared up. When I came back, I would tell him what I had done, but there wasn't much of any direct supervision. As far as advice, he never gave me much. He would tell me the problem was here or there and come back when you get it solved, which was very much of an unusual benefit for me because the number of times you can get a job like that right out of law school are few. Usually, you're in a position

*Stevens' principal agent in France during the 1930s was Anatole Vidal. In 1931, the sixty-two-year-old Vidal bought a Parisian bookstore of which Stevens was already a customer. Stevens had had little rapport with the previous owner, who had not been particularly interested in art or in his foreign clients (letter of Paule Vidal to Samuel French Morse, February 6, 1956, private coll.: Samuel French Morse).

Vidal, on the other hand, was indefatigable in satisfying Stevens' wants, from bonbons to books to an occasional painting. Indeed, they established such rapport that an oil painting of Vidal by Jean Labasque hung in Stevens' bedroom, part of the furnishings mentioned in the poem "The Latest Freed Man." The war interrupted Stevens' contact with Vidal; when the poet again became a client of the bookshop after the liberation of Paris, the Librairie Coloniale was run by Vidal's daughter, her father having died in 1944. Paule Vidal, as her father before her, was equally dogged in fulfilling Stevens' requests until just before his death in 1955.

where somebody's looking over your shoulder all the time. He put me in these sink-or-swim situations.

He had several honorary degrees about then. He got one from Mount Holyoke, which I remember vividly. Because he didn't know how to drive a car and he didn't own a car, whenever he went anyplace somebody had to go with him. I picked him up at his house, but I didn't get in the house. I never did get in that house. His wife was sort of a recluse. I never did meet her; I never met his daughter. It was a standing matter of astonishment at the office that no one ever got to see his family. I always had the impression that he and his wife were not very well suited to each other and were certainly not very compatible. I'm speaking strictly from hearsay that his wife had some emotional problems. He never discussed it. That certainly was the general impression. Just knowing him, I think he would be a pretty difficult man to live with in a domestic situation. If his wife had any neurotic tendencies to start with, living with him for a few years might accentuate [them]. It was a nice June morning [1952], and we drove to Mount Holyoke.

The ceremony was in the chapel. When we arrived we were taken in tow by some official who took him into the academic procession. I was really a chauffeur, but the people at Mount Holyoke figured if I was with him I must be a close friend, so I ended up sitting with the faculty at commencement and going to this big luncheon attended by all the recipients of honorary degrees and by the senior faculty and administration. Stevens made some comments at the luncheon; they were supposed to be facetious, and he evoked some surprised reactions from some of the people. He was a very sardonic person who tended to make comments he thought might shock other people. You get used to this after a while, so I don't recall vividly what he said. That lasted until about two or three in the afternoon; then we drove back to Hartford.

He was a very difficult person to figure out. He was a sort of sane schizophrenic, because he had these two compartments in his mind, poetry and law, and they never got together. I mean he wrote beautifully lucid legal writing; and on the poetry side, I can't understand it, which may be my deficiency, but the two never interrelated. He never brought his life in the world of poetry into the office. When I was working there [a magazine] did an article on him, and they sent a photographer up to take pictures of him in his office. That did bring up some discussion of his career and his poetry, but aside from that he really didn't talk much about it at the office. He got the Bollingen Prize and several other things; he sort of downplayed these things: so what? I don't really think he felt that way. I'm not a knowledgeable person in poetry, and I had never heard of him before I found out I might be working for him.

At that point I found out he was a pretty well known poet. I got hold of one of his books, and I tried to read it, and I didn't get too far. He didn't discuss it, and [there was] no way I could have brought it up without looking like a fool.

He used to eat lunch one day a week, and that one day he would frequently go over to a place called the Canoe Club in East Hartford. Since he didn't drive, I frequently took him over there. It was a delightful way to start a business career, because it was always the end of the day as far as work was concerned. He was a very shy person, basically, and as many shy people are apt to do to cover up their shyness, they adopt an air which can be mistaken for arrogance, aloofness or just plain coldness. He was not what I call a hail-fellow-well-met person. He could put away a good many martinis and he would try to relax, but he didn't succeed very well.

His sense of humor was one that a lot of people did not understand. What he would think would be funny when he said it would be taken by the person who heard it as an insult. I can vividly recall that one or two of his subordinates in the office, whom I'm sure he did not mean to insult, felt that he had insulted them on occasion.

He used to do some things that caused complete anxiety at the office. There was some truckdriver who was a principal in a surety bond up in Vermont. Stevens thought he was going to default on this bond or he was going to be unavailable. At the time, the law of Vermont allowed something called "bodily execution," where you could actually pick up a person and take him to jail for certain things that had nothing to do with crime. Anyhow, on his own authority, without checking with any of the other senior people in the insurance company, he tried to have this fellow picked up and tossed in jail for what he owed the Hartford Accident and Indemnity. When that was found out by the senior management, there was real consternation. The truckdriver had about eight kids, and the management could see the big newspaper stories: cruel, heartless insurance company takes little truckdriver and tosses him in jail.* There was a lot of furor about that. So he didn't have what I'd call the modern corporate executive outlook on a lot of things.

*Stevens was undisturbed by the company's adverse publicity the morning the story broke that Hartford Accident and Indemnity had actually had the man arrested after he had defaulted on the bond by failing to show up in court, according to Herbert Schoen, then a fellow lawyer at the home office who later became company president. "On the front page of the Hartford *Times* or the Hartford *Courant* was this man with all eight children, and this big insurance company ripping him away from his family in the middle of the night. I came into the office that morning and said, 'Mr. Stevens, this is a terrible thing for the image of the company. We should not have done this.' He looked at the picture in the paper, at the eight children, and he said, 'Herb, how many children has the plaintiff?' "

Looking back and knowing what I know about what it takes to be a practicing lawyer, I think he probably would have been very unsuccessful because his personality was the type that would not have given him, if you will, the bedside manner to acquire clients. His technical knowledge of the law was pretty great, but he certainly would not have been the type of person who could develop a law practice.

I always had the impression he was a little enclave in the Hartford Accident. In other words, he didn't fit into the pattern of a senior executive of an insurance company, personality-wise. And I had the feeling the company was proud to have this world-famous poet as a senior officer and would go out of its way to avoid interfering with him.

Mary Kennure

When I started to work there [1938], I didn't have much contact at all with him because I was just a claim clerk. In our [surety] department there were about nine or ten stenographers and clerks, and then the lawyers. If he had a claim to be typed, that was our [job]. He had a wonderful vocabulary; some of it I couldn't understand.

I don't think he realized that I was there for quite some time; later on, when the boys were in the service, I was made head of accounting [for the department]. Then I had a little more contact with him because the drafts every day had to be okayed by him. But he was a very stern man, hard to get acquainted with. I got along very well with him, but I was, frankly, a little afraid of him.

[Every afternoon Kennure would go in with the day's drafts once she was head of accounting.] I was kind of shy, and I blushed easily. He got a big kick out of that, especially if somebody was in the office. He would say, "Watch now." And he'd start a conversation up, and then naturally I would blush. He got the biggest kick out of that. [It was] very embarrassing to me. I had to make the best of it and laugh about it, but I didn't appreciate that.* [After

---

*Depending upon which side of the joke one was on, Stevens' office humor could be either amusing or distressing. "We had just returned from lunch and were talking about nothing in particular," recalls Stevens' colleague Wilson Taylor, "when this young lady [a message girl employed for the summer] appeared at the door to his office with a handful of checks to be signed. Stevens waved her in and proceeded to sign each of the checks. About half-way through, and without looking up, he said, 'This is that girl I was telling you about at lunch today, Taylor.'

"For fear that some future students of Wallace Stevens might think that the young lady was, in fact, discussed at lunch, let me hasten to assure them that such was not the case. It was a typical Stevens remark, made in fun, and, of course, for the purpose of embarrassing the girl. Needless to say it fulfilled its purpose. Such was his delightful sense of humor." (Letter to Daniel Woodward, July 5, 1975, HL.)

work] he used to walk from the office up to Westerly Terrace. I used to see him once in a while 'cause at that time I was living on Sigourney Street, and he used to walk down Sigourney Street to Albany Avenue [which finally connected with his home on Westerly Terrace some two miles from the office]. If I saw him I would say, "Hello, Mr. Stevens"—very gently.

Leslie Tucker

I joined Mr. Stevens in 1925. I was an assistant superintendent of bookkeeping up in the agency department, and they were paying me such a lousy salary I had given my notice to leave the company. He heard about it, and sent for me and said, "Don't worry about the money. Come down, and I'll take care of you," which he did. When I went to work for him, he gave me a big boost, more than I really expected. They finally had a salary committee [at the company], but he said, "Look. This man is worth this much to me, and that's what we're going to pay him." And nobody would object to it. I think our men were paid higher salaries than [for] comparable positions in the rest of the company. [On such matters] Stevens was very fair.

I stayed with him from 1925 to 1934. I did [bookkeeping] for about four years, and then he wanted me to go to law school, so I went to the Hartford College of Law. But during the law school period, I was head of his salvage department. That entailed recovering any money we could from losses that we paid on the surety bonds and the fidelity bonds. He wanted me to go to the New York office and go to Columbia [Law School at night]. He had it all set up for me to go down and live at the YMCA. He was a little bit peeved because I wouldn't take the chance to go down there. [When he was peeved, he was] sullen, very sullen. He wouldn't speak to me for a couple of weeks, but then he got over it. It wasn't usual.

To me he was wonderful. He treated me like a gentleman always. But he did have a caustic tongue. He never did or said anything I could take offense at really except on a couple of occasions he was kidding with me. For instance, when I'd go on a trip out of town for him, he'd say, "Be sure to stay at the YMCA." But of course I never did. You didn't know sometimes whether he was kidding or whether he was serious. I think that was one of his shortcomings: he didn't let people know.

I wasn't aware of [Harmonium, published in 1923] until maybe a year after, when people would bring in books and want him to autograph them. A lot of people tried to see him, autograph seekers, and he didn't want any part of them. The receptionist used to call me and say, "There's somebody out here that wants to have a book autographed." So I'd go out and get it and duck in his office. I hated to go in and interrupt him; he hated to be interrupted over anything. Once he got his mind going on something, he was like a bulldog. I'd go in and stand there for four or five minutes, probably. He'd look up and say, "What the hell do you want?" I'd say, "Here's a book I want autographed." And he'd sign it, "Sincerely, L. Stevens." It was a **W**, but it looked like an **L**. He handled a pen halfway up the handle, so when he wrote it was just scratch, more or less. But he would never see anybody or talk to anybody.

I asked him about "The Man with the Blue Guitar," a few things about it, and he wasn't too anxious to discuss them. He'd answer my questions, but in a way that [indicated] he wasn't interested in talking about it.

Very little [stir was made at the office when a new Stevens book was published]. When the announcement came out in the paper, his picture was in the paper. A few people went in and congratulated him, but that was all. Not until he received the big awards [starting in the late 1940s were his colleagues at the office aware that he was as important a poet as he was].

He was neat as a pin himself. He always dressed beautifully; always a gray suit, though. You couldn't tell whether he had a new suit or not. And usually a red tie. He always wore a crew cut, short hair.

He used to love black Russian tea. He'd import that from an import house down in New York. I usually took [such packages] out to the house for him. I was one of the few persons that got inside the house: in the nine years, maybe three times. He had a beautiful white rug in the living room. I used to say, "That's a beautiful rug, Mr. Stevens." And he'd say, "Look at it, but don't walk on it." He had a bedroom area that was furnished up like a library and a sitting room, and he spent most of his time in there, reading nights. He had a nice desk* in there, lamps and a sitting chair, and, of course, his bed. He had loads of books; he read almost all the time. On several occasions [Tucker met Mrs. Stevens]. I'd only see her when I went to take him out to the house or pick up something for him.

She seemed set back, more or less. She was always very much reserved. And I don't think many people knew her. All the time I knew him they never were seen together anywhere. She never called him at the office, all the time that I knew him. She was a very plain person: she wore her hair straight down, a little bundle in the back. I don't think she ever went to the hairdresser.

Occasionally on Saturday, he would have lunch with Ralph Mullen and I over to the Canoe Club. We'd be going over for lunch, and he would call

---

*According to Stevens' daughter, at home the poet did not compose at a desk but, rather, wrote sitting in an easy chair.

Ralph and say he'd like to go with us. He'd sit over there and gab with us, oh, until about three o'clock in the afternoon, when we'd take him home. He'd have a nice big lunch, usually lobster or something of that nature. He made you do most of the talking, as a matter of fact. He never did much of the talking. He'd draw you out with questions: every time I was with him he asked me about the family, this, that and the other thing. Stevens finally got in the Canoe Club after a great deal of controversy. He had tried for years and years to get in. I don't think enough of the men liked him. Most of those men who belonged to the Canoe Club were all Masons and all Shriners. They were a cliquey bunch, and they were wonderful men, high-type individuals. For years [Stevens had been trying to get in before he was accepted in 1948]. Starting in the late twenties at least, he went over there. We had more or less a Friday-night club: it was Ralph; Stevens, sometimes; Bill Liedike, Ted Armstrong—these were all officers of the company—the cashier, Whitman. Stevens would go occasionally, but not too often with us. About two or three times [a winter]. But almost every Friday night during the wintertime, five or six of us would go over to the Canoe Club and have dinner and then go over to the wrestling matches [at] the Armory. He didn't care too much for them; he only went because the rest of us went, I think. He was very jovial and enjoyed everybody's company—seemed to, anyway. We all had a lot of fun, laughing and kidding all evening. That was the time he let his hair down.

Marguerite Flynn

When I went to work for the Hartford in 1927, Mr. Stevens was in charge of the surety bond department, consisting of perhaps twenty people. In those days he was rather a forbidding character, given to sudden, unreasonable and unpredictable fits of temper and criticism. At that time he was one of the key men and was consulted about many of the major issues of the company. He had a very logical and orderly mind.

It wasn't until about 1941 that I went to work directly as his secretary, except for times when his then secretary, who had a temper of her own to match his, would walk out on him, but of course, the final flare-up came and she [Mrs. Hester Baldwin] didn't return to the company. I think he was a little more careful with him[self] and maybe I didn't annoy him in so many ways.

Wallace Stevens was a very interesting man to work for. His command of English was perfect and if you took his dictation just as he gave it, you never had to hesitate in transcribing it. He corresponded with many people about the world; bought books in England, paintings in France, tea in Ceylon.

Instead of traveling to all of these countries, he got his knowledge of them from reading and correspondence. Besides having an unusual knowledge of the French language, he spoke and read both German and French.

In spite of the fact the he was held in awe throughout the office, after his death I received several letters telling of nice things he had done for people.

During Mr. Stevens' later years he became more friendly although he still wanted his privacy and didn't allow his literary activities to mix with business. No one in the office knew when he would be getting honors, such as degrees and prizes, until it appeared in the newspapers. He even came to Wesleyan [University] in Middletown, my hometown, for a degree without telling me.

Mr. Stevens was a perfectionist in his work and expected everyone to pay as strict attention to business as he did, although if one of the adjusters in the department made a bad decision, he didn't criticize him. He arrived at the office punctually at nine o'clock and left again at four-thirty, never leaving things to be done after closing. When he was in good health he walked to and from the office to his home, a distance of three or four miles. It was on these long walks that he jotted down lines for his poetry, polishing it up later.

It was a great privilege to work for Mr. Stevens and to know him in a different way than academically.[41]

Richard Sunbury

In the summer of 1931, I was in my second year of college; my father became ill, and I had to discontinue my college course. After contacting various places for six months, I was hired as a mailboy [in the bond-claims department, where Sunbury worked through 1934]. That's when I first knew Mr. Stevens. He was a large person, of urbane manner, and his general appearance demanded respect. He was a man of dignity. He had a good pallor, high color and a ruddy complexion.

He made this quite plain right at the start: he demanded care. Now, care not only in your work but in everything you did. All the time it was care. I've seen him read his letters over and correct them one case after another, very methodically. He'd go through and make his corrections on each one, page after page. If you had five reinsurers on a contract, why, you would have a lot of correspondence to get out. And each letter, if there was one mistake in it, that meant five corrections. At the same time, he'd go to his dictionary and check his words.

Very probably Mr. Kearney had told Mr. Stevens about my situation at home. And that gave Mr. Stevens a kindly feeling toward me. It was after the first two or three months that every once in a while he'd ask me, "How's your father, and how's your mother?" Because Mother had cancer then, and Dad had had a stroke. He would keep in touch, but he wouldn't intrude. He didn't get personal; I mean he didn't pry into your personal affairs unless you had a crisis, or maybe some of the other people in the department indicated to him that things were tough with you. He might make some comment: "I'm sorry. What can I do to help?" In March 1933, my brother died. It was in the middle of the Depression. He called me in and asked what I was going to do about it. I said, "I don't know, really, 'cause I don't have any money to go up to the funeral." He reached in his pocket and gave me fifty dollars. I said, "Well, I can't pay you back very soon." He said, "Well, don't worry about it. You'll pay me back." Dad died in December 1933. They took up a collection at the office because there was no money. Mr. Stevens started it out with fifty dollars, so when Les Tucker came over to my house, he gave me a check for one hundred and fifty dollars to help out with my father's funeral expenses.

And after that Mr. Stevens asked me what I was going to do, I just had Mother to take care of. I told him I wanted to go to law school, so he gave me a raise of five dollars a week and had me transferred to the judicial department. He knew [that] there I'd get a start on what I wanted to do. In the following summer, he contacted me again. He asked me, "Well, are you going to law school?" I said, "I don't have any money." He said, "Why don't you borrow some?" And I said, "I can't borrow what I can't pay back." He said, "Well, we'll see about that." So he took me by the arm and walked me to Mr. Kearney's office. He said, "Jim, this boy has to go to law school. He has to borrow some money. Do you think we can fix it with Merriman [an officer at the Bankers Trust Company] across the street?" Kearney said, "I think we can. You see about it, will you?" He did, and Merriman loaned me enough money to go to law school at night. However, there wasn't enough money for books, so I used to do my studying in the office law library. Well, he came in one day and said, "What are you doing?" I said, "I'm looking up law because I've got a class tonight." "Well, where are your books?" "I don't have any." So right there he took me by the hand and showed me how to look up law and the various reporting systems. As a matter of fact, several times. Because of what he showed me, next year I was able to be librarian in the Hartford College of Law and earn my books and tuition.

He used to call me down every so often, ask how I was doing in law school. I'd say, "Lousy." "Well, what's the trouble?" I said, "I have to work too darn hard." He said, "Well, that's true enough, but are you passing?" I says, "Yes, but that's just about all." I had to work all the way through; it was terrible. But he was the motivating force. He would call me down and say, "What are you studying?" I'd say torts or constitutional law. "Now listen, there's just one point in all that course," and he'd give me the focal point to look for [in] each course. "If you keep that in mind, Richard"—he always called me Richard—"you'll have no trouble."

Before I even went to law school, I'd take his cases and read them noon hours. He came out one day and he said, "What are you doing?" "I'm reading your letter of yesterday before it goes back to the file room." Well, that was the start. I'd ask him, "Why do you do this?" He said, "I'll tell you about it some other time"; he had no time, but he was nice about it. Other times, "Well, Richard, when you come in tonight, we'll talk about it." So instead of going in at ten after four, I would come in at four o'clock, waiting for the mail. "Sit down," he'd say. "Now about this case. This is why we did it." I remember asking him one day, "Why do you take exceptions?" He said, "That's to stop people. That's to give you the go-ahead. If you take your exceptions there, you'll stop them right there, for the moment anyway, and that gives you something to go ahead on in the next higher court." One time I said, "Why do you keep appealing all the time?" He said, "There's only one reason. You hope for the unexpected. If you have judgments against you in the lower courts, when you get to the Supreme Court your prospects are only three in ten of overturning that." He knew that eventually I'd be trying to go to law school; he was just breaking me in gradually.

Yes, [Stevens talked about his own years as a law student when Sunbury was studying law. Also] he talked about being in a law firm in New York City. He said, "I had a very unhappy time in some respects." I said, "Well, why?" He said, "Well, Richard, I wasn't doing the type of work I would like to have done." He didn't give me any of the details; he'd indicate that he just wasn't in his groove, something like that. And he said, "Then I used to take my trips over to New Jersey on Sunday." He told me about some of these trips and what he'd seen on the ferryboat. They were the highlights of his week. He lived alone when he was in that law firm, in a hall bedroom. He said he despised living in a hall bedroom. A hall bedroom is about the width of a hallway [and lacks a window]. I guess for a while there he was obliged to just secure that sort of accommodation. He said that he walked around with his feet on the pavement, through the holes in his shoes, most of the time while he was in New York. I heard that in the course of conversation with other people.

He said that he had some of the best times of his life at Harvard. When he was in college, he said he used to get a great deal of pleasure out of this: regularly, he'd go to different parts of Boston to the pawnshops. He'd see how much they'd give him on his watch. He said the highest he ever got was thirty-five dollars. He was quite delighted because that was a pastime with him.

He was a very smooth man. He had a soft voice, and his diction was beautiful. His vocabulary was something you just sat down and said, "Oh, boy!" If you could sit down and listen to that man talk, you'd be entranced. It was almost like music to listen to the man talk. He was a master of metaphor.

This man would take a case [in bond claims], size it up: he had a psychic intuitiveness about him. He'd say, talking with the other men, "I think we're going to have trouble with this case." They'd say, "Why do you want to put up a reserve of so much?"—like $500,000. He'd say, "You wait and see." And sure enough, that case would run into trouble. He'd say, "Now, I think that this case will settle for about so much." The figure would be all out of proportion to what they had before them. But sure enough, it would come pretty close to what he said. Then they would have some cases, everything black as coal; there's nothing good about this case whatsoever. He'd say, "We're going to get out of this one with just expense money." And so help me, many times they did. They would have some involved cases come in; Mr. Ladish and "Doc" [Ivan Daugherty] would come in and talk to Wallace Stevens. And before they would get halfway through laying the bare facts of that particular case, he would say, "Well, now, what about this?" In other words, he'd be fourteen miles down the road. He'd say, "We'll appeal this to the last ditch," [or] "We better pay and get out just as soon as we can." That is a psychic something or other that the fellow had about this type of work which made him so wonderful about it.

The Christmas of 1933 he called me in and showed me a white leather-bound book; it was Chinese poetry. He had bought it for two hundred dollars, and he was extremely delighted with it. And in our talks, he would tell me about poetry. I remember he showed me how much could be said in so few words. I couldn't understand it then and I can't understand much of it now, but he did awaken my interest in and my desire to write poetry, which I do in half-fashion now. Now, up to that time I had small acquaintance with poetry. [My fiancée] got me a book of Edgar Guest when we graduated from high school. Once I mentioned Edgar Guest, and he just looked aside. I guess he was just not interested in Edgar Guest. When we used to talk, I'd say, "What about scanning and all that sort of thing?" He'd say, "Richard, scanning doesn't mean a thing. It's what you feel, and what you sense, and how you say it." He read me things [sometimes] that he would be writing or if he'd received [a poem] from old Judge Powell. "How does that sound to you?" "It sounds beautiful. Tell me what it means." And he would do that.

He'd be writing them right there at his desk, because he would stop dictating
to Mrs. Baldwin. He would stop right in the middle of dictating, and he
would reach down in his right-hand drawer, and he would just write down
[something], put it back. I've seen him do that. He had a peculiar filing
system. He always filed his poetry notes in his lower right corner of his desk,
which was open most of the time to a degree. It seemed to me there were
sheaves and sheaves. And sometimes he would reach down, and he'd shuffle
through three or four. He'd scratch out something or put something in. Or
he might take the top one and just add a line or two. All of a sudden, he'd
be reading a case, and I've seen him reach down in his drawer and just pick
something up. His private copies of his commercial work or his business
letters would go in his lower left-hand drawer. And when he finished signing
the mail at night, the signed copies of his letters would be thrown on the
right-hand side of his desk and the cases that were to go back to file would
be thrown on the floor on the left-hand side. He called it his "freight-yard
method." That's how he trained me when I first came in there.

But most always he got it [his poetic inspiration] when he was walking. He
came back [from his noon-hour walks], and I'd go in immediately at one-
thirty. "Don't disturb me, Richard." He was writing. Then, he'd give it to
Mrs. Baldwin and say, "Would you run a transcript of this?" She'd bring it
in: "I don't know what this is all about, but here it is." She didn't hesitate
to tell him off. When he'd had a particularly tough morning, he'd say, "Well,
we'll drop this now, and we'll go dance around in the sunshine." He'd go out
and walk during the noon hours; now, some of the men down there walked
with him. He would have no lunch; he just walked sometimes. He enjoyed
that lunch-hour walk. He would get away from things. He said, "This is my
time." If I saw him in front I hurried up to catch up; if he were in back, I'd
wait for him. I do know that in his walks there [was] generated a considerable
amount of his thinking along [poetic] lines. He most always had some en-
velopes stuffed in his pocket, and he'd just pull them out and write on the
back. Just walking, he'd say, "Wait just a minute, please." He'd pull out an
envelope. He always had about a half-dozen in his pocket. Probably half a
dozen times he took his noon-hour walks, and I used to join him [when
Sunbury worked under Stevens]. I remember one time he was telling me that
the prior Sunday he had walked to Farmington. "You can tell where I went
by the sweat that dropped off the seat of my pants." He had a very delicious
sense of humor.

I think that time, that was between 1932 and 1934, he was just reaching
his stride [as a poet]. I found out he was a poet just looking over Mrs.
Baldwin's shoulder, so to speak. I was coming up every night to Mrs. Baldwin

to get the mail. Sometimes she would have finished her work and she would have been working on some of his poetry. She would let me read it, and that's how I first became acquainted with the fact that he had this particular interest. The ones that I saw were typewritten copies that Mrs. Baldwin kept, and she'd show them to me when they were stricken off. But that was a confidential matter, because she knew my feeling for Stevens. I bugged her often enough; she knew I was interested. Before some of his letters went in, she'd [also] say, "You were inquiring about this, wondering how he'd answer it," because I'd talk to her at times. "I'm going to take this in. Do you want to read the file copy first?" I suppose I was the fair-haired boy between the two of them. She was an older woman, and she was a humdinger. She didn't hesitate to tell him when he was wrong [in his business correspondence]. He made grammatical errors. He didn't like it awfully well, but she was almost always correct. She'd say, "Mr. Stevens, do you really want to say this?" Her form of shorthand was extremely accurate. He'd say, "I didn't say that." She'd say, "That's what my book says." And before that letter went out, she would have him change that. I never saw such a terrific worker as Mr. Stevens. He'd have a stack of cases that high, and she'd come in, she'd take dictation for five solid hours, all morning. He worked late some nights, but I don't recall his being a briefcase man.

· IV ·

A MAN AND HIS PAPERS

When Stevens reflected on his life at the office, he thought of it, like his colleagues, above all in terms of a daily stack of thick files and his litter of letters and cases. At times, indeed, it seemed to him that he had grown into something of a caricature, a man made out of paper inhabiting a world of words. "A man in the home office," he reflected in a 1938 article for *The Eastern Underwriter*, "tends to conduct his business on the basis of the papers that come before him. After twenty-five years or more of that sort of thing, he finds it difficult sometimes to distinguish himself from the papers he handles and comes almost to believe that he and his papers constitute a single creature, consisting principally of hands and eyes: lots of hands and lots of eyes."[42]

Curiously, despite the hundreds of letters he wrote and the scores of files he compiled over the years, Stevens the insurance man of letters has not survived. Hartford Accident and Indemnity routinely destroyed almost all of this material to make space for new cases before any scholar thought to apprise the company of its value in re-creating this essential aspect of Stevens' life at the office.[43] Fortunately, however, Stevens on paper made an indelible impression on men such as Charles O'Dowd, whose job at the home office for a number of years entailed reading Stevens' correspondence, and on field men such as A. J. Fletcher and Arthur Park, whose main contact with Stevens was by mail.

Charles O'Dowd

My boss believed that you should know everything and where everybody sat, so you started out as a runner—filing, doing errands. I'd been there about three weeks, and he called me in one day and handed me a file. "Would you take this over to Mr. Stevens' office? It's around the corner." But he didn't give me any warning, and the warning that everybody knew was that when he was dictating you didn't interrupt him. So I walked in about ten steps— it was a big office—and stood there. I didn't say a word, and he finally looked up. I says, "Mr. Stevens, Mr. Armstrong asked me to give you this file." And in his best Harvard accent, he says, "Could you, by any *chawnce,* be speaking to me?"—as if there were a great many people in there with him. I says, "You're the only one I am speaking to. And here is the file." Went over and put it on his desk and walked out. But he didn't want to be interrupted and I can understand, as I later found out, why he didn't, because he would get a train of thought going, and sometimes that would take you up some byways if you do get interrupted.

About 1928 I became Mr. Armstrong's assistant, and part of the underwriting job was to review all the claim cases. Always when a contract claim was finished, I would get the file and review it from stem to stern, not to check on Mr. Stevens' handling of it but to find out what we [underwriters] did wrong and maybe correct it. So I reviewed for years all the files with his correspondence as it related to contract claim files, and it was very interesting. As a matter of fact, some of the time I'd make copies of them, they were so beautifully written. His letters were as clear and precise as his poetry was obtuse—at least, obtuse to me. Sometimes I'd run across a word that struck me that it was out of place; it didn't quite seem to fit into what he was trying to say. And I would do exactly what he used to do all the time: go out into the law library and get Webster's big dictionary, look [up] the word, and sure enough, it was right on the spot. It was a word that was unusual, and it would make one think, He's missed it here—but you found it eventually. Maybe it was the tenth or twelfth meaning, but it would be exactly the word that fitted what he was trying to get across. It gave you quite a vocabulary, because he would go after a precise, even though remote, meaning. The guy I saw using the big dictionary in the law library more than anyone else was Wallace Stevens.

He was very precise. He was only colorful when he was writing to some old friend, and there was repartee between them on something. There was an old judge [Arthur Powell] in Georgia who became a lawyer, if I remember correctly, at age fifteen. They used to have some delightful correspondence when a case was over. I had copies of some of those made, and they were tremendous. I remember one [that] Powell wrote about going to the Supreme Court of the United States. The question came up, what he should wear before the Supreme Court. Powell said, "I finally dusted off the swallow-tail coat which is indiginous to a great many Southern lawyers and which, when I was presented with the same problem when I was presented to the King and Queen of England, I dared to wear."

I remember the shortest letter I ever read was one Stevens wrote. We had a claim around Minneapolis, and there'd been a lot of correspondence back and forth with Stevens [and the lawyer representing the Hartford]. The lawyer evidently had never been east and wanted to get east, and thought it was absolutely necessary to have a personal interview with Stevens, which Stevens didn't think he needed. After two or three letters—and the guy kept insisting—Stevens finally wrote him a letter in reply: "Come ahead." That's all that was in it.

He didn't interfere in underwriting, and you didn't interfere in claim handling. Very precise in that. I don't think he ever asked any advice on claim handling; he might ask about some facts. Now that brings up a story. We had given a contract bond to a Baptist church in Oklahoma City. The contractor got into financial trouble, and the thing got into claim. There was a lot of bickering back and forth. The attorney for the Baptist church not only wanted performance but he wanted the company to pay the labor and materials bills, which had been unpaid and which the church was going to have to pay if we didn't. Stevens says, "No soap. You got a performance bond, period." He called me down. He says, "What's this? They insist that we pay labor and materials bills. There's no bond covering labor and materials bills." "Mr. Stevens," I said, "it was a mistake we made. They should have given them a labor and material bond." "Okay, Chawlie." He rang the buzzer for his secretary to come in, and he wrote the letter to Walter Downs, one of his assistants, who was in Oklahoma City: "Pay the Jones claim as though a labor and material bond had been given. You fire everybody in the Oklahoma City branch. I'll fire everybody in the home office." He was absolutely straight-line, very fair. If there was a reasonable doubt, he would favor the claimant; but if there was no doubt, he was just tough as nails, as he should be.

His colleagues knew he didn't attempt to inject himself except in his own line. He was, you might say, a prince in his own principality. I don't think they messed around with him much, and he didn't mess around with them. In those days in the Hartford, most of the top men were very independent in their own lines. There was, of course, quite a bit of socializing, but it was purely social and voluntary.

Sunday mornings, I'd leave [home to play golf] around nine, and I'd run into Mr. Stevens, who was a great walker. I'd toot the horn and wave, and he'd wave. One Monday morning I walked into his office; I said, "Mr. Stevens, I saw you taking your usual walk yesterday. Sometime when you're walking Sunday morning, why don't you stop by the apartment? Carmy [O'Dowd's wife] will buy you a drink. Give you something to get started with on Sunday morning." He said, "Chawlie, I won't do that, but I'll accept a rain check for some martinis; let's say, tomorrow night." I says, "Fine." So I came home and told Carmy. She was a little flustered because [of] Stevens and what have you. She'd heard some weird stories. Stevens had some real fine paintings; he had an agent over in Paris. I knew he had a lot of them, because he'd mention it. So Carmy was all worried. This picture she'd picked up at an auction—I guess it's a good antique painting—it was hanging over the mantel. She said, "What'll he say when he sees that?" "Well, he'll look at it probably and say, 'Chawlie, why don't you hang the goddamn thing in the cellar!' "—which didn't make her anymore at [ease]. Sure enough, he came the next night. He put Carmy completely at ease. He had asked me the previous day what her maiden name was, and I told him. Well, he walked in and for a half to three-quarters of an hour [talked about] where her ancestors came from in Europe and where they settled. He had, in that twenty-four-hour period, done a complete genealogy. She was entranced with the guy—as he could make you. He mentioned to me that at one time he undertook to have his family genealogy traced. "After they found a couple of bastards, I told them to lay off. I paid them off and quit," which was probably untrue. He was a funny guy.

He mentioned to me once that his roommate at Harvard was a famous football player who, when he finished, went to West Point and played four more years and was later coach at West Point and Harvard. He said, "He had absolutely no interest in literature, and I had absolutely no interest in athletics. We were the most compatible roommates anybody had in college. We had nothing in common." He was a funny guy.

Seven or eight years before [his death], we were sitting in his office one day talking poetry, and poetry isn't exactly my dish. The *Rubáiyát* I like; *Don Juan* I can understand. Talking about his poetry, I said, "Mr. Stevens, I just can't understand your stuff. If I had to choose between you and Robert Service, I'd take Robert Service because I can understand Robert Service."

He says, "Chawlie, it isn't necessary that you understand my poetry or any poetry. It's only necessary that the writer understand it. I've got paintings hanging in my house, and I don't understand. But that isn't necessary; I think they're very beautiful. What the painter is trying to say, I don't know. But it isn't necessary that I understand it; it isn't necessary for you or anybody else to understand my poetry. I understand it; that's all that's necessary." It used to hang me up. I tried to read it, but I was all tangled up like a skein of yarn. I bought one book, *The Necessary Angel.* I said, "Would you autograph it, Mr. Stevens? I don't understand it, but I'd like your name in it." "Tickled to death. Glad to do it!" In the twenties and the early thirties [O'Dowd learned] that he was a poet, and I attempted reading some of his stuff. He never mentioned his poetry unless you brought it up. He always seemed a little reluctant, certainly at first, when I talked to him. I didn't attempt to force it. I might say, "Mr. Stevens, I see you had a write-up in the New York *Times,*" or something like that. He'd say, "Yes, Chawlie. Now let's get down to business." [Some] magazine wrote an article on Stevens, and they called him a literary snob. His comment to me: "If you like the Democratic party, are you a Roosevelt snob?" And then he went on for two or three other kinds of snobs. [In other words,] "Why call me a literary snob because I like poetry?"

It was in 1937 or '38 on Good Friday he wanted to go up to Pomfret, [Connecticut]. There was a garden in a private estate that he had heard about and heard it was very good, so he asked if I would drive him up. We spent a couple of hours in the garden. He was intensely interested in the flowers, the structure of them and whether they were scented or not, the colors. Then we went over to the Ben Grosvenor Inn for lunch. We had to wait a few minutes to get a table, and we were standing in the library. Like most resort-inn libraries, it had all last year's best sellers and the best sellers for the previous ten years on its shelves. So I said, "I suppose you have read most of these, Mr. Stevens." He says, "No, Chawlie, all I do is read French novels." When we came back from Pomfret, we went over to the house on Farmington Avenue, looked in his flower garden, and he brought me into the house. I don't remember much about it except the bronze statue of Mrs. Stevens, which is on your ten-cent piece. I think I recognized it and mentioned it. She was working out in the yard when we pulled in. I don't know how much conversation Mr. Stevens had with Mrs. Stevens. One time, and this was when he lived on Westerly Terrace, he said, "Chawlie, I'd invite you over for a drink, but our house hasn't been dusted in months. You can run your fingers across the piano and draw a furrow in it." He told me, "That's a lie." Then, "Mrs. Stevens and I went out for a walk yesterday afternoon. We walked to the end of Westerly Terrace, and she turned left and I turned right."

I think somebody that was friendly with him took him at face value. I don't think he was particularly keen about somebody kowtowing to him, and I certainly never did. I just took him as I found him. I tried to respect his wishes, but I used to let him have it a little bit because he was just another damn poet. In my book, he wasn't John Keats.

A. J. Fletcher

Someone recommended that Wallace Stevens refer a bond claim to me for handling [in the 1920s]. I apparently handled it to his satisfaction, and for a good many years after that he sent me all the cases that he had in North Carolina. I suppose the relationship continued for at least thirty years. I had more surety clients, I believe, than any other firm in the state; that's a speciality I engaged in. [As a surety lawyer Wallace Stevens was] first-class. He was just amazing when he'd come to handling a bond claim. He just thought straight through; there wasn't any extra energy.

[When Stevens referred a case to a lawyer] he analyzed everything in his first letter so he didn't have to go back if anything should come up later concerning the case that had to be clarified. He just got that letter and read whatever part of it was applicable. His analysis of the case in his first letter [was peculiar to Stevens among the surety lawyers Fletcher knew]. It made it awfully easy to communicate with him or get an answer to a question. It would have been, nine times out of ten, already set forth in the letter by which he sent the claim to you. As to the character of the letter, I'd say that he never wrote one to me that didn't sound exactly like a prose poem: he was just that clear, and concise, and beautiful.

He would just relate the facts, and I had to do the rest of it myself. I'd report to him what I'd done; he uniformly approved it. I was in his office one day in Hartford, and this young man connected with his department came through. Wallace Stevens said, "Mr. So-and-so, I want you to meet Mr. A. J. Fletcher. He's the best surety lawyer between Richmond and"—I was afraid he was going to say Petersburg; that's right next door—but finally he came out and said, "the equator."

[When Fletcher visited Stevens at the home office,] we went over the cases we had and, ordinarily, what I would recommend we do next. Even if he offered suggestions, he'd follow my advice. I never knew him to raise the point that I had done wrong. Once I told him that some [of his poems] were sort of hard to decipher. He said a woman recently asked him, "What does this particular poem mean?" I'm not sure he didn't use a cuss word, but he said, "I don't know. I don't know what it means." On one of my visits there, I was congratulating him, I think, on having a book of poems published. I wanted to sound him out about my activity as promoter of an opera company [in North Carolina]; I raised the point in congratulating him. He said, "I think I remember seeing somewhere about your being engaged in some sort of idolatry." We were probably on even a more firm business [footing] than before because I was as crazy as he was in having an avocation to which I was devoting a good deal of time.

When I was trying a case for Wallace Stevens in Nashville, Walter Downs, his successor, called to tell me of his death. I couldn't go back [to the courtroom] to continue because, while I didn't see him often, I knew that I had [had] one of the best friends in Wallace Stevens. It was a real personal loss. I guess I just loved the fellow: the friendliness toward me, his willingness to trust to my judgment, his offering me a job on his staff in Hartford. It was a brilliant opportunity, but I didn't want success that far away from home. Just one act of courtesy after another. He was just a fine gentleman.

Arthur Park

I was in the surety-claims department, which was, considering the size of the company, a very, very small department. The result was, the management, the president and the board of directors didn't pay much attention to our little department. Other than the home office, there were less than a dozen employees in this particular work, whereas there'd be hundreds in the automobile department. I was in the San Francisco office, which was in charge of the business in the thirteen Western states; I was the only one who spent my full time on surety-claim work.

I was taught by Mr. Stevens, if there was any doubt about the validity of a claim being presented against the Hartford, to always resolve that doubt in favor of the person making the claim. He was basically a very honorable man —a man, in a business way, of high integrity. The only time Mr. Stevens got upset about a decision opposed to his decision was where it would be made by someone who had gone over his head for business or policy reasons. He treated claimants the same way whether it was Ford Motor Company as the insured or some little organization down the corner. A broker who handled a claim for a very large insured would occasionally go over Mr. Stevens' head and get approval to pay the claim. In those instances, Mr. Stevens was very incensed. Very very much so [would he make his feelings known. How often

Stevens would be overruled in other parts of the country] I wouldn't know; maybe once or twice a year here in the Pacific Department.

[Stevens was difficult to deal with on cases] only as people misunderstood what they considered sarcasm. It was [like] Wallace Stevens to have this sort of suave sarcasm if he didn't agree with you. It was a pleasant sarcasm. People did not understand. I recall the first two or three letters I received from him: I misunderstood this sarcasm, and I was about ready to resign I was so mad, when it was explained to me that this was his way of joking. As an illustration of Stevens and his ability to be sarcastic, I recall an instance when I was back in Hartford when I wanted to get a copy of a paper that was given by the vice-president and general counsel of the Aetna [insurance company] at the American Bar Association. Mr. Stevens attempted to get this paper by telephoning Mr. Braxton Dew, the author. The conversation went something like this. "Mr. Braxton Dew, please." "Mr. Dew is not in." "When do you expect him?" "I haven't the faintest idea." "Well, will he be in tomorrow?" "I haven't the faintest idea. Who's calling, please?" Mr. Stevens replied, "I haven't the faintest idea."

I don't think he was aware [that people took offense]. I've talked to many people in his old department who worked for him for years who did take offense, and I know from talking to Mr. Stevens that he did not realize they were offended by that. One individual would get so incensed, and I would tell him, "He doesn't mean that." [Among his colleagues at other companies,] some people who did not have much to do with him did not understand him; felt he was pompous, arrogant and sarcastic. I know of other people who had similar positions with other companies, such as the Travelers, the Aetna and so on, who felt that way about him, but I'm convinced [that it was] only because they never really had an opportunity to understand him: we who worked directly under him did.

I was asked to go to Hartford [for the first time] in July or August 1927. I recall very well going into the building on Asylum Avenue and was ushered into Mr. Stevens' office. Having chatted for ten or fifteen minutes, he then brought in the various people in the department and introduced them to me, people I'd been corresponding with. He had a [company] car and a chauffeur, and so he invited me to luncheon. We got in and drove and drove, at least a good half-hour. I said, "Mr. Stevens, my time is your time, but where are we going for luncheon—New York?" He said, "No, there's a nice little inn down a few miles from here that has wonderful cheese. I just love the cheese, and I thought you'd enjoy it." We had a lovely lunch in a little New England inn that was built in the 1600s. That was my first meeting with Mr. Stevens. Each time I would go back there, it was a very generally accepted rule that you always went in to see Mr. Stevens first, and then he would bring in all the boys that I knew even better than I knew him. Nonetheless, it always started with him. Very frequently [Stevens would invite Park to the Hartford Canoe Club for lunch]. That would be when he would invite the other boys along. It was a jolly afternoon, a certain amount of kidding back and forth. He liked to needle the boys. My first trip, I didn't realize that he was just needling them, because he looked rather serious when he was doing it, but I later learned that he was just having a good time. I don't recall any lengthy discussions on business matters. He would call the boys in, and we would sit around in his office and that's when the business was discussed—never at luncheon. I don't think [there was much talk of politics or the events of the day at lunch]. It was more like a family discussion: what these boys did . . . about their families . . . somebody just became a father. Very little [would Stevens talk about his own background]. That's the one thing I've often wondered about, why he didn't. Anything I learned about Wallace Stevens' early background was learned from somebody other than Wallace Stevens.

I'm quite sure it was some years after I'd been employed by the company that I realized he was considered an outstanding poet. It was never discussed by any of the employees or any of the people who worked under him. [One day Park opened his office mail to find that Stevens had sent him a poem:] "Ode to a Butterfly." I don't know how that came about, but I read it a dozen times. It was just one page; it wasn't a lengthy thing. I remember trying to understand it. It was handwritten. I think that was when I first learned he was a poet.

· V ·

THE POET AT THE OFFICE

In 1947, *Life* magazine wanted to do a feature about the poet on executive row and got in touch with Stevens' New York publisher. Stevens was hardly as pleased at the prospect of a photo spread about him at home and at the office as was the publicist at Knopf, and he refused. "It doesn't take much imagination to see what happens when a man in a large office permits the sort of thing that *Life* is thinking of," he explained to William Cole. "His associates take it for granted that he is promoting himself and the whole thing tends to alienate him from them. I cannot think of anything more imprudent and will have nothing to do with it."[44] While Stevens was politic in down-playing his other career while he was at the office, he did not, as some critics have suggested, try to conceal that he was a poet from his Hartford colleagues, who had known this from the very spring he had started working at the home office. Paul Dow, Richard Cross, Hazel Kuhnly, Naaman Corn and Herbert Schoen represent a cross section of the home-office staff—chauffeurs, secretaries and fellow lawyers—who daily encountered Stevens the poet at the office.

It was another matter, however, with the men in the field, with whom Stevens had little personal contact. He was inclined to keep his poetry a secret from these men, many of whom knew him only by mail. In the mid-1920s, for example, when it was common knowledge among home-office staff that he was a writer, Stevens cautioned a lawyer in the field who had stumbled upon *Harmonium* "not to speak of his literary efforts among our acquaintances, as it might hurt his business influence."[45] Among his fellow businessmen, who sized him up from the distance, say, of Sinclair Lewis' Zenith, Stevens was concerned that his reputation as an insurance man not be tarnished by stereotypes of the poet among the Babbitts of business. Ironically, when young Stevens had begun writing seriously, he had not been altogether free from at least some of these American images of the poet as eccentric. "Keep all this a great secret," he cautioned his wife, who was away from New York on vacation that summer of 1913 when he began working again at his poetry, evenings after work. "There is something absurd about all this writing of verses . . . you see, my habits are positively lady-like."[46]

Richard Cross

His office was about fifty feet from where I was, right off the rotunda, so I would see him come and go. The one thing that I came to recognize quite readily, that Mr. Stevens was very much a man unto himself, even at the company, because he was always very busy. But he was always very pleasant, would have a word to say. Other than that, why, it was all business with him.

He stopped in the law library one day [in 1942], and I was carrying on a conversation with [Neil] McGiehan. Very frequently he had [McGiehan] go over to the State Library with respect to his poetry and [look up] certain words. He was Stevens' errand boy. I can't recall what we were talking about; there was something [about] poetry that started this. But in any event, he said, "How would you two gentlemen like to come over to my house for dinner some night?" We looked at each other in astonishment. "Well, thank you, Mr. Stevens." And it was three days later that he asked me if I was interested in poetry, and I advised him that I had written poetry in high school, which of course didn't amount to anything. I think he asked me who my favorite poet was, and I told him it was Francis Thompson and T. S. Eliot. He nodded, and he invited me over.

There was some poetry before dinner. Mrs. Stevens was preparing things, and there was that interval of time. [There was also poetry after dinner. In all] I would say an hour at least. He read us "The Man with the Blue Guitar."

And then he asked for our idea of this other work that he was engaged with at the time. I don't know what poem it would be; it had no title, or nothing was mentioned. He covered the same subject, but there were two [versions]. He'd ask us, "Well, how does this strike you? Let me try it this way." And that's when he asked McGiehan and myself to make comments as to our preferences. He apparently wanted someone to give him a criticism, particularly with regard to the imagery created, you might say. He wanted some company to just check some things out.

It was a lovely house. His wife was rather charming. The thing that predominated was poetry, but we didn't talk poetry at the dinner table. We had a lot of repartee at the dinner table, but it was just conversation. I can't remember what subjects we covered, but she was very gracious. She wasn't holding anything back in reserve. She was a consummate cook: asparagus tips, creamed, with this pie covering; then another vegetable, creamed and with pie covering.

Then [the men] retired to the other room. It was off the living room, a study. We had a wonderful dinner, and after dinner some fine wines. There was no hard liquor [that evening]. And he took us through his wine cellar. The shelves were ten or twelve feet in length on either side, and it was sizable. Then we had a discussion on wines. He told us how the American wines were improving vastly and had great merit as compared with the past.

It was August of '42. I would say we were there for about two hours. It was about nine-thirty or ten [when they left].

Hazel Kuhnly

I was interested in poetry. I wrote poetry myself and so I tried to read his poetry. And I remember one particularly was "The Man with the Blue Guitar." Everybody [at the office] was trying to figure out what was meant by that. Many people, especially those who were not interested in poetry, somewhat ridiculed it. They would quote passages that they thought were far-out. They would quote him [the way] they would quote Gertrude Stein. But I think, in spite of the fact that they did this, they knew that it was their own ignorance, because obviously he was getting known for his poetry. I knew quite early in the game, because it got around the office that he was writing poetry. Then, of course, his poems were being published, and I was taking creative writing lessons [locally], and he was under discussion.

I got the courage to go see him one day and ask him if he would be willing to look over what I had done and see if it was any good. If it wasn't any good, I'd forget about it. If it was, I might pursue it. He was quite frank with me that he was a writer, but he was not a critic. He didn't feel that he would be capable of doing that. He did tell me not to expect ever to earn any money writing poetry. It was not a remunerative vocation. It was something you did as an avocation, which obviously he did. And I told him that I had read some of his poetry, but that I didn't understand it. He said he was very glad I was honest, because most people pretended that they understood it and didn't. He told me that he had given his secretary an autographed copy of his book, and she had come back afterward and said how much she enjoyed it. He asked if she read this certain poem, and she [had] said, oh yes, she had. He happened to know that the pages where that poem was were stuck, so he asked her to see the book, and when he found out that the pages were still stuck he knew that she hadn't really read the poem. He said people were always trying to pretend, that they thought they would please him by pretending that they understood it.

I found him very cordial and personable in my interview, even though everybody was in awe of him. That was my impression seeing him walk around the company. He was a big man and he carried himself very well. You had the impression he was not too easily approachable, but in his office he was quite the opposite. He wasn't in the field that I was in, so I had no reason to make contact with him, and I don't know where I got the courage from, because I didn't usually walk into a vice-president's office. He was very cordial, and I didn't feel rushed out or anything like that. Probably not more than fifteen or twenty minutes; it wasn't a long interview. He gave me encouragement. I don't remember the words, but I remember leaving there feeling encouraged to continue to write. I'm not sure what year that was, probably in the 1940s.

Paul and Kitty Dow

PD: In May of 1924 I went to Hartford in the home office [to work] right across the hall from the office occupied by Wallace Stevens. He would come in and chat, and liked to look at the girls and offer a few observations, and go on back. Then, as time went on, I moved out on Kenyon Street [a few blocks below Stevens' apartment at 735 Farmington Avenue, West Hartford]. I walked to work in the morning, and very often Mr. Stevens would walk along with me. He would sometimes chat and sometimes not. Of course, he was an inveterate walker. Then very often at noon, we were both trying to keep our weight down, we would walk downtown. He would go to a fruit store where they had great big grapes; he just loved them. Then he'd go to the Bond Hotel and get a Henry Clay cigar, and we'd walk back to the office and get back into harness.

It was just common knowledge [at the home office in the mid-1920s that Stevens was a poet]. For instance, there was a story at that time that some Frenchman was going to visit Mr. Bissell out at Farmington, and that this person specifically requested that Mr. Stevens be included in the gathering because of his literary status. Mr. Bissell [the company president] brought this request to the attention of Wallace. He said, no, he wouldn't go. And he didn't. I knew he was an important personality at that time. I was impressed by him, and I knew nothing about poetry. I did [collect his poetry over the years]. Certain aspects of *Harmonium* I thought were very interesting. Although I am no judge of poetry, I think the finest book written by an American is *John Brown's Body.* Once I told him I had purchased one of his books, and he said, "Well, I'm glad to get the royalty. It might be as much as ten cents." I said, "It's missing one thing. It doesn't have your signature." And he said, "Well, you can get along without that."

My first winter was spent working up material for a booklet in our agency kits. We called that *The Undertakings of the Hartford Accident and Indemnity.* That's when I got acquainted with him: part of the time I had to work in the board room—there was no other place for me; it was right across the office occupied by Wallace Stevens. I would write up the material I proposed to recommend for the booklet, and then have it passed on by the heads of the various departments. I wrote up an article on court bond, and I took it to Mr. Stevens and asked him if he would review it for me and make any changes that seemed expedient or proper. He said, "No, I wouldn't do it." "Well," I said, "I'm sorry. I hoped you would because of your knowledge of the subject." He said, "I mean I won't correct what you've written here, but I'll give you an article on court bonds." And one day he handed me this legal sheet, and I looked at it. It was his penmanship, which no one but his secretary could decipher. I looked at it, and I turned it upside down, and I said, "This is just fine. Thank you very much." He laughed like hell and went out. It went in that booklet and stayed in as long as it was published. They changed everything else in the pamphlet, but that one thing did not change.[47] I don't think anybody dared change anything he did, afraid he might leave. He was absolutely the diamond in the tiara, and he was so recognized in my time as the showpiece. No [not in the 1920s]; this is later. But he was not overlooked in the twenties, either.

I did see him right along [after Dow left the home office for work in branch offices]. He came to see me in Louisville [on surety business], and he wanted to be shown around the town. He commented on the architecture, which he thought was shabby and insubstantial. It hasn't got the Bostonian, Stanford White imprint that you find in a Northern city. We have such different [designs], very airy. He said, "How can you stand to live in such a place?" I did come up at least once a year, and I'd always drop by. He might be busy; he'd just wave his hand, and that'd be fine. But very often he'd say, "See you in a few minutes." Or we'd go to lunch. Then we'd go to the YWCA right around the corner: he was a gourmet, all right, but very often he'd descend to a corned-beef sandwich. If Kitty was along, why, that was a cinch he was going with us. He'd soon spend half a day, talking to Kitty mostly. Remember the time he took us to see the Farmington Reservoir, out there where that big castle used to be?

KD: One day he took us on quite a tour of the country. He always had a driver; it was usually [Ivan] Daugherty. We had lunch in some country place. [He was] just a very attractive, charming person. And he had the twinkliest eyes I ever remember. They were just sparkling. 'Course, he was a great big man; he looked sort of like a big teddy bear. I never heard him speak of Mrs. Stevens.

PD: I'd hear there was difficulty; and if you ever met Mrs. Stevens, she was not a warm person. The last time I saw him was out at his own home. He was sick. [John Ladish] went out there with certain papers to show Mr. Stevens, and I asked him if I could go along. We were met by Mrs. Stevens at the door. "Now I must tell you you can't smoke where Mr. Stevens is." We said, "We don't intend to smoke," so she took us up to the second floor, where he was in a bathrobe. There was a table there, and on that was a picture of a bowl of flowers [by Pierre Tal Coat]. He had quite a bit to say about it. He thought it was a beautiful thing, quite stimulating, and it had great value. "By the way, I've written a poem ["Angel Surrounded by Paysans"] about that picture." His mother was Pennsylvania Dutch, and his father was a Scotsman. Now, my mother was a Pennsylvania Dutch, [and] my father was a Scotsman. So he would discuss this with me, especially our Pennsylvania Dutch background. He said on several occasions that he'd made a study of the Pennsylvania Dutch business, and he was certain they were German refugees, religious dissenters, who were forced to the seacoast. Some of them were taken to England, some to Ireland and to America. He said, "We might even have some Pennsylvania Dutch Irishmen!" Also, this day he gave us this [pamphlet] from Yale University. [It said] he was to be one of the speakers of the occasion [the sesquicentennial celebration of the Connecticut Academy of Arts and Sciences, 1949], and he was to read what he had prepared of the "Ordinary Saturday [*sic*] Evening in New Haven." He read part of it to Ladish and myself, just a few sections, and commented on it. And he jumped around to show us how healthy he was. Picked up the tails of his bathrobe and jumped around. I was amazed.

Naaman Corn

They were all talking about this book [*Transport to Summer*, 1947] that Mr. Stevens had written. One of the officers told me, "Naaman, I saw your name in this book." And sure enough, he had some poem ["Certain Phenomena of Sound"] in there with my name on it and [that of] one of the officers that used to live out on Asylum Avenue. This poem was about him in one spot, and then one little spot in there he brought me in the poem.

> So you're home again, Redwood Roamer, and ready
> To feast . . . Slice the mango, Naaman, and dress it
>
> With white wine, sugar and lime juice. Then bring it,
> After we've drunk the Moselle, to the thickest shade
>
> Of the garden. We must prepare to hear the Roamer's
> Story . . . The sound of that slick sonata,
>
> Finding its way from the house, makes music seem
> To be a nature, a place in which itself
>
> Is that which produces everything else, in which
> The Roamer is a voice taller than the redwoods,
>
> Engaged in the most prolific narrative,
> A sound producing the things that are spoken.[48]

That's the one about the Redwood Roamer. That was a man by the name of Addison Posey. He was one of the vice-presidents here, but he went back to California. You know the redwoods grow in California. [Posey was born in Oakland, California, near the redwood forest.] Then he used to roam up and down Albany Avenue, coming to work. Mr. Stevens used to come into the office that way, too, and he would run into Mr. Posey. They never did get together because Mr. Stevens was a loner: he'd always walk by himself. He wrote this poem, and the people saw this name about Redwood Roamer. They didn't know what it was all about: what's a Redwood Roamer? So they had to go to Mr. Stevens and get him to decipher it. I didn't even know I was in the book until some of the officers were telling me about it. I never discussed anything with Mr. Stevens; some of the officers had found out who the Redwood Roamer was. I found it out by some grapevine. I never did ask him any questions about anything. If I wanted some information, I would usually go to somebody like Mr. Jainsen or Mr. Heard. Mr. Stevens, I tell you, was a loner; to approach him you had to have a certain something to get up to him some way. No [Corn had never served Stevens at home, as is implied in the poem]. He just used his imagination. 'Course, Mr. Stevens liked wine. He used to go up to the Colonial Package Store [in Hartford] and he would order wine by the cases. I would take the car up there and get two or three big cases, take it to the house, drive around the back, and put it in the wine cellar. He kept a lot of it.

I met Mr. Stevens when I first came into the office 'cause he was one of the officers. Actually, I didn't just work for Mr. Stevens 'cause I worked for the general executive office there, the long corridor from end to end of the building. My job was on the east side, that was the Hartford Accident and Indemnity Company; and on the west side was the Hartford Fire Insurance Company. I took him to be just another insurance man; I didn't think of him as being a poet, an artist of some kind. And people would come in from other offices, and they'd want to know what kind of man was that Mr. Stevens. They couldn't understand him. And they couldn't read his writing. He wrote so badly. He said one time he used to write good, but then he started studying law, and he couldn't take the notes fast enough, and he couldn't write shorthand, so he had to write so he could get down everything the instructor was talking about. Couldn't anybody read his writing: if he'd sign his name, you never would know it was Wallace Stevens.

It was my job to get along with anybody, especially in that corridor because that was my assignment. I had to try to keep everybody happy, so anything anybody in the corridor wanted, no matter what it was or when it was, I would have to see that they were taken care of. At one time he used to get big shipments of Gramophone records; they came from Europe. He would have me to go down to the post office and pick up this big box, and he'd go down with me and pay out quite a bit of money. We'd go out looking for strange types of flowers. We went up to Pomfret. At one time there was an opera house there. Mr. Stevens knew about everything, I guess. Mr. Stevens said, "An Italian opera house used to stand right there, but it burned." And in the back of the opera was a big florist, a garden. He'd spend half of the evening walking around this greenhouse looking for oddball flowers, something that no one didn't have in the gardens some other place. He would get in touch with some people around Hartford to find out some of the better places to go and look for things. He would go into the older towns and look around, like Pomfret, Wethersfield or Windsor. Just ask questions, look around some

of the old garden places, and maybe he would find something he was looking
for. [On these gardening trips,] he'd be mostly silent, and he was a very good
observer. He was just looking around all the time—the scenery and stuff like
that. There was another garden he liked to go at Marlborough, called Marlborough Garden. It was just a little place, and he used to order strange flowers
from California, and England, or Switzerland. He had all sorts of things
around his house. Usually, whenever we'd go to look for flowers, he'd go by
himself. But most of the time [Corn chauffeured Stevens,] it was taking him
out someplace with his family to eat.

I took him to a couple of football games. I took him to Yale, and it was
Yale-Dartmouth playing. We sat halfway up on the stadium there. Well, the
people that were in back of us were drinking beer, and every time they would
empty a beer can, they'd put it in the aisle, and it would go down from way
up there, *kerplunk!* Mr. Stevens got so furious. When we left the football
game that was his whole conversation back to Hartford. He was so mad. It
was like he wouldn't get along with other people's way of life. He'd just get
irritated like that, and he'd be over with it just about as fast. He'd see you
the next day as if nothing ever happened. He didn't carry no grudge.

He never would sponge on the company. When it was time to work, he
was ready to work. If you were in his office on some other reason than
company business, and Mr. Stevens would see me coming with an armful of
checks to be signed, he'd look up, "C'mon in, Naaman. Little more won't
hurt. Naaman, you blot 'em whilst I sign 'em." He was holding you up, taking
up your time: he was doing the company's work.

I had to take him over that evening [June 9, 1955 when Stevens received
an honorary degree from Hartford's Hartt College of Music]. He was at his
home; I had to pick him up and take him over there at a certain hour. He
was getting where he didn't walk so much. I lived up in the north end of the
city, and lots of times we'd be over there in Keney Park, and look around,
and here come Mr. Stevens through Keney Park [a seven-hundred-acre park,
the largest in Hartford]. He done walked from Westerly Terrace on over, and
he walked all up through the park by himself, through the woods, any old
place. He didn't care about snakes and things 'cause he had on walking shoes.
He used to wear high-boot shoes all the time; he didn't wear the low-cut
shoes. He had lighter ones when he was just coming to the office. He didn't
never talk about honors and things; he'd let the other people do the talking.
I didn't know what a humanitarian award was [that June evening, Stevens
received an honorary Doctor of Humanities degree at Hartt College of
Music] because I figured the humanitarian award should be given to somebody that had done something for humanity. The name kind of threw me

off. I said, my goodness alive, look like they could [have] picked on somebody
else.

Herbert Schoen

I was a research lawyer at the time [1947], and I was in the library directly
across from his office. I'd only been with the company a few weeks, and this
very impressive, large gentleman came in and said, "I'm Wallace Stevens. I
am told that I should meet you. Why?" Naturally, I've thought of many
brilliant things to say since, but I couldn't think of anything to say at that
particular moment. He was a real word merchant. He liked to play with words
even in the commercial world, such as the very true story [that] when a long
letter was written, he would send back the reply, "No," which, of course, was
very effective. He was a word merchant because he would try, obviously try,
to say things in a way that would call your attention to the way he was
describing. And why I don't think he led two lives is that he would do this
in everyday speech or perhaps in his humor. The breeze happened to catch
this girl's skirt, and he said, "What an inquiring wind!" Now these are very
commonly used terms, but most people would not have expressed it that way.
But he did this constantly.

[As a bond-claims lawyer he] was knowledgeable in his field; it was a very
narrow field, very complex and with huge sums of money involved. It was an
interesting thing to see a poet of his capacity—and we knew he was a poet
with great capacity then—devote so much real energy to something that was
so distant. Actually, Wallace Stevens was proud of this facet of his life. As
a matter of fact, he thought other poets who had chairs in universities and
read to women's groups or men's groups were kept men. He was very proud
that he earned his living—and it was a good living—that he did it on his own;
he did it separately and apart from his writing of poetry.

He was not a warm personality as far as those in the office went. He wanted
his privacy and respected the privacy of others. But at times I would drop
into his office and say something if a squib appeared about him in *The New
Yorker.* One time they wanted to do a profile on him. I said, "Mr. Stevens,
why don't you let them do it?" And he said, "They always try to portray you
as a damn fool." And that was the end of the profile in *The New Yorker.* We
would chat about things, and we had a small amount of rapport. At the time
our first child was born, in 1948, I came in and told him. He said, "Herb,
let's go over to the Canoe Club and celebrate." We came in, and he said,
"I will have one martini." I believe they brought out about a quart pitcher
that was filled with martinis. And we had a good lunch. When my son was

born two years later, we did the same thing again. I only had three children, and I don't know if I could stand any more lunches of this type. But he was extremely gracious at such times. He would discuss the words that he would want to discuss; he would not discuss his poems or poetry. I frankly tried to open him up on these things, and he obviously did not want to discuss them. I don't think it was a lack of desire to communicate, but he just felt, as he did say, [that] to try to explain a poem is to spoil it. Some others felt that he was acting intellectually in a superior way when he said that, but I really don't think he was. I think he intended you to have your own imagination flowing out of his words. He did at times talk about the fact that he was in Harvard the same time that Robert Frost was, and he saw him at Key West. I don't think there was any close rapport between the two poets. I think I remember once asking him why there was such a long hiatus between his writing at Harvard and his starting to write poetry again. I remember vaguely that he said, "Herb, I just had to begin again," as if it was some kind of upwelling of pressure within himself. I've never seen any other answer that was as satisfying, because I believe there are a great number of years in there where he not only did not publish, but he did not even write.

I think it's superficial to believe he lived two separate lives. Obviously, they were intertwined. He would not eat lunch: he would go out for a walk and think about words he wanted to use. I used to accuse him of wasting the company's money by thinking about his poems rather than surety bonds when he was in the office. He'd just laugh and say, "I'm thinking about these things [but] I'm thinking about surety problems Saturdays and Sundays when I'm strolling through Elizabeth Park, so it all evens out." I personally never felt that he led two lives or tried to ring down an iron curtain on what he was doing. [After Dylan Thomas's sudden death in New York on November 9, 1953, Stevens was one of the spokesmen for a committee that] tried to raise funds for his widow. They raised some money, but not enough. So I looked at the phraseology [of the appeal for funds] as a lawyer, and I said you have the right to proceed to give her the corpus of the trust and not try to invest it, because the income wouldn't be enough to support her for very long.[49] He would ask me about these things; it was all intertwined. What amazes people is that he had the self-discipline—which I don't think he had in all other respects—to come into work very regularly, and to work very hard and do the routine that the office work required, which is perhaps inconsistent with what the average individual believes a poet should do or a genius should do. I'm not sure that premise is correct. You don't have to be an erratic genius to be a genius. I know for a fact he thought about the words he was going to use in poetry [when he was at the office]. Once in a while he would discuss them with me, but only trying them out like a trial balloon, may I assure you. Once he came in the law library and said, "Herb, what does the word 'elliptical' mean to you?" I was a math major, so I defined what the ellipse is in purely mathematical terms. Well, it infuriated him, because he was not using elliptical, as I well knew, in mathematical terms. When he walked out, I said to myself, Well, I didn't get fully back for the first crack, but I'm halfway back. So he did not lead two separate lives; they were intertwined. He was proud that he could master two different things, and he scorned others who were unable to do so.

I tried to read much of [his poetry]. I had him sign his name to the books. Just for fun, I have one here which is not by Wallace Stevens, but [is] *The Shaping Spirit: A Study of Wallace Stevens,* by William Van O'Connor [Chicago: Henry Regnery, 1950]. This was 1950, I think, [that] I bought it. I said, "Mr. Stevens, will you autograph this book?" He said, "Certainly." He has signed it: "To Herb Schoen[,] Wallace Stevens[—]At his expense." He was gracious about signing them. He was ungracious if someone assumed he had an endless supply and would seek free copies. I was just smart enough not to try that. I went outside and bought the books and therefore told him that he at least should sign them. He'd laugh and he'd sign them.

I remember one comment [Stevens made about the honors he was receiving in his last years]. It was the year he received two honorary degrees [from Mount Holyoke and Columbia in 1952]. The last one was from Columbia. I asked him the next Monday morning how it went. He [had] told me he was going; we'd chat about these things [afterward]. He said, "It went very well. And when I came home, my wife was out in the garden, and I took the highly colored cowl of the honorary Ph.D. and hung it out the window and said, 'Look, darling, I have another scalp!' " She did not proceed to attend these celebrations with him. Although he had placed a high premium on his own privacy, he was inwardly pleased and he would cooperate with the festivities just enough to be gracious, but not much more. He did not like to [lecture at universities]. He did not think he did it well—and again, perhaps not oddly, because he was a perfectionist. He worked extremely hard to prepare for those lectures, and that was another reason he did not like to do it. It was quite apparent that he did not like that milieu. He didn't like the crowds of people, he did not like the social gatherings which they usually entailed. He told me at one point, and I forget which university he was at, but he was apparently receiving an honorary degree the next day. There was a social gathering the night before, and it was in the home either of the president or one of the senior trustees of the university. He escorted him in and he said, "Mr. Stevens, what do you think of my home?" And Stevens took a look around and said, "My wife and I have tried very hard *not* to create this effect." This is the kind of thing that Wallace Stevens would do with words. Some people really resented it. And he could be much more direct than that if he wished to be. But I, personally, always thought he was merely using words to get your attention, and he was quite capable of doing that.

To my knowledge, he took no part in civic or community events. He did take part [in] various conferences that we had in the office. I remember at one where we had all the vice-presidents in, and the president said, "I want each of you to identify the problem areas of your responsibility." And each vice-president got up and described his problems. When it came to Wallace Stevens, he said, "The surety-claims department has no problem" and he sat down. I never did see [Stevens address large company gatherings]. It was the kind of thing he avoided, simply by saying very clearly and very abruptly, "No!" It was allowed: everyone knew he was superior in the area of surety claims, and don't forget he was very verbal, and no one in his right mind would verbally take him on. He was a sort of elder statesman. Everybody knew he was very good in his work; if he didn't want to do other things, that was his privilege.

· VI ·
OFFICER OF THE HARTFORD

The late winter and spring of 1934 were especially important months in Stevens' life at the company and in the company's corporate life, for during this short period, both came into their majority. After almost eighteen years with Hartford Accident and Indemnity, Stevens was finally named an officer on February 15, 1934. It came as a surprise to him, for at fifty-four Stevens had resigned himself to the fact that he would never be an officer of the company. Being named one of its four vice-presidents at the home office was singular recognition: at the time, even the man who ran Hartford Accident and Indemnity, James Kearney, was only a vice-president. Its president and chairman of the board, Richard Bissell, was also the president of Hartford Fire, which still controlled its twenty-one-year-old offspring. All that changed, however, in a May coup in which Stevens, along with his fellow vice-presidents, put his career on the line for his friend Kearney.

John Rogers

There was an upheaval in the company at the time. [John Schmidt, head of the underwriting department,] was a very brilliant man who had become one of the leaders in the industry; he had developed new underwriting policies and procedures. Despite this, he had got off-center. Schmidt was spending money like wildfire. Schmidt got linked up romantically with the head telephone operator [though he was a married man]. He'd have altercations downtown; see, he was drinking heavier than he should have been. Time after time, reports would leak out that Schmidt was in some kind of trouble. Hartford Fire was always a staid old crowd; these [Hartford Accident] fellows had a little more life. The word came down from the chairman of the board to discharge this fellow. [Kearney, however, resisted until, in May 1934,] they found out that [Schmidt] had used the same brain that had devised the underwriting [innovations] to work up a way to defraud. They woke up one morning and found several hundred thousand dollars [missing]. Well, now you had two situations. [Kearney] had been told to discharge this guy for minor things, and here the auditors discovered a major thing, and the man is not discharged. So you now get insubordination. When the thing broke, this was Bissell's first move: get rid of Kearney, clean it up.

I don't think that the ruling power in the Hartford Fire board of directors ever realized the closeness of [the Hartford Accident vice-presidents and Kearney]. What he done was simply call in his boys. Now George Moloney was the vice-president in Chicago, [Joy] Lichtenstein was the vice-president on the Coast; Paul Rutherford was the vice-president in New York [and Wallace Stevens was the new home-office vice-president]. He tells me, "All these men are coming. Now this is all confidential. I want you to meet each man [at the train], take them to the Bond Hotel, and say nothing." Then they went to Farmington, to the Country Club, to lay down their strategy. They walked in the next day. Everyone was ready for action. They all walked in unison into [Bissell's] office, and all offered their resignation. "Now, where he's going, we're going." So instead of getting the top man's resignation [the Hartford Fire directors] got everybody's resignation. Here their whole corporate structure was going to fall right in their laps. When [Kearney and his fellow vice-presidents] knew they had the upper stick: "We want this and we want that." I remember Kearney telling me, "Well, you know I'm the president of the corporation now." I said, "I suspected you would be." He smiled. He'd been the vice-president and general manager. That Kearney was a fantastic guy. He could have gotten that loyalty from the lowest charwoman in the place.

As a result of the coup, not only had Kearney become the first president of Hartford Accident from its own ranks but Stevens, in turn, found himself in an especially influential position. He was now one of the top officers in a company that was a partner and no longer a subsidiary of Hartford Fire. Manning Heard and Harry Williams, both later presidents of the Hartford, observed how disinterested in corporate power Stevens was, however. He resisted a broader role in the company and flatly refused to share the company presidency during the war years, when its actual president was incapacitated by a long illness. Stevens' one official responsibility outside of bond claims was a paper one, his fellow director of Hartford Live Stock Insurance Company, Arthur Polley, explains. Content to remain head of the small bond-claims department, Stevens the businessman had found at the company what Stevens the poet once said he sought to find through his art as well, a unique and solitary home.

Harry Williams

During the war, I was in charge of all the war projects. Mr. Rutherford, who was then the president of Hartford Accident and Indemnity, had been sick, and so he established a committee of vice-presidents: Mr. Wilson C. Jainsen, who at that time was head of [casualty] claims; Manning Heard, who was [a vice-president]; and Wallace Stevens. Before I could commit the company to a war project, such as a containment or an explosive plant, I'd outline them to these gentlemen. It involved some secret work at times, such as the Manhattan Project and some work in Tennessee, which eventually led to the development of the reactor underneath the University of Chicago. I spent a good amount of time during the war in Washington; if I came home on Friday and had to clear [a project] with these three vice-presidents, I'd go to Wallace Stevens' house Saturday morning. He took the position that I knew more about it than he, and it was kind of useless, and he proposed to Mr. Rutherford that he be dropped from the committee. Mr. Rutherford said no, he wanted his input. I must admit sometimes he handled the responsibility perfunctorily. But he did ask intelligent questions when he did get interested in a particular project. When we bordered on some scientific development, why, obviously he was interested in it, but [in] a pure containment or an explosive plant he was not.

[Rutherford had] left here in September before Pearl Harbor; they treated him in the Mayo Clinic and New York, but he didn't return until almost after the war was over. In the meantime, Jainsen and Heard were running the shop as a pair, and Wallace Stevens was not included in that. It wasn't a triumverate. Heard used to be an assistant to Wallace Stevens at one time; now he was assuming a superior position. Jainsen was a claims man [whom Stevens had helped to bring into the company in 1935 and who now was also in a superior position]. There were a lot of agents who found it very difficult to ask favors of Stevens but who would come in to Jainsen. Jainsen, in turn, would talk to Stevens about it. Stevens was the senior man, but I don't think he desired to run the company. He was very jealous of his own authority in his own area. He didn't seem to want to expand beyond that.

In those days there were very influential agents. We had an agency in Houston that would produce four and six million dollars; we had another agency in St. Louis, very difficult to handle, four million. They'd come directly in here if they had a question, and if it was on bond claims, why, they would contact Stevens. Sometimes Stevens would look into this situation but preferred to have Jainsen handle the contact because Jainsen would know these people much better than Stevens. These people would make an annual visit to the company, and you were always assigned one night to take them out so that you could get to know them and they got to know you, so they could talk to you. Stevens did not participate in this at all, although there were one or two people that he enjoyed.

Mr. Rutherford every Christmastime used to have a group that he would call together, which was primarily senior executives and people that he liked particularly. And he would always invite Wallace Stevens. And Wallace Stevens liked to have a drink and Wallace would enjoy himself—and at times be a little pugnacious. [At one such holiday gathering] one of our employees was sort of a drab individual and was going along, without any point, extolling the virtues of Mr. Rutherford. So Stevens grabbed the guitar and started strumming it; it was his way of saying stop it! But he was very sociable to talk to. The great problem was to find the medium to talk about. He loved a good story, but he didn't tell one very well.

I loved his letters. He'd attach a note to the bond, and it would say yes or no, and that was it. When it came to business, he didn't mince words. He was very shrewd. The problem that he had with other people was a communication problem: he was concise to the point of almost being rude to them. He was a man who had close friends or no friends.

[While war projects brought Williams to Stevens' home on several occasions, one Saturday morning Stevens invited Williams, a ham radio buff, to look at his radio, which was out of order.] After looking at this I [explained] to him there were two things I thought were wrong with it. He said, "Before you leave, do you know anyone whom I could get to repair it?" I gave him [Edward Hunt's] phone number, and so he called him up and had him come over to the house. He said, "I'd like you to repair the FM radio and amplifier. I know you fellows always pad the bill. Harry Williams told me that there were two things wrong with it. I will pay for your repairing these two things, but only that." Hunt complained, "Supposing I find something else?" He said, "I'm only going to pay for those two things." So Hunt called me up and said, "What kind of a guy did you introduce me to? Very fortunately, you had happened to hit on the two things that were wrong with it, but on the other hand, I was going to follow his instructions completely and just repair these two things." Wallace Stevens was always suspicious of being taken by something where he had no knowledge.

Arthur Polley

His work at the company was as an attorney essentially liquidating claims under defaulted bonds. We also had at that time a company known as Hartford Live Stock. He was on the board of directors and I was on the board of directors of that company, merely to build up the directorship—that's about all it amounted to. The policies were laid down by the parent company [Hartford Fire]. Practically, all we did was to meet three or four times a year to pass on the dividends and to receive the statement as made up by the accountants of Hartford Fire. Really, it was a legal board without any great responsibility. As long as it was Hartford Fire that owned it, the owners said, "We think you can afford to pay a dividend of a certain amount," the money seemed to be there; it was just a routine. There was really no essential responsibility. But there was a responsibility to have all those things in proper legal form. That's where Wallace Stevens came in, because he was the attorney that kept everything in proper legal form and saw that it was recorded in proper shape. We had to hold [the board of directors' meetings] in New York. Wallace always went down because he conducted the meeting. He was not only the attorney, he was the secretary to the whole thing.[50] This was an hour session, and it was over with. It was a routine formality, and he would go his way. [Both Polley and Stevens were also vice-presidents of Hartford Live Stock.] That didn't mean anything either. The Live Stock was essentially run by a man out of Chicago; he was a good veterinarian. I could almost have forgotten that I was ever vice-president of Hartford Live Stock.

I don't think he was typical as an insurance executive at all, because he had little sense—or if he had, he didn't exercise it—of cultivating agents or cultivating insureds to create business. Like this agent, almost insulting him: Late one afternoon, one of our agents came in that represented us someplace in the Midwest. He said, "I represent the Hartford and have for a number of years. I just would like to call at the home office." James [the receptionist] was up to the niceties, and he started to look around for some officer he could take him to visit with or perhaps show him around. It was late in the day, and [he thought] everyone had gone until he went down past Mr. Stevens' door. So he took him in. "Mr. Stevens, this is Mr. So-and-so, who represents us and has called at the home office." Mr. Stevens' greeting was, "What the hell am I supposed to do about it?" We probably lost a good agency. A typical officer [was] one who had come up through the ranks and been out in the field trying to get business, trying to underwrite in a way that would make money and still create good will. [In Stevens' work,] he didn't do that at all. In his liquidation of claims, well, there we just had a bad mess on our hands someplace that he was working out of, and he didn't have to think about business methods. He didn't have to think about pleasing some agent or somebody else. He had to think about saving the company dollars. And that wasn't a typical officer, other than the officers in the claims department. And even in the claims department, not so much because there again they tried to adjust claims in a way that would be satisfactory to our producing staff in order to keep their good will. But when it comes down to a bad bond situation, not so much so. His temperament and the whole thing he did was unique. [The other officers] understood him. In his particular line of claim work, even if he wasn't diplomatic about it—or diplomatic at all—it didn't come back to harm. The rest of us thought it was a helluva thing to do [to that visiting agent], a joke in a way, but it wouldn't happen often enough to be serious. If I had done it, I'd have been very seriously criticized. He just loved to shock people, just to see their reaction.

'Course, I knew him well enough that it didn't bother me. I just laughed about it. He used to like to go out and commune with nature, take walks in the woods. He was around Farmington one day, and he ran into the president of the company walking along. His greeting was, "My God, can't a man go anyplace but he has to meet people he knows!" He loved to shock people, and he didn't care a damn who they were. [Sometimes] he used to stay in the office after hours, and I was there oftentimes. He'd run on to something that amused him, and he'd come walking from way over on his side of the building [to Polley's office on the Hartford Fire side]. He came once and said, "You know, I just had a funny experience. One of these"—as he termed them— " 'sob sisters' came in, and she wanted permission to review our loss files to get human interest stories." I can't remember what he said to her, but it was something decidedly insulting. She said, "I've never been more insulted in my life," and got up and stomped out of the office. He said, "Why do you suppose she did that?" It seemed essentially [he] loved to see the reaction of people, that he could shock them.

He used to like to walk to work. Sometimes he would come out and stand at the corner on Fern Street. He walked over there to get the bus, and I'd kind of slow up and wave at him, and he'd tell me to go on, the deuce with me! Once in a while he'd get in and ride with me, maybe one out of four times, and go down to the office. Well, this particular morning, he wasn't standing on the corner, he was one block east of it. I waved at him; he nodded, and got in the car, and said, "City Manager Sharpe was up on the other corner there, and if I got on the bus with him, he'd talk my head off all the way downtown." I looked over at him. "Yes, sir, Mr. Stevens!" He didn't say one word; I didn't say one word. When we got down to the office, he said, "Thank you, Mr. Polley." I said, "You're welcome, Mr. Stevens." And he went in. Now, if he had been my boss, I never would have picked him up in God's world, because every once in a while he'd just get the idea that he wanted to go someplace, and by gosh you drove him there. One of the men that worked for him [once] picked him up, and it was the time of the World's Fair in New York. Wallace was very much of a gourmet, and he says, "Well, now, it's a nice day. I guess we won't go to the office. Just keep driving." And, my God, he made him take him down to the World's Fair to have lunch. But then he didn't have lunch with him. He says, "You get what you want, and you meet me here an hour later." I'm quite sure it was [Ivan] Daugherty told me. And it wasn't only once but twice he made him take him down. The other time he wanted to go to one of the art galleries. And after he got there, he told him, "You go someplace else. You wouldn't understand these things."

I'll say this about him: I've tried to read his poetry, and to me it's the biggest bunch of gobbledygook. In fact, I've said to people, Wallace was a great kidder. In his astute way, he'd say something to you, and you'd wake up about the next noon that you'd been kidded. Never cracked a smile, never. You'd never know what was going on. And I've often wondered if he didn't write a lot of these things with his tongue in his cheek, and the country picked up on him and said he was a great poet—and probably he was—and he was having the biggest private laugh of anyone in the world. [In 1950] I read in the paper or heard over the radio news where he had been awarded some prize for poetry, I think by Yale [the Bollingen Prize]. They called him up and said, "Well, Mr. Stevens, what is your comment?" All he said was, "Hurrah!" The next day I says, "That was a great reply you made to being congratulated." "Well," he says, "what else was there to say?"

I think he was basically a kindly person, probably a selfish person. Never in my life when I've taken him home [did he] invite me in the house and say, "Come in and have a drink." I don't know if he dared 'cause the rumors around [were] that he and his wife used to fight like cats and dogs.

Manning Heard

When Mr. Stevens offered me the job [as his assistant in 1933], he said, "Now there's one thing I want to tell you. The company will treat you fairly when it comes to pay, but if you ever expect to become an officer of the company, don't accept this job because you never will." The reason for that was, up until that time there were [very few] officers in the Hartford Accident and Indemnity. [Stevens] had never been made an officer, and he was one of the oldest employees of the company. He thought there was somebody who was an officer standing between him and being an officer. That must have been true because the man [J. Collins Lee] resigned suddenly, and shortly [before] he resigned, Mr. Stevens was made a vice-president of the company. I think there was a tremendous amount of animosity between them. It was something that neither Collins Lee nor Stevens ever disclosed to me, but it was apparent. This is an example of it. Mr. Collins Lee hired a man whom he put in the bond department under Stevens by the name of Iasigi. Now, Stevens didn't like Iasigi, but he was Collins Lee's man, and he couldn't do anything about it. Collins Lee resigned, and it wasn't a week later that Stevens fired Iasigi. [Lee] was right under James L. D. Kearney and second in control; practically, the administration of the company was left entirely to him.

We had a little party at the Canoe Club after [Stevens was made a vice-president]. It wasn't a very big one, because he didn't like them. He wanted to select his friends, and he particularly didn't want anyone to give him any adulation. He was very peculiar that way. I know he was very proud of it, because it was a long time coming. Yes [he had wanted to be a vice-president for quite some time], but Mr. Stevens never showed his feelings to any great extent. He was a self-disciplinarian to the nth degree. He did his job; he left his office; very rarely did he fraternize with the people around him, although he went to many of the male parties that we had. A very fine man, but a very eccentric man.

I don't think he had the slightest desire to go any further [in the company than a vice-presidency]. I don't think he was temperamentally suited for it; I think he knew it. As a matter of fact, I don't think he would have accepted an overall executive position if it had been offered to him. [During World War II, the company president, Paul Rutherford, became ill, and it was necessary to select a few men to head up the firm during Rutherford's prolonged absence.] Stevens wouldn't have any part of it. Jainsen [head of casualty claims] and I ran the company. He preferred not to. At one time we asked him; he said no. Mr. Stevens had his own niche, and he didn't want to be involved in anything else. At that time in his life, he wasn't looking for other jobs.

[After Stevens hired Heard as his assistant in 1933] we worked together for many years and got along very well, although on occasion he was quite difficult. [For example,] one day, one of the bond men came down, and Mr. Stevens was busy. Liedike said, "Will you give this claim to Mr. Stevens?" I went to give it to him and said, "Mr. Stevens, Liedike brought this claim down and you were busy, and asked me to give it to you." He blew his top, indicating that he thought I was trying to take his cases. I said, "Well, Mr. Stevens, if you feel that way about it, my usefulness around here is gone." And I walked out and went into my office. He came in a [little] later and apologized; he said he was grumpy, said he didn't mean it.

He was a good lawyer but he didn't want to practice law. From the time I came there, anytime he had any legal situation at all, he'd turn it over to me; a few to [Ivan] Daugherty. We had quite a big piece of litigation with the Mormon Church in Salt Lake City, Utah, and I spent quite some time out there participating in the trial of that suit and a number of others. He was interested in law, but I don't think he had any experience in the practice of law; and for that reason he didn't want to expose himself to it, because he was a perfectionist, and he didn't want to do anything he didn't think he was fully capable of doing. Very seldom did we work together on a case. He had almost an unbroken rule that when he turned a case over to you he expected you to handle it. He didn't even want to discuss it with you after that. Those files he gave to you, those files were in your hands. No [Stevens was not difficult if a case one handled turned out badly]. I don't recall that he ever called me down or anything of the sort.

He was a very imaginative claims man. I mean that he was never satisfied to handle cases entirely according to routine. One of the things in the old days was, if you had a contractor that defaulted, don't try to finish the contract; you'll lose your pants. Well, Stevens very often violated that principle, and he finished contracts, and he was always pretty successful. He was at the time and for many years before his death, the dean of surety-claims men in the whole country. To be a successful surety-claims attorney you have to be highly practical, realistic; you have to watch a dollar because you [can] throw away money handling surety claims like nobody's business, like taking over a contract when you shouldn't. I've always wondered how he could separate his mind between poetry and all that's involved in poetry and this mundane, realistic surety-claims world. They're just two ends of the pole: one is fantasy and the other is real as real can get.

One day he called me into his office, and he said, "Read this." This was in his own handwriting. I could see it was a piece of poetry, and I found it difficult to read. He had the most peculiar handwriting of anyone in the world; anybody that could read it could almost read Egyptian hieroglyphics. And what I could read I found difficult to understand. It was something about mice or rats going up a statue. I looked at it and I handed it back. "Mr. Stevens, I'm sorry, I don't understand this." And he smiled and he said, "That's all right. You haven't got that kind of a mind." I think "Dance of the Macabre Mice" is the poem he read to me in his office. That's the first and only time he ever did that. I think you'll find that his poetry, to a great extent, was a poetry of words. When I first came to Hartford, they had no legal library in the office, and very often, maybe once or twice a week, I would have to go to the [Connecticut State] Library. Before I went, I'd go into his office. He'd say, "Wait a minute. Will you do me a favor?" This is every time I went. "Will you look up in the Oxford Dictionary the meaning of this word." And I'd go and I'd just copy the definition, the whole thing, drew the Greek and all that business. He probably had it in mind using it in his poetry.

He never said anything which would be that derogatory of anybody's poetry, but he just said, for instance, that he didn't like Frost, didn't like his poetry. But he [never] said anything that was derogatory of anybody's efforts or their character; he would just say, "I don't happen to like it." There was a lady that he used to meet who was very fond of him. She was a very favorable critic of his poetry, Marianne Moore. He mentioned her on several occasions.

I went in and congratulated him [on the Pulitzer Prize in 1955]. He said, "Well, thanks," and that was about all. When he won the Bollingen Prize and then he got the National Book Award, I remember that he was very proud of those. If you ever saw him excited, [though,] I'd like to know it. He indicated that he wasn't interested in [publicity. These were] all indications that you would expect of a shy man. Just didn't want to be in the public eye. He was happy about the Pulitzer Prize, the Bollingen Prize, with these acknowledgments and these [honorary] degrees, but he didn't want anybody to give any hullabaloo. He didn't want any part of it; on the contrary, he would have been very uncomfortable [as a Hartford celebrity].

When Stevens went out socially, business was the farthest thing from his mind. He talked business in business hours, but when he was out he enjoyed himself very much. He liked a little drink, and he was a connoisseur of wines. He loved the right wine at the right time in the right place. And the very best. No favorite topics; he'd talk about any subjects that came up. I don't think that anything could interest him less than politics. We never talked politics at all that I recall. He was, as I said, a disciplinarian. He'd tell you what he wanted to tell you; he wouldn't tell you anything that he didn't think you ought to know or you had no need to know.

He was very fond of symphonies, very fond of them. I remember going down [to the Bushnell Memorial Hall, Hartford's main concert hall] with him one time. I told him later that I didn't enjoy them very much. He was handicapped because he didn't have an automobile, and he either had to go in a taxi or get somebody to go with him. [In the 1930s, Heard was one of the group Stevens organized for occasional weekend trips. They] wandered around, went to this place and that, things that Mr. Stevens was interested in. We had a lawyer in Manchester, New Hampshire, who invited Stevens to bring a group of his friends up to the cabin that he owned on the northern tip of Lake Winnipesaukee. Up on the Cape, near Barnstable, Massachusetts, there was an old tavern named the Blue Tavern that we spent one Columbus [Day] weekend. Usually [these trips] were over Columbus Day. On these trips there was Stevens, Ralph Mullen, [Anthony] Sigmans and [Ivan] Daugherty. [Such trips went on for] about four or five years, until, as a matter of fact, my wife got sick and tired of being alone on Columbus Day. We'd get in the automobile and drive, between two and three days. Even a loner sometimes gets lonely.

· VII ·

ONE OF THE BOYS

The little socializing that Stevens did in Hartford was with a small circle he organized at the office. Stevens selected his friends from the Hartford Accident's junior staff; they were younger men, such as John O'Loughlin, Manning Heard, Anthony Sigmans, and Ivan Daugherty, most of whom had worked under him at some time. As their senior and superior, Stevens was the center of a circle of associates who deferred to him as he organized occasional male weekends in the White Mountains or the Adirondacks, overnight stays in Boston for the Harvard-Yale games, or weekly luncheons at East Hartford's Canoe Club. Here, most Wednesday afternoons, Stevens invited a few of these friends to join him as his guest at the large fraternal table in the center of the log-cabin clubhouse. He savored the camaraderie as much as the food at this exclusive men's club, of which J. Tansley Hohmann was long-time secretary, for despite his reserve, Stevens took keen pleasure in the image of himself as one of the boys.

The value Stevens attached to this role was set in his youth by his father's example. Although Garrett Stevens was a quiet, reticent lawyer much like his son, he had made much of the fellowship of his male circle of friends who gathered at Kuechler's Roost, a rustic watering hole atop Reading's Mount Penn. The elder Stevens celebrated this camaraderie in several poems, some published anonymously in the local Reading newspaper in 1906, when the only writer in the family was Stevens *père*. Garrett Stevens' "A Foosganger's Evening" suggests the masculine pleasures of Kuechler's circle, into which Wallace Stevens was himself initiated as a young man.

> The Judge and Tom, and Doc and I! We four afoot
> For Kuechler's Roost one snowy day quite late set out.
> The snow was deep, the paths were hid, and only marks
> We long had known on tree and stone made sure our route.
> We struggled hard and puffed and swore, while many a fall
> Forced groan suppressed; and it was dark when round a turn
> Of garden wall we struck a place well known to all.
> Leading to gate, always a-swing, to Kuechler's own.
> The Judge and Tom, and Doc and I.
>
> "Ho, Kuechler! Ho," loud we shouted. Door we battered.
> *"Schlofuht du,* Louis? *Bisht du od?"* Low voice we heard,
> And soon a shuffling sound, as snow we scattered
> And at the door the lantern lit, without one word.
> Like bear disturbed, old Kuechler stood, and peering out
> With hand 'bove eyes, with draggled beard, wondering he
> What fools these be, this time o'night, to cause this rout.
> And there we stood, a famished gang, half shamed stood we—
> The Judge and Tom, and Doc and I.
> . . . .
> But glasses clink and gurgling soon, in each parched mouth
> That sparkling wine, not Kaiser's now, but our own prize,
> Reaches the spot where spirits weak grow quickly stout.
> A flow of soul, each genial friend in friend confides.
> Tom recited then his choicest bits, and Doc, he sang.
> I stories told, and the Judge he—well, he moralized,
> And sniffed the smell from kitchen door. A jolly gang
> This Judge and Tom, and Doc and I.*

*Reprinted in the Reading *Eagle*, July 20, 1924, p. 14. The Foosgangers, or "goers-on-foot," was a hiking club made up of Reading professional men, among them Garrett Stevens; Daniel Ermentrout, a local judge; and Colonel Thomas Zimmerman, editor of the Reading *Times*. Most paths in the woods around Reading seemed eventually to lead the Foosgangers to the wine house on Mount Penn operated by Jacob Louis Kuechler, a German immigrant who had settled in Reading, perhaps as early as the 1850s. Although he had come there as a woodcarver, Kuechler later opened a restaurant-saloon in downtown Reading, and around 1882 he built a simple frame building on the eastern slope of Mount Penn, about three miles from town, that soon became a popular tavern. "There are Wine Houses and Wine Houses. This one was most unusual," an habitué later recalled. "It became widely known because of the personality of the owner, whose sociability gave it atmosphere. Those not feeling it, did not fit. . . . Companionship, not commercialism, was the keynote. There were no elaborate menus, rye bread and cheese being favorites. Roast pig was served at banquets. . . . The place slowly acquired a literature

To the end of his life, Wallace Stevens was very much Garrett Stevens' son; among his boys at the office, he enacted a role he had learned from his father, as he perpetuated so many other aspects of his father's style.

There is a sense in which Stevens dealt with his boys at the office as perquisites of his position. And yet, most of the few intimate relationships of his Connecticut years developed out of his life at the office. Fellow lawyers Wilson Taylor, James Powers and, above all, Judge Arthur Powell were among those singular friends with whom Stevens was comfortable, as he was with few people, to be the businessman, the man of letters and the family man.

John O'Loughlin

The company started back about [1913]. There was a lot of youth in the company in those days, and Mr. Stevens and Mr. Kearney and Mr. Armstrong were about the oldest of the group in there. The balance of the organization was all youth. If you'd have gone over [to the Hartford Fire side of the building] it was antiquated, with people who'd been there twenty-five or thirty years. But when the A&I started, it was all youth, mostly.

I went to work in the bond department, and Mr. Stevens was head of the

---

—both in prose and poetry—with much of the latter in Pennsylvania-German. . . . Mr. Zimmerman was the official poet and dedicated several of his poems to the Roost. . . . After the wine had passed a number of times these poems became songs. The Foosgaengers were very vocal but not very lyric." (Benjamin A. Fryer, "Kuechler's Roost," *The Historical Review of Bucks County,* October 1935, pp. 15–16.)

There was a decided taste for literature among Kuechler and his intimates at the Roost, which made it seem to some visitors that Shakespeare's Mermaid or Johnson's Mitre had been rebuilt on Mount Penn (Reading *Eagle,* February 14, 1909, p. 7). The tone was set, in part, by Kuechler himself. Indeed, among Wallace Stevens' vivid memories of him was Kuechler "as he recited from Schiller some loved line" ("In Memoriam of J. L. Kuechler," Reading *Times,* January 7, 1904, p. 2). Kuechler was, as one of the Foosganger poets, Colonel Zimmerman, recalled, "a man of artistic taste and capabilities, a lover of classical German poetic literature" (Reading *Eagle,* February 14, 1909, p. 7). While Garrett Stevens was a Foosganger who published anonymously in local newspapers, Thomas Zimmerman gained a considerable local reputation as a poet, especially through translation of German classics into English and of English poetry into Pennsylvania German, some of them preserved in the two-volume collection he published in 1903, *Olla Podrida.* With his dual career as both a newspaperman and a poet, Thomas Zimmerman may have served as one of the models for Wallace Stevens at the time the young poet left Harvard to try for a newspaper career in New York, Zimmerman having encouraged him along these lines when he hired Stevens as a special reporter during his vacations from school.

Kuechler's Roost is a particularly interesting spot in the literary life of Reading during the years Stevens was growing up there. It was, among other things, a congenial gathering place for local businessmen who were also, in a loose sense, men of letters. Given his familiarity with these men in this setting as a young man, it is understandable why Stevens later found it surprising that his public would find it remarkable that a businessman could also be a man of letters.

bond-claims department. We got to know each other because I used to do a little running for our department—go down and pick up files. He and I then struck up an acquaintance. When I left in 1930 to go to Glens Falls [Insurance Company], he was instrumental in bringing me back to [the] Hartford in the New York office in 1933. But during the period that I was associated with him, [from] '24 to '30, we had a very fine acquaintance. He had his likes and his dislikes, and he had his friends and his enemies. He was a very outspoken man. If he liked you, he liked you; if he didn't like you, he didn't like you. You had to understand the man. [A friendship] had to initiate on his part, not on your part. If you wanted to get close to him [and] he didn't, you might just as well forget it. You couldn't impose upon him. It was his observation of you that brought him to you. But you had to understand him to appreciate his values 'cause he had many attributes that weren't on the surface, but they came out.

When I was there in the early twenties, he got to be quite a connoisseur of tea. Three o'clock every afternoon, he used to call me. We used to go down to the medical department [where there was a stove] and have tea. I used to travel with him on weekends. He was quite a horticulturist in those days before he moved out to Westerly Terrace [1932], and we used to visit nurseries. He had to give up the horticultural end because Mrs. Stevens took that over, and there was a clash over what she wanted and what he wanted, so he bowed out of it. He'd call you up at noontime and say, "Let's take a walk."Until later years, he never ate lunch. And we'd walk over as far as Trinity College and back. [Even in blustery New England weather, on these walks] he never wore an overcoat, and he never wore a hat until later years.

He was very meticulous about his dress. All his clothes he had made, over in East Orange, New Jersey, by a Norwegian. All his shirts and underwear and socks he had in Newell's on Park Avenue. Even his denture powder he had from a special pharmacy on Park Avenue. In those days he was quite a cigar smoker, but he gave it up. He used to get his cigars out of Tampa. He was a great one for ordering fruit from California, dried fruit. And he was always looking for the unusual. When he would go to New York, there was a place up on Madison Avenue, a fruit store. He'd go up there and order fruit; they'd put it on the train coming [to Hartford]. Maybe he'd call me up and say, "I've got some fruit down here [at the Hartford station]. Would you drive down?" [O'Loughlin would then take Stevens home] but as far as the door; that's as far as it went. Never got inside the house. When he had me transferred to New York, he used to send me down the catalogue of the Parke-Bernet Galleries: he'd want a painting or he'd want a book, or something else. He'd send me the check and say, "This is the maximum you can bid for this." Every once in a while I'd pick it up. Or he'd call, "Pick up such-and-such when you come up this weekend." I used to bring up fruit and wine from New York when I'd come home and visit my own people. So over the years we had a close association.

When his first book came out, he gave me an autographed copy of it. "To my good friend," he [wrote]. "When you read this, you won't know what the hell it's all about." That was part of his humor. He was very proud of [*Harmonium*], but he was very disappointed, too, because a lot of people just didn't understand what he was trying to get across. You could see it by the fact that his books didn't sell as rapidly as he thought they should have sold. You'd never know about [a new book] until you read about it in the newspaper. He never publicized it in the office—very reserved. He'd be in demand sometimes for a few lectures and speeches. The only one I ever went to was at Mount Holyoke. [O'Loughlin drove Stevens there.] He wouldn't stay around for lunch. Most of his address was just taken from little notes that he had scribbled down, and when he got through he just disappeared. Walked right off. That was him. You had to understand the man. He could come in here, sit down, and he'd say what he wanted to say in three minutes, get up, and walk out. It wasn't any reflection on you; this was the way he operated.

He wore glasses later in years, but he used to keep his own counsel about his eyes. He would use drops; I do know that he was going to somebody in New York about his eyes, not locally. He had the old-fashioned glasses; they were very small and wire [-rimmed]. But he never wore glasses on the street. He only wore glasses in his work, and he always had them hanging down off his nose. He and I often talked about his eyes. I never mentioned anything, but I was under the impression that there were some problems with cataracts, maybe, forming. He had the same idea, but he wouldn't admit it to himself.

He was very vigorous. He would walk an average of a good five to ten miles a day. And it wasn't unusual for him, when he was in New York, if he was up around Madison Avenue to walk down to the office at John Street, which was a good eight miles or so, just for the walk. He'd come in the [New York] office, walk right by you, say "hello" and "good-by," and keep right on going, walk right out. You had to understand him.

When I came back to Hartford [from the New York office in the late 1930s], he had broadened out, got a bit mellower, a little more considerate of people. He got out of that shell of isolation. He joined the Canoe Club. [It] used to be a weekly event to go there Wednesday, and he always wanted two friends to go along, either "Sig" [Anthony Sigmans] or "Doc" [Ivan Daugherty] and me. He had very few friends beyond that. And once you left the office, then it terminated. About eleven o'clock he'd call up: "Jack, you got your car today? Well, we're going over to the Canoe Club. We'll meet outside at twelve o'clock." We'd go over to the Canoe Club, and he'd have a couple of martinis. Wednesday would be the cold-roast-beef day, and this would be his bill of fare. And he would leave over there by one-thirty and be back in the office by quarter of two. That would be the only lunch that he would have during the entire week. You couldn't take him to lunch. You could never buy him a meal if you were in his company. He'd kid around with you, but no business. Never got into serious discussions; maybe he'd be talking about the weather or about some incident that came up, and national events. No shop. He could always come out with a crack, and he'd laugh very heartily for three or four minutes. But he would never insult you; he would never make fun of you. He had a very strong, husky laugh.

He used to go down with Judge Powell to the Keys and [they'd] have a hilarious time between the two of them. He would never tell you [anecdotes of these trips] other than this was an event to let himself loose. When Mr. Stevens used to take a little bit too much aboard, he got very hilarious in many ways. I was with him one time at an affair when he had a little bit more [to drink]. The waiter came along with a tray of hors d'oeuvres, and he kicked it right out of her hand, and it went right up to the ceiling. Mr. Stevens was not a drinking man, and when he got a little bit more, he'd become very joyous and not mean or cantankerous.

J. Tansley Hohmann

[The Hartford Canoe Club] is a limited-membership club. It used to be eighty or eighty-five; now it's a hundred. In Stevens' time, the limit was less than that. We had quite a few people in the manufacturing business, and we had lawyers, and we had lots of people in the construction business. All types. But I can't recall anybody that was really in the literary end, writers or whatnot.

Now the Canoe Club is not a place where the membership is going to listen to any poetry. Everybody knew [Stevens was a poet]. We called him the Poet Laureate, in fact. There weren't any inhibitions over at our club: you might get needled as a guest, even. Many a time, I've warned my guests, "You can expect anything from anybody over there. [Don't take] any exception to it, because you never know what somebody is going to tell you." Stevens wasn't backward about saying things. Well, nobody is over there. Someone gives you a barb, he knows you're going to give it back to him if you can think of anything to say. But all in fun. That's what the club is for, a place to relax. The idea was usually to keep business out; and as far as the general group is concerned, there was never a business discussion. You might discuss some stupid things, like how fast is the river going, five miles an hour or ten? It wouldn't be anything serious, however, so that anybody could very well enter into the conversation. It was just a period when you can forget everything.

Probably the dues at that time were twenty or twenty-five dollars a month. It wasn't too much, and the prices of the meals were on the lower side, two-fifty. We had a chef in those days; he was one of the best chefs we ever had. Every Tuesday he would have hot roast beef for lunch. Wallace did not come over on Tuesday, but he always came on Wednesday and he had cold roast beef. And he liked to have it about half an inch thick. And then he covered that with English mustard. He'd really enjoy it. Every week he did that. He'd be at the round table [at the center of the lodge]. People sit [at the smaller tables lining the walls of the clubhouse] if you went over with a guest and just wanted to talk to him. There're no cliques at all.

I don't think Stevens did anything in particular for the club except attendance at lunch and at meetings, and that's true of the majority of people. There're only a few who are going to get involved in the work.

He wasn't one you were completely familiar with. That's about the best you can say. He was always welcome, always went through and spoke to everybody. But he wasn't one that you made a real friend out of, let's put it that way. Some people you really get very friendly with quick and others you don't.

Anthony Sigmans

Having been a close friend and associate of Mr. Stevens for many years, I take pleasure in giving my impressions of a great man, a man I admired and who is largely responsible for the success I achieved in later life. Certain it is that we had very little in common either educationally, socially or religiously. I haven't had any formal education; all mine is practical experience. [Having left school after the seventh grade, Sigmans was later admitted to the Alabama Bar after working as a clerk and secretary in a law office.] And yet my deficiencies did not alter our friendship. Hate to break down [here Sigmans was unable to continue for a few moments], but it shows the closeness.

It was in 1934 that I first made his acquaintance, and it came about in an odd sort of way. At that time I was employed by the Glens Falls Indemnity Company; my work was similar to that of Mr. Stevens, except that he was with a large insurance company. On occasion, both companies would be involved in a major loss, and we exchanged correspondence. One day a mutual friend got in touch with me and stated that he had a call from Mr. Stevens, who wanted to see me and had suggested New York as a place to meet. His exact message to this friend was: "I want to see Sigmans. You don't know what I want to see him about, so it don't concern you. Have him call me." We had a brief phone conversation, and it was agreed that I would meet him at the Commodore Hotel on a day certain and to come up to his room immediately on arrival.

[About] six o'clock I knocked at his door. What I saw was a towering figure over six feet tall, weighing two hundred and fifty or more. To say the least, I felt insignificant and immediately developed an inferiority complex, which existed more or less until his death in 1955. Mr. Stevens greeted me cordially and immediately inquired if I had [had] dinner. And with that he commented he had just consumed several pounds of Pennsylvania Dutch sausages, one of his favorites, and consequently did not have much of an appetite. He suggested that we see the town, which was something new to me, although he was well acquainted with the city. Nothing was said concerning the purpose of the visit.

We left the hotel and got in one cab after another, visiting night spots and having drinks. He never failed, upon entering a club, to tip the orchestra leader and have the orchestra play "Have You Ever Seen a Dream Girl [sic] Walking," which was popular at the time and one of his favorites. During the course of the evening nothing whatever was said concerning the purpose of the meeting. Toward midnight I told Mr. Stevens I could drink no more and that my drinking habits were conservative. I think one reason why he gave me such a test in New York was because the company was known for its alcoholics; he had one or two in his department, and I think he wanted to make damn sure that I was not an alcoholic. He could handle his, and he liked his drinks. Sometimes when I'd take him to a company shindig—I'd always see that he got home—sometimes he'd say, "Let's drive to Windsor. I want to sober up a little before I go home."

Seemingly pleased, he immediately urged me to start drinking coffee, commenting he would have another drink or two. At this juncture, I made it a point to inquire what he wanted to see me for. He bluntly replied that he wanted to offer me a position with the Hartford. I told him I was very happy with the company I worked for. He elaborated both as to position and salary, and I countered by saying that I did not think I would be interested for several reasons. "Think it over, and call me in a day or two," which I did, with the same answer. He then urged me to visit him in the home office when [I was] next in the area. This happened to be a couple of weeks later. I still was not happy thinking of leaving my present employer, although the offer finally made was attractive. He asked me to see the president of the company.

Introducing me, he stated, "I would like you to meet Mr. Sigmans, who has just decided to come with the Hartford." This statement rather stunned me, but not wishing to embarrass him in front of the president, we left. On the way out I asked Mr. Stevens what he meant by making such a statement. His reply was, the company was going to employ me and we might as well finalize it now. He also asked me to meet his first assistant, Manning Heard; he pulled the same stunt in his office. At any rate, Mr. Stevens asked me again to think it over, and with that he apologized for having to leave promptly: he was taking the train to [Kansas City]. He'd go out on very large bond cases which required conferences with very influential people. He might go to Kansas City today and not go again for six months. There'd just be an occasional case, because he'd delegate to his other men. But he'd go to New York once or twice a month even if he didn't have any business there. He loved New York; he knew every part of it.

I discussed the offer with my superior, who knew Mr. Stevens and his prominence in the industry. He certainly was the most outstanding surety-claims man in the business; I think I'm prepared to say that, because I was in the business for a number of years and had occasion to meet a lot of the big surety men. And Stevens, whenever his name was mentioned, "Oh, hell, he must be right." [Sigmans' superior] urged me to accept the offer, as it undoubtedly offered me a great opportunity. This I did.

At the time we were in the depths of a depression, and banks were failing on all sides. The company took over a lot of bank obligations and assets. I was hired to organize the [salvage] department to recoup some of these assets. But I wasn't with him long. It shows you the man he was. After I worked like hell in this department, which was something he admired—he liked somebody to work hard because he was a prodigious worker—it wasn't but a matter of three or four months before he said, "The president wants to see you." We had an agency situation in the South, and [the president] wanted me to take a tour of all the agents and evaluate the manager we had in Atlanta. When I came back from that, they called me to go to Philadelphia. Then I got back to the harness again, I was loaned to the casualty-claims department. Well, I never got back to Mr. Stevens, but the point I make is he wasn't selfish. He hired me, but he was that kind of man—[his first loyalty was to the company]. Definitely so.

And he appreciated the company doing for him what they did because he was an odd sort of individual, let's face it. I don't think he'd have been a practicing lawyer. Hell, he couldn't have talked to a jury or clients. He wouldn't last two days in business. On one occasion they had a big case down in Washington. Mr. Stevens made some comment: he didn't think the man [representing the government's claim] knew what the hell he was talking about. And here's a stranger; you just don't say those things. You may think them. But [he spoke] just what he had in mind, just like he did with my wife. In the early days, she found it very difficult to be around Stevens, which happened on one or two occasions when we had business guests from outside the city. On one occasion we went to the Turkey Inn for dinner, and my wife was called upon to pour the tea, which Mr. Stevens was very fond of. [In] his odd sort of way, he criticized the way she was holding the teapot. She immediately commented, "If you would hold your cup properly, I wouldn't have to hold the teapot this way." Normally you'd say, she's making a social error, but he works for me [so] I'd better keep my mouth shut. But that was Mr. Stevens. On the way home he started a conversation with her, and she finally said, "Mr. Stevens, I wish you would come down to earth. I don't understand half you're talking about." With that he placed his arm around her, and they were bosom friends. Very definitely [Stevens respected that type of directness].

Even though I transferred to a different department, I was constantly in touch with Mr. Stevens. He'd call me up: "Let's go over to the Canoe Club." Frequently, if he had an errand to do or the weather was bad, he'd call me and see if I'd take him home. It was not an employer-employee relationship; we were just friends. I'd do anything for Mr. Stevens. I wasn't trying to ingratiate myself with him in order to advance in the company, because he had his department and I got into this other type of work. We went to New York and Boston a number of times: we used to go to the Harvard-Yale games a lot. Sometimes there'd be [Ivan] Daugherty with us, and [Manning Heard]. He'd always get the tickets. We'd make a real affair out of it. We'd go to the Statler and have a big dinner; he loved that and he loved to listen to the music [of the hotel orchestra]. Come home the next day. Mr. Stevens had a sense of humor that was often misunderstood: instead of being funny, it could be construed as sarcastic. I remember an occasion when he and I planned a trip to Boston, which was one of his favorite places to spend a night or two. He wrote the Statler Hotel for reservations and stated, "I would like a room overlooking the [Boston] Common. I will have with me Sigmans, who could be assigned a room overlooking most anything." He meant no offense; he thought that was a joke, because he wouldn't hurt me for all the tea in China. He wouldn't have asked me to go with him if he was going to do that. And to his good friend [John O'Loughlin] when he was trying to set up a date with me: "You don't know what I want to see him about, so it don't concern you." O'Loughlin understood: that was his way of being funny. And the longest trip was when we went up to New York State, up Fort Ticonderoga and all around there. That was around '35 or '36. We had a happy time on that trip, eating, sightseeing, and chewing the fat. He could admire the women, but on our trips never became involved with any women or anything. That was purely a man's affair. But I mean he liked to joke and all that: a girl walking down the hall or something, he's just as apt to make some curt remark to whoever was there about this or that. When we got up in the 1940s, it was purely New York occasionally, particularly if he wanted to bring a case of wine home. We'd pick up the French wine and get it in the basement door late at night: he didn't want Mrs. Stevens to know. And then the Canoe Club innumerable times.

Now, in later years, he was invited to join the Canoe Club. He loved it because he could sit around and listen to the fellows crack jokes, and he always enjoyed a joke—the dirtier the better—and have a few drinks. The surroundings were rather crude, and he loved that. I don't know this directly, but the story goes, a man was delegated by the members who said, "We're not getting much out of Stevens as a member. He never joins in the conversation, and he just sits there and looks at us and listens." This man was delegated to try to bow Stevens out of the club. Shortly after that, he saw Mr. Stevens standing on a rainy day, and he stopped. "Can I give you a ride?" He said, "You certainly can." And the man says, "Where do you want to go?" He says, "I want to go to the Canoe Club. I love that place. I love the atmosphere. I love the members." And that dropped any ousting proceedings. They'd never tell him.* And I know that he belonged to [the Century Association] in New York. He'd go up there and rub elbows with some of the literary people.†

His entertainment, socially, was practically nil except for the occasions when he would ask me and others close to him to chauffeur him on short trips and outings. He would pay the bills. We had many such trips over the years and always most enjoyable.

Mr. Stevens' family consisted of wife and daughter. His wife was an odd

*Sigmans read of the alleged ouster movement in Ralph Minard's review of the *Letters of Wallace Stevens* in the Hartford *Times*, March 11, 1967, p. 20. However, according to the secretary of the Canoe Club during Stevens' years as a member, "There was never an ouster movement. None at all." (Taped interview with J. Tansley Hohmann.)

†"The saying in New York was: 'It's easier to get into Heaven than [into] the Century Association,'" according to Kurt Roesch, a member of the club and an acquaintance of Stevens during the 1950s. "It is very difficult [to become a member]. You have to have six recommendations. Then you are suggested and there is a vote. [There are] monthly gatherings, with black tie. The whole club is a very civilized thing. There are quite a number of literary people in there, poets and writers. Everybody reads his poetry, but practically nobody knew him," so reserved was Stevens after he became a member in June 1951. (Taped interview with Kurt Roesch.)

sort of person. They had very little social life. She did not have anything to do with Mr. Stevens' business associates. Hardly anyone ever came to their house. In fact, I was invited in the house only once over a period of years and that was when Mr. Stevens was seriously ill. I brought him flowers. He called me to his bed. "I appreciate the flowers, but don't ever bring me flowers again." Mrs. Stevens probably said something about it. I'd bring him home, for example, innumerable times, and he'd say, "Oh, there's Mrs. Stevens in the yard. Don't drive up there. Let me out here, and I'll walk up." And he'd apologize constantly. "I'm sorry. I'd like to have you come in, but Mrs. Stevens won't permit it." Now, there was nothing I did to Mrs. Stevens. Hell, I only saw her twice in my life; unless she took a dislike to me because I was spending so much time with Mr. Stevens because I could get away easier than some of the other fellows. As I say, we'd take the car and go here and there, and have dinner and a drink or two. He didn't find me noisy; I didn't say a helluva lot unless he said something, 'cause I couldn't keep abreast of his intellect. I wouldn't dare say to Mr. Stevens, "I can't do it."

[When] Holly was growing up, she must have experienced a lot of want in her life because, her father being what he was and her mother being queer, she didn't see much of life. Once in a while he'd say—this would be on a Monday when we'd come back—"Well, we had a good time yesterday. We all stood around and sang a song after dinner." Now Holly, he sent her to Vassar. He told me one day, "I feel bad today. Holly has left Vassar." "Oh, what's the trouble?" He said, "She thought it was too snooty." He was keenly disappointed. So he got her a job with Aetna Insurance, and then she fell in love with one of the service men for one of the dictating-equipment concerns. And that hit him hard. And he would talk to me about it. "I'm going to break it up; I'm going to get them divorced," which he did. And then after Mr. Stevens died, Holly married again, and Mrs. Stevens didn't like the boy. She was going to break that up. So the poor girl had a helluva time.

He never talked to me about his poetry because he knew I didn't know a damn thing about it. [Once] I says, "I don't understand a damn thing about [poetry], and you know I don't." And that was that. The only thing I knew about his poetry was that it was on the order of Gertrude Stein; now I've forgotten who the hell she was. So he never bothered talking about it other than "Well, I just published a book" and so forth. There'd just be casual mention of it. More would be made in the press. *Ideas of Order,* quite a bit was made of that at the time. I've got a lot of newspaper clippings and write-ups of him [going back to the mid-thirties, which Sigmans began collecting shortly after joining the company]. He would tell me sometimes when he was going to Harvard or Yale and talk. Just a passing remark. I bought a few [of Stevens' books], but in those days it didn't mean anything to us. When [*Ideas of Order*] came out [1936], it was just talked about around the office, so you went down [to the bookstore] just because he happened to be in the office. We didn't think he'd ever be the celebrity he was. I was surprised [when Stevens received the Pulitzer Prize in 1955] because I didn't know who Pulitzer was. We just accepted Wallace Stevens as another man at the office—smart as hell—who liked to write poetry.

To sum it all up: he was a very lonesome man in many ways, and that's why he built his life around a half dozen of us pretty much. And we revered him. That I broke down here shows my affection for him.

Lillian Daugherty

My father-in-law [the late Ivan Daugherty, who worked under Stevens as a bond lawyer for twenty-five years] said once that he was not a friend of Stevens because Stevens didn't have any friends. But he called himself an intimate: he was as close to him as Stevens was to anybody. And I think he rather enjoyed that.

Stevens would confide in my father-in-law. Stevens and his wife had a terrible row once. She was so angry that she threw something at him. Stevens came into work and said, "Doc, I just don't understand women. I don't know what to do. What do you think I should do?" My father-in-law told him, "Why don't you go home, put down your briefcase, put your arms around her, and tell her you love her? Buy her a bunch of roses and send them to her." "What the hell for?" He was puzzled, but he said, "All right, I'll do it."Apparently it did the trick, because he came into work afterward and said, "Gee, I don't understand that, but it worked." That story sticks because I remember thinking at the time, Here's this tremendously sensitive man, and the idea of showing his wife a little appreciation or affection comes as "Gee, how come it worked? How come she was happy about these flowers?"

My father-in-law said she was a beautiful woman and very high-strung. I think he often pitied her. My father-in-law was very gallant. My father-in-law's marriage was a romance, and he pitied Mrs. Stevens because she had to live with this burly guy for whom, in the order of importance in his life, she was pretty low. Stevens talked to my father-in-law about Holly and Holly's husband [John Hanchak] and told him that he didn't approve of that marriage.

There were oft-repeated stories about being taken to the Canoe Club by Stevens; there were stories about football games they attended. My mother-in-law was very resentful of the time that he spent with Stevens away from home. My father-in-law was a devoted family man; his weekends should have been devoted to entertaining her. She was really quite spoiled by him. It seemed to be an influence that took him away from her and away from the family, and she resented it. She resented Stevens, always. I think there was a lot of drinking going on on these weekends, and that bothered her. Ivan would verbalize to his wife [that] he didn't really want to go, but Stevens had the tickets: it was the political thing that he had to do. The impression I had was, he sort of enjoyed himself, although he wasn't about to say that, not with her saying, "Wasn't it terrible that Stevens dragged you here or made you take him there?" He didn't contradict her, but my impression was that he rather enjoyed some of these outings. My father-in-law was proud of his part of the relationship with Stevens; he felt that he did not kowtow to this man. He told him what he thought, and he felt Stevens respected him. He didn't feel he was pandering, himself, by taking him different places.

There is this one incident they both told me about with great glee. Stevens was at their house one night. There was a painting on the far wall of the dining room. Stevens walked in and said, "Oh, it's an interesting picture." And he walked over a little closer and said, "Oh, it's a reproduction, isn't it?" and [then] he said, "Everything in your house is a reproduction, Doc." And my father-in-law said, "Yes, and it always will be as long as I work for you." Nobody ever told me what Stevens' reaction was: they were so pleased that he really told Stevens off that time. I wondered if Stevens had said it in humor. If he did, they took it as an insult. Another little story that's coming to mind is Stevens saying to him, "Doc, why aren't you a member of this Canoe Club?" "I'd be a member if you'd pay me enough money so that I could afford it."

In line with this humor, Stevens inscribed his books as they were published to my father-in-law. I do remember one of the books autographed, "To Doc, who never understands any of this stuff anyhow." This never impressed my father-in-law: so the man wrote a book of poetry and it was published, so what? He certainly was not impressed with Stevens' poetry. He didn't understand it; he always made a point of saying, "Well, I don't know anything about that."

My father-in-law was anti-Semitic in the way that unthinking people are. He used to say things to my father like "Gee, Herman, you're a great guy. You're different from other Jews." Apparently, Wallace Stevens was the same. I'm sure that was something that he and my father-in-law had in common. The Canoe Club was restricted. I remember a conversation I once had with my father-in-law about Stevens' poetry. I was talking about a poem and giving a little bit of this great, sensitive-man [approach]. He changed the subject real quick to the Canoe Club and the fact that Wallace was anti-Semitic—which was telling me: don't like him.

The whole family idea was that Stevens was the villain who kept my father-in-law from getting anywhere in the company. My father-in-law said he wasn't the only one. Stevens was the kind of boss who did not care for his employees: he didn't fight for them with the big shots, he didn't try to get my father-in-law raises. If my father-in-law had ended up in any other department, other than working for Stevens, he would have been a vice-president. I'm in no position at all to judge that. My father-in-law was a very bright, very intelligent, very conscientious man. My mother-in-law had a great deal of resentment against Wallace Stevens. But my father-in-law would argue with her mildly. He'd say, "Well, now, Mary. There's good in every-body. And you have to feel sorry for a man like that." Or, "He's got no friends. I'm the only one." What I really felt was that he was allowing her to ventilate these feelings for him and that he really believed that Wallace Stevens was to blame for the fact that his raises were low, that he never did become an officer, and that he never received the recognition that he should have [had].

Ivan felt that Stevens should have had more of a hand in preparing somebody to be his successor. As a matter of fact, I'm remembering now his talking [about how] Stevens thought he was immortal. That most of the department heads would have had somebody lined up and would have paved the way. Stevens didn't do that; he kept everybody down under him, so that when he died there was sort of a scramble. No [her father-in-law's lot did not improve after Stevens' death]. I think that my father-in-law had the reputation of being Stevens' man by that time with the rest of the people.

My father-in-law told me from time to time that he suspected one of the men or other [in Stevens' department] accepted gifts from contractors. Stevens did not know and was not involved. It bothered my father, but he kept it to himself. Some contractor once bought him an automobile, drove it right out in front of the house. "This is a gift for you." My father-in-law was outraged and refused the gift, wanting no part of anything like that.

The two families did not associate; it was the two men going off together. But occasionally, when my husband was a teen-ager, he would have to go and pick them up after work. Stevens never referred to him by name, always as "the boy." When they were in the car, the three of them, he would never address Bud, "How are you?" or anything like that. It was: "Tell the boy maybe he should go that way." My husband's feeling was a lot of resentment. I don't think that anybody in the family likes to talk about Stevens, not because they don't want to say bad things about him. I think they just have so little regard. It just irks my husband when someone inquires about Stevens: here's the great poet—who was just a bastard, a seriously flawed man.

Wilson Taylor

I didn't know him then as anything but a lawyer and a business executive [in 1931, when Taylor, an experienced surety lawyer, began working in the Hartford Accident and Indemnity's surety department in New York]. I didn't realize what a thoroughly educated and refined man he was. It didn't take me long to learn, and it was then I began to save his letters, over a hundred of them. Getting to know him was a gradual affair that took place over a period of years. Lots of times when he came to New York, he'd call me up and we'd have lunch, sometimes dinner, and spend the evening together. If he was going to be down on a Saturday, very frequently I would meet him, and we'd go to various of the small galleries. He used to seem to know the people at the Wildenstein Gallery; I can't think of another where he really spoke to the people as though he knew them. One day we were having lunch, and I brought up the subject of the exhibit of Walter Gay at the Metropolitan. "Oh yeah," he said, "we must see that today."[51] He had planned that. He used to get those current exhibits from *The New Yorker*. I don't think he ever came down that he didn't read *The New Yorker* on the way. I don't profess to be the connoisseur of art that he was, but I appreciate certain types of it. I didn't appreciate our visit to the Museum of Modern Art; I don't know whether he enjoyed it.

To him [gallery going] was just part of life. And Stevens enjoyed life. I don't care what aspect of it, he enjoyed it. A few times we'd go over to some concert in the Times Square area: he used to like Stravinsky, and we'd go to some Stravinsky concerts over there. I don't think we ever went to a musical. I don't think we ever went to a play. He enjoyed things from Forty-second Street north to the Carlyle Hotel, and in between there were bistros and there were galleries; this, that, and the other. This is mostly on the East Side, up and down Madison Avenue.

Sometimes, he'd come down and he'd just walk around by himself. He loved to walk. [Once] he was walking down Madison Avenue, looking at the antique stores. This particular one was closed. He called me Monday morning, said he'd been down Saturday and he saw this lamp. He recognized it as a choice piece of pottery, porcelain I guess it was, and some kind of a fancy shade on it. He wanted to know if I could get up there that day and see if I could buy it for him. So I went up and the price on this little old table lamp was two hundred dollars. That was a lot of money in the thirties. "Oh, good

God!" he said, but he sent two hundred dollars down. He said, "Make them pack it well, and they'll have to pay the cost of shipping." And they did; they were probably darn glad to get two hundred dollars. [On another occasion, in auction rooms, with Taylor along,] he was looking for a sofa, and this girl was showing him this handsome sofa. She said, "That's a good-looking sofa for two hundred dollars." And Stevens' reply was, "You don't know how good two hundred dollars looks." He was very comfortable during the Depression; about '34 he was made a vice-president and vice-presidents in those days . . .

He wasn't [a home-office politician] but he was very well liked by Jim Kearney [president of the Hartford in 1934]. And then by Paul Rutherford, who succeeded Mr. Kearney. Some of the presidents that followed I don't think were quite as fond of Stevens. Stevens was so far superior to anybody there that he very frequently stepped on some toes, rather tender toes, and some of those tender toes became vice-presidents and one of them became president. So it made, eventually, a difference.

In the industry he could make an awful lot of enemies by way of his letters. I remember one fellow in the Fidelity and Deposit Company just refused to answer any of Stevens' letters. You have probably heard about the letter he wrote about some lawyer he took a particular dislike to. He described him as showing a smile that was like the silver plate on a coffin. [Again] Stevens was at a football game at Yale one Saturday and ran into an officer from the home office of the Aetna [Life and Casualty Company, also in Hartford]. So Stevens and the home-office man greeted one another. Then Mr.——— said, "Stevens, you know Mr.——— from our New York office." It was a mystery how Aetna put up with him so long; he used to pull some of the most crooked things. And Stevens said, "Oh, yes. I've heard that Sing Sing lost its quarterback!" Whammo! It's just this type of thing he'd say; he knew this fellow, and he had no use for anyone that was off-color. I often wondered why he became friendly with me; certainly it was not on the mental level. I think one thing he would require of anybody he was either going to work with or be friendly with was trustworthiness.

I reported to him out here [when Taylor took over the West Coast bond operation of the Hartford], such as it was. He didn't want to be reported to very much. One of the funniest things that happened in that respect was during the war [when Taylor was still at work in New York]. We had some whopping big antiaircraft-shell contracts for the navy [that needed capital to complete]. I went to the higher-ups in the New York office, but nobody would take responsibility [to release $200,000]. Finally, I said, "By golly, I'm going to sign for it." I did, and the money was released; then I began to wonder whether I still had a job. So I thought I'd better get on the train to Hartford and see Stevens. I went in his office, gave him the whole story on the contract, the amount involved, what I had done. He never said a word. When I got all through, he said, "That reminds me of the story of Mrs. Webster's dog." I've never yet heard the story of Mrs. Webster's dog! But that was typical, that was his way of saying, "Okay, you've done a good job." He never interfered with anything that I had to do. I wrote to Stevens one time, wanted him to give me an answer to what he thought I should do. He said, "I'm not going to make any decision in this matter." He would delegate—if he had someone to delegate to. I didn't know anyone in the field that had as broad an authority as I did. He was always very nice to me; I never had any trouble.

He would have a great deal of compassion for any fellow who was having trouble—up to a point. He had a fellow in one of the offices that was having a drinking problem. Stevens didn't want to fire him, so he told him to come to Hartford, he wanted to talk to him. So the fellow went to Hartford and registered in the Bond Hotel with a quart of whiskey, and Stevens didn't see him until the next day. Of course, the next day, he just looked like the wrath of God. Well, he was fired; Stevens knew then that there was no hope.

It's not often that he came down [to New York] on cases. We discussed work, of course, at times. Not too much [shoptalk, however]; you see, shop to him was a means to an end. His real interests were in other things—largely, his poetry. Sometimes we'd talk about his poetry. Things like that he would have to bring up. If he brought them up, we might spend an hour or two talking about them. If I brought them up, why nothing further was said. I wouldn't say very much. The most outstanding [conversation] I recall was the time he had a book of poems all ready for publication, and he hadn't decided on the title. There were two titles under consideration. One was *The Man, That's All One Knows.* The other was *Parts of a World.* He told me that when Mrs. Stevens asked him whether "Knows" was spelled "Nose," he [decided] he'd better name it *Parts of a World.* He frequently would mention a specific poem. We were having dinner one night at the Carlyle [Hotel], and Stevens looked up at the waiter. "My God! It's Bruno Richard Hauptmann [the Lindbergh kidnapper]." He just looked exactly like him. So he laughed and he said, "Two Egyptians being served by a Nazi." And then he said, "Gee, that's a good title for a poem. I must write that down," so he pulled out a little card. I don't think he ever used it. I read a lot of Stevens' poetry; I've read more of his poetry since I've been out here than I ever did back East. No [Taylor did not ask about particular poems]. I knew this from my conversations with him: it wasn't necessarily his idea that anybody should know what he intended. They could read it for what it was worth, get some enjoyment out of it, put their own interpretation on it. To me, the most outstanding example of that is "The Comedian as the Letter C." If anybody can read that and come to any conclusion as to what was in his mind or what he intended, I'd like to know what it is. And yet, there are some beautiful lines in it. His words and the way he uses them can, in so many instances, be the most beautiful thing that you can imagine. Probably the outstanding example of that would be "Peter Quince at the Clavier."

I knew that he lectured at Harvard, that he lectured at Yale and probably at some of the smaller colleges. One time he went down to Princeton [1941] and gave a talk. He was laughing about it when he got to New York on his way back to Hartford. I met him, and we had dinner that night. He, evidently, [had] proceeded to insult everybody on the campus; he laughed and said, "I'll never be invited back there again."*

Lots of times the conversation would be on matters that I considered rather personal. Wallace Stevens never once told me, "Now I don't want you to repeat this," but I knew when it was confidential and I've never repeated it. There are certain things that I know that I will never repeat. A quite personal thing, which I don't mind telling, was the fact that his wife was on the coins [the Mercury dime and Liberty half dollar].† I knew Wallace Stevens twelve years before he ever mentioned that to me. It was one of those personal things that I would never bring up. His personal life was, I've always gathered, rather a quiet affair. Very seldom [did] Mrs. Stevens ever come down [to New York]. She was very much of a homebody. Stevens told me one time, "We never have any company. We don't have any friends in Hartford." He told me once she would not have anyone in the house. He had this big home; I've seen it when we drove by there one night and dropped him after one of the [com-

---

*When his host at Princeton, Henry Church, did not write for several months after Stevens' lecture there, Stevens was distressed to think that his behavior at Church's dinner party had offended his host, whose friendship meant a good deal to him (letter of Wallace Stevens to Henry Church, January 28, 1942, *L WS,* pp. 400–401). "No there is absolutely no need to have anything on your conscience," Church replied reassuringly to Stevens, who had worried that among his list of offenses might have been his bearing that evening toward Princeton composer Roger Sessions. "I'm sure of Sessions you made a real friend for you made him sit down at the piano and play again his own composition—That rarely happens to him—That was just before the evening broke up—I dont [sic] know what else you could have done to him—I am deeply grieved that you have had so much *mental torture.* . . ." (Letter of February 11, 1942, HL.) While Stevens made light of his behavior at Princeton to Wilson Taylor, worrying about how he had comported himself once he had returned home from a university event was not uncommon for Stevens.

†The sculptor Adolph Weinman, who owned and resided in the building on West Twenty-first Street where the Stevenses lived during their New York years (1909–16), modeled the figures on these coins after Elsie Stevens.

pany] stag parties. [Taylor never was invited inside.] In my early days with
the company, we used to work half-days on Saturday, until twelve or one
o'clock. I know that Stevens liked to get the fellows together and go out to
his home Saturday afternoon, just sit out on the lawn and have a drink and
talk awhile. They were just the fellows in his department; I wouldn't say they
were cultured gentlemen, but Stevens liked them, and they were good, loyal
fellows.

One night Mrs. Stevens and Wallace and I were having dinner together
in New York. It was the only time I ever met her. That was in the early
thirties; I hadn't known Stevens very long. He was lamenting the fact that
he didn't think he was doing much for society that he'd be remembered for
after he was gone. That's when she reminded him of his poetry. Mrs. Stevens
mentioned that his poetry would probably survive him.

Margaret Powers

I was part of the fun-and-frolic side of Wallace Stevens' life. We'd been
married two months, and he came to meet Jim's bride. He had to see what
kind of a person that boy of his had married. I didn't realize then that this
was going to be part and parcel of my whole married life. Jim was in the
shower when the guest arrived, and I had to meet Wallace Stevens all by
myself. He was always on time. There I was, this little girl absolutely in awe
of this man. [Her husband had given her *Harmonium* during their courtship.]
I thought, Oh, my lord—I'm as intellectual as the *Reader's Digest.* Well, he
realized the situation, that here was this little girl scared to pieces, so what
did that darling person do but just have me rolling on the floor telling me
about somebody's funeral. It sounds blasphemous, but he made it so funny.
When Jim came out, I was just madly in love with Wallace Stevens. He
certainly put me at ease, and I enjoyed him ever since. But I thought how
considerate to understand that here was a young girl absolutely green. That
was '29.

We went out to dinner and the theater, or something. He was always
finding new places for us to go. He loved the theater, musicals and so forth.
A year or so later, in the summertime, he took us to *The Third Little Show.*
I think it was [with] Bob Hope and all those who were top comedians.[52] We
sat in the third row, not the balcony the way the Powerses would do it. He
just loved the theater. He was always taking us to things like that. He knew
all the comedians and appreciated their humor—oh, boy, yes! He liked the
music, too. He took us and Henri Amiot, a Frenchman who had worked at

the Hartford; he was back in New York to visit [after having returned to France].

[During their New York years, the Powerses saw Stevens] every few months. He'd just say, "I'm coming down. Tell Jim." And we'd just have a fine time. We'd go to a speakeasy, always one of those fancy ones. It wasn't one of the Joe-sent-me [kind]. He was known; he could always get in. Then we'd have dinner someplace; he knew about all the good [restaurants] and the French ones. He was always well known. Then the theater or a concert, something special. His field of knowledge was so extremely wide. [At night,] we used to walk up and down Madison Avenue, where all the antique shops were—lighted, and beautifully so. Then he'd point out these *objets d'art*, particularly Oriental art. He knew a great deal about it, and he was dippy about Oriental rugs, spent fabulous amounts on them. [He never bought anything when he was with the Powerses.] He did that by himself; I think he didn't want anybody to know how much he spent. [In those Depression days he was] very flush. He spent money high-handedly. He treated us always. Then, of course, he knew modern French painting. It was just fascinating to be with him. I can't remember the names of the private galleries we stopped at. [He would say,] "There are some pictures in here I'd like you to see." He knew so much about them, the technique and that sort of thing. His knowledge was encyclopedic about all the arts. I was so surprised that he knew so much about music, the form of a fugue and that sort of thing. He was very familiar with whatever we were hearing that night, and he said, "Now you watch that theme; it's coming up later." There wasn't any one of the arts that he didn't know a lot about.

Jim wasn't interested in the arts, really, left all that sort of thing up to me. The theater he adored. They got along perfectly; they were just deeply fond of each other. He felt that Jim was his boy. He used to say it several times: "How's my boy?" He felt very close to Jim, and Jim absolutely idolized him. Jim loved working with him [in the late twenties]. Jim learned a lot about succinctness, not this gobbledygook they put into briefs nowadays. Wallace taught him that, very decidedly. Jim traveled a great deal in those years [under Stevens]. Wallace Stevens kind of talked Jim into the West Coast when he wanted to break away from New York to practice law. He talked about their [Wallace and Elsie's] trip to California [1923], that they'd had such an unusual trip and loved it so. He talked [about the] open spaces; he thought the scenery was beautiful, and he liked the climate in San Francisco. He wanted Jim to go to San Francisco [to work for the Hartford again. Because of the traveling involved, Powers finally settled in Portland, Oregon]. Whenever we were in New York [after moving to the West Coast in 1933], Wallace would come down, and they'd just talk, talk, talk. They'd go into cases, all kinds of things that were current. They did [talk about Stevens' poetry]. I didn't get in on that. Jim understood more of it and knew Wallace Stevens' philosophy, which was beyond me. Jim was not an avid reader of poetry, but if Wallace Stevens wrote *A B C,* he loved it. Jim was extremely well read in all kinds of things. He sent us copies [of his books].

After we came out here [to Portland], we'd go back east about every year. Then we'd see him a couple of times the week we were in New York. He would always come down and see us. [Our] first year back we had that memorable evening [resulting in "A Fish-Scale Sunrise"]. Jim and Wallace had been together all afternoon, and I met them about six or so. And then we started out. We went to a couple of speakeasies, then the place where we got the singer to play "La Paloma." That's where we had our dinner. When we got through there, it was about eleven-thirty or twelve, and we went on to the Waldorf Roof, which had just opened, and did the dancing. First time he had ever danced, so we danced. He was doggone good; he had a wonderful sense of rhythm. He seemed to enjoy it thoroughly, and that was a new experience for him. This was at twelve o'clock, and yet he insisted on having the pickled herring in cream. That's from Reading German, I suppose. We tried it, but he loved them.

It was an impetuous evening. I think we just meant to meet and have cocktails, but we went on and on and on. He'd [do things] on the spur of the moment. For instance, walking from Lewisohn Stadium [after a concert] to end up at two o'clock in the morning at the Carlyle Hotel [a ten-mile walk in New York City], that type of thing. Just "Let's do it!" Or that Waldorf Roof. He hadn't planned it; it was just something that came up. [He liked it] because it was impetuous, doing things that he'd never done before. I think he felt quite close to Jim and me that evening. He kissed me—the only time in his life—he wasn't that type. I understood the evening and what it meant to all of us, but I can't when he put it in poetry.

A FISH-SCALE SUNRISE

Melodious skeletons, for all of last night's music
Today is today and the dancing is done.

Dew lies on the instruments of straw that you were playing,
The ruts in your empty road are red.

You Jim and you Margaret and you singer of La Paloma,
The cocks are crowing and crowing loud,

And although my mind perceives the force behind the moment,
The mind is smaller than the eye.

The sun rises green and blue in the fields and in the heavens.
The clouds foretell a swampy rain.[53]

That must have been about '33. We didn't know about "A Fish-Scale
Sunrise" until *Ideas of Order* came out [1935]. He sent us copy number 13.

When he was trying to get me interested in my ancestors, he wrote this
limerick he'd been looking up about them. It was something about a lady
from Thistle went to wet her whistle, something faintly bibulous about it. He
could write them like nobody's business, in the perfect limerick form. He did
reminisce more in the later years when he got into the genealogy business.
He had a woman [Lila James Roney] working full-time on his genealogy [in
the early forties]. One time he found a will, and one of his ancestors had left
his silver shoe buckles to "my friend, Thomas Carhart," which would be one
of my ancestors. In the later years, he was still going on about the genealogy.
He gave me up as a lost cause. There is a thing called the Holland Society
in New York which he insisted I could claim to belong [to]. He was very
disappointed I wouldn't join up. I don't know why he was so interested in
genealogy. It was a puzzle; he liked that—and the surprises that came in. He
was so interested in old graveyards, and he found more little old graveyards,
he and Jim, in odd places [in New York]. He wanted to read the old tombstones.

[In the 1930s the Powerses vacationed in Paris.] He sent all these wonderful letters to introduce us and have Mlle. Vidal and her father [Stevens'
French bookseller] take care of us. Jim had been in Paris for two years at the
end of the war and had gone to the Sorbonne. He and Wallace seemed to
know a lot about Paris; you'd think Wallace Stevens had been there three
or four times. Henri [Amiot] and Jim had a beautiful time. Henri lived in
Hartford for a year or so and worked at Hartford Accident and Indemnity
[becoming one of Stevens' many informants on the Paris he never visited].
They did [see] a great deal [of each other in Hartford], and they walked all
kinds of places, Jim and Henri and Wallace Stevens. Of course, Wallace
Stevens always walked to work, and Jim walked, walked, walked; both loved
to walk, [taking] great big strides.

Elsie was never part of our [times together]. I don't suppose Elsie knew
much about our expeditions. I didn't go to Hartford more than once or twice.
[Once] I went to the Stevens house and met Mrs. Stevens, and saw the
famous statue [a bronze bust of Mrs. Stevens by Adolph Weinman]. When

I go into a house, if I don't care much about it, I pay no attention. If I get in and am intrigued, I can tell you everything that is in the house. The only thing I remember is the statue in a kind of bay-window effect. It seems to me he showed us some books. We were just there half an hour or so. It was afternoon. She apologized for some mess. There was no mess. Kind of flitted; she wasn't at ease. Twittered. Unbalanced. She was a recluse, absolutely. It was tragic. I have a hunch there was a little bit of jealousy about the way people accepted him. Now that was a private thing: he did not gossip; he did not run her down in any way. But once in a while you'd hear a little remark that made you know they didn't have great rapport. He never criticized her, ever. He was a gentleman, completely and totally. Now maybe Jim [was a confidant], but Jim never talked. [The afternoon of the visit] Holly was in school. 'Course Jim knew her as a little girl. I didn't meet her until Cornwall [Connecticut, where the Powerses summered in the 1950s]. I didn't get into any of the worries he had over her; that was Jim. [By the time Mrs. Powers met Holly] he was very proud of her. He beamed bringing Holly, knowing that I'd never met her before.

When we had a vacation house up in Cornwall, he was always bringing up goodies, real croissants [from] a place in Hartford, great batches of those, and brioches. Always treats for the Powerses; things we'd never think of having. He loved Cornwall.* We lived there all summer long for several years, but he knew these fabulous places to eat that we'd never heard of. We'd drive, but he'd take us. [In Cornwall] Lewis Gannett, the [book] critic of the New York *Herald Tribune,* was one of our neighbors. Thurber lived there, too. [Stevens and Thurber met] through one of our neighbors. We'd have luncheon parties. We introduced Mark Van Doren [a Cornwall-area resident] to him. He saw him only a few times that I know of. Mark Van Doren was one of the kindest people; he always brought out the best in anyone to whom he was talking. I asked Wallace Stevens about [an] author that lived up in Cornwall that wrote poetry. He said, "Just a writer of verses, not poetry."

I remember one time in Cornwall we were sitting out on our veranda in this 1810 house. He'd come up in the middle of the day, and so Jim said, "Well, it's time for a martini." But he didn't know how to make a martini. We had a guest there, and the guest said he'd manufacture a martini for Wallace. But he got it mixed up and used sweet vermouth. Wallace took a sip of it and said, "The sachet is wonderful." Can you think of a more beautiful description of a *sweet* martini? He would use an unexpected word

---

*Stevens memorialized one of his return trips from Cornwall to Hartford in "Reality Is an Activity of the Most August Imagination" (*OP,* p. 110).

that would just send you rolling. He was the farthest thing from a stuffed shirt, and he could unstuff any shirt he met. Just a little word. He wasn't mean but delicious. Once I was expounding on some evergreen that was quite new in those days. I got very erudite. So he said he had just put in some denticulatas—and looked at me. I knew there wasn't anything like that: he was telling me that I was being a pompous ass. I just loved it; just the one little word, that was it. He was not unkind about people: he'd talk about situations and would be a bit sarcastic, and describe things.

[Soon after the Powerses were married] we lived in Florida for a year. The early part of '31, he was en route to Key West and Judge Powell was with him. It was a blissful evening. Judge Powell was on a diet. The doctor said he could only have one drink a day, but he didn't say anything about half-drinks, so [Powell had] half-drinks all day. I never saw Wallace Stevens appear even faintly drunk, no matter how much he drank. He was dignified to the nth degree. Much laughter but never . . . Well, maybe in Key West; I don't know. We used to hear a few remarks about what they'd been doing in Key West. The Key West episodes always sounded like the most fun in the world.

CHAPTER TWO

An Affair of People:
Judge Arthur Powell and His Friends

"Life is an affair of people not of places," Stevens admitted in a moment of self-criticism of his solitary ways. "But for me life is an affair of places and that is the trouble."[1] And yet his relationship with the South, so central in the life and art of his Connecticut years, was very much an affair of people as well, largely through his thirty-year friendship with Arthur Powell. Indeed, on his business trips with Judge Powell, head of the Atlanta law firm that often represented the Hartford on bond-claims cases in the South, Stevens enjoyed the closest friendship of his mature years.

Though Stevens delegated most long-distance traveling once his department became more than a one-man operation in the early 1920s, he continued to go south on business each winter through 1940, ensuring an annual escape from the harsh New England climate for a few weeks each year. While it was a standing joke at the office that Stevens kept an insurance claim open for years to ensure this escape at company expense,[2] the cases that brought him south were legitimate, though many of them could as easily have been delegated to one of his assistants. *Harmonium* records how rewarding the poet found these trips from the outset, though the poetry inspired while he was in the South is by no means a complete account of the satisfactions that made his excursions there singularly appealing to Stevens year after year.* The friendship with Judge Powell that developed on these business vacations deserves a closer look, for it highlights the less solitary side of Stevens, a side overshadowed by the usual view of him as the loner he more often was.

*As early as January 1917, only ten months after his first trip south on Hartford business, Stevens published "Primordia" in *Soil*; this contained a sequence of lyrics entitled "In the South," the first of many poems that were inspired by his visits to that part of the country.

Though Stevens had begun to travel south on business less than a month after he joined the Hartford, he did not meet Arthur Powell until the early 1920s. A difficult case had brought Stevens to Florida on three occasions before Powell, in early January 1922, arranged a conference among the principals and resolved the contention. Impressed, Stevens retained him as his main Southern counsel until Powell's death in 1951. Because his home-office staff was always small, Stevens usually hired local lawyers to represent the company on claim matters in their area, and Little & Powell of Atlanta was in many ways typical of the prominent firms Stevens chose.

Powell, who was in his late forties at the time they met, was a senior partner in one of Georgia's most prestigious law firms, the reputation of which was understandable, given the Judge's formidable legal experience and political connections. Born in 1873 in rural southwest Georgia, Arthur Powell was a short bantam from the pinewoods who passed the bar at eighteen with little formal legal training. He had learned much of his law as a boy, riding the rural court circuit with his father, a country lawyer he idolized. At thirty-three, Powell left the successful practice he had built up in his hometown of Blakely when the Georgia Bar Association asked him to run for one of three seats on the newly created Georgia Court of Appeals, the second highest court in the state. During the next few years on the bench, his colleagues later agreed, Powell established himself as one of the "three . . . greatest judges Georgia has ever produced."[3] He resigned from the bench in 1912 and moved permanently to Atlanta to enter private practice with John Little, the well-connected son of a former Georgia Supreme Court justice. Elliott Goldstein later became a partner in the firm.

Elliott Goldstein

Both Stevens and Judge Powell were good lawyers. They would have discussions on legal points; Stevens seemed to rely heavily on Judge Powell's opinions. In those days, lawyers didn't really have specialties. Lawyers were supposed to do everything, and a lot of [bond claims] came in, so we did a lot of surety work. These things come in waves. There was an awful lot of surety work during the early thirties, extending into the forties: a lot of businesses went under, and a lot of buildings that were contracted for insurance companies had to complete.

Some people insist on a lot of reports and not taking any action without getting approval. It's quite true of Stevens that you'd get a letter from him beginning this case, and then he pretty much expected you to handle it. He didn't interfere and pretty well would go along with whatever you said.* He

---

*In this regard, Stevens' administrative style at the company was distinctive; at the same time, it kept his department small, as one of his staff, John Ladish, points out. "It was our practice, whether it was a fidelity or surety [claim], to refer it to a law firm, and then we'd almost forget it, leave it entirely up to them. That was foreign to the casualty-claims department's way of doing things. Stevens would have had to have a much larger department if [his staff] had

put the responsibility on you to make the judgments. He wouldn't try to second-guess you, or say, "Why didn't you do so-and-so instead of doing this?" In that sort of business you could be pretty awful. The fellow that succeeded Stevens [Walter Downs] was awful. He was the kind of guy that wanted to make sure that if there was a mistake made, you made it; if it was something right, it was his. We quit representing the Hartford [under Downs]; it just wasn't worth it.

As I remember Stevens' letters, they were quite short. Judge Powell loved good writing. He didn't have much use for people that couldn't write. He never used a word unless it was precisely the right word; he never used long words if he could use a short one; every sentence he wrote was perfectly crafted. [Once] some lawyers came in from Americus [Georgia]; they had a controversy down there and they came in to consult Judge Powell. Judge Powell said, "Well that's very simple; file a bill for declaratory judgment." They said, "Would you mind drafting it for us?" He took a yellow pad and wrote the thing out in longhand. Most of us will write a first draft and change it, but his every word was exactly right.

Judge Powell was to a large extent self-taught. He tried his first case when he was a boy. They tell the story that about 1914 we represented a group that wanted to put an insurance company into receivership; in order to do that, they had to prove that the insurance company was insolvent. Well, the insurance company hired all the actuaries in this area that were available, so there was nobody that understood insurance-company accounting that could testify whether it was solvent or not. Judge Powell went to the library, got all the books on actuarial accounting for insurance companies, spent about six weeks, and became an expert. Then proceeded, with his knowledge, to prove the company was insolvent. In his forties, he taught himself French so he could read certain authors, probably where there were no translations. He was extremely well read, and their friendship was really concerned with literary things.

They were very much alike, from what I know about Stevens and what I've read about him: they were both men who had a very broad intellectual capacity. Some lawyers are just specialists and technicians. Neither one of them was that. Both of them really were just as much interested in things outside the law as they were in law.

Once or twice, perhaps, Judge Powell might have met Stevens in Florida, but in most instances, he came by Atlanta and they went to Florida together.

---

to keep control of certain claims. Although you had to pay attorneys' fees, it was still less expensive than traveling and having a large department."

Now that was over a period of a good many years. I don't believe Mr. Stevens spent a lot of time here in Atlanta.

Powell gave a special character to Stevens' business trips to Florida from the outset. While they were waiting for the final contract to be drawn up after the Miami conference in the winter of 1922, the Judge invited Stevens to relax for a few days with some of his Georgia friends at Long Key Fishing Camp, a resort for affluent sportsmen in the Florida Keys. The camp's score of yellow cabins, brilliant against the white coral, were set along a narrow boardwalk that led through a grove of coconut palms to the Gulf beach. Long Key's owners boasted that these waters had "big 'uns thick as minnows," and the huge tarpons, tunas and sailfish mounted in the main hall, the blackboard that posted the day's record catch, and the cabins themselves, each named for a fish to be had in local waters, emphasized the mythology of the place. Stevens so enjoyed his stay there that Long Key became one of his favorite winter vacation spots throughout the 1920s. Indeed, this trip set the pattern for Stevens' Southern business-vacations for the next twenty years. After zigzagging from Atlanta to Miami on claims, Stevens and Powell usually enjoyed some days' rest in the Keys, either at such exclusive fishing camps or, more often in later years, at the elegant Casa Marina Hotel in Key West. After this rest, Stevens often saw to bond matters along the route back to Hartford. Such trips kept him away from home for two or three weeks almost every winter until 1940.

On his first excursion to Long Key, Stevens wrote to his snowbound wife at home only of the tropical pleasures of the midsummer scenery he was enjoying. He did not mention how much he was also enjoying the camaraderie at Long Key. Because Elsie Stevens strongly disapproved of drinking, Stevens' letters home from the Keys did not refer to the rowdier pleasures he engaged in there as one of the boys. To his novelist-friend Ferdinand Reyher, however, Stevens wrote with gusto of his initiation into the Powell circle. A few weeks after his first visit to Long Key, he had taken the first opportunity he could to return there following business in Washington.

> Now, that trip to Florida would have unstrung a brass monkey. I went down there with half a dozen other people from Atlanta. I was the only damned Yankee in the bunch. I was christened a charter member of the Long Key Fishing Club of Atlanta. The christening occupied about three days, and required just two cases of Scotch. When I traveled home, I was not able to tell whether I was traveling on a sound or a smell. As I remember it, it was very much like a cloud full of Cuban señoritas, cocoanut palms, and waiters carrying ice-water. Since my return I have not cared much for literature. The southerners are a great people.[4]

Mrs. Frederick Cason glimpsed the rowdiest side of Stevens' Florida jaunts one evening in 1936 when she overheard the poet, then fifty-six years old, recount the fight he had just had with Ernest Hemingway in Key West. It was the one time she met Stevens, when her husband, a Miami lawyer, invited his business friend from Hartford to a small dinner party at his home.

Mrs. Frederick Cason

He brought a book out; it was poetry. I understand that he wrote several other books of poems; I think it was his first. It came as a surprise to me. Judge Powell was there and Mrs. Powell; Mr. Stevens, Mr. Cason and myself. It was just a social evening. It was nothing except fishing and hunting tales. That dominated the conversation because they'd talk business at the office and business wouldn't come home. Stevens had a lot of fishing tales. They were all funny, and they were all very clean. My husband was quite a storyteller himself, and Wallace and Judge Powell kept right up with him.

Stevens and Judge Powell had been down there [Key West], and Hemingway was there at the same time. They disagreed on certain things and had quite a fight. They were both pretty well lit. He said he was a fool to get that drunk. He was laughing. Stevens himself was telling it. What it was about I don't know.* I was in and out of the room. He and Judge Powell and Fred were talking. Mrs. Powell and I had gone upstairs, so when we came back down, they eased off on that.

Mr. Stevens and Mr. Cason saw each other quite frequently. Every now and then Mr. Cason would say, "Well, it's time to send Wallace some wild lemons." He had some when he was down here, and he said they were the most delicious things he'd ever had put in drinks. So we'd send him some of those big, rough lemons.

[Like Stevens, Mr. and Mrs. Cason had been occasional guests at Long Key Fishing Camp in the 1920s.] Long Key was open only to members. It was

---

*The fight occurred in February 1936. According to Hemingway, his sister had come away from a Key West cocktail party in tears because Stevens had spoken badly of him. Hemingway then set out to confront Stevens, meeting him just after Stevens had left the party boasting that if Hemingway had been there he would have flattened him with a single blow. Stevens tried to do just that but missed, whereupon Hemingway knocked him down several times. When Stevens finally did manage to land a punch, he broke his hand on Hemingway's jaw. Before leaving Key West, Stevens reconciled with Hemingway, who agreed not to tell anyone about the fight since Stevens was worried that the story might get back to his insurance colleagues. The official story was to be that Stevens had fallen downstairs. (See *Ernest Hemingway: Selected Letters, 1917–1961,* ed. Carlos Baker [New York: Charles Scribner's Sons, 1981], pp. 438–40.)

Apparently Stevens was less worried than Hemingway thought, since he told the story on himself even before he returned to the home office. In any event, the news soon reached his Hartford colleagues, as Manning Heard, then Stevens' assistant, recalls. "I was in Florida and I met somebody. He knew that I was with the Hartford, and he said to me, 'You know about Stevens and Hemingway? They had a helluva fight.' I said, 'Is that so?' And that's all I said to him. But I do remember that Stevens came back with his hand broken, and he did have a little puffy eye. But I didn't [comment on it], and neither did he."

bowl and pitcher and outside toilets, just really rough. There was no water down there, no lights. It was a camping outfit. You were comfortable [though]: you had good friends.

On Stevens' first visit to Long Key in January 1922, the affable and well-connected Judge had initiated his new friend into a circle of railroad executives, bankers and lawyers, into a masculine idyll of fishing, drinking, eating and lounging that appealed to Stevens, who liked to imagine himself as one of the boys. He particularly liked the camaraderie of Powell's circle because the Georgia men of affairs he met at the camp roughed it in style, whether feasting on doves and a haunch of venison in a club member's private railroad car or cruising along the Florida coast aboard the yacht of Powell's law partner, as Stevens did on a month-long jaunt south in 1926. Above all, however, he enjoyed the Judge's company. Powell quickly put people at ease with his warm country ways and soon succeeded in overcoming even Stevens' notable Northern reserve. Stevens admitted that he often found it difficult to meet new people,* but he found the Judge was not "a man with whom you have to take any trouble, because he needs no thawing."† Despite his legal and social prominence in Atlanta, the Judge's true sophistication lay in remaining faithful to his roots in the red clay country where Georgia, Florida and Alabama corner. Indeed, Stevens was particularly susceptible to the charm of Powell's country character on their first Long Key excursion. During the last months of 1921, he had been preoccupied with writing his most ambitious poem to date, which he was then calling "From the Journal of Crispin." It was not simply that, in Powell, Stevens had found "a grand old rummy,"[5] as he once complimented Powell, for the Judge impressed Stevens from the outset as more than a genial drinking companion with whom to relax after the artistic concentration of the previous months. Stevens recognized that he was in contact with a man who embodied an ideal he had just celebrated in the Crispin poem, a man who was, above all, spokesman for his land. On this and subsequent business trips, the poet enjoyed the company of a friend very much made out of "the substance of his region,"[6] who gave it voice.

Powell was a gifted raconteur, especially noted for his local tales and aphorisms, which grew out of the red clay country where he had grown up. Such tales were part of Stevens' pleasure in relaxing with Powell from the

---

*"Getting acquainted with people is difficult for me," Stevens wrote apologetically after first meeting J. Ronald Lane Latimer, the young publisher of two of Stevens' limited editions in the mid-thirties (letter of November 2, 1936, Chicago). Stevens had found meeting Latimer difficult even though they had been in frequent and friendly correspondence during the previous two years.

†Letter to Hi Simons, April 4, 1945, *LWS*, p. 493. If Stevens found Powell easy to meet, he seems to have found this true of Southerners generally. When advising his protégé James Powers on an area where to resettle and practice law, Stevens recommended the Carolinas, since "It seems to me that Southerners are a good deal more willing to make advances than other people." Unable to resist the pun, Stevens added, "certainly that is true of some of the handpainted waitresses at the Hotel Charlotte." (Letter of May 11, 1932, HL.)

start. "After breakfast in Mr. Pidcock's car Judge Powell and I sat on the verandah of our cottage," Stevens wrote to his wife on his 1923 visit to Long Key, "where I read the Sunday Tribune and listened to stories of Georgia life."[7] Indeed, some twenty years later, Stevens tried to interest his publisher in these first-rate yarns that had entertained him for years and that the Judge had collected into his autobiography.* In this collection of anecdotes and reminiscences, Powell vividly depicted the life of a rural Southern county from Reconstruction to the start of the twentieth century. When *I Can Go Home Again* was published in 1943, Stevens wrote praising his old friend's book as a piece of vintage Americana, a classic of place.[8] This was high praise indeed, for in the 1940s Stevens was himself a connoisseur of the local, steeping himself in his own regional lore as he traced his genealogy and tried to recover a sense of his Pennsylvania past. Such praise was not merely a reflex required by twenty years of friendship. Stevens so enjoyed the Judge's idioms and descriptions of Southern life that he began using them in his poetry after their first business trip together. In a hitherto-unknown memoir of his relationship with Stevens, Powell noted that the poet used one of his new friend's Southern phrases as the title for one of his most important early poems, later telling the Judge that he borrowed " 'A High-Toned Old Christian Woman' . . . from a passing speech of mine in describing an acquaintance of ours."[9] The Judge's Southern accent continued to be heard in Stevens' poetry almost a decade later. "We were walking in Key West," the Judge recalled, "when I stopped to look through a fence. I explained that I thought it enclosed a graveyard, as some of the rubbish looked 'like decorations in a nigger cemetery.' He was interested when I explained the custom of negroes to decorate graves with broken pieces of glass, old pots, broken pieces of furniture, dolls

*While he had tried to interest his publisher, Alfred A. Knopf, in Powell's memoir, Stevens had originally urged the Judge to submit his manuscript to the University of North Carolina Press, which eventually published it. In recounting this episode to his colleague Wilson Taylor, who had inquired about publishers for a friend with a manuscript, Stevens gave some of his views on the New York publishing scene of his day.

"I tried to tell Judge Powell what he ought to do with his book; he did everything but. First he tried his friends in Atlanta, all of whom had friends in New York, etc.; then he tried publishers' agents in New York. About the time when he was thoroughly discouraged, only because there was nothing else left for him to do, he went where I told him to go in the first place. They took his book and made a great fuss over it, and the old man has been pleased with himself ever since. All there is to say about it is that he finally sent it to the right place. Probably your friend has written a novel. In that case, the question immediately after the question relating to some one likely to be interested is the question in respect to the publisher by whom he would *like* to be published. Harcourt-Brace are very decent people. Personally, I like Knopf, although, since I only publish poetry, the business end of it is slight. Simon & Schuster are great money makers, but, personally, I wouldn't allow them to publish anything of mine, even if they wanted to and, since they have written me several times, I assume that they would be willing if I had anything in which they were interested. They are vulgar advertisers and they keep a very fair share of what they make, or so I am told. Harper is much interested in new people. All your man has to do is to write, say, to Harcourt-Brace and say that he has a manuscript, describing it, and ask whether they would be interested in seeing it; if so, that is all there is to it." (Letter of August 15, 1944, HL.)

heads, and what not. The poem ["Like Decorations in a Nigger Cemetery"] itself is an olio, and the title is fitting." Stevens, of course, acknowledged the source of the title for this poem, which he dedicated to Powell. Beyond the title, however, the Judge also contributed at least one line as well. "I recall that in February, 1934, when we were in Tampa, we provisionally handled a business matter with a friend of mine in that city. He [Stevens] later wrote me that he could not get any answer to his letters to my friend and asked for a suggestion. In the course of my reply, I suggested that my friend is a 'hen-cock that crows at midnight and lays no eggs.' You will find the phrase in division xxx of the poem."

Instances such as these testify to the attraction of Powell's regional character for Stevens the poet: just how impressed he was from their first meeting seems clear from a revision he made in "From the Journal of Crispin" as he prepared it for publication as "The Comedian as the Letter C" the summer after that first Long Key vacation with Powell. The change occurred in that key section where Stevens asserts that the ideal poets are the truly indigenous poets, the responsive men who speak for and from their region. In "From the Journal of Crispin," submitted for the Blindman Prize a few weeks before meeting Powell on that January trip, Stevens placed the figure of the pine-spokesman in Mississippi. After meeting Powell, however, he decided "The man in Georgia waking among pines / Should be pine-spokesman."[10] For a poet who responded to the anecdotal form as much as Stevens' titles indicate he did, for a writer who admired the pithy, colorful phrase as much as Stevens' "Adagia" testifies, Powell was a businessman Stevens the artist could admire.

Getting to know the Judge better on their trips together, Stevens was, in effect, getting to know better a region of the country that stimulated his imagination. Through their friendship the disjunction between people and places that Stevens felt was somewhat mitigated. That the Judge's character as a regional spokesman was an important element in his developing friendship with the poet from Connecticut is underscored by the fact that this was also a prominent feature of a friendship that developed between Stevens and a Florida lawyer who began to join Stevens and Powell on these business-vacations in the late 1920s. Like Powell, Philip May had a deep interest in local lore and, also like the Judge, published works on his region, though of a more historical and less personal cast. "I am counting on showing the two of you about a bit on Sunday," May wrote on the eve of one of Stevens' trips through May's hometown of Jacksonville, "in exchange for your complete repertoire of recent stories, and hope that you will let me make one or two contributions, in our study of American folklore." Stevens, in turn, christened May "high-priest of the red clay hills of Gadsden county and you chant their name like a mystic saying Lud! Lud! Lud!"[11] May, like Powell, acted as a guide, putting his Northern friend in touch with aspects of Florida that meant much to them both—its history, its landscape, its cuisine. The itinerary May proposed on one of Stevens' business trips south, for example, included side trips to "one or two places of interest to poets near Jacksonville which you haven't seen—Fort Clinch, at the entrance of Fernandina harbor, and just beyond, some sand dunes covered with the most remarkable and lovely wind-blown trees I have ever seen; St. Mary's, an old English settlement . . . where there is a country hotel, which makes oyster stew from unwashed oysters. . . ."[12] Years later, May reminisced about Stevens' visits to north Florida to his friends the Stevens scholars, Frank and Dorothy Doggett.

Frank and Dorothy Doggett

FD: When Stevens came here, Phil told me, he always went to the best hotel [in Jacksonville], called the George Washington Hotel. There are places you can identify that Stevens went with Phil May, that he mentions in the *Letters*: the Kingsley Plantation on Fort George Island, the Gerbings Oyster House and Hibernia. He talked about going to the jasmine-scented island, which of course he quoted in "Asides on the Oboe." From what he said about what he saw there, I knew it was Fort George Island. Phil May had written a pamphlet on the slave smuggler Zephaniah Kingsley. He was trying to interest Stevens in Kingsley, and Kingsley had a plantation on Fort George. Then Stevens told Phil he might come to Jacksonville. He was going with Judge Powell to North Carolina, and he would like to eat oysters with him among the violets beside the swamp, near Fernandina. Just south of Fernandina, on Amelia Island, was a famous oyster place called Gerbings, and the proprietor's hobby was flowers. You could go there, in the days Stevens did, and eat all the oysters you could eat, any way you wanted them, for a nominal price. South of Jacksonville [is] Hibernia, which was a plantation in the Civil War period owned by the Fleming family. There is a novel by the woman who was in love with Henry James, Constance Fenimore Woolson; part of it is set in a hotel in the Hibernia area. There was a tearoom there at the time Stevens came to Jacksonville.

DD: Phil said that he and Stevens were coming back [from Ormond Beach one time], and he wanted Stevens to meet a certain couple on the east bank of the St. Johns [River], south of Jacksonville. Phil knew these people well; they weren't home, but he walked right in. In the living room there was *Modern American Poets,* that anthology by Conrad Aiken, lying open on the table. Stevens picked it up, opened up to his own name, and started reading his own poetry. Phil was standing there beside him, and he said, "Why, Wallace—do you write poetry?" He hadn't known it. And after that he began to send Phil books. They had been associated a long time before he knew that.

FD: Phil was a very literate person. He was a friend of Marjorie Rawlings [who won the 1939 Pulitzer Prize for *The Yearling*. In 1936 May arranged a dinner at Rawlings' farmhouse at Cross Creek, Florida].

DD: They knew that Stevens was on a diet. And the way Phil told it, she put this food before Stevens, and all the other people began eating this other food. And he actually picked up his food and threw it over by the fireplace, then ate what everybody else ate.

FD: He had a lot to drink, that's what Phil told us, because he wrote Marjorie Rawlings and apologized.

DD: That's not the way it's described [by Rawlings].* And then they asked him to read a poem. He read "Domination of Black" to them, but he did it all the time as if he were making fun of himself for being a poet. And he loved [that poem]; he said it was his favorite poem.

During the first years of the Powell-Stevens friendship, in which getting to know the Judge meant getting to know better the South that stimulated him as a poet, Stevens had kept his poetry a secret from Powell. "Our acquaintanceship, even from the first, was rather intimate and yet until 1927 I did not know he had ever written anything, other than a business letter or a legal document,"[13] Powell recalled in an account of his friendship with Stevens that he sent to critic Hi Simons. "Accidentally learning of the Harmonium, I cited him for contempt of friendship for not telling me of it, and he sent me a copy inscribed, 'To Arthur G. Powell with the affectionate regards (in all sobriety) of his friend, Wallace Stevens.'" This incident marked the beginning of their closest period of friendship, the years from 1927 to 1940, when Powell became one of those rare individuals with whom Stevens was comfortable as both poet and businessman. The Judge proved to be something of an audience for new works Stevens completed on their winter trips during this time, mostly throughout the years they vacationed at Key West. In his memoir to Hi Simons, the Judge noted that "In February, 1932 or 1933, at Key West, Wallace read me in the hotel the 'Mud Master.' . . . He had just finished it and was trying it out on me, as the dog. He was specially

---

*"The occasion irks me still," Rawlings wrote in *Cross Creek Cookery*. "My friend Phil May asked to bring his friend, Wallace Stevens, the poet, to dinner at Cross Creek. The great man was on a strict diet, he wrote, and must be served only lean meat, a green salad and fruit. I planned my best baked-in-sherry ham for the rest of the company, and wracked my brains for a method of making of lean meat a delicacy. I decided to prepare the heart of a Boston pot roast of beef in an individual casserole, with sherry. The poet proved delightful but condescending. He began on his beef, looked over at the clove-stuck ham, and announced that he would partake not only of that, but of all the other rich dishes on the table. His diet, it seemed, was not for purposes of health, but for vanity. He was, simply, reducing. I snatched his sherried beef from him, pulled out the bone and tossed it on the hearth to my pointer dog." (*Cross Creek Cookery* [New York: Charles Scribner's Sons, 1942], pp. 106–7.)

While Stevens may have explained that evening that he was not dieting for health reasons, that was not the case. The year before, Dr. W. W. Herrick, a New York diagnostician who had begun treating Stevens for high blood pressure in the mid-1920s, had indicated that weight loss was a necessity. Stevens then weighed 234 pounds, and Herrick advised him to shed twenty pounds to bring his pressure back to the safe level it had been at in 1932. (Letter of W. W. Herrick to Wallace Stevens, January 2, 1935, HL.)

pleased with the word 'pickanines' in the third verse. As you know, sound effects are a part of his artistry; especially sound effects produced by making slight changes in a word." Indeed, Powell was one of the few who were privy to Stevens' work-in-progress.

In February, 1935, we were at Key West again; and his poem "Mozart [1935]" . . . was forming in his mind. In the second and third lines, for sound effect, he uses the phrases, "hoo-hoo-hoo," "shoo-shoo-shoo," and "ric-a-nic." I now have in my possession a scrap of brown paper, a piece of a heavy envelope, with this written on it in his handwriting:

> "ses hurlements,
> ses chucuotments, ses ricaments.
> its hoo-hoo-hoo,
> Its shoo-shoo-shoo, its ric-a-nic."

The Judge also apparently had easy access to manuscript works that have since been lost, or, as in the case of "The Pleasures of Merely Circulating," perhaps preserved by him because of his regard for Stevens' work.

In February, 1934, he and I were to meet at Tampa, Florida, to go from there to Key West. He spent the day there ahead of me. When I arrived, I found on his table in the hotel room, written on hotel stationery, a skit and a poem. The skit ran this way, as I recall it:

> "The humming bird is king among humming birds;
> But Vitis is a castor bean
> And a ticket seller."

(Vitis is a small junction point on the A.C.L. Railway just out of Tampa; and he gave a full description of it, as seen by the naked eye.) So far as I know, this skit has never been published. . . . I captured the originals [of "The Pleasures of Merely Circulating"], had them typed in my office and sent the copies to him. I intended to keep the originals, but a servant, thinking they were mere useless scraps, burned them.

Seven years after the Judge had indicted his friend for hiding the fact that he was a poet, Stevens had grown so comfortable in his role as a poet around this businessman that he became part of evenings spent with Frost at the Casa Marina the winter of 1934. "One of my pleasantest experiences was at Key West," the Judge remembered, "when he and Robert Frost on two successive nights came to my room, and under the kindly influence of small doses of the Georgia corn I dealt out to them, discussed each others poetry and how each went about writing his own." Various accounts of Frost and Stevens at Key West have filtered down, none more engaging than Powell's poetic snapshot.

> There they sat,
> Drawn together by fire's love of fire;
> The one—his fire lit of fat light wood,
> The other—his fire lit of the slow-burning oak wood.

They did not parse;
They merely glowed, subduing flame,
They spoke of Dowson and British poets,
And Harriet Monroe and others of the ilk.

And I,
Untutored in arts like these,
Feeling my incompetence to speak a part,
Merely poured the corn and smiled a smile.[14]

Powell's concluding stanza registers the amateur's understandable sense of inadequacy in the company of two master poets. Yet while the Judge insisted that he was no man of letters, the sheaf of poetry and short-story manuscripts among his papers show that he shared Stevens' commitment to the creative act as one of "the sanctions of life."[15] "He did a tremendous amount of things of this type, but it wasn't done for publication," notes a grandson who grew up at the Powell home. "He did these things for his own personal pleasure and for the pleasure of a group of his friends [the Ten Club of Atlanta] . . . who enjoyed literature and who were creative a little bit themselves."[16] The Judge's short stories, such as "DeWeese and His Trial," which expands on an anecdote about a French bigamist in his autobiography, draw portraits of characters in the best tradition of the humorous eccentrics who populate Southern fiction. Though Powell's poetry is less accomplished, it demonstrates the type of responsive reader Stevens found in the Judge. In the frolic of sounds and the repetitious play of phrasing and imagery in "'The Stream Lined Train Passes Lake Istakpaga," one of his more successful poems, for example, Powell shows his sensitivity to Stevens' technique in such poems as "Earthy Anecdote," its apparent model.

Coming! Coming! Coming!
The Valkyries! the Valkyries!
The shriek is the scream of the valkyries,
But the clatter, the clatter, the clatter,
Is the clat-clat of the hoofs of the does
The swift-footed does from Okechobee.

They ride, they ride, the valkyries ride
On the sleek-limbed does from Okechobee;
And the hair of the valkyries, swept back in the wind,
Covers the does, the fleet-legged does from Okechobee.

The serpent that follows the does,
Speeding, speeding, speeding to keep up with the does
Has long sinuous sides as of varnished steel,
And scales that are as the glass of many windows
All hiding as the fan-dancer hides
In the swiftness, the dazzling swiftness of the motion.

Going, going. Gone!
The valkyries, the does and all

> All but the blunt tail of the serpent
> Fading to a dot in the distance.
> Gone to Valhalla![17]

Powell's autobiography reveals that the Judge was particularly attuned to the play of language so central to Stevens' art. Powell often resorts in the course of the book to the verbal riches of his region, relishing with a connoisseur's palate the mix of Indian, Negro and country dialects that contributed to developing his ear as he was growing up. Powell's response to a new book of Stevens' poetry, as in his letter of thanks for *Esthétique du Mal,* typically stressed his pleasure in "the elegance of the language—the choice and combination of words; and, as Robert Frost says, 'the per-form-ance.' "[18] Such comments and such poems as "The Stream Lined Train" suggest, in part, why the Judge's brief memoir focuses on incidents involving the verbal play in his friend's work. Stevens came to recognize in Powell a reader sensitive to that "gaiety of language"[19] that meant so much to him as a writer.

Arthur Powell, of course, was not an aesthete with the refinement of Henry Church, the only other friend to whom Stevens dedicated a poem. Church, an American expatriate who spent much of his life among the Parisian avant-garde as editor of a French literary magazine, was Stevens' ideal contemporary reader. "I belong to an old era," Powell wryly boasted in a 1937 paper he read before like-minded members of the Ten Club, his Atlanta literary group.

> In poetry, architecture, painting, drawing, music and other of the arts, the movement is toward the abstract. . . . Or, as Wallace Stevens in one of his poems has said it:
>
> "Music is not yet written but is to be,
> The preparation is long and of long intent
> For the time when sound shall be subtler than we ourselves."
>
> . . . So that when new things in government and in these other things seem strange to me, it may merely mean that I am not up to date . . . that I am lacking in culture; that there may be more art or higher art in surrealism than in realism; or in dadaism than in Greek sculpture.[20]

While "poetry fascinated him," as his grandson recalls, Powell's tastes were traditional and not contemporary; Browning and Tennyson were his favorite poets. Indeed, he admitted that his initial interest in Stevens' poetry had sprung largely out of friendship. The authors on whom he delivered papers before the Ten Club over the years—Shakespeare, Molière and Holmes, for example—reflect his conservative interests and those of his fellow members of the distinguished Atlanta study club to which he belonged and before which Stevens spoke. Like Powell, the other members of the Ten—which included the presidents of Emory University, Agnes Scott College and Georgia Institute of Technology; a former Georgia Supreme Court justice and an ex-governor; bankers and lawyers—had traditional literary tastes. The club might study Sidney Lanier but not the Fugitives. While their literary analyses might not have dazzled Stevens on his visits, he might nonetheless have heard the member assigned *The Scarlet Letter* introduce his talk with reminiscences of his boyhood experiences with Walt Whitman, who had first encouraged him to read Hawthorne but insisted he take a walking tour of New England beforehand. Another might tell of his father's close friendship with Joel Chandler Harris. If not modernist in outlook, neither was Powell's Atlanta group provincial. Men of contemporary connections, the club members enjoyed the company of two modern masters, for Robert Frost, too, much more often than Stevens, would spend an evening with the Ten on his annual trips south. Dr. Louie Newton was secretary of the club when these poets visited, and he noted their different styles.

Dr. Louie Newton

The first time I recall having met Stevens, he came as a guest of Judge Powell at his home on Peachtree Street. He impressed me as not reticent but rather a little bit shy, which did not surprise me, because I've always thought it was the role of a poet to listen rather than to make much noise. Mr. Stevens impressed me that afternoon. Judge Powell introduced him very warmly and said, "I predict that he is going to become a man of acknowledged worth in the area of poetry." Mr. Stevens came again; I believe we were studying some area of poetry. He did make a comment, and it was very well received. Judge Powell, more than any other member of the Ten, kept our thoughts alive about Mr. Stevens. He was very jealous for Mr. Stevens to be known and accepted as a poet.

Robert Frost was an annual attendant at the Ten. Robert Frost was a very close friend of Dr. James Ross McCain, who was president of Agnes Scott College. Mr. Frost read every year when he'd come in February on his winter vacation. He would read us the latest poem he had written. Mr. Stevens was asked to read, and he was very reluctant. He said, "Let me read from somebody else." But they would always say, "No, we want to hear you read some of your own poems." I remember an evening at Agnes Scott College that was a most impressive evening of Stevens. He read his own poems as the evening's program. [It] might have been in the thirties. As I remember it, they had invited him again and again. Dr. McCain presented him as having been finally persuaded to come, that he did not like to read his own poems publicly. Dr. McCain introduced him in a very warm tribute. He didn't read very long; he must not have stood up there over twenty minutes. He was not a good reader.

Such a public appearance before the audience of students and invited guests that filled the college chapel was extremely rare for Stevens in the late 1930s, the probable period of this reading, and indicates his regard both for Powell and for his Atlanta circle of friends. For Powell, this group offered an opportunity for that fellowship of the mind that was as important an aspect of friendship to him as the revelry at Long Key. Giving the 1908 commencement address at Mercer University, his alma mater, the Judge had set aside his down-home style to articulate his profound sense of friendship.

> . . . the paradox of my existence [is], namely, I know myself only in-so-far as I am known or may be known by another than my present or momentary self. Left alone to the sole self-consciousness of any given moment, if such a thing were possible, necessarily my whole personality would shrivel up into a mere atom. . . . This is the status of man's relation to the inner self. . . . Free me from my fellow men, leave me to myself alone to work out the salvation of my isolated self, "the world forgetting, by the world forgot"; and shall I for the first time show who I really truly am? . . . This is the heart and the reason of the Hegelian postulate that "all consciousness is an appeal to other consciousness."[21]

Powell's references to Royce, Dewey, Nietzsche, William James, Herbert Spencer, Coleridge, Byron and Plautus in this speech suggests, as his membership in the Ten Club testifies, to an intellectual vitality that was part of what made him such a good companion to Stevens during their many business-vacations over the years. There was far more to this businessman than passing the corn. If he was not Henry Church, a modern man of letters, the Judge was, without sentimentalizing Stevens' concept, a version of the "all-round man" he described admiringly in "The Whole Man: Perspectives, Horizons." Delivering a lecture on *Le Misanthrope* to professors in Atlanta; regaling friends with local lore at Long Key; issuing one of his thousand court opinions, some of them legal classics; composing poetry or a still-standard text on land law, Powell was the figure of Stevens' whole man with "breadth of character and, say, diversity of faculties."[22]

This friendship was mostly a man's affair. There was also a family side to it, however, especially as Stevens came to know the Judge's family, either when his wife and daughters occasionally joined the men in Florida in later years or when Stevens accepted invitations to stay at their home on fashionable Peachtree Street, where the Powells' neighbor and family friend was Margaret Mitchell, author of *Gone with the Wind.* Though Stevens did not choose to stay frequently on Peachtree Street, Powell's family remembers him as a constant presence, a friend often referred to at the dinner table. Powell's anecdote about Stevens' "Depression before Spring" was one of his favorite stories, told with a good deal of laughter.[23] He kept a straighter face when relating it in his memoir than when telling the anecdote to guests at dinner. "Speaking of Mrs. Stevens, she is a decided blonde, with a very classic face. . . . Wallace once told me that the words 'The hair of my blonde / Is dazzling, / As the spittle of cows / Threading the wind' . . . were suggested to him by seeing his wife's hair streaming in the wind when she was a girl." At the last meetings between Stevens and Powell, Mrs. Stevens, too, was part of the company. In the winter of 1940, the Stevens family concluded a lengthy trip down the East Coast with a visit to Key West, where they joined the Powells. This was the fulfillment of a long-standing promise that Stevens had made to his wife some eighteen years before, during that first vacation at Long Key with the Judge: "We must come together as soon as we can and every winter afterwards."[24]

That 1940 trip proved, in fact, to be Stevens' last trip to Florida, the final vacation he and the Judge shared in that Southern setting, which had done so much to nourish their friendship. For some years prior to 1940, Stevens had been restless for a change of scene. The war, which was declared the following year, made the decision for him. It not only interrupted his routine trips south but also radically altered the character of the Keys that had delighted him. The navy, for example, had requisitioned the elegant Casa Marina Hotel, so much a part of his later Key West holidays, for officers' quarters. By the winter of 1943, Florida had so lost its appeal for Stevens that even when a record cold wave of twenty below zero, coupled with fuel rationing, made it quite likely that the Stevenses would have to close their Hartford home and move to a warmer climate, the poet was cool to the prospect of a Southern stay. This was the same bleak winter described in "No Possum, No Sop, No Taters." The Northern landscape in this "deep January" poem evokes the feeling that "Bad is final in this light."[25] The folksy title is meant to heighten the sense of *mal* by contrasting this winter scene to the down-home version of paradise, the South, which had meant so much to Stevens over the years. As he wrote to Philip May, "How happy you all seem to be down there; how you go on living in a land of milk and honey, or, to be more exact, possum, sop and taters."[26] The Southern paradise referred to in the poem's title, however, no longer tempted Stevens in real life. About the time he wrote "No Possum, No Sop, No Taters," he also wrote May that the prospect of actually being forced south was unappealing. ". . . I have a great many irons in the fire right now and the last thing in the world that I want to do is to loaf."[27]

Indeed, by 1943 a new passion, for genealogy, had made a scene much closer to home far more attractive when Stevens had the leisure to travel. Pennsylvania supplanted Florida as the locale of vacations in the last years, as he sought to do what Powell had boasted of in his autobiography, to go home again. Curiously, it was Mrs. Powell's urge to retrace her Northern ancestry that brought these two friends together for their final visit—not in Florida, but at a Pennsylvania resort—in 1946. Suggesting a summer visit, the Powells met the Stevenses at the Hotel Hershey, where they were joined by the Mays. It was this reunion of old Southern friends that contributed in no small way to making this one of the happiest holidays that Stevens and his wife had ever spent. During the next five years, however, age, distance and the Judge's declining health were partly responsible for reducing the contact between these two old friends to a Christmas correspondence. Powell's death from a stroke in August 1951, at the age of seventy-seven, marked the departure of one of those rare individuals who made Stevens' world a more human place.

P·A·R·T II

>>>>>>>>>>>> <<<<<<<<<<<<

THE MAN OF LETTERS

CHAPTER THREE

Hartford's Writer in Residence

In early May 1952, William Carlos Williams came to Hartford to address the New England professors who had gathered at Trinity College for the spring meeting of the College English Association. It had been a year since Williams suffered the severe stroke that had kept him from another literary weekend and a reunion with Wallace Stevens at Bard College, where Stevens received an honorary degree in March 1951. The friendship between the two poets went back to their *Others* days at the beginning of World War I; they were among the young writers publishing in the pages of that avant-garde magazine funded by Walter Arensberg, at whose apartment the *Others* crowd socialized until the early 1920s. Williams had seen little of Stevens in later years; at most, they exchanged occasional notes, such as the one Williams wrote in December 1949 to tell Stevens how he had enjoyed his remarks on Marcel Gromaire in a catalogue for the French painter's current New York show. Thinking how long it had been since they had been together, Williams extended a standing invitation to the Hartford poet to visit him at his home, just minutes from Manhattan: "if you're in New York at any time why not come out to Rutherford. . . . There are 3 extra bedrooms any one of which is at your disposal at any time for as long as you want to stay."* Such

---

*Letter of December 22, 1949, HL. Writing this letter, Williams may well have had in mind the very different hospitality Stevens had offered him on his previous visit to Hartford years before. Williams had recounted that incident only a few months earlier to exemplify how odd he thought Stevens' ways could be at times: "we all knew, liked and admired him. He really was felt to be part of the gang. But he was funny: He asked me on many occasions to stop off at Hartford to see him on my way through when I'd be going north on a vacation. Once I did stop. I met his wife, casually, and spent the night—at his expense, at a nearby hotel—with my little dog!" (Letter to William Van O'Connor, August 22, 1949, Dartmouth.)

hospitality was typical of Williams and the opposite of Stevens' reserved response, three years later, when he learned that Williams was now coming to Hartford. Perhaps Williams could stop by Westerly Terrace for a few minutes on his way out of town, Stevens replied guardedly to a mutual friend who had tried to arrange a visit between the two poets.* Attending any function for Williams at the local college was, of course, quite out of the question, Stevens said. "I want to keep Trinity at arm's length (to be plain about it) because I want to keep everybody at arm's length in Hartford where I want nothing but the office and home as home."[1]

He was a typical New Englander, Dr. Williams commented disparagingly in the obituary he published in *Poetry* a few months after Stevens' death. "He was in the midst of a life crowded with business affairs a veritable monk . . . a frightened man drawing back from the world as if he had been in fact a New Englander."[2] In one respect, however, Stevens was not typical of the New Englanders among whom he lived: his antisocial ways were out of place in Hartford, at least among its writers. By the time Stevens moved there in 1916, Hartford had been accustomed to prominent writers among its citizens for more than a century, men and women who had developed a tradition of the Hartford writer as a sociable man of letters. This tradition dated from the early days of the Republic, when the Hartford Wits were America's first literary coterie. During Stevens' first years in town, he was reminded of this tradition almost daily on his way to work as he walked by Nook Farm, the classic instance of Hartford's literary life style. In the 1920s Stevens lived just above that cluster of Gothic mansions on Farmington Avenue where Mark Twain, Harriet Beecher Stowe and Charles Dudley Warner had spent their gregarious and civic-minded lives in late-Victorian Connecticut.[3]

Indeed, one of Stevens' hosts on his first visit to Hartford, in the summer of 1913, had been a member of that Nook Farm circle and one of the city's most sociable writers. Stevens learned of Hartford's literary ways from Annie Eliot Trumbull, even before he moved there. Three years before the young insurance executive found himself, unexpectedly, a citizen of Hartford, he had come as a weekend guest of an insurance associate from New York, Heber

---

*A few days before Williams came to lecture in Hartford, Stevens was at Harvard to give a poetry reading; visiting with his young Cambridge friends Richard and Betty Eberhart beforehand, Stevens confided how anxious he was about Williams' upcoming stay in his hometown. Richard Eberhart recalls that "Mr. Stevens was visibly perturbed because he'd known Williams for a long time [and] he had no way to entertain him. This really aggrieved him. He told me how it was. He asked my advice. 'What can I do? I can't have him at my house.' He seemed quite unable to cope with the situation. This is interesting to me that it troubled Stevens, even though he was seventy years old. And he still didn't know what to do to make Williams happy in Hartford." As Betty Eberhart notes, "I don't think we really questioned him much about it at the time because I knew there was something funny about Mrs. Stevens, that she didn't want to have people in the house. Wallace felt very bad. He said, 'What do I do with him? I have no place.' Of course, Bill Williams had just the opposite kind of family. He had Flossie Williams, which meant anybody could go to his house. My feeling of Wallace Stevens at home is a little like a feeling of a novel by somebody like Thackeray: Wallace was the prosperous businessman with a big house, but his wife was always upstairs in some mysterious way." (Taped interview.)

Stryker, who had recently moved to the Connecticut capital. Stevens had readily accepted the invitation to escape the heat of Manhattan and spend the Fourth of July holiday in New England. Stevens was not yet an author, having published nothing since undergraduate days at Harvard, but Stryker knew of his friend's literary interests and had invited Annie Trumbull, Hartford's most notable writer at the time, to fill out the party. The career of this fifty-six-year-old author had peaked just before the turn of the century, about the time Stevens was making his literary debut in undergraduate literary magazines. In 1897 a collection of Trumbull's short stories from the *Atlantic Monthly* and *McClure's Magazine* was brought out, followed two years later by her next-to-last novel, *Mistress Content Craddock*. ⁴ This spinster, who had once been part of the younger generation of Twain's Hartford circle, was the daughter of his friend James Hammond Trumbull, Connecticut's secretary of state. Annie Trumbull was a decidedly sociable author, like those of the Twain circle generally. Twain, for example, had joined in enthusiastically when this young woman and her friends had set up the Saturday Morning Club of Hartford for the women of Nook Farm and the daughters of Hartford's better families in 1876. The idea of forming such a circle along the lines of Boston's original Saturday Morning Club was something the gregarious Twain approved of, and he gave no less than fifteen lectures there before his death in 1910. While its aims of promoting culture and social intercourse for women may now sound a bit quaint, there was nothing provincial about the roster of writers, from Bret Harte to William Butler Yeats, who spoke before the club in its first years.⁵ The Saturday Morning Club was just one of the many literary and social groups in which the energetic Miss Trumbull was active while working on such plays as *A Masque of Culture* and publishing such regional fiction as *A Cape Cod Week*. With her wealth of stories about the gatherings at Nook Farm, young Stevens doubtlessly heard a good deal about Hartford's gregarious literary circle that first weekend in town as he junketed by automobile with Trumbull around the New England countryside during the day. He also dined with her at the country club fete she gave the evening before he returned to New York. "*The* Miss Trumbull," Stevens wrote to his wife, who was vacationing in Pennsylvania at the time, "was, after all, a most agreeable person, with very pleasant manners and a sense of humor."⁶

While Trumbull was a formidable example of Hartford's sociable literary women, Hartford's gregarious men of letters were also to be seen. There was a small circle of regional writers, traditionalist poets and novelists, among them Odell Shepard, Wilbert Snow and, for a time, Robert Hillyer. Not much read today, they had standing as writers in the 1920s and 1930s: both Hillyer and Shepard, whose books were issued by Stevens' own publisher, Alfred A. Knopf, had won Pulitzer Prizes long before Stevens' award in the last months of his life in 1955. The gathering place for these Yankee writers was a bookshop in a converted Greek Revival home on a cobbled lane just a block below Stevens' downtown insurance office. Soon after Edwin Valentine Mitchell opened his Lewis Street shop in 1921, it became not only the best bookstore in town but also the literary center of Hartford. Mitchell, a former lawyer with ambitions to be a man of letters himself, also started a small publishing house and literary review, *Book Notes,* shortly thereafter at the same address. The literary ventures at 27 Lewis Street were a throwback to the mid-nineteenth century, when Hartford was one of the publishing centers of America. Although the writers who sat around chatting in the back room of Mitchell's bookshop on a Saturday afternoon conversed mostly in New England accents, occasionally an arresting foreign voice could be heard. One might hear Padraic Colum, a frequent visitor, gossiping about James Joyce and James Stephens after returning from one of his Dublin visits, or Wyndham Lewis, having come from London for a visit with Mitchell, pronouncing that Sinclair Lewis was the American Balzac. Sinclair Lewis, too, was a regular at the bookshop during the year he spent in Hartford following the appearance of *Babbitt* in 1922.[7]

The only writer from the Lewis Street circle with whom Stevens had anything to do, however, was a poet with a decidedly Maine accent, Wilbert Snow, from Wesleyan University in nearby Middletown. After one of Snow's lectures on modern poetry before a women's literary club in Hartford in the early 1920s, Mrs. Stevens had come up to this lanky professor to say that this had been the first time she had heard her husband's poetry read publicly. Stevens, whose "Peter Quince at the Clavier" Snow had read admiringly that afternoon, was one of the new poets that young Snow regarded highly. Taking the initiative, he promptly called Stevens and invited him to lunch, the first of several such meals they shared over the years. Not surprisingly, Stevens took to this regionalist poet. With a face as craggy as the Maine coast he came from and celebrated in his poetry, Snow was one of those individuals whom Stevens truly admired: a man made out of the substance of his region and who was its voice. This Maine expatriate was also the quintessential figure of the Hartford writer. A sociable and civic-minded man of letters, Snow was a force in Democratic politics and eventually became governor of the state.[8] Hartford was used to writers who were active men of affairs. What was eccentric about Stevens in a Hartford light was not so much that a writer should be an insurance man but that he should be so determined to ensure his privacy, that he should be "the damned monk" Williams had thought all New Englanders were.

After graduating from Smith College, Elva McCormick began working at the Lewis Street Bookshop the year Stevens' first book appeared; for the next thirty years there, she was able to gauge how little known Stevens was in his hometown by the small demand there was for his books. James Thrall Soby, however, was one of the early local admirers. This wealthy young Hartfordite was avid for modern poetry and painting when, in the late 1920s, he became a partner in Mitchell's bookshop. He soon began to acquire the notable collection of modernist paintings that led him into museum work, first as assistant director of Hartford's Wadsworth Atheneum and then as assistant director of New York's Museum of Modern Art. In the midst of the sociable Lewis Street circle of writers, Soby learned firsthand how determined Stevens was not to play the role of one of Hartford's writers-in-residence. This remained the rule throughout Stevens' Connecticut years, as the director of the Wadsworth Atheneum found out as late as the 1950s. When Charles Cunningham asked Stevens to repeat at the local Atheneum the lecture he had given at New York's Museum of Modern Art, Stevens refused. One was much more likely to encounter Stevens the poet in Hartford if one were simply passing through town, as the young literati Donald Stanford, I. L. Salomon, Frank Jones, William Van O'Connor, Peter Lee or José Rodríguez Feo did. In his last years, however, Stevens mellowed somewhat, at least in the case of two young poet-professors, Richard Eberhart and Samuel French Morse, who lived in the area and with whom Stevens cultivated the few literary friendships he had in Hartford.

James Thrall Soby

I had a bookstore with a man named Edwin Valentine Mitchell. We knew all the local authors. They would sort of hang out at the bookstore. Stevens came in quite often. I admired him enormously, but he was a very strange and difficult man. He didn't like people very much. I think he liked Wilbert Snow personally; Snow was around the bookshop all the time. Not much [fraternizing between Stevens and the other poets there, however]. Not with Odell Shepard at all; they never got along well. Stevens never would relate to people.

I talked to a couple of his colleagues, trying to find out more about him when I had an idea to do a book about him [in the early 1930s]. He was in a way a terribly civilized and urbane man; he was also, which scared me a little bit, a terribly hard-boiled businessman. They all said he was the toughest one that came through the office. But I gave up [the book] after a while. I saw it was hopeless: I couldn't get anything out of this man. Mostly [the conversation between Stevens and Soby at the shop] was about poetry. Most of the time it was, "No! No!," that he didn't want to talk about poetry. I would have remembered [had Stevens bought any books by his contemporaries] because it would have interested me very much. But not at all. He was a browser. Stevens was a dead end on a lot of points, and that was one of them.

We used to try to sell his books in the bookshop. We never did very well. We did [stock the 1931 edition of *Harmonium,* for example]. I displayed it prominently; I had it all over the bookshelves. I sold about three. He didn't show any emotion at all about it. He sort of picked up the book, took a quick look at it, and put it down again.

[About this time] I tried to get Mitchell to publish a book of his poems. Stevens said, "I have no new material." Extremely rude. He said, "I'm not at all interested. I'm not that poor a poet that I have to look around for local publishers." He was a very proud man, and he felt he was entitled to be published by the best persons there were. Here I was, a small-town bookseller embarking on publishing.

A number of people called him up. Sometimes they called from the book-shop and tried to get an appointment with him. They never succeeded. He'd just say, "I'm terribly busy." I think he would have been the same anywhere. I talked myself blue in the face about him, but I soon gave up. I'd recommend people to him, and then Stevens would be rude to them. That would be the end of it.

I didn't have that many [contacts] with Stevens, but he knew I admired him. Except that I had one contact that was more or less constant. Stevens was a genuine lover of art. [Between 1931 and 1941, Soby worked at the Wadsworth Atheneum.] It [was] one of the best museums in the country and had the best museum director [A. Everett Austin, Jr.].* Stevens went to the museum all the time. At noon hour, he'd wander around alone. He was almost furious if anyone interrupted him. He'd come every holiday. Very often on weekends. He wouldn't talk about the exhibitions. I kept trying to find out what artists he liked. There wasn't any way to tell except to follow him around the gallery and see where he stayed longest. He came [to the 1931 Surrealist exhibition, the first such exhibition in the country]. Not just once, but quite a number of times. I saw him there [at the 1934 world premiere of *Four Saints in Three Acts*] but, as usual, he was alone much of the time. Austin gave a series of parties before and after, and so did I. I don't think he came to either [though he was invited].

[On one occasion, Stevens did accept Soby's invitation to a party in honor

*During his years as director of the Wadsworth Atheneum (1927–1945), A. Everett Austin, Jr., transformed Hartford's provincial museum into a center of the avant-garde movement in America. Between 1933 and 1935 alone, Austin mounted the first Picasso retrospective in America; brought George Balanchine from Paris to found the School of American Ballet in Hartford; organized the world premiere of the Virgil Thomson-Gertrude Stein opera *Four Saints in Three Acts*; acquired the Diaghilev-Lifar collection of ballet designs; sponsored lectures by Dali and Gertrude Stein; mounted such exhibitions as "Drawings by Eugene Berman," "Works by Tchelitchew," "Cubist and Futurist Art from Collection of Leonide Massine," "Pevsner, Gabo, Mondrian and Domela"; and gave May Sarton's Apprentice Theatre a home in the new wing he had recently built. To some, such as Eugene Berman, Austin was America's Diaghilev.

Austin lived only a block below Westerly Terrace, and his Palladian-style mansion on Scarborough Street was the gathering place for modern artists visiting Hartford. One of the more memorable evenings occurred in 1935 when Virgil Thomson, Aaron Copland, George Antheil, Paul Bowles and Roy Harris could be heard there playing one another's compositions (*A. Everett Austin, Jr.: A Director's Taste and Achievement* [Hartford: Wadsworth Atheneum, 1958], pp. 10, 46). Whenever Austin called his nearby neighbor on Westerly Terrace, hoping to introduce Stevens to someone who wanted to meet him, the poet declined (interview with Helen Austin). In Hartford, Stevens kept his distance not only from the traditional New England writers who gathered at the Lewis Street Bookshop but also from Austin's avant-garde circle.

of Carl Sandburg, who had come to read before the local poetry society.] It was at my house. It was just a little gathering. He never mingled at parties and was always off in a corner [by] himself. I was a little shocked [when phoning to invite Stevens]. He said, "I'll come, but on one condition: that you do not invite Archibald MacLeish." This was a terribly trying situation. I knew MacLeish. We both lived in Farmington. I never got along well with MacLeish, but I did with his wife. I didn't dare ask him [why] because he turned purple with rage whenever you mentioned MacLeish's name. I dropped the subject. He admired [Sandburg], which is very odd, because they're very opposite poets, God knows. But he thought Sandburg was very real, and that appealed to him. He had an overriding sense of reality in everything he did.

[In 1942, Soby moved to New York to work at the Museum of Modern Art.] I'd pass him in the gallery, and we'd talk a little while. It wouldn't go far. He'd ask me what I liked and what stood out. And he'd tell me what he liked most. Then he moved on. He was always a man who was frightened of being trapped into a new friendship. He was very [much interested in Paul Klee]. I know he was, because when I used to follow him through the gallery, he always stayed longer in the Klee gallery than anywhere else. That's how I knew. There wouldn't have been any other way to find out.

Elva McCormick

I can remember his coming down the street. We had windows in front of the bookstore, so that we saw everybody. He was such a great big fellow, six foot three or four, and weighed two hundred and fifty. But he didn't look fat, just a big man, tightly bound and fully packed. I could never imagine Stevens running. It was this stately, measured walk. I can't imagine he'd ever hurry; he'd always plan well ahead to get wherever it was he wanted to go. I remember his coming in and ordering a book occasionally. I got him to sign [The Auroras of Autumn]. He tried hard to explain "The Irish Cliffs of Moher" [when McCormick asked him about the poem in this late collection]. He said, "I don't think you'd understand this unless you wrote it." I think that's true of many of his poems. He never stayed very long. Generally, he came with a specific errand in mind and would be on his lunch hour.

[Elsie Stevens] was just a mousy little creature. You almost felt that she was afraid to say hello to you. She came in with Holly by the hand and went into the little room devoted to children's books. She bought books for Holly, but I have never known her to buy a book for herself.

Those were the days when you made real sales. The big executives and several others used to come in for their weekend reading. They'd read the New York *Times Book Review*, and then they'd go out with an armful of books, make a thirty-dollar purchase. In those days, books were two dollars and fifty cents. They didn't read poetry. They read biographies, autobiographies and history. We had one small section of poetry. We did sell some Stevens, of course, but we didn't sell him the way we sold Edna St. Vincent Millay. When a new one of hers came out, you had a big list of people who wanted to be sure to get her first editions. But we never had a waiting list for Wallace Stevens. I took care of Mrs. Russell Johnston [a local judge's wife who was a director of the local poetry society and a Stevens fan], saw that she got everything. There were a few other people, but none that were real collectors: H. Bacon Collamore, he was the great modern-poetry collector [a friend and collector of Robert Frost and Robinson Jeffers, among others; he lived in Hartford]. I don't think he collected him. You wouldn't find one in a thousand [among Hartfordites interested in the arts] who knew him by name, who he was.

I drove to New York the night he read at the Museum of Modern Art [January 15, 1951]. Isabel [Wycoff] wanted to go; [she] was a woman in Hartford who was crazy about Wallace Stevens. She used to telephone him, and she'd write to him. And another girl who worked in the shop, and Holly [Stevens]. We got there in plenty of time—and tense, because it was icy and snowy. Wallace told us that he always ate at a restaurant close to the Museum of Modern Art, so we did. I remember the note he wrote me before we went. "I understand you are planning to go. Well, if you go, you might as well get in."* So he gave me two tickets. There was a little reception afterward. (Later we did talk about it.] He thought we were crazy just to go down for that.

I always treated him like a regular guy; we just passed the time.

Charles Cunningham

When I went to Hartford [in 1946 as the new director of the Wadsworth Atheneum], my father was still alive. [He said,] "I don't know many people in Hartford, but I have a classmate and a friend by the name of Wallace Stevens." They used to meet at the Signet Society. My father was a member and he was a member. I'm not sure I knew who he was before I came to

---

*Stevens had, at first, tried to dissuade his daughter from attending the talk in a note that reveals the stage fright he suffered as a lecturer even late in his career. "Please do not come to my reading in N.Y. It would make me nervous and self-conscious at a time which, for me, is bad enough already. Moreover, I have engagements before and after." (Letter of December 4, 1950, HL.)

Hartford. Actually, my first wife's family were great friends of poets, particularly [John] Masefield, whom I knew very well.[9] Masefield was then Poet Laureate of England, and I think Stevens told me that he admired Masefield.

Stevens didn't like to talk much about his poetry. We lunched together three times. When he'd go off to literary circles in New York, he would talk a good deal more about poetry. We talked much more about Hartford. He asked me my ideas about the Atheneum. It had a marvelous reputation as a museum. I had known Chick Austin, who had been the previous director, and had a great admiration for him. Wallace Stevens, although I'm not sure he approved of everything Chick did, was rather fascinated by him because he was an extraordinary man. Stevens was always very interested [in the Atheneum]. He was one of the more generous annual contributors, but aside from that he didn't usually have much connection with the museum. He visited the museum from time to time, [but] he wouldn't come to the desk and say, "Is Mr. Cunningham in? I'd like to just say 'hello'." He never came to any openings. Good God, he would have avoided that like the plague!

He told me [about his manner of collecting] the first time I met him. He had a friend [Anatole Vidal, the French bookseller] in whom he had great faith. What he did was to send what he could afford and told him to buy what he thought was good and send it to him. He said he'd never been disappointed. I can't say that the friend was all that much of a world-beater, because in those days the prices were not what they are now. You could pick up some pretty marvelous things. I bought Henry Moore watercolors and two Wyndham Lewises for one hundred pounds or less; the Wyndham Lewises were thirty pounds apiece. Holly asked me to come up to the house [after Stevens' death]. She didn't know what [the paintings] were, and she was wondering what she should do with them. I probably told her that there was none for which you'd paid two hundred dollars that was [now] worth forty or fifty thousand.

He knew about art. Now, when I came to Hartford, I don't think people took art very seriously, except a small few. The attendance when I came was something like twenty-eight to thirty thousand people a year. He enjoyed the collection; he enjoyed the museum. I'm not sure that if we'd put on an exhibition of Rococo painting in Italy and France this would have psyched him up enough to come, but he was interested in modern painting—primarily, I suppose, between the relationships of poetry and painting.

I know he did lecture once at the Museum of Modern Art [on "The Relations between Poetry and Painting"]. I saw this [newspaper notice] and said if he lectures at the Museum of Modern Art, it would be a wonderful drawing card to get him to lecture at the Atheneum. He said, no, he would not lecture, because "in Hartford I'm known as an insurance [man]."

Donald Stanford

I had written to Wallace Stevens [1937], requesting a meeting. I pointed out that I, too, wrote poetry. I mentioned Yvor Winters' name; he had been my teacher at Stanford. I think it was the Winters connection that did it. I may have sent him a poem of mine; at any rate, he said he had not read my poems in the magazines—I'd published quite a few at that time—but that he would look out for them in the future. He wrote back and set a time. I arrived at the appointed time; I think it was in the afternoon. He himself met me at the door, and we proceeded directly to his backyard, where there was a lawn and a garden. I'm sure I did not meet his wife. Then we talked awhile there. [Stevens did not invite Stanford into his home during their two-hour talk.] He looked like a rather prosperous Rotarian businessman, just a bit overweight perhaps.

At that time, I was very enthusiastic about his early poetry, the poetry in *Harmonium,* particularly "Sunday Morning." I expressed my enthusiasm for the poem, and he was a bit noncommittal. I was, of course, eager to talk about poetry. He seemed not to want to talk about poetry very much. I had the impression that poetry was not his major interest at that time, although I realize he'd just published *Ideas of Order.* We did talk in a general way about poetry. I could not tie him down to anything specific about his own poetic career. The names of Pound and Eliot came up. We talked briefly about Winters because I knew Winters well. He had been reading Winters to some extent, and he made one remark that sticks in my mind. He just said, "Well, Winters wants to start things all over again." I don't know exactly what he meant by that; perhaps he meant that Winters was reevaluating the history of the short poem in English, or words to that effect. But, of course, he may have been looking forward to "Notes toward a Supreme Fiction," because he thinks there the poet should start things all over again. I was conscious of that break [between 1924 and 1930, when Stevens had published no new verse]. I knew that it was sort of forecast in "The Comedian as the Letter C," and I realized he'd gone out of the poetry business, as it were, for some time. I did try to get started on that, but he always turned to other matters, such as gardening.

Gardening was one of his main passions at the time, and it took up a good deal of our conversation, as a matter of fact. He talked about the great variety of lilies he had in the garden, and he was very angry at a great white rabbit that was eating his lilies. I didn't know much about lilies and that ended the conversation. I didn't realize that tiger lilies were weeds. But he was very polite and kind throughout.

We started talking a bit about politics. This was the depths of the Depression. I was one of the angry young men, more or less inclined to Marxism, although I never became a Marxist. And I expressed the notion that capitalism was in a bad way and that the lower classes were being exploited. He wasn't having any of that. He just said "exploitation" was the wrong way of saying it; that was unfair. I don't remember the conversation in detail, but he certainly opposed my political views, no doubt about that.

I lingered on and on and did not leave until he indicated he had other things to do, although toward me he was very polite and tactful and kind. The thing that struck me most was his reluctance to talk about his own poetry. I left him with a very good feeling; I felt he'd enjoyed the talk. My last impression of him is leaning through my car window [as] he helped me find the best route to Hanover [New Hampshire, where Stanford had accepted a teaching position at Dartmouth College]. He bid me a very cordial good-by, and that was it. I do have a vague recollection he mentioned he was familiar with New Hampshire, and he wished me the best of luck at Dartmouth. He thought I would like it there.

When I was at Harvard, from '33 to '34, where I took my master's degree, Stevens did not have a very high rating with the people I knew. I was the exception there in thinking highly of him. I knew Theodore Spencer quite well, that is, in a student-teacher relationship. I knew F. O. Matthiessen quite well. In our conversations, I was always promoting Stevens; I said Stevens is one of *the* major poets of America. I got rather shrugged off on that. Spencer's remark was, "Well, he has a kind of underground reputation, but he is just too precious and affected to be very important." And of course Spencer and Matthiessen were high on T. S. Eliot; about all they could see was T. S. Eliot.

Frank Jones

When my friend [Arthur Blair] and I were editing *Diogenes* at the University of Wisconsin—I was a graduate student at the time—we got to know Howard Moss, who had been kicked out of the University of Michigan, apparently for trying to organize the chambermaids into a union—that's what was said, anyway. So he moved to Wisconsin; later on, I visited Howard Moss at his home, somewhere outside of New York, and he would take me up and down Rockaway Beach and recite from memory long stretches from Wallace Stevens. He was particularly fond of "The Paltry Nude Starts on a Spring Voyage." This was what really turned me on to Stevens. Before that I'd known about him and read a few of his things. This got me excited about him, so I immediately started reading *Harmonium* and all the Stevens I could get hold of. This must have been around 1940. The only person I can remember in New York that talked a lot about Stevens and was really wild about him was Moss. [He said] simply that he regarded him as the supreme poet of our time, that he was continually thinking of him, that Stevens' lines kept coming to his mind. He really knew a lot of him by heart: that's one of the few cases where I met someone who has all that of a poet ready to spout along the beach. Then, when I got this poetry reviewing job on *The Nation*, this Stevens book, *Parts of a World*, happened to come along, and they asked me to do it. That was the background to this whole thing.

If I hadn't done that [review] I wouldn't have dreamed of looking Stevens up. I was a totally unknown person to him, but I made myself known on the basis of having written that review. I really thought the book was rather bad, but I didn't have the courage to come out and say so, so I said things rather indirectly [in the review]: "Mr. Stevens doesn't really come up to Yeats," and that kind of jazz. I did feel he was trying to come to grips with the so-called actual world, the real world, and it wasn't really his line.

[Jones made the following notes immediately after his meeting with Stevens. Later interpolations by Jones are added in brackets.]

Hartford, September 5, 1942. I have an appointment with the immigration authorities, and, it being Saturday of Labor Day weekend, I decide to spend the day in town. My business over, I wander around, sampling a few of the excellent book sections of auction marts, picking up, among other things, Henry James' *The Tragic Muse* for a dime. Perhaps this stimulates my boldness, for soon I look up Stevens in the phone book, then in the city directory to see if the Wallace Stevens on Westerly Terrace is indeed the "vice-pres lwyr Hartford Accident & Indemnity Co." It is.

"Hello"—a deep rich authoritative but not ungentle voice.

"Mr. Stevens?"

"Yes."

"This is Frank Jones. You doubtless don't know who I am, but I have the honor of reviewing your new book in *The Nation*."

"Yes."

"And as I happen to be in town for the day I would like to come and pay my respects."

"Well, yes—if you don't stay too long." (A chuckle.)

"Oh, no, I assure you I won't. You can time me by the clock. . . ."

"Where are you now?"—Directions follow, showing a highly accurate offhand knowledge of bus movements.

The house is handsome, but simpler than most on the Terrace—a beautiful street, and actually a terrace, one lane of the road being about ten feet above the other. It is a district of huge quiet lawns, flower gardens, big houses in excellent architectural taste.

[Stevens was dressed casually but with great elegance. I think he was home for the day. He had a tweed jacket and nonmatching pants. A general air of affluence—not opulence, but affluence—about him that I liked right away.]

"Mr. Jones, I take it? How do you do?"

"How do you do? I am very glad to see you."

"I—er—have to go in here"—leading the way to a little study projecting from the house at one side. [He was in this sun room, I think it was called, where there was a lot of light pouring in the windows and (chairs) with very beautifully flowered cushions. I immediately felt very comfortable in there. It was a great spot to relax and chat. There were a lot of books on the wall, which he pointed out toward the end of the hour I spent with him, fine bindings and things.] I am practically commanded to sit down in a roundish green chair, from which I get a good side view of my host. As he sits down, an ample six-footer, in a high-backed easy chair, I notice how round his face is—the benign cheeks of an almost elderly Cupid—and that he has a respectable bay window. Otherwise he is unlike the Business Man: a geniality quiet and gentle, a smile and slow-coming laugh not deliberate. He suits perfectly the charming little study—rather a relaxing or reading room: His main study is upstairs, I learn later—with its walls a shade pinker than his face, its welcoming chairs with their mellowed flowered upholstery. At once I am at ease. [We stayed in that one room all the time, I didn't move around the house.]

"To begin with—of course you realize—this is *not* an interview."

"Of course."

"These young men—you know, some of them regard this place as a sort of railroad station; they think they can come through any time." The sternness melts as I smile agreement; the chuckle travels slowly up and becomes a full-grown laugh; the subject is dropped.

"I am not a journalist," I explain, "except in the most amateur of ways . . . I do occasional book reviews . . . I teach classics for a living."

"Oh. Yes, reviewing is no way to live. I've been reading about Edward Thomas, the English critic and poet—"

"Yes. He tried to live on it entirely, didn't he?"

"He had a pretty bad time of it—of course, they pay nothing at all over there. Do you find it pays you anything?"

"Well, my last review brought in $23—it was quite a long one, though—"

"Twenty-three is good, very good! Where do you teach classics?"

"At Yale."

The Harvard man's words suggest relief: "Oh, well, then you know your way around!" I am not, then, necessarily one of "those young men." [I think he was immediately willing to talk to me as soon as he found out I was at Yale: not having gone to Oxford, not having written the review, being at Yale —that really put him on. He really began to open up at that point. That put me somewhere within the reach of civilization. I got this job in classics in the fall of '42. (Members of the English Department) were notorious for not giving a damn about anything in the nineteenth century, let alone the twentieth century. At least that was the impression we got in the Hall of Graduate Studies. So obviously, if you don't care about the twentieth century to begin with, you're not going to care about Stevens.]

"I have taken the English *Nation,*" he resumes—meaning *The New Statesman and Nation*—"for many years now. I still keep it up, though it's not been much since the war began. I began my subscription a long time ago, but dropped it because it came to seem as if it would go on forever. Then I missed it, started again, and have had it ever since."

"Yes, I've been familiar with it since my days in England—I lived there for several years."

"Oh." A further improvement.

"By the way, another magazine I've had to do with is one you may remember—*Diogenes.* Arthur Blair and I started it in Madison, Wisconsin, in 1940."

"Certainly I remember it—and liking it, too! I was looking at one the other day. It seemed very vigorous to me. They wrote me, I think . . ." A laugh. "I'm afraid I wasn't very nice to you. . . ."

"On the contrary, I remember a very kind letter."

"It was, I think, because I had nothing ready at the time. Sometimes I send things off that are not quite finished, and then regret it. You know how it is: I put the thing down after it has started in my mind, just to get the swing of it set; but then it needs the polishing, and sometimes one neglects that. Then, too, I'm a poor correspondent—only write when I feel like it."

"Yes—Blair and I are like that, too. Perhaps it has something to do with the lapse of *Diogenes*!"

The laugh is very sympathetic this time. "Yes, so it goes. I read all the little magazines—have been for years—and when they stop, there's nothing to read." A quite sad silence follows this, Stevens looking into the middle distance as if he saw the ghosts of all the dead little mags knocking wistfully at the window. [I remember I was greatly moved by what he said, that he read all the little magazines; he was sad when they expired.] "The periodicals in this country are really dreadful," he resumes. "There's none that one cares to read regularly."

"Yes—an occasional article, maybe, in things like the *Atlantic* or *Harper's*. But the poetry they publish! All the dull fellows, conservative."

Another silence. I wonder if I have been tactless—try to remember if Stevens has ever been in either of these—decide it is not impossible, and resign myself to having blundered. But what emerges seems not to confirm this sinking feeling.

"Well, I suppose poetry is always a matter of groups, cliques, rival sets."

"That's as it should be, isn't it?"

"Yes"—doubtfully. A change of subject is indicated. Somehow we arrive at Indian literature. I announce an enthusiasm for Hindu poetry.

"I don't like that Indian stuff."

"Not even the poetry?"

"What, for instance?"

"Well, Kalidasa, and the two epics, of course—they're magnificent."

"Hmmm. I was given a book recently about Indian philosophy and civilization, and I read the sections on their theories of poetry, very carefully. They're a nuisance."

Since I know as little of Hindu poetics as he seems to know of Hindu poetry, still another tack is naturally to be taken. By way of England, Oxford, and kindred topics, he comes to reminisce about an Oxford man he knew [Leonard van Geyzel], who started as a lawyer but turned to growing coconuts in Ceylon. A very sensible decision, I remark; he agrees. The coconut planter has sent him physical and intellectual delicacies; a native liqueur ("wasn't fit to drink—make out of wood or something"), candies ("We left them about the house—they were fine things to spring on people"), a book of poems in English by a German monk, printed at Colombo ("There was an exquisite poverty about the book's appearance"). He mentions a letter from the planter describing the mobilization in Ceylon recently—"A very British affair. They all went out and bought dollar uniforms, brought them home, and so they were ready for the Japs." The ensuing laugh is one of affection for the casualness, not mockery of the inadequacy. In accent and manner, in much of his attitude, Stevens is the most English American I have met: the more so for not being consciously imitative. [At that time I was hardly fresh out of Oxford, but I had completed my work there in 1937, so it was still pretty fresh in my mind. He had what I call this British tact. When I got there, there was this very elaborate mutual exploration, where you'd stick to one topic for about a minute and then dash on to something else. 'Course there was no particular point in my going to see him anyway; I just wanted to meet him. He reminded me of English people who behave like that: even when you do have a specific purpose to see them, they never mention it for the first five or ten minutes. They talk about anything rather than what you're coming to see them for. That's the quality I found in Stevens.] Indeed, this very tentativeness, this seeming reluctance to argue about literary matters, this apparent recourse to comic relief by talking of eccentric acquaintances—it is all like the English way, the way of skating around the topic closest to one's heart, inviting one's guest to join in the fun, the trial spin, before getting down to business. Having found by this time that I have at least the makings of trustworthiness—that I, too, like France, and mangoes, and papayas, and am not unimpressed by the fact, emerging from one of his reminiscences, that the world is, after all, a small place—it is he who now abruptly changes the subject, and with a little sigh, as if to say, "Well, that's done," asks:

"Do you write poetry yourself?"

The impact of this, from a major poet, leaves me able only to mumble something apologetic, "Yes . . . I indulge." The "yes" seems to reassure him and launches us into what we have been wishing to discuss.

He declares that he reads, or at least samples, all the verse that comes his way, even if sent him with requests for advice. He clearly has sympathy for anyone who makes the effort, and seems actually to regret that the results of the effort are so often incorrigible. But he doubts whether advice should be offered at all.

"It's an impossible business—what can you do? I'm not especially tactful —no more than anyone else—and the poetic ego is so tremendous! If you tell them anything else than that they're brilliant, overwhelming, the most amazing stuff you ever read, they resent it; and if you say nothing, they resent that too."

By way of American poets, we come to speak of their country. [I may have been trying to draw him into (a discussion of other American poets), but I don't think he bit.] I mention California in some connection. He expresses an amused, New England reflection of it. "Here, between Boston and New York, you're in the center of everything. In California it's easier to go to China than to New York; and who wants to go to China?"

I agree that even now there is a solid culture, a being in the current, in what I have seen of New England. In half-serious confirmation of this, I mention my good luck in Hartford's bookstores.

"Hartford," Stevens says, "is a very American city, but here that includes, yes, a strong cultural tradition. Our businessmen are well educated, they read books, some of them even write: there's Mr.———, for instance, the chief Mififi of a company . . ."

"The chief what?"

"Oh—" laughing—"Mififi, panjandrum, headman, you know. He goes away each summer to live the life of a painter." [Reviewing this, it seems to me probably his mood at the time was somewhat double. On the one hand, he likes the notion that there are educated men he can talk to; on the other hand, he knows that he's by himself as far as writing poetry is concerned. "They read books, some of them even write" as I recall it was gentle irony, but nevertheless irony.]

He goes on to express the view that the acute antagonism in this country between business and poetry, the arts in general, is overdone. He thinks it silly that a man's ability to live in both worlds should be so widely doubted, on both sides of the gap between commerce and culture. But his ensuing remarks hint that the artist is nevertheless critical of his surroundings.

"I was the first in my company to move out to this district."

"A very beautiful one."

"Yes, I like it. Alfred Knopf visited me sometime ago, and was much impressed by it.[10] If I had been a real-estate man, I'm sure I could have sold him some land! He was looking for a place for Thomas Mann, who wanted to live not in New York, but in some genuinely American place. But he finally decided on Princeton, and now he's in California. Several men from the company followed me out here, so I do know my neighbor, you know, to talk to. But—I gather you like to walk—"

"I love it."

"Then you will understand—I like walking to work, so I don't drive in with them; and I like walking alone, so I don't walk with them! I've grown a great deal heavier of late years, and prefer to walk very slowly—at will—stopping when I care to—"

"That puts me in mind of something in Sherwood Anderson's memoirs. When he was becoming a writer and slowly breaking away from business, he forced himself to walk slowly, to look at things, instead of rushing around. Have you looked at his book?"

"I haven't read it. It must be interesting. Anderson was a very interesting man. Do you know how he died?"

"No."

"I thought it might interest you. Apparently he was coughing, and while coughing he swallowed a toothpick, and it got stuck inside him, and a day later he was dead."

"Good heavens! I was wondering what carried him off; he seems to have had a terrific constitution."

"Yes . . . Did you come to Hartford to see the museums?"

"No, I had to"—explaining my business. "There are some excellent collections here; I saw one of them last Christmas."

"Yes. I used to do a lot of that when I first came here. I was rather forlorn then."

In further comment he speaks of the many excellent art collections, public and private, scattered about the region; and this brings up the memorable Mrs. Gardner of Boston.

"You know, I'm old enough to remember her. When I was at Harvard— I was in [the Class of] 1901; what a very long time ago it seems—she was being very active socially, especially as patroness . . . helping promising young men, a whole trail of them. George Copeland, the pianist, was one, I believe."

"That's interesting. She was the princess of collectors, I suppose. But one of the guides in the Gardner museum told me that about half of what she bought was trash."

A definite raising of the eyebrows at this, which anyway is an exaggeration of the guide's estimate, as I subsequently recall.

"Oh, I doubt that. She was well guided. Boston is a city of advice."

Mrs. Gardner's memory vindicated, we pass from her to her hunting grounds. Talk of Paris leads me to mention *Lettres Françaises*, a review recently established at Buenos Aires. A circular from it is on the endtable in front of me. Stevens tells me its editor intends to come to New York to gather contributions, of writing and of funds. I ask him if he recalls an article in *Partisan Review* in which I mentioned this magazine, along with several other French periodicals. [I wrote an article about French magazines that were coming out during the Occupation and called it "Writers in Defeat." No (Stevens didn't meditate on conditions of the artist as World War II was beginning), not with me; of course, he does some of this in some of his poems. As I recall, there was very little discussion of contemporary events. We didn't really much care about that at the time; we were talking more about literature, and magazines, and things like that.]

"In *Partisan Review*? Well, then, I must have read it; I always read it, all of it. An excellent magazine, isn't it? The only exception to the dreary scene."

"Yes, I suppose we may rightly commend it, as fellow contributors." This statement does not completely restore my vanity.

"But really," he continues, "I hardly read at all. I like to buy books, and look at them; then they go on my shelves, and I look at them there. When I do read a book, it seems a waste of effort. Take this, for instance"—holding up one of two handsomely bound volumes on the desk. "It's a history of the county in Holland where my ancestors came from. I had to have it bound to read it at all; it was falling apart when I bought it; and recently I read the whole thing, the whole two volumes. Afterward I wondered why. . . . The strangest impulse . . . For a time I wanted very badly to get a complete set of Turgenev, just to have it around. But what would I have done with it when I had it?"

"Yes, I know those impulses. You probably read all the Turgenev you needed years ago."

"Exactly; I read most of him in French."

After some further desultory chat, I remember my promise not to stay too long.

"Well! It's been very nice; I'm glad you came. When I go to New Haven next I won't look you up, but I'll think of you."

"That's kind of you. I look forward to feeling my ears burn."

"I often get away to New Haven for a weekend—find it a good place to relax, entertain myself."

"You mean you actually find New Haven a relief from Hartford?" I am incredulous, having inhabited New Haven for a year.

"Why, yes."

"Strange. That's just the way I feel about Hartford."

"There! That shows how silly it is, really. A state of mind."

As we pass through the living room, in which I notice two photographs of his very good-looking daughter (on the desk), he opens a big glass-front bookcase.

"As a fellow poet"—this fully reconstructs my vanity—"you may like to see these. My bookseller in Paris, Vidal, had them done. I've dealt with him for years; I always wanted to know what he looked like, so finally I had a fellow go 'round and paint his portrait. Now, whenever I publish a collection, he has it specially bound. A sort of automatic arrangement; nothing in writing."

I am delighted over the exquisitely bound *Man with the Blue Guitar*, noting especially its end papers, dark blue with stripes of silver that look curved and straight at once.

"Yes," chuckles the author, "they dither." Then, with an air of finality: "Well, I won't show you any more. It's bad form—although the New Deal, I'm told, was devised so that people with fine bindings can show them to people who can't afford them."

"Or to decrease the number of fine bindings they can show?"

"Yes, that too. But here, I'll show you one more. I wanted an eighteenth-century armorial binding, not over one thousand francs. Vidal hunted all over the place for this one—*La Siège de Calais, Tragédie,* by some obscure laborer in the polite drama. Yes, a handsome job. You should take up something useful like that, instead of teaching classics to people who only want to forget them."

"How true."

"When you do, I shall send you a book to bind."

"Agreed."

[I met no one else in the house; I think I caught a glimpse of his wife somewhere else, in the background.]

At the end of the garden path, he speaks again of little magazines.

"They're the best thing, the only thing—and they die, and people don't wake up until it's too late to do anything about it."

A half-turn back towards the house, and with a parting smile he raises a big hand to mine. Shaking it, I venture that if he changes his mind about looking me up in New Haven, I shall be most happy.

"Well, I'd like to, but you see, I usually go with some of the fellows to the Yale game, that sort of thing."

"I see."

"Good-by, then, and come again!"

As I walk back downtown I keep seeing Wallace Stevens in the Yale Bowl, rooting for Harvard with the fellows. It is pleasant to meet a poet who enjoys his world.

[He was the most likable poet I ever met, on the basis of that one hour, the one with the best manners.]

I. L. Salomon

I went up to Hartford [1952], and I decided to call him one day. He was affable but distant. He asked me why I wanted to see him. I said, "I was born in Hartford, and I write, and I would like to come by and say 'hello' to you." He asked me when I could come. I said, "At once." "Well," he said, "come over."

When I got to his home on Westerly Terrace, he was not exactly affable, but he seemed content to see me. When I met him on the lawn, he was wearing his porky-pie hat. That's what Robert Frost called it. He asked me what I had written. I said, "I don't have books, but I've written a great deal of poetry." "Don't you believe in having your work printed?" I said, "Occasionally, it's printed, yes." But I told him I didn't care whether my work was printed or not. I just wrote because I had to write, and I liked what I wrote, that I was fundamentally a traditionalist poet. Then we got into a discussion of the philosophy of poetry in itself. He was a very difficult man to get near to. The only time he perked up was when I talked of my philosophy of poetry. He asked me whether I had written those things out. I said I started essays that I felt I wasn't competent to finish. He said nothing. He was interested, but that was all.

Now all that time there was his wife at the door and his daughter, Holly, on the lawn. He never once invited me into the house. Holly said—I don't remember whether she called him "Papa" or "Father"—"Well, don't you want to invite him in to see your library?" He sort of shrugged his shoulders, and he invited me in. He didn't show me the books. In fact, I looked at them myself; I just looked, I didn't take a book down. He had a beautiful place; he had a beautiful library. I didn't object to his being rich; I would have liked to have been in that position myself. But he treated his wife as if she were ash. I saw her at the door, and she disappeared; but Holly remained. She just disappeared, vanished. She was a dear-looking woman, seemed very much cowed. When he talked, I could see there was a shudder, a trembling effect on her. I looked at both of them: you could tell he was the master—with a broad *a*.

He told me that he very often wrote poems on scraps of paper. I said, "So do I." And he asked to look at what I had pulled out of my pocket. "Well," he said, "I write them, and my secretary types them up. I don't have to type them."

He did tell me, "You mentioned Williams. What do you think of Williams?" "I think he's one of our important writers. He's done something to change our language. He's done something to cadence." I mentioned one of Williams' poems, the one about the country funeral. I said, "I've always felt strongly about that." "Well," he says, "I took his books when they came here and dumped them in the fireplace." I didn't know whether he was showing off or just wisecracking.

Then we talked of *The Necessary Angel.* We got into the business of what a poem was and what made it click. He says, "Don't you believe this and this?" He mentioned his poem that talks about the nigger cemetery ["Like Decorations in a Nigger Cemetery"]. I told him the truth: I found the title offensive. He just ignored it.

I didn't bring him anything to sign. I said, "I have a first edition of *Harmonium,* and I have the *Ideas of Order.* I didn't bring them for you to sign." He said, "Why should you? Why should you want them signed?" I did bring his poetry up, and he didn't say a word. I mentioned several of the pieces in *Ideas of Order.* I asked him why he made that title. He said, "Don't you like it?" I said, "It's too intellectual." I praised "Harmonium" as a title. He sort of frowned. I think he felt he was well rid of me.

I'd say we were at the house thirty, forty minutes. Then we rode together to Elizabeth Park, and then we went downtown. He said, "I'd like you to see a tree. We'll go to Elizabeth Park." He evidently had been much attracted to [the tree]. I remember his voice clearly, when we were moving maybe twenty miles an hour. "Slow up. Look at the larch!" He asked me to wait there. We both sat in the car and looked at it. [Then] he said he wanted to pick up some fruit. [On the way to buy it downtown], he talked of fruit, G. Fox [a local department store], and "the bleak meanings of poetry." I did put down the sense [of the conversation] in a poem.

HARTFORD POET
(Essence of an Encounter)

Desire for the apogee of sun
is in this light; the pyramidal larch
gathers to its yellowing linear leaves
the flash of brightness given by sun and air.

The brown pagoda in Elizabeth Park
is a mandarin in harsh habiliments
of dry sharp thorns and twisted briers towering
over rose arches where no roses are.

It is not yet noon; day vaults to solar height;
the autumnal atmosphere is shifting from
warm to cool to warm in tried responses.
Slow up, said Wallace Stevens, look at the larch.

The way the light encrusted the gold glints
shut out the logic of the busy world
a traffic-jam away, where none had time
to note the season's affluence in foliage.

On Westerly Terrace an old neighbor died,
making him visible to eternity;
a voice in me cried *stop* before a church
as we drove on; a voice beside me spoke

of fruit, G. Fox, insurance, and the bleak
meanings of poetry. I: meaning in words

unmake a poem's sense; a poem lives
in newness, is unique as any "I" who is.

He: configuration is the thing that counts,
mine as against just anyone's notation;
I've come to terms with no one but myself,
and so I hear a purer water-music

someone will overhear. There was accord
between the light in us and light in day;
my hometown glittered in the man I spoke to;
my hometown his, a business life's adoption.

He knew this city, took full being from it,
no less than from the panoramic larch,
its boughs sun-sinewed with fecund nodes of fire,
than from the things we talked of into town.

Speech stilled us to accomplished silences,
and when I left him at the fruiterer's,
an old-timer's place as modern as old age,
on Front Street affronting by its architecture,

the keen clean sound of him was in my head,
the opulence of sun a coronal
for the rock crystal brilliance of his mind,
deft as the captured concept in a poem.*

His quotations and mine, I made up all of them. They're my own, based
on what I read of Stevens. I found him like a good businessman, all business.
It was difficult for me to see him as a poet when he talked. He had a business
attitude in everything he said. But in what he said, the way he said it, the
poetry came through. I think there's a mirror of him in the poem that really

*Trinity Review, May 1954, p. 40. When Salomon sent Stevens an earlier version of the poem,
Stevens was less than enthusiastic. "I suppose I ought to say that the poem is the works. But it
seems to me that a poem of this nature presents a problem: how to write a poem intended sooner
or later for the eye of a poet—not a poem about a poet but a poem to a poet. My guess is that you
have to write it as one would write to another and that the excess of poetry is out of place.
However, it is interesting to see what you have done. What a memory you have. Many thanks."
(Letter of April 10, 1952, Beinecke Library, Yale University.) When Salomon later sent off the
poem to Rolfe Humphries in October 1952, Humphries asked Stevens' approval before including
it in an anthology he was compiling. Reading between the lines of Stevens' reply, Humphries
decided Stevens preferred that the poem not be published and he returned it to Salomon. It
finally appeared in the Festschrift to celebrate Stevens' seventy-fifth birthday because Marianne
Moore, who liked the poem, suggested Salomon submit it to Trinity Review.

reflects his thinking, but I didn't include in the poem things that I might have included. What I couldn't put into the poem were certain characteristics of him that I took note of. For example, when we went past the fruiterer's, he took out his wallet. And like the rich man that he was, he riffled the bills in such a way that I could see that he was tight with money. He was very careful at what he selected in the fruit and made sure that he took out one ten-dollar bill and not one twenty. As he riffled those dollars, one could see dominance there. The man knew exactly what he did. The Italian fruiterer showed great courtesy, and Stevens simply acted as if [to say], "Well, I'm bestowing money on you, and I'm getting some good fruit."

Robert Frost, with whom [Salomon was] very friendly, said to me, "He's a swell from Harvard. How did you find him?" And I said, "I like his poetry, but I didn't like the man at all, the man as man." Frost, who himself was on a pinnacle and knew he was, said, "He looks down on everybody."

William Van O'Connor

The sole occasion on which I met Stevens was in the summer of 1946. We stopped off in Hartford to visit with friends, the Edward Hirshes. At that time they lived in Unionville and he taught at St. Joseph College. The day before we arrived they had had a visit from a Hartford Accident and Indemnity Co. man who wanted to find someone who might talk with Mr. Stevens about a phrase he was using in an essay—the phrase was "from [the] chromatic to [the] clear."[11] Ed Hirsh said that a friend of his (me) who was interested in modern poetry was arriving the next day. The upshot was that Ed Hirsh and I visited with Stevens in his office. He was writing the piece on William Carlos Williams that later appeared in *Briarcliff Quarterly*, and he was trying to explain how the poet moved from the concrete to the abstract. We talked about a lot of things. I told him that we were going to visit with the Karl Shapiros, who were then in Connecticut, at Gaylordsville, and he asked me whether Shapiro needed financial help of any kind. He didn't, but I gathered that Stevens was offering to help if he had needed help. We also talked about a scholarly book on Crashaw that had received a good deal of attention. He was noncommittal about it, but from the doorway, as we left, he said he wouldn't be found dead in bed with the book. I also remember his making a point about not having literary people out to his house. Someone—my recollection is that it was Norman MacLeod—had phoned him a couple of times and on the second occasion Stevens was quite abrupt with him.[12]

Peter Lee

In March 1951 I sent a group of my own poems to Stevens at the suggestion of the late William Van O'Connor, who thought that mine resembled Stevens'. When I came to Yale in September of that year, I wrote to Stevens if I might visit him in Hartford. He told me to come to his office at twelve-fifteen. When I got there I was led to his office by his secretary, and behind a huge desk sat Stevens, a well-dressed man with a silk tie the color of azalea or coral. Our conversation was mostly social. We went to the Canoe Club; he had a martini and cold roast beef. Then we went to Elizabeth Park in a chauffeur-driven car.

We sat down and talked about poetry in general. He was quiet, reflective, contemplative and wise—and, perhaps, also a bit lonely. I saw him several times thereafter. He usually avoided discussing his own poems; when I would ask him about specific passages or poems he would reply that they are too easy to require any comments. When I asked him whom I should read he recommended Randall Jarrell and two French poets, Francis Ponge and René Char. He was always happy to help me; he wrote recommendations, read some of my translations from Korean poetry, and he would jot down his suggestions, occasionally in French, such as *"c'est beau, n'est-ce pas?"* His knowledge of East Asian literature was based on Arthur Waley's translations from Chinese and Japanese poetry. But he had a strong taste for Oriental paintings and old books. When I made presents of two Korean paintings, he was delighted and told me that he had kept them in his own rooms to look at. He seldom talked about his own family. He regretted, however, that he could not take me to his home. He told me that he loved long evenings of reading and listening to music, particularly opera.

His abiding ambition was to make a trip to Europe; when I went to the Continent in May 1954, he was excited. When one writes one cannot be as relaxed, free and casual as [when] one talks to a person next to you, but his letters were full of wisdom, candor, warmth, and sometimes melancholy, as when he wrote me about his seventy-fifth birthday:

> I could answer you in French but, if I did, you wouldn't know it. It was wonderful to have your postcard in French. More than anything else it made me understand how much a Korean student, or, if you like, a young Korean scholar, and a somewhat old American student who never had time to become a scholar resemble each other. I wanted all my life to go to Paris but what would have been important when I got there was

the ability to leave the hotel in the morning and wander around all over the place all day long before returning to the hotel in the evening. There used to be in the town in which I was born in Pennsylvania a young man who died young but whom I knew very well. Somehow or other, London had captured his imagination and there are thousands of places in London that he wanted to visit but never did. I suppose the world is full of people like that and that in this very building practically everyone spends part of every Sunday reading the travel supplements in the newspapers. The travel supplements, nowadays, relate chiefly to well built girls in bathing suits and while that sort of thing is an immense attraction, what with the ship's bars and bathing pools and dancing salons, all it does to me is to make me feel old, like spilling tea on my waistcoat or finding that I have eaten too much for breakfast when I have hardly eaten anything.[13]

José Rodríguez Feo

When I started this [Cuban] magazine in '44, *Origenes*, I tried to make a selection of the best modern American poets, and I wrote him and asked him for permission [to translate "Esthétique du Mal"]. I knew I wouldn't have any difficulty because all the other famous poets like Eliot I had written to had said it was all right because they knew it was not a commercial magazine. It was a very select and small magazine. I suppose they were, too, pleased to have their poetry translated into Spanish and maybe the exotic thing of having a magazine in Havana publishing their things. He was very generous and nice in writing me immediately and saying that it was all right.

[After corresponding for some two years, Stevens met Rodríguez Feo in New York in 1947.] Everybody has a sort of romantic idea of what a poet looks like, so I was very amazed in a way when I saw this gentleman. I knew he was an older man, but I didn't know he was so much older. At that time he was sixty-eight. And then you imagine, too, the presence and the way that poets dress, disheveled-like; that, too, is a romantic conception. I knew already he was in business, and he looked a true businessman in a way. But at the same time he didn't give you the impression of the typical American businessman in his appearance, who is more aggressive-looking, because there was something of the gentleman. I think we met at the Ritz Towers.

Once or twice I do remember going to Hartford. I didn't feel very happy. He never took me to his house, and he was very mysterious about his family. When I went to see him for the first time in Hartford, he said, in sort of an apology, his wife wasn't feeling very well and he didn't think I'd enjoy going to the house. That's when I had a first inkling there was something wrong with her. He took me to his club. I had the impression we were sort of isolated in this place [the Canoe Club], surrounded by these things that didn't have anything to do with us. He transformed himself in a way; he'd change when somebody that was from this other world of business [came over]. As if he was trying to hide the fact [of his literary life]. Of course this is typically American, because a Cuban, a Frenchman would not feel ashamed to be known as a good poet. So that's why he always said, "Let's meet in New York."

At that time I was a very literary sort of person. I read a lot, and I was involved like all young men in this idealistic world of letters. So naturally all my conversation had to do with literature. I remember asking him about different poets because I wanted to get some orientation about the people that I would publish. At first he was very cautious when he talked about somebody. For instance, he would say something praising somebody, but at the same time he would have this ironic smile, like he gave you the impression that he wasn't really telling you all that he meant, really. You might ask him, "Well, what do you think of this poet X?" and he'd say, "He's fine, he's written a book that is nice," and so on. But then he'd have this little smile and make you think, Maybe he's kidding me. Of course there was always this vein of mockery in him, and of humor, because he had a wonderful sense of humor. I remember, on another occasion, when I asked him about Eliot he gave me the impression that he didn't like Eliot very much. But he said to me that he was a good poet in the sense of the *métier*, he knew his poetry. When you talked about a poet that he didn't like, he never said outright "I don't like him," but it was the way he talked. I don't think we ever talked about any American poet in which he was sort of affirmative in saying "Yes, I really like him. I think he's a great poet." Never. He was at first a little coy because, I suppose, I was asking him questions, so he was somewhat cautious. But after a certain time—you know how it is when you know somebody after a half hour or maybe an hour of conversation. . . . Although we didn't talk very long that time, because we went out somewhere; we went into some fruit store after that; he wanted to see some fruits. He was always going to fruit stores to buy things.

I remember from his letters and from his conversation, when I asked him about American writers, especially if they were alive, he was very coy and very reserved in making any statement. But when he was talking about foreign writers, French or Italian or English, I believe his opinions were very, very good. And he might discover things that not even a man who speaks the language [did]. I was always amazed at this marvelous perception he had of these things when I talked to him. To be frank, that is one of the reasons I became such an admirer of him, and why I always wanted to see him again, because I was fascinated when I talked to him. I met other important poets in America and in England many times on account of having this magazine, like Eliot. Eliot, to me, was a complete bore. I met Stephen Spender, who was very intelligent, William Carlos Williams, so many others, critics and so on, but none of them impressed me so much as he when he was talking about poets and literature. For instance, one of the most incredible things was [after] he received that bunch of *Origenes* that I sent him so he would know the kind of magazine that I was doing. [Even] if he didn't know Spanish well enough to read the magazine, he wrote to give me his impression of the magazine. He had this wonderful phrase, "Man's fever is not present here."[14] That's incredible, because today in Cuba the people who have criticized that magazine and the poets who were around that movement in *Origenes*— because *Origenes* was a movement, besides [being] a magazine—have criticized it precisely for that. Man's fever is not present here because it was not exactly a magazine of writers who belonged to that pure poetry tendency that is exemplified, for example, by Henri Brémond, [yet] they were poets [who] were not interested in the daily, the realistic sort of literature. They were Catholics, they were idealists, who had the idea that poetry was the most important thing.

Another very interesting thing was when he read the essay by Aníbal Rodríguez. I don't know if he knew that Aníbal was the brother of Mariano Rodríguez, the painter whose painting he liked so much, but he read that essay on *alegría* and immediately he was fascinated by that idea [of] *alegría, felicidad. Alegría* is not exactly happiness; *alegría* is something like *gaiety*. He could see that, because he is the poet of the enjoyment, in the sense that those realities that he speaks about—for instance, when he talks about fruits or when he talks about pictures, or looking at something in nature—those are the things that make life enjoyable. He's a hedonist, in that sense. That's what I noticed immediately, because Cubans or Latins by temperament are very much in that wave—in that *onda*, as we say—of enjoying life as different, for instance, from the Americans who are by their backgrounds puritanical. To the Americans, anything that is joyful for itself—for instance, sex or enjoying a meal, wine in itself—they don't consider that to be completely good. For instance, the first time we went to the Chambord, a very good restaurant, he said to me, "José, we will have one of your tropical fruits because I see on the menu they have avocados, alligator pears." They brought us half of the avocado, which was very expensive; in the center they had cheese. To him that was a beautiful thing; it became almost a poetic object, to be eaten, but to be enjoyed, to be looked at. Then the wine. He gave me the impression of being a Frenchman or an Italian, not an American, and I asked myself how did he come by that. I don't know: the poet in him, the aesthetician? So from the very beginning, I noted this love of life in his enjoyment.

Then, too, when we talked for the first time about Cuba, and he told me he had [also] been to Florida and his nostalgia for this. [The] first time he came to Cuba [1923], in the letter he wrote he gives you the impression he didn't enjoy Havana very much; it's a very strange letter.[15] He said [to Rodríguez Feo] he enjoyed Havana very much, but the thing he enjoyed mostly was the climate, nature, the sky, the natural aspect. Not the city, the tropics. And the air. He said he thought the air in Cuba had something very special about it. I said, "Are you saying about the air something similar to what is said in *The Tempest*? It's a wonderful description of the air in the Bahamas. There's something soft and sweet about the air." He said, "Yes, and how funny that you should talk about *The Tempest*," because obviously he was remembering that, too. He always talked with nostalgia about the South and south Florida. And the climate, too. Of course, this is typical of the people who live in the cold country, but to him it was not going to Florida [or] going to Havana to get away from the cold. It was something sensuous in his appreciation of being in Florida: what he felt in the skin. He said that [there] you live with your senses more than [you do when] you live in a cold place. This has to do with his poetry; it was part of his personality. It is interesting, for instance, to compare other American poets, like Elizabeth Bishop, who lived in that world, and the things they have written. If you read that, you see that nothing of that appears. Why? Because they didn't have the same sensitive response that he had. You might say anybody who comes from New England, where it is so cold, when they go to the South, naturally they enjoy it. Yes, but it is not the same thing.

All this goes to show, and in his conversation it was very evident, this man was, inside, something very different from the outside. I remember that he mentioned Mariano, when he saw his pineapple [Rodríguez Feo had sent Stevens some of Mariano's watercolors]; he said that Mariano must be an exquisite person. But he's the exquisite person who saw in this pineapple what probably Mariano didn't see. Mariano saw lines and color, but he saw this exquisite thing of the pineapple.

We would walk a lot when we were in New York. He would say, "Oh, José. You Spaniards, you get tired of walking." I'd say, "Oh, Mr. Stevens, but you've already walked fifteen blocks." He'd say, "Yes, but it's so nice to walk and look at the stores, walk down Fifth Avenue and down the streets in the

Italian sections, look at the fruits, look at the shops, look at the flowers." And he would never get tired. I said to myself, this is a very healthy man, and he was very energetic in that way.

I was about twenty-seven; I looked much younger. He knew that I was a young fellow that read a lot so I could talk to him on a par about French literature and about American literature, so in that way he felt a certain respect. I don't think he gave me much advice. He always advised me that I should live more. That was in accord with his philosophy of life. I kept saying, "Don't kid yourself. I enjoy life more than you think." He'd say, "Oh, yes, but you should be more in contact with the real things of life, not be so absorbed in literature." I never talked about my amorous life, so I think he got the impression I was more or less of an asexual sort of Platonist. Doesn't he say in one of his letters, a little bee going from flower to flower to acquire a lot of knowledge on literary matters? But he was never with me the preceptor, the teacher. We always talked as equals about things.

He always would emphasize when we talked that I had to think more. In a letter he said it once, "You have to think two or three hours every day." When we met he said, "You have to think [not only] about what you read, but you have to think about your life and the things around you." This has a connection with his poetry, that he's really a philosophical poet. Although once, when I mentioned Santayana's book [*Three Philosophical Poets*], he said he didn't think a great deal of the philosophical poets. But he was a philosophical poet; he was not only a philosophical poet, he played with ideas.

We never talked about his poetry. I never asked him those silly questions that Renato Poggioli asked him about what does this mean and that mean because I never tried to find a meaning in poetry.[16] I enjoyed the poetry in itself; I wasn't trying to find the clue. Our conversations were very untranscendental. We'd talk about food; we'd talk about a beautiful necktie, or about a show. We talked about Cuba. We talked about the books we read; mostly they were foreign. As you notice in the letters, they were not American; I was not reading at the time American books. He always wanted to talk about other things, not literature. One of the last times we met, we were having a lot of drinks and I said, "Oh, Mr. Stevens, but I want to talk about literature and you keep evading the issue. You say you don't read and you read a lot." He would say, "No, let's talk about what you were saying about Cuba." I said, "I have the sensation that you're sort of plundering me because when I talk about all these things, all the things come into your poetry." He smiled and sort of laughed. "You're a very smart young Cuban fellow." I said, "All right, if that's going to contribute to your poetry, let's talk about this [and] that," and then we'd talk all these Cuban things.

In one of his letters he remarks, "I . . . really read very much less of everything than most people. It is more interesting to sit round and look out of the window."[17] He said that to me to justify the fact that he didn't read Hemingway. And this is very funny, because this is exactly what Hemingway said to me. Later, I discovered when I went to see Hemingway at La Vigía, where he lived, outside of Havana, that he had all the latest books, all the literary reviews, and everything. They were both on the defensive; I think Hemingway did it for a different reason than Stevens. I think Stevens was a man so well read, who read an incredible amount, if you go through the letters you can see how much he read, so many things that weren't even worthwhile reading, when he got together with me in New York he wanted to talk about other things that interested him as a poet. But in the case of Hemingway, this attitude was the attitude of machismo, of the tough guy: "I'm a very manly guy, I have nothing to do with literature, I write but . . ." So, in reality, Stevens read much more than he would admit; now, when I read the collected letters, I realize he was fooling me all the time.

When I mentioned for the first time Hemingway and my admiration for Hemingway, he got—I wouldn't say angry, but he was very bothered by this. He said he didn't like Hemingway, gave me the impression he thought Hemingway was a rough sort of horrible person. I remember meeting Allen Tate [with Stevens for cocktails a month after Rodríguez Feo first met Stevens in 1947]. Allen Tate was, of course, the opposite from a personality like Stevens. I could see Tate and Stevens at a table; without knowing them, I probably would identify Tate as an intellectual, [a] professor or maybe a mathematician. At the same table I would never identify Stevens as a poet, with a man who worked with ideas. Not only the way they dressed. In the conversation, too, Tate was the sort of man [with] the sort of conversation you expect out of a professor: a little pedantic, without [a] sense of humor and that playfulness that Stevens had. I remember that Stevens was very polite but he didn't give the impression at that time that Tate was the sort of person that he would feel at ease with. I think he wanted to introduce me, because Tate was in the world of magazines and could be helpful. He was a very strange combination of a poet who, on one side, was very intellectual, very rigorous, and at the same time he had this other thing that doesn't go often with the rigorous intellectual poet, of this playfulness, [a] fanciful, fantastic sort of vein in him. I've read some essays in which they accuse him of being a very intellectual poet, but what saves him from being an arid and boring poet is this fantasy vein, this playfulness, which, in a way, is the essence of poetry. That was in his personality when you talked to him, this playfulness in words and making fun of things.

I think if Stevens had devoted himself to doing literary criticism, he would have been a better critic than most of the professional critics who were working in America at that time, because he was a very intuitive man, a very sensitive man and one of the finest poets in America at that time. The thing that I will never forget was when he wrote me when I sent him a book [*Les Impostures de la Poésie*] by Roger Caillois, whom I admired very much. "Caillois is rather a sonorous *phraseur,* and this makes him a kind of intellectual Pierre Loti."[18] Now that's one of the most intelligent and fabulous things I ever heard about Caillois. Pierre Loti is a nineteenth-century French writer who is not very well known. Imagine, to be able to make that comparison! Many years after I read that, I took Caillois's books and read them again and realized that he was very correct in his judgment, and I was the one who was wrong.

I haven't read all the letters, but I think of all the people he knew, he was more benign and nicer about me. I read a review in an English magazine when the book [*Letters of Wallace Stevens*] came, and it said the most wonderful letters in the collection are the ones he wrote to José Rodríguez Feo. I can see now that I must have been something fresh in two senses: because I was a fresh wind blowing from the tropics [and] a fresh young man, because I would be very impudent in the questions I would ask. And I would say, "Oh, I don't agree with you." He really liked that because it stimulated him. I must say at that time I was a pretty good drinker; I don't think even Stevens or Hemingway could put me down. One time we were drinking in New York; we got rather drunk, and I asked him, point-blank, "Now, I want you to tell me, frankly, do you think you're a great poet?" I just said that to provoke him, because he was provoking me, always insisting about my being this Cuban who was too Americanized. I remember we had a political discussion that day, because when he said this, I said, "Well, don't forget that we're an American colony. You still have that idea that we Latins are inferior." He said, "Well, we've had a few drinks, and when you have a few drinks you can say a lot of silly things: but I think that if I'm not a great poet I'm getting pretty near to being a great poet." That was the first time I noticed him boasting about anything. Then I said, "Why do you think you're a great poet?" He said, "I don't know why I think I'm a great poet, but I'm beginning to write great poetry." I don't think he would have said that if he hadn't been drunk, because he was very measured and he very seldom talked like that.

Richard Eberhart

The first time [1936] I saw Wallace Stevens, I was a master at St. Mark's School. I was driving down to New York and stopped on the road to see him. Since I was young and impetuous, I suppose I may have just dropped in on him. Mr. Stevens came out to the curbstone, and we talked for fifteen minutes. I told him how much I admired his poetry. He was affable, very cordial and sophisticated. I was surprised that he didn't ask me into his house. Later in our association he told me once that all he could ever do was to putter around the lawn and help his wife with the gardening, but that it was very difficult to have people in the house. I never saw his wife.

After my short visit, I went on. It was rather astounding that later I should have such a warm friendship with a man so much older, especially since poets are rather cantankerous people in general. From 1946 to 1952, I was in my wife's family business, the Butcher Polish Company of Boston. So I was being a man who was a dichotomous individual: with my rational, working hours I was learning a business; with my free hours, I was doing what I most wanted to do, which was to write poetry. I guess he cottoned to that, because he was the one who was mostly talked about as doing that very same thing. I was on a business trip, selling Butcher Wax. I got to Hartford and went in to see him in the big, marble offices [of the Hartford Accident and Indemnity Company]. They led me in. I saw Wallace Stevens sitting behind this great desk, thirty feet away. It reminded me of anecdotes of Mussolini, who was such a psychologist that he always sat behind a big marble desk at the end of a room—say, sixty feet. Whoever was coming to see Mussolini had to walk a long way, which put the man in an unfortunate position, whereas the man who was receiving him could watch every gesture. I think Stevens probably remembered that I had come to see him before, and he read a lot of modern poetry, so he knew my work, along with that of my contemporaries. He was very cordial. I told him what I was there for. He applauded that; he was a very practical man. He made some calls and told me whom to see to sell my product. He said, "Come back, and we'll have lunch."

When I came back in half an hour, he could see I was in the room but he was very busy. After he had done his job and was ready to go somewhere, we had a chat. He said, "Do you mind if I ask Mr. [Ralph] Mullen [Stevens' fidelity assistant] to come along? Then we won't have to talk shop." I learned later on that this was a ploy of his, a feint. Walking with Mr. Stevens through the marble corridors of the insurance company on Asylum Avenue was itself a great adventure. I felt as if I were a tugboat beside the *Queen Mary*. He had a magnificent stance and moved with stately grace. He was a huge man and moved with a great deal of solemnity. It was very pleasant, but he was rather awe-inspiring.

The three of us got into my little car and went over to the Canoe Club. I noticed that there were no canoes around, except for the one hanging on the wall. Wallace said that there hadn't been a canoe seen on that river for thirty years. It was so hot that day that we all took off our jackets, which you wouldn't think he would do, and there we were in our shirt sleeves. I allude to that in my poem.

AT THE CANOE CLUB
(To Wallace Stevens)

Just a short time ago I sat with him,
Our arms were big, the heat was on,
A glass in hand was worth all tradition.

Outside the summer porch the viable river
Defied the murmurations of guile-subtle
Truths, when arms were bare, when heat was on,

Perceptible as picture: no canoe was seen.
Such talk, and such fine summer ease,
Our heart-life against time's king backdrop,

Makes truth the best perplexity of all,
A jaunty tone, a task of banter, rills
In mind, an opulence agreed upon,

Just so the time, bare-armed and sultry,
Suspend its victims in illusion's colours,
And subtle rapture of a postponed power.[19]

Stevens ordered martinis. After about two, in the hot weather he really loosened up. Then it all came out that this was a great joke, that Mr. Mullen knew Stevens' poetry and knew all about his fame. Out of sensitivity to the business colleagues, he didn't want to be overweeningly fond of himself as something besides a businessman. It was shrewd, too, that he didn't want to play the poet to incoming people like myself. He had to pretend it was a business lunch. Then we just talked about poetry. He talked a little about Delmore Schwartz; he had read Schwartz and thought well of him. Then we talked about some of the then-young poets around. Mullen talked poetry, too. He was learned enough.

The most remarkable lunch I had with him was one time when Sam Morse, whom I saw quite a bit of, and I took Wallace Stevens to Berlin, Connecticut, twenty miles away. Stevens said, "There's an old German restaurant [Naher's Inn] down the pike. Would you like to go there?" We sat at a round table; it was a homey place, very comfortable, rather like some types of old Boston restaurants. Here again we started drinking cocktails. He liked to drink, and we must have had three, maybe more. Take them slowly and talk and talk about poetry. I didn't have a tape recorder, but I wish I had [had]. At such lunches it was as if there was a perfect freedom between participants. It wasn't as if one needed to talk all the time. It was as if each person, the three of us, were whole beings, and you just talked as you wanted to without any program, without any self-consciousness that you had to do it a certain way. He was so charming a man and so sophisticated. That's what I liked about him. He would give a certain trope, a sentence or something, and you would relish it. He was an aesthetician *par excellence.* And we got to know each other so well that we relished each other's silences as well as what was said.

Then we had lunch. Naher's always gave a great big German meal. Stevens said he had to be very careful about what he ate at his age because "If I indulge in too much drink and too much eating, I won't be able to eat for two or three days. It will ruin my system for quite a long time." He was so thick-bodied, I think he had a problem this way in his last years.

Now this was simply delicious: in came a man about Stevens' age who spotted him and came over. What happened in the next fifteen minutes was marvelous. He hadn't the faintest notion that Wallace Stevens was a poet of note and excellence. If he did he was more subtle than I thought, but the point of this was he wasn't subtle at all, that he was the commonest man in the world. We [Morse and Eberhart] were almost snickering because it was so strange. But Stevens was such a worldly business type that he cottoned immediately to the commonness of this old friend of college days, whom he hadn't seen for years. And they just talked the utmost banalities for twenty minutes. Then he got tired of it: "Well, nice to see you, Wally." I thought this was a marvelous example of the largeness of Stevens' world. We had recognition signs, but Stevens was a very polite man; he wouldn't run down his friend to us. I must have seen Stevens for lunches like these eight or ten times.

When we were living at 10 Hilliard Place near Harvard Square, he used to come to see us once a year and go to the football game. He'd have a few martinis with other friends and then come and have a few with us. He was always very cordial, very unprepossessing. He was a very distinguished-looking man. I was twenty-five years younger, so I think he was a sort of father figure. You had a certain respect for him due to his age, not only his position in letters. He never talked lightly; he just talked naturally. He was perfectly friendly; he didn't hold back. If there were other people around, he was just delightful. It was as if he were a businessman: he tried to tone down the idea that he was a great poet.

[Before one of his Harvard readings] Stevens visited us and wanted to be taken around to see the architecture. He was, as I said, a huge man and complained about getting into the ordinary American car as we started. Going down Garden Street, he pointed out a big salt-box and said, "When I was in college, in that house lived the last member of the Regency." I thought that was very interesting. Then I took him up to see the Walter Gropius architecture in the new graduate school complex. We drove in, and he actually got out and walked a few steps. He looked it over and didn't say very much. I tried to point out some of the merits of the building, but he was rather silent about it. Then, when we passed the old law school buildings that are made of nineteenth-century red brick, I was so amused when Wallace —as, I guess, I thought of him—remarked somewhat dryly as he cast his eyes over these old buildings, "I wonder why it is that they can't make architecture as good as these buildings were?" I thought that this was remarkable, because as an artist his poetry was not only with these times but even prophetic. He had his imagination in words, and yet he had a blind spot for Mr. Gropius, who, in his art, was considered the most newfangled of them all at that time. Of course, I didn't argue with him. He was twenty-five years older than I was, so there was quite a generation gap; I was delighted we got on so well. When we came into the Square, he pointed to a place where Billings and Stover had had a pharmaceutical place for a hundred years and said that was where Robert Frost had lived when Frost was an undergraduate there: "But I never knew him."

After taking him around the town, we got to the place of his reading, which was Sever Hall, where all these readings have been since time immemorial. It's not a very large hall; maybe it holds two hundred. There were about fifty people who couldn't get in, so the chairman moved the meeting to Emerson Hall; that took a long time. I had seen it happen once before, but this story has rather an astounding ending. Mr. Stevens sat behind the desk and began reading a few poems in his rather flat and unexpressive way. He wasn't one of the best readers of poetry; he never took the slightest trouble to project his voice beyond his normal speaking range. If you listen to his records, they're the same: very interesting voice, but totally nondramatic. By this time there were a hundred more people outside who couldn't get in. Since Mr. Stevens was well along in years and it was felt he wouldn't be reading too many more times, all these people wanted to hear him. Then they made a second decision to move over to the basement of the Fogg Museum. I remember what a strain this was emotionally and psychologically; it spoiled the effect of the reading. Forty minutes at least were taken up before the people finally got to hear the poet. What it did to him, of course, I don't know, though he got through his reading all right. It was interesting, however, that he was by this time so popular that hundreds wanted to hear him.

My admiration for him from the first time I started reading Stevens, which must have been in the middle thirties, was enormous. The more I read, the more I liked his mind and his poetry. As the literary climate established itself, the world was dominated for decades by Eliot and Pound. And, I must say, I was a great lover of Eliot. But as time went on, I came to think Stevens was the mountain peak of those times. The reputation of Eliot sank enormously for very complex reasons. One of the reasons is because his art was so intimately aligned to Christianity. As the world has de-Christianized itself, people have tended to like either Stevens or Williams. It seems obvious that Stevens has no followers; he hasn't produced a school of Stevens people. It is also obvious that Williams has had an enormous number of followers, even while he was alive. I think that's because Williams was an objectivist and because he believed in America, the America of commotion and motion, the whole zany part of America that people can relate to. Whereas Stevens became more and more aloof, more insular and more wound up in his own imagination. Williams, as a matter of fact, had more impact on the poetic language than Stevens. Williams tried to invent new forms; he was always more inventive than Stevens. Stevens was a more monumental mind; that gives him a kind of grandeur. I'd never use a word like that for William Carlos Williams. The reason Stevens will last hundreds of years, though (in contrast, say, to W. H. Auden), is because his mind was not enmeshed in the goings on of the day; it was on more eternal aspects of reality.

It's remarkable that our country has produced these two disparate characters [Williams and Stevens] at the same time. And yet my taste has been to favor Stevens, just because he is more private, more imaginary. I think he has a richer and more sensual and sensuous gift with words. There were whole decades in my life when I felt comfortable with Stevens. Now maybe I was wanting a father figure, but I felt I belonged in his ambience, to his view of the world, and I took pleasure in that realization. I remember, for instance, every time I would go to New York, I would think of New York City from a Stevens point of view, not from a Williams point of view.

Yet now, in the last few years, I regret to say that I think that's all fallen apart. The world has changed so much that Stevens is now a man of history. I don't think he speaks to the young people today, with the chaos, Watergate and the Vietnam war that we've lived so horrendously through in the last ten years. As a matter of fact, I wrote a poem the other day, trying to put this into words. I think of a man just the opposite of Wallace Stevens, Stevens Wallace. And I think of poetry as perhaps poetry of the people, not of the elected, the elite intelligentsia. I tried to compose that poem by seeing it two or three ways with different protagonists. Now, I couldn't have written that poem ten years ago. This is not a poem against Stevens, but with all that's happened, it seems to me that poetry has to be vitally associated with the commonweal, with what people do and with what goes on in the world. We're not going to have a Wallace Stevens in the next twenty years; we're going to have an entirely different kind of poetry. He lived in a world of grand Republicanism, of big houses, of wanting to make a large salary and of living with noble people.

One of the most provocative things that Eliot said was that in poetry there is no competition. In a sense there is no competition, say, between Wallace Stevens and William Carlos Williams. I mean, we've got them both; you don't have to say one is better than the other. On the other hand, from a practical point of view, it seems that there is nothing but competition in the arts and in poetry. You can say that the prizes and all that are not a good thing, and there is a lot that's bad to be said about them. But another, more charitable, way to look at it is that a big prize draws the attention of many people to a good book. He didn't try to play the game, as Williams did, trying to be better known. As a matter of fact, that's where Stevens' aloofness really came in. Some of his best books were published by little presses. Think of the difference between Stevens and Frost in that regard. Stevens would never have demeaned himself to want to go to a presidential inauguration and read a poem. Now that doesn't mean he was a snob. He had a much more private idea of what art was. Wallace would have thought the best thing would be the real intimacy of a reader in silence with his book. He gets the man, he gets the poet just from the purity of the page. You don't have all the readings, the audiences, [the] prizes, belonging to the societies and the academies. I know, for example, that he didn't have the boyish reactions that William Carlos Williams would have had or I had to prizes. He wasn't that ebullient, or that outgoing, or that simple. He took it in stride.

I was appalled to learn that after his death his wife burned up two or three hundred letters. Holly told me she thought she had gotten all the main literary things out of the house, but in the attic there was a stack of things. Now maybe they were only personal letters, when he was courting her, which she didn't want the public to know. I thought that was an absolute crime.

We passed [many] letters back and forth in the last eight years of his life, the time of my chance friendship with him. It was delightful to get these, though sometimes you couldn't read his writing. It was a real literary-intellectual correspondence. I'm sure it would have gone on for years, just talking about anything that we were interested in on a [given] day. Nobody was trying to get something out of the other.

I think the reason why we had a friendship was because of his humor. He had a great sense of humor, and there was a certain comic sense in the fact that here was a younger fellow who was also in business and a poet, too. I think that the first meeting—when I came, not to interview him or to be pompous and ask about the meaning of poetry but wanting to sell some wax —he cottoned to that. That set the stage. Then we just had an affinity; he had affinities with other kinds of people, all different.

Samuel French Morse

I had won the poetry fellowship [to the Cummington School of the Arts, Cummington, Massachusetts] in the summer of 1936. I went to Cummington '36, '37, '38, in the summers. I was one of the people who thought that Cummington not only ought to have a good chamber group, but it should, since it was teaching literature and painting and sculpture, try a press. Katharine Frazier [the school's director] got excited about this, and eventually they were able to get an old press. Harry Duncan had come to Cummington in '38, and he, of course, became the printer. We talked about people we'd write [asking for poems to publish: William Carlos] Williams, Stevens, Allen Tate and [R. P.] Blackmur. I was on the board of the press and the one who wrote Stevens [in] 1940 that we'd like something. He was fascinated by fine printing and elegant books, so he sent for all the things the Cummington Press was publishing. Having approved, he commented that he had commitments to Knopf, but, when these commitments were fulfilled, he would be glad to send something to the press.

I was so flattered when I first wrote that we'd like something, and he said, "Well, why don't you do a book of your own?" and he'd be glad to write a preface.[20] I had published about a dozen or so poems, a number in *Poetry*; I was appearing a little bit. But I waited. [In 1944, Cummington Press published Morse's *Time of Year*, with a preface by Stevens.] He was not one of the proud possessors, but he grew up in the world of the proud possessors. He did not want to be known as a patron of anything; he avoided that. He would not be on the list when *Four Saints in Three Acts* was done. But it would have given him pleasure to be the discoverer of somebody who amounted to something—even as a collector of paintings; one can see this in his correspondence with Mlle. Vidal [Stevens' Paris bookseller, who bought paintings for him in later years]. Yet he was not about to be imposed on, not about to waste much time from his own work on this.

There was that first flurry of contact in '40; then, two years later, just as he was getting ready to do the preface to *Time of Year*; and one or two letters when I was stationed in Florida during the war. Then nothing until I got to Hartford. [In 1951, Morse joined the faculty of Hartford's Trinity College. The year before, however, he and his wife first met Stevens, after writing that they would be passing through town.]

Elsie came to the door, peered around, and said, "He's around *back*!" There he was, sitting out enjoying his garden. What is it: "One must sit still to see the world"? We talked and had lemonade, or something to drink. Elsie even then didn't like schoolteachers: she came out, we were introduced, and that was that. It was the iris season, and there were magnificent irises that had been bought, I suppose, from a grower out on the West Coast. Elsie had cultivated them, and they were handsome indeed. But Stevens did not think of them in terms of color, and shapes, and sizes—things that one might have thought he would have commented on. He talked about them in terms of money. I think of William Carlos Williams' poem, "Late for Summer Weather": walking through "heaps of fallen maple leaves / still green— and / crisp as dollar bills."[21] Everything was in terms of dollar bills to Stevens. How expensive the garden was, not in an offensive way, but just surprising. [There] was that materialistic streak in him. One of his aphorisms, "Money is a kind of poetry,"[22] is a very nice way of putting it, but it's materialism. This is perfectly all right; it's just a little surprising in a poet, that's all. [At the time, Morse was working on his dissertation about Stevens.] I did ask him one or two questions that Ph.D. candidates would ask. I knew [from] that first meeting that I shouldn't ask him academic questions.

I heard from him first [after settling in Hartford], that amusing letter about why I hadn't come to see him: "When I noticed in the newspaper last fall that you were coming to Hartford I thought that I should see something of you but I suppose that it is like living in Boston without ever getting to see Bunker Hill."[23] I was working on the dissertation and didn't want to bother him with a lot of student-academic kinds of questions. I did not want to impose. We made a date, and I drove him to the Canoe Club. The first thing he told me when we went in was that "We do not talk poetry here." But, of course, we talked about poetry all the time in one way or another. It was very easy, not stuffy at all, sort of bluff good humor. [The lunch] lasted quite a long time. He liked to drink, and we had three or four martinis. Several of the men at the Canoe Club came up and talked. He was very gracious with them. That was after [Stevens received an honorary degree from Mount Holyoke]. They knew about this, and he seemed a little surprised, but they were quite intelligent about it. Again, that American business of being a little wary of his reputation. At the Canoe Club he was just one among many; people seemed to enjoy him, and he seemed to enjoy seeing them. These were business acquaintances, and he was one of the boys. Back of the bartender [were] pictures of nude girls; he wanted to be sure that people understood that he appreciated this, too, nudging me and saying, "See!" I always felt he did this [as if] "Well, this makes me one of the boys."

[A lunch with Stevens at the Canoe Club] had an aura, very civilized and pleasant. It had no great high pitches or low points. It was well-sustained, [but] it wasn't anything for Boswell to take down. Asking him questions was not what I sensed my relationship to be. I thought it was much nicer to know him as a kind of older friend. I would ask him a question now and then. For example, to me the movement of the verse line in "To the One of Fictive Movement," perhaps simply because of some analogue with "Daughters of Time, the hypocritic Days, / Muffled and dumb like barefoot dervishes,"24 was his most Emersonian utterance. There's something of that tonality. He said he had no notion of this. But then poets are always, in one way or another, slightly defensive about influence. He always seemed to me [though] in a very basic way an original. Our conversations were very informal, a little bit of gossip sometimes. He talked once [for example] of Marianne Moore's endless revisions of the fables of La Fontaine; she used to send him revisions. He never got very much [into gossip] about other poets. He did get very angry at Austin Clarke's review of the pirated edition of *The Selected Poems*. He thought Pound was awfully silly, had just made a damn fool of himself—and perhaps was really a traitor. He was very conservative, essentially. Eisenhower was his man, not Stevenson. And that's all right; one didn't have to think of liberal or conservative political values with Wallace Stevens. We had a relatively unliterary relationship, and yet it was all pertinent to my sense of what the poetry really is, which is not that it's so terribly profound, not all literary theory and metaphysics. It seems to me full of a kind of *joie de vivre*, rather intellectual *joie de vivre*. No [impassioned discussion] that I can remember. He did most of his best positioning by letters. His best social relationships were essentially through letters, until the very end of his life. But [our] relationship, which was all right to begin with, got easier and easier. It reached the point where he called me "Sam." And this was not easy for him, to address people by first names.

I saw him most often by himself; we had lunch together. Two or three times Richard Eberhart came; once, Norman Pearson. Stevens was very amusing [when Stevens met a college classmate, while lunching with Eberhart and Morse]. Stevens knew the conversation was banal, but he enjoyed this, the way he enjoyed writing down banalities overheard at the office, which make up some of those "From Pieces of Paper" [a collection of jottings, some of which Stevens later used as titles or lines in poems]: "It's going to be a beautiful day," or "Red Loves Kit"; in "Connoisseur of Chaos," "things chalked / On the sidewalk so that the pensive man may see."[25] Graffiti, if you like. "The News and the Weather": the title of that poem is from the newspaper or the radio. He loved to listen to the radio. There was one program that intellectuals would be very snobbish about, but Stevens was perfectly capable of listening to some of these things and finding them amusing. He wasn't so insecure he had to make an image of himself as appreciating only the best. He did not like Mozart very much; Berlioz was obviously more to his taste. I said something once about Haydn, [whom] I liked, and he sort of muttered, that was all.

He had quite an elegant [record] collection, not huge by any means.[26] Of course, 78s always took up much more room; you had to be discriminating. He was a great buff of the Schnabel Beethoven: he had the famous thirty-two sonatas Dr. Schnabel did, the original [Beethoven Sonata] Society set. I don't remember much opera. I know he had the Maggie Teyte recordings, particularly the Berlioz songs from *Nuits d'Eté*. Then he'd been listening to Mahler toward the end of his life; I don't know, maybe this is one of the things people say for the hell of it.

The only public appearance [of Stevens'] I ever saw was [at] the [1954 YMHA] reading in New York and the autographing afterward. He loved the landscape going down [as Morse drove him along the Merritt Parkway to Manhattan]. The feeling that he has in that little piece on Connecticut that he did for the Voice of America and in "A Mythology Reflects Its Region," that kind of feeling was there. He gossiped a little about some writers. I remember his asserting that E. E. Cummings had behaved better than anybody else during the war. It wasn't anything malicious at all, perhaps a little skeptical about the accomplishments of some of our poets. He, again, could be very generous, always very generous with Delmore Schwartz [for example]. I'm not sure how deep his interest in the work of other poets was, because he was so much concerned with making the next poem himself, in spite of the fact he had dry spells like every other poet. But from *Parts of a World* [1942] on, there were very few times when he wasn't writing or thinking about writing.

He was not a good reader, but [that evening at the YMHA] he made things go very well: could people hear? and so forth. He wanted to be sure he was heard. As he read the poems, I learned something about the way certain lines went together and a little about his sense of stress and organization. You had to get this from watching and listening. He handled himself easily on the stage and was able to keep it from being a run-through. He had a little bit of manner, not anything that was noticeable. [At the autographing] he was very short with someone; he had the feeling that someone wanted the book signed to make it more valuable rather than because he really cared about the poems.

[In 1954 Morse, faculty adviser to *Trinity Review*, organized a special Wallace Stevens issue to celebrate the poet's seventy-fifth birthday.] He said it was like a very rich chocolate cake; he was impressed by my having unearthed some of the rejects from back in the *Harmonium* period. Two or three of those I never knew why he rejected: "The Indigo Glass in the Grass" is great fun; I liked "Peter Parasol" and other things that disappeared. I was surprised that he didn't say anything about [T. S.] Eliot's letter, because you knew Eliot was sort of lying between his teeth: I didn't realize that Mr. Stevens wasn't published in England.* Eliot knew perfectly well that Mr. Stevens wasn't published in England; Faber and Faber would be the only company that would publish him. We asked a number of people [to write in appreciation] who didn't contribute. The most notable one was Mark Van Doren. I thought because of the Cornwall poem, "Reality Is an Activity of the Most August Imagination," that Van Doren [who lived in Cornwall] would have been willing to say something. He said he thought that Mr. Stevens had more than sufficient attention.

There was very little association with Trinity until the *Festschrift*. Then Don Engley [the Trinity Librarian] urged Mr. Stevens to exhibit his hand-

---

*In 1953, Faber and Faber published the first authorized English edition of Stevens' verse, *Selected Poems*. "I am rather ashamed of the fact that Stevens has not been published in London before," Eliot noted in *Trinity Review*, May 1954, p. 9. "I had taken for granted that some other firm had published his work, and wondered at their incompetence in taking so little trouble to make the fact known: it was one of my fellow directors who first called my attention to the fact that Stevens, although his name and some of his poems were very well known to the élite who really know, had had no book to himself." On November 22, 1950, Knopf's London agent, Pearn, Pollinger and Higham, had sent a copy of Stevens' latest book, *The Auroras of Autumn*, to Morley Kennerley, Eliot's fellow director at Faber and Faber, pointing out that the author had recently received the Bollingen Prize and inquiring whether this English firm would like to publish the work. The matter was then brought to Eliot's attention. He proposed that instead of publishing *The Auroras of Autumn*, it would be better to do a selection from Stevens' poetry as a whole as his debut volume in England. Eliot indicated that if that book sold well, his firm would also consider bringing out a volume of Stevens' collected poems at a later date.

somely bound copies of his own books, which he agreed to do. Stevens once did say something to the effect that Trinity had ignored him for a long time, [but it was] nothing so desperate as a prophet without honor in his own country.

[After Stevens' death in August 1955] I went to the house with Don Engley as people appointed by the bank to go through the library [to] put a value on it. It seemed a very conventional upper-middle-class house. What did he say about Westerly Terrace: not a very edifying neighborhood? Mrs. Stevens fed us, and it was quite true that she was a very good cook. Mrs. Stevens was perfectly willing to let us look through things. When we went through, things had been obviously picked up, but nothing had been very much disturbed. There was a great deal of correspondence, obviously, at the office; he didn't bring a lot of things home. Papers were in bureau drawers. The letter from [Archibald] MacLeish inviting him to be the Charles Eliot Norton Professor of Poetry was probably under some socks.* That letter from [William Carlos] Williams about "The Worms at Heaven's Gate"† was up in the attic in the famous red folder, along with other odds and ends. The red folder was the biggest collection of early material that remained. In his closet were some of his books: his first edition of *Ulysses* was on a shelf. There was a [sitting] room [connecting with Stevens' bedroom] with a piano [on which was] some of the silk material Mr. van Geyzel [a planter-correspondent of Stevens'] had sent in from Ceylon. Those little bits [Oriental figures] that Harriet Monroe's sister sent him [from China] were on a desk in that room,‡ along with the big collection of the writings of Alain. He collected Alain because Alain was an aphorist; he had book after book of proverbs in languages many of which he couldn't read, obviously, [such as] Armenian. It was a nice collection in a kind of breakfront the Alain collection was in [also]. There were other books in that room, some of the things he liked very much and, I'm sure, valued

---

*In November 1954, Archibald MacLeish invited Stevens to be the Charles Eliot Norton Professor at Harvard the following academic year. Partly out of concern that a leave of absence from the insurance company would force the issue of his retirement, Stevens declined, with great regret.

†On June 8, 1916, Williams sent a letter to Stevens, suggesting some changes in the manuscript of this short lyric. "For Christ's sake," Williams urged his friend, "yield to me and become great and famous." (*The Wallace Stevens Journal*, Fall 1979, p. 73.)

‡In September 1922, Mrs. Lucy Monroe Calhoun, the widow of a former U.S. minister to China and the sister of *Poetry*'s editor Harriet Monroe, shipped a package to Stevens, who had asked her to do some shopping for him in China. She sent a small table screen and tiny figure, both of white jade; a pair of black crystal lions; and a wooden figure of Hson-hsing, god of happiness and longevity. Years later, Stevens remarked to Harriet Monroe that the statue was "one of the most delightful things that I have." (Letter of April 5, 1935, *L WS*, p. 280.)

considerably. His copy of Tom McGreevy's *Poems* may have been there,* certainly some of the Cuala Press books, things of that kind. The books were hither, thither and yon. One could, perhaps, have traced his interest in poets by seeing who had been relegated to the attic. He had every book of good color reproductions of Paul Klee up to 1955. He really did like Klee very much; I always felt there was kinship in spite of some of the things he says about modern art. That was a crucial thing for him: "One cannot spend one's time in being modern when there are so many more important things to be."[27] And although he is an innovator and a discoverer, I always felt he belonged to a line of continuity, that he was not turning things upside down deliberately. He wanted to do something new, but he did not feel a Poundian compulsion to make it new at all costs.

I don't think that [Elsie Stevens] liked the books and paintings very much. He did say once that he had to be careful, and explained he sort of sneaked the new paintings into the house: a new painting would go into his room. He did also complain once about Mrs. Stevens throwing away things that he cherished, particularly his literary magazines, which he collected. Stevens knew before he died that I wanted to write a book about him and had begun something. He was not offended by this; quite the contrary, he was most generous about what he gave me and the encouragement he gave. But Mrs. Stevens very much resented anyone's wanting to know anything about their lives. And she insisted that poetry was a respite for him.† I would say it was the only thing that really concerned him, even more than all the good things that made poetry possible. He was very loyal. I was convinced that his great pains never to involve anyone with him at Westerly Terrace signified domestic discord of some sort. In the later years, when he was invited to go to Paris for [a] UNESCO meeting of artists and writers, he refused, partly by saying Mrs. Stevens was not a good traveler. In other words, he may have used her as an excuse to avoid doing what he really didn't want to do, because he preferred the Paris of his imagination to the real thing. On the other hand, with the certain amount of tongue-wagging that has taken place, it seems to

*For a profile of Stevens' largely epistolary friendship with Dublin poet and art critic Thomas McGreevy, see my "The Irish Connection: Wallace Stevens and Thomas McGreevy," *The Southern Review*, Summer 1981, pp. 533–41.

†When Elsie Stevens learned that Morse was at work on a biography of her late husband in 1960, she wrote, "I must say that a critical biography is not needed for the understanding of Mr. Stevens' poetry. Mr. Stevens' poetry was a distraction that he found delight in, and which *he kept entirely separate from his home life,* and his business life—neither of them suitable or relevant to an understanding of his poetry. Particularly with his home life, which I would regard as an intrusion and an intervention. The publicity that Mr. Stevens' renown offers, is offensive to me. . . ." (Letter of December 20, 1960, HL.)

me he was also being very much the gentleman about allowing no distemper or rancor to be visible. He very often made it seem to be his shortcoming rather than anything of hers.

Donald Engley

I recall going to the chairman of the English Department when I first came [as Trinity College Librarian in 1951] saying, "I am amazed that Trinity has never given Mr. Stevens an honorary degree. What's wrong here?" It was something to the effect, "Well, we should have, but now it's too late." My reaction was, "It's never really too late." It was because the English Department at Trinity in the thirties and forties was traditional, stodgy, not rooted in the twentieth century at all. It reflected Hartford's failure to recognize Stevens. At the point [Morse and Engley were visiting with Stevens] we were pioneers.

Sam Morse had arranged for an exhibit of Mr. Stevens' books in Trinity Library, his personal copies of his books, with their fancy bindings. Mr. Stevens wanted to see the exhibit, so Sam and I picked him up. In the process of showing him the Trinity College Library, he mentioned that he would like to see the Watkinson Library also, which was on the top floor. This is Hartford's version of the Boston Atheneum; it was removed to Trinity in return for fireproof housing in 1952. [In the course of the conversation] I explained what a pioneer George Brinley was [whose Americana collection is a highlight of the Watkinson holdings]. Brinley was the kind that would attract Wallace Stevens. Brinley was a peddler; going around the countryside during the Civil War, he found that people's attics were full of what passed for ephemera. Brinley collected for twenty or thirty years. He would give a housewife pots or a new petticoat in return for "junk" in the attic. He realized before he died that he had a major collection of Americana, and in his will directed that the entire collection be sold at auction. This is a landmark sale. Wallace Stevens knew all about George Brinley. I took it as evidence that he was a man of the world of books.

I found out after we arrived upstairs and were standing in the rare book room of the Watkinson Library that he had had a great attachment to the Watkinson Library in its previous existence downtown. He used to go in there during the noon hours to look up things. After this visit [as I was] telling the curator of the Watkinson Library, Miss [Ruth] Kerr about it, she said, "Oh, yes, I remember his coming in at noon quite often, and indeed just a few noons before we were to start to move the books away from its Gothic environs, Mr. Stevens came in and walked around the place for the last time.

I recall his telling me that he hadn't really approved of the Watkinson being moved because of the loss of that architectural background." It [had been] part of the Wadsworth Atheneum on Main Street. It always struck me that for somebody who was so modern in his writing, so avant-garde, he treasured the traditional about Hartford. Maybe this wasn't so surprising after all, because in his own work he reworked the past.

[The tour of the Watkinson Library] followed lunch at the Canoe Club, one of several. Sam and I found ourselves being invited to go to lunch, but it was only on Wednesdays. We had the same menu each time: a martini or two and then lobster stew. He wouldn't get back until three in the afternoon, having left at twelve. We were young men in our thirties; we stood in awe of this man, and when he said, "We'll go to the Canoe Club," that was good enough for us. This got to be embarrassing after a while. We couldn't reimburse him for this. [One afternoon on the way to lunch] I veered to the right instead of going over the Charter Oak Bridge [to the Canoe Club]. He told me I had missed my turn. I said, "No, I didn't." He got more vociferous as we went down the road. He said, "I want to go to the Canoe Club!" We [Morse and Engley] were saying we had something else in mind. We had checked on a place [Naher's Inn] way down on the Berlin Turnpike. My knees were knocking because it's a pretty far piece down the turnpike when you have a protestor. We [had] talked to the host and told him what we were up to. [Afterward] Mr. Stevens agreed that it was a very nice lunch, but he wasn't too expressive about anything. We found shortly thereafter that when a fellow poet or publishing friend came to town, he would say he had just discovered a very nice restaurant and would like to go [to Naher's].

[At their meetings] he seemed very aloof. I wouldn't want to say withdrawn, but he was very enigmatic to me. Of course, how old was he then, seventy? And I was in my thirties. It was probably more my own making, because I had less to say to him than Sam Morse. Yet I found him reasonably easy to talk to because he was interested in the world of books, and I was part of that world. [After his death] for estate purposes Sam and I were [at Stevens' home] to look at the books and paintings, but primarily the books. My general impression is that he would have the complete works of a French poet, Apollinaire, people like this, and he would have them in their original condition. He wouldn't put fancy bindings on them; he wasn't that kind of collector. He reserved Gerhard Gerlach for [some of] his own work, asking that binder to do something special that would fit the books. They were there to be read; he wasn't a paper collector as such. It was a working library. It covered modern literature and the arts and philosophy. There weren't very many rare books.

I don't think I originated very much conversation [at these luncheons]; I enjoyed what I was hearing. I was getting more explanation from him than participating in a poets' corner. [The luncheon discussions had a decidedly literary flavor:] poet-acquaintances that Sam shared with Wallace, a discussion of poetry itself. We would discuss the meaning of a word; we'd work it over and over. It was a typical poet's occupation to be playing with the meaning of a word or the relationship of a couple of words. This would come up sometime [say] from his describing having gone to New York to meet Marianne Moore, as he used to do. He told us one of his favorite customs was to take the train on a Saturday morning to Grand Central, walk up to the Plaza, and meet Marianne Moore for lunch. She'd come over from Brooklyn. Then they would stroll down Fifth Avenue, hit Broadway, and keep on going all the way to the Battery. Sometimes she would take the subway from there; other times, if they hadn't finished their discussion, they'd turn around and work their way up. I remember his describing meetings with Frost in Florida. One thing stands out: Stevens said to Frost, "The trouble with you is you write about things." And Frost replied, "The trouble with you is you write about bric-a-brac."

He was very positive in his likes and dislikes of people. He either liked people or he detested them, that's the way it seemed to me. He particularly seemed to object to people arriving unannounced in town and saying that they just happened to be passing by. Could they come to see him? I recall his being rather emphatic that he wasn't available.

CHAPTER FOUR

A Private Poet in Public

"Authors are actors, books are theatres,"[1] Wallace Stevens once quipped. During his later years, however, Hartford's extremely private man of letters actually found himself on stage, facing the large audiences that had come to hear him perform. Beginning in the 1930s, Stevens occasionally assumed the role of a public man of letters, though always outside Hartford. He appeared most often in four locations within easy driving distance of his home: to see him in Cambridge, New Haven, South Hadley and New York is to see the preparation, the strain, and the reward, as Stevens found himself in the unlikely position of center stage.

· I ·

CAMBRIDGE

Stevens made his debut as a lecturer on December 8, 1936, at Harvard, before the audience that gathered in Sever Hall to hear "The Irrational Element in Poetry."

On April 27, 1936, Theodore Spencer, temporary chairman of the university's Morris Gray Committee, had invited Stevens to talk on poetry or to read from his poetry, perhaps both, in three weeks. When the invitation arrived, however, he was putting the final touches to his long poem *Owl's Clover*, which he sent off to his publisher J. Ronald Lane Latimer less than a week before the date Harvard had set, May 21, for Stevens' appearance. This schedule left the poet little time to prepare a lecture. Nonetheless, he certainly had abundant new material to draw on for the reading Spencer had suggested as an alternative. Not even the honor of taking part in Harvard's 300th anniversary year, however, could entice Stevens onstage simply to do that. At the time, a reading hardly seemed worth the toll a public appearance exacted of him: "I suffer like a child with something 'coming on' as the time for such a thing approaches," he explained to May Sarton when declining her invitation to read in New York a few years later, "and it all grows worse when the time actually arrives. Accordingly, I had rather not. It isn't worth reading in public unless one reads as one reads to oneself, and I can't imagine doing that."[2] Unwilling simply to read at Harvard, then, Stevens declined Spencer's invitation but left the door ajar should his alma mater care to have him lecture at a later date, for lectures were a different matter. "I like to do these papers," he later confided to a friend, "because they clear my mind and make it necessary to take a good look at ideas that otherwise would drift about, vaguely, with no place to go."[3] In less than a week Spencer replied that Stevens would unquestionably be invited the next academic year.

As a result, Stevens was ready, topic in hand, when a letter came from Harvard on November 2, 1936. "If it would suit you to have me write a paper, I shall be glad to do my best," he replied. "In a general way my subject would be the irrational element in poetry. After Mr. Spencer wrote to me last spring, I thought of writing a paper on that subject, but have not yet actually done so. However, there is plenty of time between now and December 8th."[4]

Despite a heavy work load at the office and the onset of the holiday season, Stevens did not feel pressed when the invitation arrived only a month before his scheduled appearance, largely because during the previous year and a half he had unwittingly been jotting down notes for the lecture as he corresponded with the young publisher of *Owl's Clover*. Latimer had put several questions about poetry to Stevens in the preceding months, which had set Stevens thinking about many of the topics he now touched on in this paper, such as the irrational element in poetry: those unaccountable choices that make up a poet's style and subject matter. The invitation to appear at Harvard appealed to this extremely private poet, then, precisely because it was an opportunity to address formally issues he had been writing about offhandedly in spare moments at the office. Composer Arthur Berger, a Harvard graduate student in music at the time, found Stevens' remarks particularly potent. Almost twenty years later, Berger paid his respects to the memory of that day in his musical setting of *Ideas of Order*.

Arthur Berger

Delmore Schwartz, who was a very close friend—we kind of shared a couple of rooms—urged me to go [to Stevens' lecture] and gave me to believe it was a very important occasion.* He had already introduced me to *Ideas of*

---

*The talk provided Schwartz with one of his favorite anecdotes about Stevens, which gained wide currency in New York literary circles in the 1940s. As Schwartz's friend, William Barrett recalls in his memoir, *The Truants: Adventures among the Intellectuals* (New York: Doubleday,

Order, and I was very much taken by it. Delmore admired Stevens greatly.

Stevens was a polished businessman in looks and yet very gentle in his voice, almost like a preacher. For a composer groping for justification, what he preached—and I say preached advisedly—seemed very cogent: "it is probably the purpose of each of us to write poetry to find the good which, in the Platonic sense, is synonymous with God. One writes poetry, then, in order to approach the good in what is harmonious and orderly."⁵ The words *harmonious* and *orderly,* which was advice he was giving to the poet in musical terms, certainly left an impression, because I remembered it vividly when I read the essay again in the posthumous collection. Not perhaps the part about God so much, except in a metaphorical sense. We were in the shadow of Irving Babbitt around Harvard. The implication of some of the things he said could be disturbing—that perhaps in a statement like this, poetry might be spoiled religion. And according to Babbitt, spoiled religion was a very bad thing: one should be a poet in his poetry and religious in one's religion. It was a very loaded [lecture] in those days.

Especially when Stevens got to the subject of escapism: "the greater the pressure of the contemporaneous," Stevens said, "the greater the resistance. Resistance is the opposite of escape."⁶ Now his denial of escapism was itself suspect, and later, of course, in 1941 [in "The Noble Rider and the Sound of Words"] he qualified this remark. "My own remarks about resisting or evading the pressure of reality mean escapism, if analyzed." But he made it clear it's not escapism in a pejorative sense, for he added in this Princeton talk, "The pejorative sense applies where the poet is not attached to reality, where the imagination does not adhere to reality."⁷ His views on escapism or resistance had very sympathetic listeners among us because we were very much aware of this problem: those of us wanting to be artists [were] being pressed that we had to have a message to the people in our art, influence the people. It was never quite clear whether we were supposed to express our

---

Anchor Press, 1982), "Apropos of the alienation of Wallace Stevens, Delmore used to tell the story of Stevens's remark after he had delivered a lecture on poetry at Harvard: 'I wonder what the boys in the office would think of that.' The point seems to be that there was such a disparity between Harvard and the 'boys in the office' that Stevens must have suffered from a sense of alienation" (p. 237).

When asked about his remark a decade after that Harvard lecture, Stevens retorted: "I feel quite sure that there is nothing to the point that I said something in that lecture by way of commenting on the oddness of an insurance man reading a lecture on poetry. I have never made any such comment and have never felt that it was odd for me to be doing such things. Other people say that sort of thing. . . . Is any man supposed to be engaged in his business to the exclusion of everything else and, if he is, what do people think of him?" (Letter to Thomas C. Lea, September 24, 1948, Dartmouth.)

political views or influence people to have other political views. What we wanted to do was to be musicians and poets and painters, not primarily to profess some particular commission no one seemed to have given us. That we should take this upon ourselves didn't exactly appeal.

I myself found it very disturbing and even stopped writing music for a while. What Stevens had to say touched some very sympathetic chord in us, because we were grappling with these problems. I'm not sure I realized at the time how much help his words [were] for me, but I think, later, as I look back, I realize they did a great deal to straighten me out on things like that.

My impression [at the lecture] was that he was very gentle, very sweet; the feeling of a very fine sensibility came across. It was a cool occasion; I don't recall very much hoopla. It was quiet.

There is another aspect I am reminded of. Delmore talked about Stevens a great deal; I'm sure he explained his poetry to me. Delmore [also] read me his [own] book of poetry, *In Dreams Begin Responsibilities,* right about this time. I was curiously surprised that anybody would write poetry nowadays [that was] so conservative. I probably felt even Stevens was a little conservative. I had been brought up on Cummings and Carlos Williams and the *transition* crowd. I'd been around with the really avant-garde composers and painters and musicians and poets in New York, so I had a certain feeling that maybe these people were old-fashioned. It was only when I came to Harvard in 1935, and then through Delmore, I came to know Stevens. It was only later I appreciated how wrong I was, that one doesn't judge a poet by such superficial aspects.

When Stevens was completing "The Irrational Element in Poetry," the week before he was to read it in Cambridge, he found to his dismay that the lecture would not take up the hour set aside for it.* In spite of himself, he had to round out the time by reading from *Owl's Clover,* though he had resisted doing so the previous spring. It was apropos, of course, for his remarks on the predicament of the artist in unsettled times like the 1930s had their roots in

---

*Stevens wrote "The Irrational Element in Poetry" in nine sections, each about a typewritten page. This was in keeping with his taste for the adage and the aphorism, and the lecture reads like a collection of Baconian essays, brief forays into a subject. Like Stevens' subsequent talks, this first lecture looks at its subject as if through a prism, catching varying facets of its theme. As a result, Stevens' essays are often not so much tightly-knit logical sequences as they are montages, with some sections adhering rather loosely to the canvas of the argument.

The danger of composing in such brief units as Stevens used in "The Irrational Element in Poetry" was that this montage might turn into a miscellany of ideas. This may partly account for the fact that in later years Stevens looked back rather harshly to his first lecture, deciding not to include it in his only prose collection, *The Necessary Angel: Essays on Reality and the Imagination* (New York: Alfred A. Knopf, 1951).

the poem itself. When Stevens arrived at Theodore Spencer's home in Cambridge for a cocktail party in his honor after the reading, he found the poetry had been additionally apt to the occasion. One of the guests he met at the gathering on Oxford Street was the poet who had set Stevens composing *Owl's Clover* the year before by asking for a long poem to include in a series of chapbooks put out by a London publisher. "When we were introduced," Conrad Aiken recalled, "he at once said that he regarded me as the godfather of all his recent work, and that it was my request for a book for Dent that had started him off again."*

Mary Aiken

Ted Spencer asked Conrad and me to come around; Conrad wanted to meet Stevens. [Aiken had not attended the lecture.] Conrad never made any public appearances; he did the Gray lecture once and that was one too many. He never went to other people's lectures. When Tom [Eliot] was reading or lecturing at the Library of Congress, Tom had lunch with us. Conrad said, "Now look, don't get mad, Tom, but I'm just not going. I never do." So he didn't even do that, and, after all, Tom was practically his best friend. Conrad hated the whole notion of people getting up and making exhibitions of themselves. Conrad and Stevens were quite alike about that. It might have been the first time they met, but Conrad was a great admirer of his work. He preferred it to [that of] any other American poet; he talked about him a great deal to everybody. Conrad thought he had a miraculous use of language and a great sense of color; that's what I chiefly remember.

It wasn't a big party, because it was in the study. There were only about eight: [Richard] Eberhart, Conrad and Ted, Stevens and me. There were two or three others; I don't remember who they were, probably people from the English Department at Harvard. Stevens was rather shy and couldn't look less like you'd expect a poet to look. He really did look like a businessman. I remember him extremely well; it's very funny, considering I've only actually

*Letter of Conrad Aiken to Herbert Stern, *Selected Letters of Conrad Aiken*, ed. Joseph Killorin (New Haven: Yale University Press, 1978), p. 305. While Aiken was indeed the godfather of *Owl's Clover*, his recollection of what Stevens said is misleading on a key point, that Aiken had been responsible for Stevens' starting to write again after his silent period during the late 1920s. This silence had already been broken for some time by the time Aiken wrote Stevens in the mid-thirties. When Aiken requested a long poem for Dent on January 5, 1935, Stevens was already collecting the lyrics he had been writing during the past few years into the manuscript of *Ideas of Order*, to be published by Latimer. What Aiken's letter did do, however, was to start Stevens thinking about writing his first long poem since "The Comedian as the Letter C," published twelve years earlier.

Stevens' compliment to Aiken points up quite accurately, of course, the important part that requests for poems played in spurring Stevens to write throughout his career.

seen him in the flesh twice. It was either his bulk or that he had a very powerful personality inside that silence that I liked.

Stevens and Conrad had a good deal of conversation. Ted was very talkative, and so was Conrad; they knew each other extremely well. I don't think Stevens and Ted knew each other very well, so Stevens didn't talk as much as the other people did. Someone there said how much he wanted to come to Hartford to see Stevens. Stevens just looked at him, and then he turned to Conrad and said, "I wish *you'd* come, Conrad. I would very much like to have *you* come." He could be a little rough on people.

I expect it was one of the rarest invitations that was ever given, to directly ask Conrad to stop [by]. Stevens wanted to see him and he wanted to talk to him by himself. There wasn't any way at this party that he could. It was Ted's study: a fireplace, a sofa, three or four chairs, so you couldn't depart to that end of the room and have a private conversation. I liked him very much indeed. He seemed extremely amiable, except for that particular incident, which was hard on the other person, but it wasn't hard on Conrad. I would have liked to have known him very well. I always regretted that we didn't actually stop. I think if he had actually written and invited us [we might have]. We went through Hartford a million times, but we were always going through at the wrong time.

I never saw him again until he [received] the National Book Award [on January 25, 1955]. We always got asked, but Conrad wanted to go for once because he was so pleased that Stevens had received it. Afterward, he went up and congratulated Stevens. Stevens said, "Well, Aiken, justice has never been done to you, but I'm not going to do it here and now. Sometime I will." I don't know exactly what he meant. He said it in front of a lot of people; whoever gets [the award] is always surrounded by thousands of people, so everybody heard it. I think that's the reason he said it: in a sense, he was doing justice to him.

The guests that Spencer had invited to the cocktail party after Stevens' first lecture were typical of the people Stevens met as a public man of letters: not only fellow poets like Aiken but also a younger generation of professors who admired his work. That December evening in 1936 Spencer had asked two young colleagues from Harvard's English Department to join the small party, Harry Levin and F. O. Matthiessen. Four years later all three professors contributed pieces to the first collection of scholarly essays on the poet in the *Harvard Advocate*'s special Stevens issue.* Levin continued to meet Stevens

---

*After reading this first collection of essays about himself, Stevens had reservations about such scholarly attention. "It makes me feel that a lot of more or less perfect strangers are becoming uncommonly intimate with me." (Letter to Hi Simons, December 27, 1940, Chicago.)

casually over the years when the poet returned to Harvard to lecture, to read, and, in 1951, to receive an honorary Doctor of Letters degree, an award Levin had initiated.*

Harry Levin

He was, perhaps because of his diffidence, a poor lecturer and an even worse reader of poetry. He threw away all the great lines, it was almost painful at times.

At a cocktail party after the [1936] reading, in Spencer's house, Stevens was rather shy, and I can't say we exchanged more than a handshake and a polite word or two. He came across very much as a gentleman of the old school, one very like the New Englanders of his generation that one met on Beacon Hill, proper Bostonians. I never realized, until relatively late, his Pennsylvania Dutch background, which had been completely obliterated, as far as personal style was concerned, by the old Harvard tone. From what I know of the Harvard [Stevens attended], though it had become a university in its periphery in the graduate school under President Eliot, at the core of that university, in the Harvard Yard, it was still a sort of provincial academy for the gentlemen's sons of New England.

[At Stevens' reading at Harvard on May 1, 1952,] I had charge of the arrangements. And I daresay it was the case, [as] on other occasions, when we offered him the honorarium, he gave it back. He said, "Let this go to some young poet who needs it more than I do." I believe he consistently shied away from talking about his work with other people. He liked to talk about painting, and given the difficulty of any conversational gambits with him, the easiest thing was to talk about French painting. That was the topic of conversation. [Also] that was the occasion he gave me to understand that he had read [my] review of the book of prose, *The Necessary Angel,* in the *Yale Review.* It was a review with reservations. I myself do not follow the present line, which regards each of his successive works as an advance on the last. I think I stopped somewhere in the middle, with *The Man with the Blue Guitar.* I'm very fond of some of the earliest things he did in *Harmonium.* Consequently, I don't take him very seriously as a philosopher. I think he was

---

*"The awarding of honorary degrees was, in the past, a closely guarded privilege of the Harvard Corporation," Levin recalls. "For a long time they didn't even accept suggestions. Later they invited a few faculty members to dinner once a year to advise them. I happened to complain to Henry Shattuck, who was for many years senior member of the Corporation, that the arts were insufficiently honored among the annual honorary degrees, that the antennae of the Corporation were not spread out in that direction. He said, 'If you have any ideas, we'll see what we can do.' I did have a couple of ideas: one was Thomas Mann, the other was Wallace Stevens. Shattuck remembered Stevens; they were in Harvard together. And that perhaps had more to do with it than my original recommendation."

doing almost the converse in those critical essays, using prose discourse but making a kind of poetry out of that. With great respect, in an omnibus review where there were only a few paragraphs about the book, I expressed that sort of reservation. He let me know, very quietly and gently, that he had read the review and the comment registered. It was more in sorrow than [in] anger.

Richard Wilbur was one of the Levins' guests on the afternoon that Stevens gave his last public reading at Harvard. Wilbur had first seen Stevens when the elder poet came to Cambridge in 1947, to deliver the talk "Three Academic Pieces."

Richard Wilbur

I don't think Stevens had any idea of what kind of celebrity had suddenly developed for his poems among the graduate students and young people interested in poetry. Of course, the interest wasn't confined to such people. I don't think he had any idea what he was letting himself in for, in agreeing to come to Harvard on that occasion. We all crowded into Room D in Emerson Hall, which was a philosophy classroom suitable for holding maybe one hundred people. It was full an hour before the reading. F. O. Matthiessen, who was introducing Stevens and in charge of arrangements, came in and told us to move to Sever Hall. Everyone rushed over there in a rather impolite way. People were pushing and shoving. Sever soon filled up, and once again it was announced that we were going to move to the big hall in the lower part of the Fogg Museum. By that time, nobody in the audience had any manners left, and people were pushing old ladies aside and rushing across the places where it said DO NOT STEP ON THE GRASS. And there was a great jostling crowd that poured through the door of the Fogg Museum. I had never seen Stevens. I don't know whether I'd seen pictures of him, but I knew which one Stevens was: he was the man standing there aghast as something like a Yale-Harvard game crowd flowed past him on its way to that big basement lecture hall. I can remember that André du Bouchet, who is now so well known a French poet, was then a very young man doing a bit of graduate work at Harvard and running from room to room to try to hear Wallace Stevens.

[Five years later Wilbur introduced Stevens at his 1952 Harvard reading.] Sometime during that visit we were [at the Levin home]. I have a mental image of Stevens, Harry Levin and Elena Levin and myself in the Levin living room, and of Stevens being extremely courtly, toasting his host with a highball and thanking him for his hospitality in a very old-world and elaborate way, like the sign-off of a French letter. Except that he kept insisting on calling Harry Levin "LAY-vin," it was an extraordinary display of courtesy. Now as far as the reading proper went, there were two microphones. One led to a recording apparatus—thank God—on which his beautiful reading was recorded. And the other was dead. [The New Lecture Hall] was absolutely full, so acoustics weren't as good as could be hoped in that structure. I got up and introduced him. Billy James, William James's painter son, was down there in the second row, with his hand behind his ear. But I thought, He's always been deaf: things are doubtless well enough arranged here. Then Stevens rose to read, and I sat on the platform. Because I did, I didn't realize that nobody out there was hearing Stevens at all. His voice was splendid, but because of his age, it didn't project. I suppose it's a measure of the enormous respect people felt for him that they sat there hearing nothing for an hour. It was a great pity. Stevens knew very soon after the reading that the sound equipment had not been operating. He was very disgruntled by that, and he said, "I'll never read again."

Then we went to Jack Sweeney's house [Sweeney was director of the Poetry Room at Harvard and a friend of Stevens']. I can't say who all were there: I think the Jameses were, William and Alice James. And the Levins. There may have been some other people there for a drink or so, and then it thinned out, because I can recall that things became very quiet. Stevens became very comfortable, sitting in a corner chair as he talked at great length about the Harvard of his days, about Royce and Santayana. We were all so interested that we just asked him questions that made him talk a little more. I cannot remember anything save that it was all about his teachers in philosophy. Those were the people he talked about, and we went out feeling *that's* what happened. Not the publication of a few poems in the *Advocate,* but his philosophy courses.

There is a terribly little thing, but it interests me about him. After the 1952 reading, when we were at Jack Sweeney's, Stevens was annoyed with over-hearing people saying "I couldn't hear a thing." And he said, "As for the fellow's introduction, all I heard him saying was 'Mist' Stevens. Mist' Stevens.'" I don't know why, I had just gotten into that rhythm of elision, and it annoyed him. That little bit of asperity reminded me that Holly Stevens told me her father was always correcting her speech, very scornful of mis-pronunciations.

Then we drove him to his hotel in our old '36 Ford, which was very uncomfortable for him. We said we hoped he would come and see us some-time. "I won't, but you're very kind to invite me." There was no severity in that at all. He was just being honest. In the same way, during that day he spoke, not with any great animus but with a certain firmness, of two classes of people: those who bother you with letters and those who do not. He didn't like people who wrote him letters and made him either answer them or feel guilty about not answering them. I had had a very brief postcard exchange [with him] once, and I recall him saying he thought the postcard was the ideal form, something like the sonnet, in which people could send each other signals without unnecessary pain.

Then we had another little exchange by postcard. I had been reading Gaston Bachelard, the Sorbonne philosopher and aesthetician. Bachelard says somewhere that the human imagination simply cannot cope with polar conditions, and so I shot off a postcard to Stevens. He wrote back some splendid sentence about Bachelard is wrong, most art is created out of a condition of winter. I must hasten to add that the number of words that passed between him and me was not very many, ever. But it seems to me that he was the sort of person (rather like me, to tell the truth) who would rather talk about something else and not about poetry all the time. I remember sometime, heaven knows when, saying, "There's a poem of yours I'm crazy about. It's 'Le Monocle de Mon Oncle.' I never get tired of it. Do you like it?" He said, "I like all my poems." Then he either went on to say, or I went on to understand, that when a poet reaches a certain age he becomes more self-forgiving and can accept the faults of his previous self and enjoy the virtues.

[Wilbur last met Stevens, a few months before his death, at a Harvard dinner for the English Department Visiting Committee.] We had one of those evening banquets that are intended to disarm the advisory committee: you give these advisers a lot of drinks, you tell them what a wonderful department you've got, and you don't really ask their advice at all. John Mason Brown was presiding at this affair, and he was doing a very good job of telling lots of smoking-car jokes—though they weren't truly smutty. At any rate, he was a good raconteur. *The* person in the room who was booming with laughter at every joke was Stevens. Some of the members of the English Department, I thought, were showing a little bit of prissy restraint. Stevens contrasted with anybody else you might have named in heartiness. I've learned since, from the anecdotes of others, how devoted Stevens was to jokes. We exchanged a few words about tennis and growing older, at what age you should stop playing singles and start playing doubles. What impressed me was, once again, that jocund side of him, which was so extraordinary, considering the ascetic side of him.

Harry Levin

Stevens was very conscientious about coming up for the Visiting Committee meetings, though in the questioning of the department he never said anything. He was one of the appointed members; we always had some writers and scholars. On one occasion, after dinner and after the speeches and questions at the Harvard Club, we adjourned to the rathskeller. A relatively small group, two or three people in the department and Stevens. He was really very glad to have a stiff drink or two. I have the impression that because of his shyness, he sometimes relied on this to break the ice. At any rate, he then began to talk, and he told us one or two smoking-car stories. They wouldn't be considered anything today, but in those days they might have been considered slightly risqué. My colleague Walter Jackson Bate was there. He'd always had a very good sense of humor, but with each joke he grew grimmer. Stevens finally said, "I'm afraid I'm not amusing you, Mr. Bate." And Bate, who was then very much the *enfant terrible* of the department, said, "You'll have to be funnier than that to make me laugh, Stevens!" Poor Stevens was quite humiliated, got very red, and stopped talking.*

· II ·

NEW HAVEN

This was not the first time that the poet had returned to Hartford red-faced. Wallace Stevens' appearances at Yale offer the best vantage point for seeing, behind his imposing façade, the distress that this extremely private

---

*As Walter Jackson Bate recalls that Visiting Committee dinner, Stevens "kept quiet, obviously ill at ease, most of the time. He had not bothered to notice anything about the English Department since he left college. He was unaware that the old tyranny of Germanic philology, especially for the Ph.D., had been destroyed by 1940–1947. One of the people most responsible for replacing it with a more literary and humanistic approach was the famous Douglas Bush, the distinguished humanist. Stevens turned to Bush and said, 'I guess you are one of those philologists that dominate Harvard.' Bush was offended and said nothing.

"After the meeting, Harry Levin, I and someone else (I forget who it was) took Stevens to the bar at the Harvard Club and tried to get him to talk. As I recall, he made a few off-color jokes. This got tedious, and I said, 'Stevens, we were able to come up with better jokes of that kind in the 4th grade.' Stevens then became quiet—I think that he was a little drunk." (Letter of Walter Jackson Bate to Peter Brazeau, February 8, 1977. For another account of Stevens at this dinner, see Edwin Honig's "Meeting Wallace Stevens," *The Wallace Stevens Newsletter,* April 1970, pp. 11–12.)

poet often experienced on and off stage as a public man of letters. Stevens first came to Yale as a Bergen Lecturer on March 18, 1948, to deliver his lecture "Effects of Analogy" and to read from his newest poem, "A Primitive Like an Orb." He arrived on the two o'clock train from New York, where, earlier in the day, he had presided over the annual stockholders' meeting of the Hartford Live Stock Insurance Company. His faculty host that afternoon was Louis Martz, who, Stevens was pleased to learn, hailed from his hometown of Reading. Martz, an admirer of Stevens' poetry since Theodore Roethke had introduced him to *Harmonium* in his undergraduate days, had in fact suggested Stevens to the Bergen Lecture Committee that spring.

Louis Martz

He came up from New York with a big briefcase because he had been down doing legal business and came directly here to give a lecture. As he was arranging to give his lecture, I took him back to my office. He opened up the briefcase and said, "Now you see everything is neatly sorted out here. Over in this compartment is my insurance business with the farmers, and over in this compartment, this is my lecture and some poems that I want to read. I keep them completely separate." This separation of the two aspects of his life—even to the fee—was a very clear principle that he followed. Beforehand, it's customary to go into the university secretary's office at Woodbridge Hall and be presented with the check for the lecture, then sign the [guest lecturer] book. This is all very formal. Norman Pearson and I and Carl Lohmann [then university secretary] were there. Stevens opened the envelope, looked at the check [$150], turned to Norman and said, "What do I do with this?" Mr. Lohmann said, "Most of our poets use it to eat with." Stevens said, "I couldn't do that! Oh, I never use my poetry fees. Take it. Give it to some worthy cause." And he turned it over to Norman Pearson, and Norman gave it to some little magazine. That was his view toward his poetic profession. He didn't make money out of it. He just gave the checks away.

Generally, in the auditorium we were using, we wouldn't need a microphone, and we had not hooked one up. This was a great mistake, because his voice barely carried beyond the third or fourth row, and it may have been three or four hundred people in this auditorium. At one point a woman raised her hand and said, "Could you speak more loudly? I can't hear a thing." He said, "I'll try, lady. I'll try." That seemed to upset him so much that his voice dropped down even lower. After the "Effects of Analogy," he read a few of his poems. The audience stayed put, though half couldn't hear. They took it, a full hour lecture, and there was a big round of applause. It was just a tribute to him because he was obviously much admired.

[In conversation before the lecture] I did speak about how many of the undergraduates were interested [in his poetry]. He nodded and smiled and said he would like to meet some of them. I had a little poetry group here; we met once a week, purely voluntarily. Stevens was one of the poets we read week after week. He wasn't taken up in university circles until the fifties, but we were doing it right after the war. After the lecture, I told my little group to come up. He talked to them, and they were terribly impressed. He could be very gracious. But he also could be very sharp.

An incident with Dudley Fitts [later that evening] was very sharp. We went to Norman Pearson's house afterward. Norman had a big, upright sofa, very stiff, and Stevens sat on it like a great, tall giant. There weren't many people: my wife, Dudley Fitts and his wife, Pearson and his wife, the [Cleanth] Brookses, one or two others. He wanted something very small. As we had cocktails and a little wine [with dinner], he became quite genial, seemed to trust us, and began to talk. At one point, Stevens launched into Fitts, rather harshly, and said, "What's a fellow like you doing spending your time there [Phillips Academy, in Andover, Massachusetts] teaching? That is taking all your energy, all your best thoughts. You ought to be doing your writing." A funny thing for Stevens to say. Fitts was taken aback by this and said, "Well, I have to earn a living." His wife spoke up, "And he has [two] children, you know. We just can't be taking off for the wilderness and let him write his poems." Stevens really backed up. "Oh, I apologize. Never should come between a man and his wife. Never. Never. I won't say any more."

Cleanth Brooks

[After the lecture] there was a dinner at Norman Holmes Pearson's, and there, after a couple of drinks, Wallace Stevens became a different man from the rather shy, rather inaudible lecturer. He was a relaxed, easy, joking, talkative, delightful companion. I remember a good deal of talk with him. I had simply remembered it as a very pleasant conversation. We talked about John Ransom, we talked about Delmore Schwartz. We talked about the good estate of letters, what was wrong and what was right about it. I think he indicated at the time that Delmore Schwartz represented a kind of hope for modern poetry. I don't think he was emphasizing Schwartz's actual poetry so much as the general stance he took. I may be elaborating what was not in the situation, but I think it was the matter of: here is a person living in New York and facing the difficulties and the facts of American life. We don't need anything escapist or remote, something of the sort. There was no undue self-consciousness. He was certainly not holding forth for the group in any way.

There was a sequel to this pleasant meeting. I began to hear stories around that Wallace Stevens thought he had mortally offended me. I really was completely shocked and surprised. We had had a very pleasant conversation: I think he teased me about some of my friends, John Ransom and others, but it was all light-hearted teasing. I found nothing offensive and thoroughly enjoyed it. It was Allen Tate, among others, to whom he said something.* I can speak for my wife; she would be absolutely shocked to hear of this report, simply because it had not made an impact on her whatsoever. She has a good sense of humor and would have laughed her head off. Anyway I did get, later on, a very formal apology from him. I was able to write back with utter sincerity that I had taken no offense, in fact, didn't realize there was anything to take offense at.

We're dealing here with a full-grown chimera, a fabulous monster, something that didn't occur except in his imagination. By that I can only conclude that Wallace Stevens was a true poet as well as a gentleman. A true poet in really letting his imagination oftentimes completely alter his picture of what a situation was. His memory of that evening was completely out of kilter with my memory of it or, I would say, the facts of the situation. A man of less courtesy, less politeness, less sensitivity would have worried much less about it.

Louis Martz

The editor of the *Yale Review* had asked me beforehand whether it would be possible for us to get the manuscript [of "Effects of Analogy"], so after the lecture I asked. He said, "Oh, do you think anybody would be interested in reading it? You know these prose things, just thinking out loud. It's really not . . . Do you think people would be interested?" I said, "I think they'd be very much interested." He gave me the text and said, "I don't want to revise or anything like that. If they want some revisions, just tell them to do whatever they want to do. It's all right with me." The editor liked it and made some suggestions. I had read it and thought it could stand some culling here and there, so I wrote him and made some suggestions for revisions. He wrote back and said, "All right. Just go ahead." It came out slightly cut and revised. I think he was very happy to have it published.

---

*A year after meeting Brooks, Stevens was still embarrassed about his behavior that evening and wrote to Tate, "About a year ago I met Cleanth Brooks and his wife in New Haven under circumstances which made a wreck of the thing. After reading a paper at Yale I went to dinner and the Brookses were there. Either the cocktails were too good or too many, with the result that I got talking to Brooks about the fact that Louisiana was not a part of the United States at the time of the Revolution, etc. The worst of it is I was probably not very respectful to his wife, who of course took his part." (Letter of March 31, 1949, Princeton University.)

Garrett Barcalow Stevens as a young man (Courtesy Henry E. Huntington Library)

Margaretha Catharine Zeller Stevens (Courtesy Henry E. Huntington Library)

Wallace Stevens as a boy (Courtesy Holly Stevens)

The Harvard Advocate *staff,
1899. Stevens is standing
at the far right.* (Courtesy
Harvard University Archives)

*Manuscript of "Cathedrals
are not built along the
sea," written while Stevens
was at Harvard* (Courtesy
Henry E. Huntington Library)

Cathedrals are not built along the sea;
The tender bells would jangle on the hoar
And iron winds; the graceful turrets war
With bitter storms the long night angrily;
And through the precious organ pipes would be
A low and constant murmur of the shore
That down those golden shafts would reach far
A mighty and a lasting melody.

And those who knelt within the gilded stalls
Would have vast outlook for their weary eyes;
There, they would see high shadows on the walls
From passing vessels in their fall and rise.
Through gaudy windows there would come too soon
The low and splendid rising of the moon.

*Elsie Stevens in Elizabeth Park, Hartford,
Connecticut, c. 1916. In the background is the
lily pond of "The Plain Sense of Things."*
(Courtesy Holly Stevens and Henry E. Huntington
Library)

*Elsie Stevens during her early years in
Hartford* (Courtesy Holly Stevens and
Henry E. Huntington Library)

*Wallace Stevens during his early years
in Hartford* (Courtesy Holly Stevens and
Henry E. Huntington Library)

Wallace Stevens in Hartford
(Courtesy Holly Stevens and
Henry E. Huntington Library)

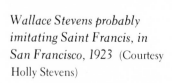

*Wallace Stevens probably
imitating Saint Francis, in
San Francisco, 1923* (Courtesy
Holly Stevens)

The home office of the Hartford Fire Insurance Company and the Hartford Accident and Indemnity Company, 125 Trumbull Street, where Stevens worked during his first years in Connecticut (Courtesy Hartford Insurance Group)

Wallace Stevens, c. 1940 (Photo by Pach Bros., New York; courtesy Henry E. Huntington Library)

On an outing, c. 1929. Left to right: Ralph Mullen, Wallace Stevens and an unidentified man (Courtesy Holly Stevens)

Officers of the Hartford Accident and Indemnity Company, 1938.
Among those mentioned in this biography are: front row (left to right),
Edmund G. Armstrong, Wilson Jainsen, George Moloney, Paul
Rutherford, James Wyper, Wallace Stevens; middle row, Manning
Heard (third from right); *top row, W. R. Liedike* (fourth from left) *and*
Joseph Broucek (second from right). (Courtesy Hartford Insurance Group)

The new Hartford Fire Insurance Company and Hartford Accident and
Indemnity Company building, 690 Asylum Avenue, at the time it was
completed in 1921. Stevens' office was on the first floor of the Hartford
Accident and Indemnity wing, to the right of the pillars. (Courtesy
Hartford Insurance Group)

*Chelsea Square, New York City: a postcard photo that Wallace Stevens
sent in January 1911 to his wife, who was visiting relatives in Reading,
Pennsylvania. Stevens drew an arrow pointing to their apartment at 441
West Twenty-first Street, across the street from the General Theological
Seminary (foreground).* (Courtesy Henry E. Huntington Library)

*210 Farmington Avenue, Hartford, c. 1924. It was during the years the
Stevenses lived here, from 1917 to 1924, that most of* Harmonium *was
written.* (Courtesy Holly Stevens and Henry E. Huntington Library)

118 Westerly Terrace, Hartford, 1953 (Courtesy Holly Stevens and Henry E. Huntington Library)

Wallace Stevens in the backyard at 118 Westerly Terrace, 1951 (Courtesy Holly Stevens and Henry E. Huntington Library)

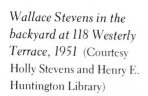

735 Farmington Avenue, West Hartford, where the Stevenses lived from 1924 to 1932 (Photo by J. R. Harrison)

Long Key Fishing Camp in the Florida Keys. On this postcard, which Wallace Stevens sent to his wife from Florida in January 1923, he wrote, "this one shows the cottages, the cocoanut palms and the immaculate white ground. . . . Each cottage is named after a fish." (Courtesy Henry E. Huntington Library)

The Hartford Canoe Club, East Hartford, Connecticut, as it looked in Stevens' time (Courtesy Hartford Canoe Club)

The Casa Marina Hotel, Key West, Florida, c. 1940 (Courtesy Holly Stevens and Henry E. Huntington Library)

Judge Arthur Gray Powell
(Courtesy Martha Powell
Power)

Wallace Stevens and his daughter, Holly, outside 735 Farmington Avenue, in 1929 (Courtesy Holly Stevens and Henry E. Huntington Library)

Left to right: *Josephine M. (mother's helper at the Stevenses'), Holly and Elsie Stevens atop the Empire State Building, 1933* (Courtesy Josephine M.)

*Wallace Stevens in the front garden at
118 Westerly Terrrace, c. 1939* (Photo
by Holly Stevens)

*Wallace Stevens and his nieces in
Pennsylvania, c. 1943. Left to right: Jane
MacFarland Wilson (Elizabeth's
daughter), Eleanor Stevens Sauer (John's
daughter) and Anna May Stevens (John's
daughter-in-law)* (Courtesy John Sauer)

*Wallace Stevens (extreme
right) at the time of the
funeral of his brother John,
July 1940, in Lobachsville,
Pennsylvania, shown with
(left to right) John Stevens,
Jr., Jane MacFarland
Wilson (daughter of
Wallace's sister Elizabeth)
and Eleanor Stevens Sauer
(John's daughter)* (Photo by
John Sauer, courtesy Jane
MacFarland Wilson)

Jean Wahl and Wallace Stevens at Mount Holyoke College in August 1943, when Stevens lectured on "The Figure of the Youth as Virile Poet" (Courtesy Holly Stevens)

The Church circle at Ville d'Avray. Left to right: *Sylvia Beach, Barbara Church, Nabokoff-Sirine, Adrienne Monnier, Germaine Paulhan, Henry Church, Henri Michaux, Jean Paulhan and Michel Leiris.*

1950 National Book Award ceremonies. Left to right: Edward Weeks,
Wallace Stevens, Newton Arvin, Brendan Gill and Saxe Commins.
(Courtesy *Publishers Weekly*)

Jury for the National Book Award in Poetry at its meeting in New York,
January 1952. Left to right: Conrad Aiken, Winfield Townley Scott,
Peter Viereck and Wallace Stevens. (Courtesy *Publishers Weekly*)

*Wallace Stevens at the
Avery Convalescent
Hospital, July 1955*
(Courtesy Anthony Sigmans)

Wallace Stevens (seated) *with Anthony and
Mary Sigmans at the Avery Convalescent
Hospital, Hartford, July 1955* (Courtesy Anthony
Sigmans)

*Stevens' gravestone,
Cedar Hill Cemetery,
Hartford, Connecticut*
(Photo by J. R. Harrison)

Then the Connecticut Academy of Arts and Sciences was going to have its [sesqui]centennial [1949]. They asked me whether I thought Wallace Stevens was a good poet. They wanted a Connecticut poet to come down [to New Haven for the ceremonies], and since he'd just been here they said, "Do you think he would write a poem for us in honor of the centennial?" I said, "I don't really know. He never has, but I'll ask him." He wrote back he didn't think he was really any good at writing commemorative poems, but if he could write a poem and dedicate it to the Connecticut Academy he would come. So that was the genesis of "An Ordinary Evening in New Haven." We talked about that, and he described how he composed it. "I wanted to have something that would relate to the occasion but not directly. So I just fixed on this idea of a poem about a walk in New Haven, but then branching out." He said it really got so far away from the base that New Haven hardly appears in it. "It's only the title, really, but," he said, "that's the way things happen with me. I start with a concrete thing, and it tends to become so generalized that it isn't any longer a local place. I think that puzzles some people." He had written many more parts of that poem than the ones he read here. He told me that he had selected sections and put them together specially for the Connecticut Academy to suit the length of time he had to read it. "Now, I read every section as is my custom to my wife as I wrote it. She put her hands over her eyes and said, 'They're not going to understand this.' I was very careful to pick out the sections I thought would go over with an audience. But even so, my wife was terribly concerned about it." It's often thought that she wasn't interested in his poetry, and perhaps at first she wasn't. It was very clear that he said he had read all the sections to her as he wrote them. "As is my custom." It was very clear it was his habit to read—at least at that time of his life—the poems he was writing to his wife and get her responses.

She was sensibly worried that maybe it wouldn't go over. She didn't come to the occasion, of course. He was aware of an aural audience, which wasn't true of all his things. The fact that he knew he had to read it aloud probably had some effect on the cadences and the general feel of that poem, which is somewhat different from the preceding poems. This time we set him up with a microphone; he read very nicely and it was a success.

There was a great shyness in him. He didn't talk easily to people. At the Connecticut Academy thing, he mingled with the people at the reception and the dinner, but he didn't speak much. The lack of contact between Stevens and Yale until the last years came from [his] own remoteness, the difficulty of access to him. He was in Hartford and was regarded as a strange, distant person, a difficult personality. Some [writers] get very close to Yale, but it's usually an outgoing personality like Bill Styron. They have friends;

they're down here all the time. But Stevens was just not that kind of person. I think he was a little uncomfortable in the presence of academicians. He had many admirers down here among the students, among the faculty, but was not the sort of person that would come down and mingle.

On March 27, 1950, Stevens was awarded Yale's Bollingen Prize in Poetry. After that, an evening in New Haven became a little more ordinary, at least on the winter weekend when the Bollingen jury of poets gathered to decide that year's winner. At first, Stevens was simply a guest at the dinner held for the distinguished jury on the eve of its deliberations. Then, in the last two years of his life, he came as one of the jury itself.* Mary Jarrell met him on these latter occasions when her husband, Randall, was one of the panel of judges as well.

When Stevens had been proposed for the award in the winter of 1950, some of the Fellows, such as Robert Penn Warren, assumed he had already received all the major prizes and suggested it go to a poet with fewer accolades. At seventy, however, Stevens had received very little official recognition, the Bollingen marking the beginning of a spate of awards that came to him, belatedly, in his last years. Léonie Adams had cast her vote in favor of Stevens in 1950; she had been on the jury that had created a whirlwind of controversy the year before, when the Bollingen Prize had gone to Ezra Pound, then interned by the government in a Washington mental institution for collaborating with Mussolini during the war. The Library of Congress, which had been awarding the Bollingen, was forced to give it up as a result of that controversy and Yale then offered the prize a new sponsor. There was no criticism now when the prize was awarded to America's businessman-poet, a choice as deserved as it was prudent after the Pound affair the previous year.

Léonie Adams

Yale came forward with the noble offer to take over the prize. And they took over the entire jury. That was a way of backing up the Fellows. It was decided to be impracticable to have the Fellows, who were scattered around the earth anyway, come there to act. [For] the actual voting jury, four were chosen: Mrs. Biddle [the poet Katherine Garrison Chapin], Karl Shapiro, Conrad Aiken and I. The others were all entitled to send in nominations, and did so, to the jury.

When Conrad arrived, he and I had a little talk. I had made up my mind that one of the most neglected good poets in the country was John Crowe Ransom. I think it was because of something Allen Tate had told me, that the year that Ransom's *Selected Poems* appeared, no Pulitzer was given

---

*Wallace Stevens was not Yale's first choice for the Bollingen Prize Committee but was proposed as a backup if Robert Frost refused to serve on the jury. (Memorandum on "Committee for Award of the Prize for 1953," Archives, Yale University.)

because the committee said there was nothing worthy of the prize. Isn't that shocking? Now [in 1949] Frost's *Collected Poems* appeared, one of the many times. Well you could hardly ignore it, but I remember Eliot's letter that said he saw little purpose in giving an award like this to the much-belaureled Frost. And it would seem to be chickening out, really, trying to say [that] after all, we're good Americans even though we did vote for Pound. Conrad spoke of Stevens. Of course, I knew Stevens' range was more, and ultimately he was the more important poet, though it is hard to make these absolute distinctions. Ransom always did what he did perfectly; he was a very fine poet and he had been neglected. Conrad said—it was a real conspiracy—"If you vote for Stevens this time, then I will vote for Ransom next time." And that's the way it turned out, because we were on the jury for two years. [During that weekend's events, Aiken] told me, with a certain pride, that he felt that during the period when Stevens had stopped writing and gone into a kind of obscurity, that he had been persuaded to come forth and that he [Aiken] was more or less responsible for his taking heart and beginning to write again. It was a very genuine feeling on his part, both his admiration for Stevens and a certain pride in having brought him forth, as it were.

We had this little talk and we went into the meeting. Conrad was not a very expressive person in speech. He simply made his pronouncement that he thought that Stevens should have it. I talked of Ransom, but I agreed it should go to Stevens. There was another nominee, one or two perhaps. [There was] very little discussion of the qualities of Stevens' work. We had absolutely none at the Pound meeting because it was assumed that all the people there knew their own minds, knew what poetry was, and wouldn't make speeches as you would to a class. Conrad's clout was behind the thing, and I acceded to it. Mrs. Biddle was willing to go along, and, I suppose, Karl was, too. So it just went through. It was for his work in general; you could do that. It was not [for] a book [since Stevens had not published a volume in 1949]. It was given for his distinguished career.

But would Stevens accept it? Mr. [James] Babb, the Librarian [at Yale, who presided at the meeting], thought we shall have to see whether Stevens wished to take the prize because the Bollingen had made such a big stink in being given to Pound the year before. The papers had been full of it, and *The Saturday Review of Literature* was roaring around.* I was sitting next to

*Stevens preferred to stay out of literary controversies and avoided literary politics. The controversy over the Bollingen award to Ezra Pound was a case in point. When the traditionalists William Rose Benét and Robert Hillyer used the award to mount an attack on modernist poetry in *The Saturday Review of Literature* in 1949, Allen Tate tried to enlist Stevens in the camp of prominent writers who were protesting to the magazine. Stevens, however, did not

Mr. Babb [who] called him when the vote had gone through. It was an instantaneous answer. I could hear Stevens' strong, warm voice coming over. He didn't exactly say, "You bet your life I will," but he was absolutely delighted and enthusiastic. "Certainly. Of course I will." My impression always was that this man had lived in seclusion from the literary world and not in it. Every Consultant [in Poetry to the Library of Congress, for example] wrote and asked him to make a recording. I remember this letter on file. He had said, "Even if I'm the only Eskimo who doesn't like snow, I wouldn't make a recording." It was absolutely contrary to hear this warm, enthusiastic voice—without a moment's hesitation.

[Four years later Stevens served on the Bollingen Committee that awarded the prize to both Léonie Adams and Louise Bogan.] They telephoned me after the decision. It was Stevens who told me about the award. Apparently he was the one delegated to make the announcement. He said, "I'm certainly glad I'm one of the gang that did this thing," which, of course, pleased me. I told [Louise Bogan] that, and she said indignantly, "He didn't say that to me." Allen [Tate, who had served with Stevens on that 1955 jury] came to see me later on his way through New York. Of course, I knew he would have been for me. He made some peculiar statement: Cummings was up that year, and he had the feeling that Stevens very much didn't want Cummings to have it.

Mary Jarrell

Stevens had just won the [1954] National Book Award and we were in New York for that a couple of days before; I was very excited to be meeting the great man. [Before dinner that first evening] Randall somehow wound up on the other side of the room, and I was next to Stevens. I didn't know what to talk to him about. I intimated something about the National Book Award, and he right away put his hand up and said, "Oh, no, no, no." He asked me where I was from. I said California, and with that he very easily began to talk about his own daughter, who, I believe, was about to take a trip out there by car with her son. He asked me what I thought of that. "Are you worried about this?" And he said, "Well, yes, I don't know if I approve of her driving

---

enjoy polemics, unlike the feisty Tate, and he declined to sign. "I don't see the Saturday Review and, even if I did, I should skip anything it might contain by Benet and/or Hillyer. So that 1. I know nothing about this; 2. care less; 3. do not believe that the Saturday Review or Benet or Hillyer, jointly or severally, or both, could possibly harm the cause of letters; 4. prefer to keep out of this and 5. intend to do just that. . . . I have recently decided to live to be a hundred. One of the ways of doing that is not to jump into bonfires." (Letter to Allen Tate, October 20, 1949, HL.)

so far with that child." I got the feeling then that this was going to be a kind of paternal conversation; he was treating me as he would treat a young woman similar to his daughter. My feeling at that time was this man isn't really interested in this subject; he's using this b⁄ ·use we can't sit here and not say something. He was interested, though, in looking at me, his full face. I don't mean to sound vain about this, but I did feel that he was on a little trip, looking at a young woman of thirty-six who was healthy and reasonably attractive. But it was disinterested looking; he had selected something he was going to think about to get through all these meetings.

[During the evening] he was very much a presence and very much globed in himself. I don't mean to say this was vanity. It's a sense of one's own being: he knew who he was and he was being himself. When there was any chance for wit, he could be witty. But he wasn't in any way dominating or forthcoming or leading the situation. Thornton Wilder, as compared with Stevens, was trying to dominate everything. He was very talky; he reminded me of Frank O'Connor. He was full of raconteur, comment and response. Other people would wait till Wilder finished, then the poets would get into it. [The talk between Marianne Moore and Stevens] was pleasant and joking and mutually very admiring; it made [for] a lot of conviviality, because Randall was a great Moore admirer. Stevens, Jarrell and Moore were a little trio. I remember coming away feeling a little sorry for Winfield Townley Scott because he wasn't treated very well that night. He was speaking up about something or other. I don't know whether it was Randall or Stevens [who] contradicted him, cut the ground out from under him, and after that we didn't hear much more from Winfield Townley Scott.[8]

The next morning we were at breakfast at the Yale Club. Randall was across the table, and I was somehow next to Stevens. We were talking generally, and I said something about seeing *Ninotchka* in New York with Randall. Stevens came alive immediately. "Garbo!" he said. He talked about always wishing he could meet her and how beautiful she was, that she really was his favorite actress in the world. There was a pause. I knew Randall well enough to know that he was being a little audacious—here it was, a table full of people—but he had a direct question that he wanted to ask Stevens. He felt he was not going to be able to ask him this question if he didn't get on with it. So he just shifted the subject entirely to "Sunday Morning" and said, "I've noticed that you have changed some lines in 'Sunday Morning.' How did you happen to do that?" Stevens pulled this famous Robert Browning thing. He began to look very vague and disbelieving, as if he hadn't remembered whether he changed them or not. He hesitated and started to say something about "I don't know why." Then he said, "Let's talk about Greta

Garbo again!" [Later] he and Randall got talking about the Colony [in New York City] as a place to buy wine. He gave Randall the name of the man at the Colony who was his wine dealer. And he told Randall that man could just give him the best of everything and to tell him he was a friend of Wallace Stevens.

That is the time Auden won the Bollingen. I don't think Auden was everybody's first choice; I don't know Stevens' views. That's when Stevens made his famous sentence, which Randall used to quote. When this other person was up for consideration, Stevens said, "Oh, but that's not permanent poetry." And he vetoed whoever that was.

Randall liked Stevens a lot, and he enjoyed the fact that when they met they had been congenial. Randall was certainly uneasy in a group of other poets; I saw it time and time again. Once we met Eliot, and to my astonishment Randall never said a word to Eliot the entire time that we were at this party. I realized later that he was just too much overawed by Eliot. With Stevens, they were congenial, they liked each other. You just regretted that they couldn't be together longer. When Randall wrote the subsequent [review], the one that treats "The Rock," he was able to be engaging about Stevens because he had met him.[9] He spoke about this "disinterestedness," and Randall admired disinterestedness above all qualities. He tried very hard to be disinterested himself about his own life, his own poetry, his own criticism. And he felt Stevens had this. He must have sensed this more than ever, because Stevens didn't hold [Jarrell's 1951 critical review of *The Auroras of Autumn*] against him.[10] When we were together the two times we were there [at the Bollingen judging], it was a pleasure, you didn't feel a strain. I noticed among poets that we met how some were easy to meet and talk to and [with] some an immediate constraint set up—for instance, with Richard Wilbur and Conrad Aiken, people who were sore at Randall's early reviews of them. But neither Frost nor Stevens was difficult in that respect; we found real warmth to be with them, no effort.

Frost used to visit us, happily, and stay the night. We asked him about his relationship with Wallace Stevens. Frost said he first encountered him at Harvard; Frost was pushing a baby buggy on campus. The two knew who they were [but] Stevens didn't even speak to him. Just looked at him out of the corner of his eye, didn't nod, left Frost pushing his baby buggy in the other direction. The implication from Frost was that he was never elegant enough for Stevens' taste. Frost would go to Florida in his later years. Somebody, knowing the two of them were down there, got them together. [Frost recounted an incident there when] Stevens said he did not have a certain book. According to Frost, he sent [an] extra copy, and Stevens never sent him a note of thanks. [There was] a deep, smoldering, incurable resentment that Frost had about Stevens. [It was partly the result] of Frost's acute sensitivity at being a nonintellectual poet, somebody [for] *Saturday Evening Post* readers or *Atlantic Monthly* readers, and Stevens being such an intellectual. Frost always divided the world into intellectuals and himself.

· III ·

SOUTH HADLEY

As it happened, Stevens lectured most often in Frost country, at Mount Holyoke's campus in South Hadley, Massachusetts, a winding country mile below Frost's academic home at Amherst College. Those who attended Stevens' lectures at Mount Holyoke College, saw that, even away from home, the public man of letters was very much Hartford's private poet. Indeed, on his first visit, in August 1943, Stevens' usual distance from his audience affected the proceeding itself.

Stevens had been invited to Mount Holyoke to participate in one of the most ambitious intellectual experiments spawned by the war, *Les Entretiens de Pontigny.* Each summer during World War II, the Mount Holyoke campus was transformed into the American equivalent of the twelfth-century monastery at Pontigny, France, where, for nearly thirty summers between 1910 and the outbreak of the war, European artists and intellectuals had converged for *décades,* or ten-day seminars. In 1942, Mount Holyoke and the Ecole Libre des Hautes Etudes, the Franco-Belgian university-in-exile attached to the New School for Social Research in New York, had sponsored the first *Pontigny en Amérique,* bringing American and European intellectuals to South Hadley as the historian-critic Paul Desjardin had earlier brought the likes of Valéry, Gide and Lytton Strachey to a converted monastery in the Loire valley.

Among the eighty scholars and artists who participated that first summer was Jean Wahl, a young Parisian existentialist philosopher. He stayed on to teach at the college and, in March 1943, organized the second summer of *entretiens.* The morning sessions that coming August were to be given over to the arts, with Lionello Venturi directing the week's discussion on painting, novelist Julien Green the week on fiction, Gustave Cohen the meetings on drama, and Jean Wahl the sessions devoted to poetry. Afternoons were for social issues, with lectures by Claude Lévi-Strauss, Raymond de Saussure and Roman Jakobson. Wahl had been interested in American culture even before he came to the United States, so it was no surprise that the Jewish refugee, who had read *Moby Dick* between interrogation sessions in Nazi Paris, invited more Americans to join this second summer of discussions than had participated earlier: among them philosophers like Suzanne Langer and Paul

Weiss and writers like Marianne Moore and Katherine Anne Porter. Wahl had recently finished Stevens' newest book, *Notes toward a Supreme Fiction*; understandably, he decided to invite this American writer as well, for the subject of the book was very much in line with the subject of the summer's *entretiens, "Permanence et renouvellement des valeurs"* ("Permanent and Changing Values").

Stevens agreed to come on August 11, in the middle of the week given over to poetry in the morning discussions. At 10:30 A.M. that balmy Wednesday, he settled into one of the chairs that had been set up under the large elms near Porter Hall and began to read his paper, "The Figure of the Youth as Virile Poet," to the men and women gathered on the lawn. Among them was Alan McGee, a member of the college's English Department, who later secured for Stevens the honorary doctorate he received from Mount Holyoke in 1952.

Alan McGee

He spoke outdoors to a group of people sitting on dining-room chairs around a rectangle. We were at least fifty people. Obviously, it was a pretty crowded outdoor exercise, and [as] with any outdoor exercise, you have to sit fairly close together so that everybody can hear. Marianne Moore and her mother sat there in tricornered hats, looking as much like each other as two women twenty years apart could conceivably look. He was sitting near the porch, and she was right beside him, in the courtyard, facing the audience.

He lent a great aura of distinction. He was one of the most distinguished-looking men I ever saw. His appearance and clothing were of the gentlemanly perfection. The intellectual quality you can tell from reading the essay.

He did not enter into a lively discussion. Marianne Moore spoke more freely, and so did John Peale Bishop, in discussion with the audience [that week], but I don't remember that after Stevens' speech. Some of the speakers who spoke later [that week]—for instance, Mr. Bishop—spoke in such a way that indicated they had been affected by what Stevens had said.

At *Pontigny* the lectures, however, were not intended as ends in themselves but as catalysts for discussion. That was viewed as an equally important aspect of each two-hour session. The official title of these summer gatherings was, after all, *Entretiens de Pontigny,* and the poets who came to speak that week knew, as John Peale Bishop put it, that "they should, when they had come to a close, hear their conclusions disputed and their dearest convictions put to doubt."[11] As usual, Stevens had found an invitation to appear in public appealing because it was an opportunity to gather his thoughts together, this time about a subject that was dear to him in the early 1940s: the need for a university chair devoted to the study of poetry and the life of the imagination.* The emphasis on debate at *Pontigny*, however, had been an additional incentive for Stevens to come to Mount Holyoke, as he explained to a friend at the time, for "It will also give me an opportunity to hear the thing discussed."[12] Though his subject changed considerably as he prepared his lecture, Stevens nonetheless had kept the argumentative character of *Pontigny* very much in mind and arrived in South Hadley that August morning with the kind of talk Wahl had urged him to write, one that would spark a lively discussion.

One senses the provocations Stevens built into the text by seeing it within the context of that *Pontigny* summer. As Stevens knew from scanning the brochures for the upcoming conference, his poetry seminar immediately followed a week devoted to philosophy. Aware that lectures by such metaphysicians as Paul Weiss would still be echoing among the audience, Stevens began his talk by asserting that "what is central to philosophy is its least valuable part." Poets, he went on to argue, live in a "radiant and productive atmosphere," while the world of the philosopher, in which many of the audience had been willing citizens just a week earlier, was disparaged as "the gaunt world of the reason." The controversial quality of the essay seems clear even in slight details. Jacques Maritain was honorary president of the group to whom Stevens was speaking and had, at one point, been scheduled to lecture the week before Stevens' visit. Rather puckishly, Stevens asserted near the end of his talk that "in spite of M. Jacques Maritain, we do not want to be metaphysicians."[13]

At *Pontigny*, Stevens gave a cutting edge to his remarks on the relation of poetry to philosophy not found in his other statements on the subject, such

*In the spring of 1940, Henry Church, a wealthy new friend of Stevens and a patron of the avant-garde, first turned to the poet-lawyer for advice about providing a trust fund in his will to help struggling artists and scientists. Stevens soon countered by suggesting that Church might also consider setting up a university chair for the study of poetry. As a result of Stevens' suggestion, put forth most eloquently in a lengthy October memorandum on the subject, Church attempted a small-scale version of this idea. In late 1940, he funded a "folding" chair of poetry, as it were, at Princeton University, endowing the annual Mesures Lectures. Stevens gave his 1941 talk, "The Noble Rider and the Sound of Words," as one of the lectures in the inaugural series.

By the winter of 1943, Church's interest in Stevens' idea of a permanent chair revived. On March 27, he wrote to the poet, asking if Stevens had any further thoughts on the subject and suggesting they talk about it over lunch at some point. The topic was very much on Stevens' mind at the time. A week earlier Jean Wahl had invited him to *Pontigny* to speak about his poetry and poetic theory; Stevens had replied immediately that he would like to deal with the subject of a chair of poetry. Though Stevens later wrote to Church that he had revised his topic, when the Churches listened to the lecture that August morning at Mount Holyoke they must have recognized, as others in the audience could not, that the talk was very much an extension of the memorandum on the subject that Stevens had sent them in 1940. As he argued the superiority of the poet to the philosopher, Stevens was, in part, using the lecture to argue for the establishment of a poetry chair, in the light of chairs already existing for the lesser subject of philosophy, to possible patrons. This private aspect of the address explains why Stevens was extraordinarily persistent in urging and arranging for the Churches to attend his talk at Mount Holyoke.

as his later and more benign lecture "A Collect of Philosophy." His rhetoric here was in keeping with the spirit of debate at South Hadley. Ironically, when it came time for Stevens to take part in the discussion he had provoked, his private nature emerged and had a chilling effect on the audience, as Paul and Constance Saintonge, Mount Holyoke professors, recall.

Paul and Constance Saintonge

CS: It was not what you'd call a give-and-take between the audience and the poet. He was very much up there and in charge. He perhaps answered two or three questions and then went off. His manner didn't encourage a response. The audience was completely docile. I think a few people dared to go up afterward and asked questions.

PS: Most of the people at *Pontigny* wanted to make themselves felt. It wasn't only the *entretiens,* morning or afternoon, it was the whole ambience: the discussions at meals and into the night that were part of *Pontigny.* That was what the refugees particularly liked.

CS: Normally, most of the speakers were staying here. There were very famous people here among these refugees. It was talk, talk, talk all day and all night long. Stevens was quite an exception.

Stevens made an impression, surely. It was wonderful to have him here. But he was like an angel who flew in for a minute and went out. [I remember] mostly the look of him, the impression as a person in this immaculate pearl-gray suit, looking very smooth and pink above it. And then the three ladies in pastel coats who bore him away afterward the minute it was over. They surrounded him and carried him off to a waiting car. I had the impression that this was to protect his privacy, not to get any more involved.

The lecture had provoked the audience, even if the private Stevens had inhibited the discussion, which went on into the night after he had slipped away.[14] Paul Weiss, the metaphysician who had spoken the week before, gives a sense of the reaction Stevens' remarks stirred. Though Weiss had left Mount Holyoke before the lecture, when he read it in *The Sewanee Review* months later he immediately wrote to the Hartford poet, arguing that the virile young poet should be matched against stronger philosophers than Stevens had cited in his essay before giving the match to the artist.

Paul Weiss

I was still at Bryn Mawr. I must have picked up the magazine in the library —I was always interested in poetry—and seen that article. When I read it, I thought he had not altogether understood the thinkers he was mentioning, and I wrote him what I thought was a kind of friendly letter, suggesting that perhaps he would like to modify it in the light of some things I might be able to tell him. I thought, Now here's a man saying some important things. I thought very highly of him, and I wanted him to see: now what were you going to do if you got a real, full-sized philosopher who's making a great contribution, one of the great historic figures? Are you going to speak in [a] derogatory way of him, as you did of Bergson?

[Among the points Weiss found debatable in the essay was Stevens' proposition that "if the end of the philosopher is despair, the end of the poet is fulfillment. . . ."][15] That is certainly not characteristic of most modern philosophers. I don't really see to whom he is referring. Even skeptics like Nietzsche, who disowns the possibility of really knowing what is the case, ends with a kind of optimism toward the future. I'd have to go back to Schopenhauer, with his pessimism. I would say certainly James was not a pessimist, Whitehead was not, Hegel was not. Maybe if you thought of Bradley, who was very critical of knowledge of this world, [but] even he thought there was a way of knowing what was actually so. I can't imagine to whom he is referring. As a matter of fact, my own attitude would have been [that] the people Stevens was most contemporary with, which were the idealists and the pragmatists, were overoptimistic. That means Royce, perhaps Hocking, and James. Santayana, of course, had some influence. Now Santayana was ironic rather than skeptical or despairing; cynical, perhaps, a little. But no, I think this was a period when Americans felt that they were in a growing, expansive period, and the challenges that were being made to established ways were merely challenges to more openness.

I met him once or twice. The time I remember most vividly was when he came to New Haven to read some of his poems [as Bergen Lecturer in 1948]. [After that meeting, Stevens wrote to the poet Theodore Weiss: "Weiss, the philosopher, came to the lecture at Yale and spoke to me afterward. I liked immensely what I saw of him. He has the same eager interest in everything that you have."][16] That's interesting that Stevens had this reaction to me, and yet he didn't move in on it. I don't remember the lecture at all. I just remember being so disappointed because I couldn't make contact with him. And the fact that I could hardly hear his poems being read and being amazed at a man who was so successful in business and who was so big in physical presence was so shy. He spoke hardly above a whisper. Had I not been in the first row, I would not have heard anything. After, I went over and introduced myself. Then a number of people came over and spoke to him. Afterward, I sat with him ten, fifteen minutes. I found him very shy, almost timid. I found it difficult to make contact with him. Then I discovered he was in awe of somebody who might be a philosopher and was sort of frightened he might have to talk to me [about] some of the things he had said. He was so damned shy that he didn't say to me, "Now let's sit down and talk about this." We spoke a little, but it was sort of polite, and he was always sort of moving away [from] rather than toward me. He apparently didn't realize the great respect I had for him, how highly I thought of him, and how willing I would have been to sit down and go over the matters that bothered him. But there was no real confrontation with me, no asking me the questions that he should have asked.

It was not unusual for Stevens to keep his distance from those he met at his public appearances with whom he felt affinities. Jean Wahl, who had been one of the brilliant prewar Parisian circle that included Valéry and Gide, lived only an hour away from Stevens at Mount Holyoke during the war. "He is precisely the sort of person that I should like to have down over weekends, talking about a thousand things," Stevens confided to their mutual friend Henry Church. "But that is out of the question."[17]

Despite Stevens' guarded debut at Mount Holyoke in 1943, he came to like the atmosphere at America's oldest women's college, its "feeling of friendliness and of being human, which women seem to create."[18] In April 1948, he returned to Emily Dickinson's alma mater to give the Kimball Lecture, rereading the paper on "Effects of Analogy" that Paul Weiss had just heard him deliver at Yale.* In April 1951, he again returned to present

*Stevens' Kimball Lecture on Friday afternoon, April 2, 1948, was the opening event in a special poetry weekend at Mount Holyoke College, the twenty-fifth anniversary of its annual Glascock poetry competition. Over the years Robert Frost, Marianne Moore and William Carlos Williams had been among the poets who had served as judges for this collegiate poetry contest, which had been won by such young writers as Robert Lowell and Muriel Rukeyser. Marianne Brock was the Mount Holyoke professor in charge of the Glascock competition at the time of Stevens' 1948 visit.

"In the mid-1940s, I wrote Stevens out of the blue. I told him about the Glascock. He refused very courteously [to be a judge]. He simply said that he didn't go in for things of that kind. But we did want him very much. It was two or three years after that [when Brock again invited Stevens to serve on the jury]. [He again declined to be a judge but agreed to give a late-afternoon lecture that preceded the evening's Glascock competition, won that year by Kenneth Koch. Stevens did not stay for the evening event, leaving immediately after his talk.] When he was leaving I asked him why he had finally come. He said he liked my letter, in which I said I could send a car for him, that he didn't have to go to the dinner, that he didn't have to take part in the affair at all, that I would send him home again. He gave us back the fee [for the lecture, stipulating that it be distributed, anonymously, to the young poets who would lose the competition].

"In 1952 we wanted Wallace Stevens for an honorary degree, but we thought it extremely unlikely he would want to come. He accepted right away [though he declined the invitation to give the commencement address]. Everything was always proper about him: he was ahead of time, no anxiety about anything. He was dignified and accepted the citation with the proper gesture. Alan McGee and I sat on the platform in the front row, tears rolling down our cheeks, we were so moved. We had almost been in tears for Marianne Moore a few years before. It an original essay, "Two or Three Ideas," to a College English Association meeting of New England professors. Joyce Horner and Elizabeth Green, members of the English Department at Mount Holyoke, attended both lectures; they got a closer view of Stevens than most of the audience at his 1951 lecture, however, when they chauffeured him the hour's drive up the Connecticut Valley from his Hartford home to the South Hadley campus.

Elizabeth Green and Joyce Horner

JH: My recollections are mainly of going to the house and meeting Mrs. Stevens. She was thin and faded—*blanched* was the word I used [in diary notes]—as if she'd been hiding in the house. It was a great surprise to me that she was a gardener, because she didn't look like a gardener at all. This was the end of April, and she must have been outside considerably, but she did not look as if she'd been outside. She was wearing a pink housedress. She received us; Mr. Stevens was not quite ready.

We had a very curious conversation. She said, "What do you teach? My ancestors were concerned with education." Here there was an interruption from Wallace Stevens, who had come in. "Need we go into that?" She went on. She said, "I never went to college, but I made good marks in composition and art, and I got an A in composition."

EG: I think this was in the fourth grade; I'm sure it was in elementary school.

JH: I thought perhaps there was some glow of remembering that she got an A on her own, but "glow" is too strong a word. As if she remembered that she had glowed before she met the man who was too clever for her. She gave us cocoa and biscuits. Wallace Stevens said, "What dry biscuits." She did not say "It is the nature of biscuits to be dry," but something like it. Then Elizabeth said, "I'd like to hear about your ancestors." She said they were Swiss schoolmasters, the first schoolmasters in Berks County. Well, at this point Wallace Stevens got up, impatiently. "He doesn't like me to talk about myself," she said, "but I do like people to know that I am interested in something besides cooking and cleaning. Oh, dear, you haven't finished your cocoa!" He certainly gave the impression of being dominant. What I surmised, probably most unjustly, was that she had been different earlier, that maybe after childbirth she had changed. She gave such an impression of naïveté, beyond any normal adult, in the language, in the sentences she spoke.

EG: My old Chevrolet barely got three people in. If one of them was Wallace Stevens, it was good the other was Joyce to balance it out. He told

---

was the quality of Stevens that did it; it was the thing we had given our lives to." (Taped interview.)

us [as we started the drive] that he had a sore throat, and he wasn't going to say a word all the way up. About all we said was "yes," or "no," and "thank you"—he talked nonstop.

JH: At the beginning he said, "I don't like to talk about poetry." That was a warning. When Sydney [McLean, a Mount Holyoke professor who had chauffeured him on an earlier occasion, had] picked him up, she had asked him why he called the poem "Peter Quince at the Clavier." He said, "It's in Shakespeare, isn't it?"

EG: He started out asking if I had any relatives in Hartford. He talked about the Greens in Hartford and environs for quite some time. I didn't have any relatives, but he explored the possibilities quite thoroughly.

He knew that we were going abroad that summer and asked us where we were going.

JH: He talked about Tom McGreevy in Dublin.

EG: "Fine young chap. Have you encountered him?" and the red-headed bookseller [Paule Vidal, in Paris] who had succeeded her father.

JH: And a refugee sculptor from Salzburg. One would have thought that he'd personally met them all.

EG: That he'd been to these places. We thought it was fascinating: what an urbane, traveled man. [Stevens, in fact, never went to Europe.]

JH: Elizabeth mentioned someone in another branch of the same insurance company, and he said, "We don't know many others. Being in bond claims is like being in Oriental languages at a university." He talked about a friend [his assistant Ralph Mullen] who was dying in the Hartford Hospital. He pointed out the Fuller Brush building and said, "I take my hat off to a man who can start with nothing. Interesting saga, the American Dream." He said at one point, "The beauty of Hartford is based on money."

If you had driven up without knowing that he was a poet and had that conversation, you would have thought he was urbane, traveled, wealthy, but you would never have suspected the poet, especially the kind of poetry he wrote.

EG: Such an intellectual and private kind of poet. It was much easier to believe the insurance company vice-president.

JH: At the end he said, "I'll tell my wife neither of you made any passes at me."

EG: I turned him over to whoever it was, probably Alan McGee [chairman of the English Department] just before the program began.

JH: Alan must have been very persuasive to get him to come up to that College English Association. When he got his program practically completed, Alan said, "But what we haven't got is the star speaker." Then he turned up with Wallace Stevens; it was a great coup.

EG: The talk was splendid. His voice was low. We all had the good sense by this time to crowd the front seats. I heard "Two or Three Ideas" much better than I heard his earlier lecture ["Effects of Analogy" in 1948]. It was a fully organized talk, complete from beginning to end. That was different from the talk he gave in 1948, which had been not so much an organized essay as a series of various remarks about imagination and about the importance of poetry. It had lacked the beautiful intricacy of the organization of "Two or Three Ideas." [In 1951] he stayed through lunch and the early afternoon; then somebody picked him up from the office and took him back.

JH: We ran into him in the course of the day. We must have asked him if he had been to any of the lectures. He said, "These fellows are probably fascinating, but I'm getting old."

· IV ·

NEW YORK CITY

It was rare for Stevens, even jokingly, to give his age as an excuse. He was much more likely to maintain that at seventy-one he felt like twenty-eight, as he did in his get-well note of April 23, 1951, to William Carlos Williams, who was recovering from a recent stroke. Indeed, Stevens' schedule of readings and lectures in 1951 hardly suggests that he was slowing down. In New York City alone that year he read at the YMHA Poetry Center, which was directed by John Malcolm Brinnin; lectured at the City College of New York; and spoke briefly at a banquet given by the Poetry Society of America, where he and Richard Wilbur received awards. Stevens also gave an acceptance speech at the National Book Awards ceremony presided over by the *Atlantic Monthly*'s editor Edward Weeks, the next year serving as an NBA juror under William Cole, who was head of publicity at Alfred A. Knopf, Stevens' publisher. Stevens' numerous Manhattan appearances in 1951 indicate not only the energy he put into his role as a public man of letters in his later years but also the pleasure he took in this belated public regard.

Stevens began 1951 with a lecture on poetry and painting at the Museum of Modern Art on January 15 that would prove far more important to his career as a public man of letters than he knew when he agreed to give the talk. Less than a week after that Monday lecture, Monroe Wheeler, who had invited Stevens to speak, wrote that the museum was eager to print the lecture. Stevens was quite willing and suggested that his publisher be contacted for the necessary permission to publish elsewhere. When Wheeler spoke to Alfred Knopf personally about giving the museum permission to issue this one lecture as a pamphlet, he also suggested that Knopf should someday publish a book-length collection of Stevens' essays. The idea appealed to Knopf, and before January was over he wrote to Stevens about the matter, chiding the poet for holding back that he had been writing prose as well.* Actually, some three years earlier Stevens had submitted his essays to his editor at Knopf, who had rejected them. In the spring of 1948, the young scholar William Van O'Connor had written to Stevens that he would like to make a collection of the poet's prose for publication by a university press. At first the idea appealed to Stevens, who suggested that for politic reasons his regular publisher should be given first refusal. When his editor at Knopf, Herbert Weinstock, rejected these essays, however, the poet's own insecurities about the value of his prose came to the fore, and Stevens scotched the idea of O'Connor proceeding any further with plans to publish through a university press. "There are just two things that made me decide not to republish the papers," Stevens later explained to O'Connor. "One is that they were not truly expressive because I had to draw them out so because they had to be of a more or less fixed length. The other is that Mr. Weinstock of Knopf's did not particularly like them and I valued his saying so because it only confirmed my own feeling about them."[19]

Now, in the late winter of 1951, as Weinstock reread these essays at Knopf's instigation, he changed his mind about their value. Knopf's interest in the project and the publicity Stevens was receiving at the time, with a gold medal from the Poetry Society of America in January and a National Book Award in March, may have helped Weinstock to read the essays in a new light. In any event, he wrote to Stevens on March 27 that he was enthusiastic about publishing the prose pieces. "I am glad that you think well of the essays. It makes me think better of them,"[20] Stevens replied in agreeing to the collection. In November 1951, Knopf issued *The Necessary Angel: Essays on Reality and the Imagination*, the legacy of Stevens' career as a public man of letters and a book that, just months before, Stevens had thought would never be published.

Monroe Wheeler

When we began having these occasional appearances of writers in the auditorium of the museum, I had Marianne Moore and Wystan Auden, so I wanted other great poets, too, and Stevens fitted in perfectly. He was fascinated by the assignment, that is, what a poet feels about painting. I discovered finally that he didn't know a great deal about painting; he really hadn't the time to study it. He visited the museums, there's no doubt about that; he paid close

---

*Alfred Knopf's letter to Stevens on January 29, 1951, written after Wheeler had spoken enthusiastically of Stevens' prose, tells a good deal about the distance the Hartford poet kept in his relationship with his publisher in nearby New York:

"I think you treat your publisher very badly. You come to New York, make speeches, read papers, receive medals and I read about it in the papers and hear of it from mutual friends. Why don't you let me know so that we could meet?

"I am told that you have taken to prose and that what you have written is not without importance and significance. And that some day you must put this prose together in a volume for us to publish. All of this sounds interesting and attractive and I hope that you will take me into your confidence one of these days." (HL.)

attention, probably, to art magazines, too. His favorite painter was Georges Braque, and we talked a lot about him. It was the style that suited him. He simply took pleasure in him; he didn't analyze [in conversation].

[Moore and Auden] simply gave readings of their poems [at the Museum of Modern Art]. But since I'd known, probably through Jim Soby, that Stevens was interested in painting, I chose the topic and consulted him about it. [At the lecture] people were polite and intensely interested. Naturally, the other poets were extremely respectful. He read ["The Relations between Poetry and Painting"], and you couldn't call it a rousing success, but people liked it.[21] I thought it was very personal, very intelligent, very subjective. I liked it myself.

He came back [to Wheeler's apartment after the lecture]. E. E. Cummings came back with us and his wife, Marion; and Loren MacIver with her husband, Lloyd Frankenberg, who had helped us arrange our appearances of poets at the museum. Loren MacIver had painted several of the pictures [in the apartment]; I remember thinking, after he'd gone, that Stevens hadn't looked at a single picture.

Stevens became quite elated and happy. Cummings was taunting him, as he did everyone; he loved to needle people in a very friendly way. Then Stevens got to talking about Key West and meeting Hemingway down there. He dwelt for some time on this Key West visit, which had made a deep impression on him. There was an altercation, that I remember. It was not to Hemingway's glory at all; Stevens was the hero of the episode. He thought that the whole thing was [funny]. And that episode, perhaps, had something to do with some story that he told that he considered off-color. He called me up the next morning to apologize for having told that raw story. I can't imagine how he could regret it; it wasn't raw at all, whatever it was. Only he was suffering, but nobody else paid any attention. I can't remember what it was; if I made a note at the time, I've lost it.

I did make a note of things that he said during the evening that related to genealogy. He had applied for membership in one of those venerable societies of pioneers, the Holland Society. They turned him down. It turned out that this woman he'd hired to compile his genealogy had faked one of the connections, and this had been discovered by the Holland Society. He said, "Imagine her taking the trouble to fake an entry for a paltry five hundred dollars."*

*Stevens paid Lila James Roney, a prominent genealogist, far more than five hundred dollars during the two years she worked on the Stevens family tree until her death in November 1944. That December, Stevens submitted the genealogy she had compiled to the Holland Society of New York; after the society questioned her findings on the Dutch-American background of

[T. S.] Eliot was mentioned, maybe Eliot had just been here or was coming to New York. He said that he made a point of not reading Eliot because he didn't want to be accused of being influenced by him. He told me, as I suppose he told everyone, how he wrote and when, on his way to work, composing the poems in his mind and then dictating them to his secretary. And then working them over evenings and weekends, especially weekends. He said he would retreat to [his] study and just come down for meals—and sometimes not even then, when he would be absorbed in his work. He mentioned a particular Sunday when he hadn't appeared at all.

I never went to his home. We had a curious conversation about that. He mentioned Carl Sandburg used to visit him and would simply call up and say that he was in town. Then Stevens would set about getting a room for him in a hotel. He heard afterward from friends that Sandburg thought it was strange that he never offered him any hospitality, that he never invited him to stay with him. And Stevens said that that had never occurred to him at all, never. He was really surprised by it and rather ashamed of himself for not having thought of it. But he must have been extremely inhospitable. I remember his also telling me about a poet named Charles Henri Ford. Apparently it was a summer day, and he entertained [Ford] outdoors. He said it soon became apparent that Charles Henri Ford wanted to get in the house to see what it looked like. He kept hinting and finally, I suppose, demanding the use of the facilities, he got in. This was very much resented by Stevens: the very fact that the boy wanted to see the inside of the house made him disinclined to show it.*

Michiel Stevenszen, from whom Stevens' paternal line was descended, Stevens reluctantly withdrew his membership application. For a fuller discussion of Stevens' interest in his genealogy and in the Holland Society, see chapter 8.

*Ford had visited Stevens at Westerly Terrace to do an interview for the surrealist magazine *View*. Commenting about that piece ("Verlaine in Hartford," *View*, September 1940, pp. 1 and 6) to a friend a few years later, Stevens confided another reason he resented Ford. "The Museum of Modern Art, at the present time, is being directed, I believe, by James Thrall Soby of Hartford. Soby is a very agreeable person whom I don't know except in the most casual way. He has a very considerable collection of modern French paintings, and devoted all of his thought and time and all of the money that he could scrape together to forming this collection up to the time he left Hartford, a year or so ago, to associate himself with the Museum during the war. He lives in Farmington [Connecticut] in a house specially arranged, I believe, to show his pictures. When young Ford came up here to see me I said, in substance, that Soby had a typical collection of modern French pictures. Ford had the cheek to report this as something very disparaging, particularly coming from one who had a mere handful of nothing at all and those things relics of nobodies. That is one reason why I don't like Ford. I had to write Soby a letter because he is the last man in the world that I would offend for any reason, since I hardly know him; moreover I am intensely interested in such of his pictures as I have seen." (Letter to Henry Church, December 3, 1943, HL.)

[A week after the Museum of Modern Art lecture, Stevens invited Wheeler to lunch at the Passy Restaurant in New York.] My recollection of that is food. He was a great gourmet, and he talked about his favorite foods and how hard it was to live in Hartford because there were no really great restaurants there. Neither were there any great grocers where he could buy the really fine fruit. That's why he loved to come to New York to buy wonderful fruit to take back with him to Hartford.

John Malcolm Brinnin

The first season that I had charge of the Poetry Center was '49 to '50. I'd written him saying it was inconceivable that we would have a season without Wallace Stevens. And he wrote back a little note saying "Thank you, but that is all soufflé." After he had refused one invitation, I made another [the next season], which he accepted with the proviso that there be no reception or any other social gathering in connection with his appearance. He came with Holly, and we met in the Green Room of the Poetry Center. He wore evening clothes and looked rather grand. When we were alone, he turned to me: "You know," he said, "on an occasion like this the voice is the actor." I said to myself, Fine, he understands that a reading is a performance. Then he went onstage and read for nearly two hours in the strictest monotone anyone had ever heard. The audience walked out in droves; they couldn't hear him, or if they did, found what he read absolutely without dramatic interest. A girl I knew left quite early. When I had a chance to ask her why, she said, "He looked like my *father*." They had come to see Wallace Stevens the romantic poet and found themselves looking at a business executive. Those who loved him of course stayed until the end. But as an evening's entertainment, it just didn't work. On the recording [taped at the reading] there's much more interest: whatever mental force directing what he's saying comes through. From that recording you'd never know the evening had been so monotonous.

[Introducing Stevens at the Poetry Center, Brinnin observed that one had to read Wallace Stevens to know what America was like, that Stevens was "in the American grain."]22 When you're very young and you come to Wallace Stevens and you begin to look at those sources, they seem all to come out of a European connection—except for a few little programmatic jars in Tennessee, or whatnot. But after a while, perhaps as I learned more about Europe and simply knew more about international poetry, I began to see that this guy was as American as Walt Whitman or Frank Lloyd Wright or Gertrude [Stein]—or any of our real home-grown, impossible people. That cranky, marvelous genius is really an American thing. It's something you sense, and when you see it, you know it. It's peculiarly American; I think we're beginning to see it now, beginning to be old enough and have enough exemplars of this thing. And yet I don't know how one would put it down in a sentence or two, just as you can't define the country in a sentence or two. But once you get away from clichés, it has something to do with both inheriting Europe and getting rid of it. I used to see Stevens as a delightful exotic. Now I see him with oats in his teeth.

My memories of him are not of any personal sort beyond the fact that I was the impresario [for Stevens' two readings at the Poetry Center]. There may have been an afternoon when he came for a drink when Holly had an apartment in Hartford and I was [teaching] at the University of Connecticut and used to go over there.

[While at the University of Connecticut, Brinnin arranged for Dylan Thomas's readings in America and was in constant contact with him, not only when Thomas was in Connecticut but throughout his tour of the United States in the early 1950s.] Like other British people, [Thomas knew nothing of] Stevens. To go to England and talk about Wallace Stevens as I did was to go to the Sahara. They didn't know about him, didn't want to. This was not an American poet; this was a sophisticate out of Paris and other nefarious influences, and [they] were very embarrassed that something so sophisticated should have arrived on American soil. They couldn't handle it, and they hardly can today. It's only been in the last fifteen years that Stevens has spoken to the younger British poets; they've discovered him for England. But it's incredible, almost as if there were a conspiracy of deliberate ignorance. Thomas had no sense of Stevens whatsoever; we talked a lot privately about poetry. If I mentioned Stevens—and I must have—there was no recognition.

[On the occasions Brinnin was with Stevens] I couldn't see the poetry in the man. I suppose, as the years have gone on, the anomaly has become less. There's no one I've known who's lived so completely outside of what his poetry might lead you to expect. When I was younger, this seemed very strange to me. As I'm older, I can see how this happens. After all, I've known enough people to realize that some of the quietest and most conventional have the most raging imaginations, and that some of the roaring boys are pretty thin, really, spending their poetic capital in life rather than on the page.

As the years go on and the picture becomes clearer, I think he's our great poet of the period. This isn't a sudden recognition; it's been a growing one, a deeper conviction.

Edward Weeks

I'd never seen Wallace Stevens read; I'd never heard him lecture, so [the National Book Awards ceremony] was my first chance to see him on view. He walked in so neat and well turned out in his gray suit and unspectacular necktie. He looked just as if he had dropped by on his way to the office in Hartford. He had great courtesy. So often it was a hurly-burly: all the book trade was there in those early days, the critics had been brought on from their various papers, so there was a great deal of greeting and quite a din. If I said five hundred, I'm sure I'm not exaggerating. They had to have a very big room for it. He remained in this untouched by the noise.

Of course, everything quieted down when the awards were made, and then each speaker rose to say why he was grateful for the honor. None of them did it as well as Wallace Stevens had done. He said everything he wanted to say in about five minutes, beautifully precise, expressive, very controlled utterance. It was a joy to hear a speech as succinct as that without any pretensions whatever.

In those days a large cocktail bar had been set up; after the formal events and the meeting adjourned, everybody flocked over to get cocktails and then moved around. It was a great example of American good will stirred up by alcohol, and a thing to avoid. I feel perfectly sure that Mr. Wallace Stevens escaped just as soon as he conveniently could.

William Cole

I was the head of the committee that pulled together the National Book Awards [in 1952]. It was traditional to make last year's winner a judge. Stevens agreed, to my surprise, because I didn't think he would like to do this sort of thing. I was pretty frightened, because he had been billed as a very imposing fellow. And he was. I think Virginia Woolf said about T. S. Eliot, he was a man who wore a four-piece suit, and that's the impression I got of Stevens. He was very austere; in fact, frightening. He was a very large man, with a great belly and a head like a melon. And a difficult fellow.

I remember the meeting of the judges very well. There were Winfield Townley Scott and Peter Viereck, Selden Rodman and Conrad Aiken. The meeting [was] very late getting started because Peter Viereck was caught in a snowstorm, and so we had to pass the time with four or five of us sitting around a table. I showed some pictures from one of the previous meetings of the National Book Awards, pictures of judges sitting around a table. One of those judges was Gwendolyn Brooks. Stevens looked at the picture and said, "Who's the coon?" Then he semi-apologized, saying, "I know you don't like to hear people call a lady a coon, but who is it?" Somebody mentioned a book by Witter Bynner that year. Stevens said, "Old Star-Spangled Bynner," which got a laugh from everybody. Then he decided to tell us a joke. "Pat and Mike were on the trolley car, and a nun came in and sat down. Mike said to Pat, 'What's that?' And Mike said, 'That's a nun.' Pat said, 'Why's she called a nun?' 'Because she never had none and will never get none!' " That was Stevens' joke! The only other thing I remember of that nature was talking about bad language in poetry. He said, "There is this poem that mentions a womb. I can't even pronounce the filthy thing."

Peter Viereck came, and we had the meeting. Stevens was a perfectly good judge but didn't have much to say about anybody but probably Miss Moore and a few other top ones. Stevens had to excuse himself early. He got up, put on his topcoat, and said, "You gentlemen will have to excuse me. I have a date with a lady." And off he went. He was Big Daddy, really. Everybody there deferred to him.[23]

The word at Knopf [where Cole was publicity director from 1946 to 1957] was leave him alone! Just do his books. He's not going to cooperate. Alfred Knopf just said, treat him carefully, and don't try getting him into publicity situations he doesn't like. But I knew that anyway. One didn't do any special publicity when a book came out for him. You just sent review copies. You didn't try to get him on the Mary Margaret McBride radio program.

[In October 1954, the Knopfs, however, did hold a luncheon to celebrate the publication of *The Collected Poems of Wallace Stevens.*]* Those luncheons were so horrible, I expunged them from my mind. These luncheons were stiff, formal, no jollity. I'm sure Knopf and Stevens were very formal with each other: no "Wally" or "Al."

Richard Wilbur

As for when I first met him, that would have been at the Poetry Society of America [January 24, 1951]. He was getting a gold medal; I was getting some kind of prize. It was at [Sherry's]. Many of us arrived quite a bit before the

---

*The guest list for this luncheon, held on October 1, 1954, included: Conrad Aiken, W. H. Auden, Jacques Barzun, Louise Bogan, Harvey Breit, Francis Brown, John K. Hutchens, Kermit Lansner, James Merrill, Marianne Moore, Norman Holmes Pearson, W. G. Rogers, Charles Rolo, Mrs. Harry Scherman, Delmore Schwartz, Wallace Stevens, Lionel Trilling, Irita Van Doren, Carl Van Vechten, Alfred A. Knopf, Blanche W. Knopf, Alfred Knopf, Jr., William Cole, William A. Koshland and Herbert Weinstock.

meeting began in the ballroom. We were all in the cocktail bar, and Stevens came in. He looked hale, jovial, rather nattily dressed but soberly so. The very embodiment of the *bonvivant*. He met everybody and introduced himself to everybody within a certain area very quickly. He organized a bunch of us around a table, bought drinks for everybody. He was very jolly. Nothing vulgar or backslapping about it, but very jolly. As I recall, he was sitting next to a pleasingly plump, middle-aged woman who was from Montana, and he kept joshing her about what he called "Mon-TAHN-a." In other words, he was in a good humor and was behaving like the noblest sort of traveling salesman.

And then, in the midst of all this gaiety, he leaned forward toward me, and he said with absolute seriousness, indeed something approaching grimmness —the look of an abbot talking to a novice—"Now, Wilbur, you're good, but you must stop publishing in *The New Yorker*." Well, I was very flustered— and happy to have him use the word "good" to me. I confusedly defended myself. I said that I didn't have any money, and that they paid the best of all the magazines. Also that to be published in *The New Yorker* meant that you got a pretty good wide readership, and apparently reached even Wallace Stevens. He said, "That doesn't matter. Money doesn't matter. If you're a poet, you must be prepared to be poor, if that's necessary. You must be like a monk. You must sacrifice yourself to your work." Now of course I'm not able to repeat what he said in his words, but he did say he felt it would be impossible for me to write over a period of years for a chic magazine that carried advertisements for Black Starr and Frost Gorham without adapting myself to their expectations. I remember countering by saying that as far as I could see, I had never adapted myself to any imagined audience. But I was much more impressed with what he said than with what I said. I was pro- foundly impressed with the ascetic and devoted view of things he took—and could suddenly switch into in the midst of all the gaiety he, in fact, had provoked.

I remember how William Carlos Williams, in the midst of saying some- thing admiring about Stevens, said, "But he's a damned monk!" The very thing Stevens said I ought to be. "He's a damned monk! He stays burrowed into his house there. He won't go out, and he won't mix in the literary life. He won't let himself have any fun." It was the ascetic side of Stevens that Williams couldn't understand, was rebelling against: why should a man give himself a miserable time?

Then we went up and he got his gold medal [from the Poetry Society]. I remember getting up and reading a poem of mine called "A World without Objects Is a Sensible Emptiness." The poem really says what Stevens says in one of his poems, that "The greatest poverty is not to live / In a physical world.''[24] And so I was in a position to say something gracious about the guest of honor as I rose to read my poem.

Among the audience at Stevens' New York appearances during these last years, at the Museum of Modern Art in 1951, say, or at the YMHA in 1954, were some who had come at the poet's invitation. They were often young admirers whom Stevens had befriended on his jaunts to Manhattan, such as the musician John Gruen and his painter-wife Jane Wilson, or the fledgling scholar Bernard Heringman. Stevens' invitation to Heringman at the time of his lecture at the Museum of Modern Art is particularly interesting in this regard. While he tried to discourage his daughter, Holly, from attending, saying it would only make him more nervous to have a family member in the audience, Stevens went out of his way to be sure that this graduate student from Columbia University was there. Heringman, who was beginning his dissertation on Stevens at the time, was a young scholar whom Stevens befriended with the idea that he would, like the scholars idealized at the end of "Notes toward a Supreme Fiction," help to "get it straight one day."

Bernard Heringman

I have a memory of him reading "The Noble Rider and the Sound of Words" at Princeton in 1941. I was a sophomore. He didn't deliver well; I couldn't hear him well. He was timid in his manner. He was too quiet; he was too impressed with the scholarly atmosphere.* That was somewhat true at the

---

*Frederick Morgan was also a Princeton undergraduate at the time of Stevens' 1941 talk. He recalls how primed some of the audience were for Stevens' visit and what the poet symbolized to some of the aspiring writers of the 1940s. "I was a member of the first creative-writing course at Princeton, under Allen Tate. This was very important in my life; in fact, it's what led me into a literary career, ultimately. In the course of reading contemporary poets like Stevens, T. S. Eliot, and so on, I developed my own literary interests. Tate spoke of Stevens' poetry with great admiration, and he spoke of his way of life, mentioning something to the effect that Stevens' associates didn't know about his poetry and that Stevens kept that whole side out of his business life. We, in the class, were somewhat favorable toward this way of Stevens, because our idea was, well, you have to make a living some way. You're not going to make a living writing poetry. This was in the days before poets could make money by getting university jobs just because they were poets—not that that's a great living even now. In those days, any of us who thought of a serious career as a poet and who did not have family money thought maybe Stevens had the answer. We had the image of this elegant man who had his life so neatly compartmentalized. This was very attractive to Joseph Bennett [Morgan's classmate and, later, co-founder of *The Hudson Review*] and to me at that time. I'm not sure that it would be particularly attractive to me now, but at that time that idea of control over one's way of life was very appealing. We had [R. P. Blackmur] in 1940–41 and read Blackmur's essays in *The Double Agent*, one of which was the great Stevens essay, so we had a lot of background on Stevens. *Harmonium* was already one of my favorite books of modern poetry. Well, of course, when Stevens came and gave this lecture, I was there.

"It was not a great crowd, maybe forty or fifty. I remember him sitting at a table and reading, almost as if it were a conference or preceptorial room, a more intimate setting. We were very

Museum of Modern Art. This is years later. He was less timid, less diffident in his manner, but he was subdued. He was a little in awe of his surroundings. He spoke, though, in a very sophisticated way: his references to art, and to philosophy, and to poetry were very high-level. He assumed a very sophisticated audience. He started with some complimentary remarks about having a select audience, a polite opening. I remember that he switched from prose to poetry, and it was hard for a moment to tell the difference. The style of it was very impressive, but the delivery was not.

[Heringman and Stevens had first met in New York in March 1949.] When I was working on my master's, I wrote him a letter importuning him as politely as I could to come to talk to him in Hartford. He wrote back a very polite but very cold rejection. After it was done, I said I ought to try again, I might want to do a dissertation on him. I sent him a copy of the thesis, with as ingratiating a letter as I could, not dishonest, but I wanted to know what he thought of it. He liked it and invited me to have lunch with him the next time he was in New York, where he would give it back to me.

That lunch he acted as if I were as rich and courtly as he. He wondered if the Passy would be good enough. He allowed it wasn't as good as it used to be, but there weren't too many talkative women there. He was taking me to lunch; I couldn't possibly have afforded that.

He had a real grace. We were both a little awkward at first. He was made less so by his efforts to put me at ease. He asked if I'd like a drink. Later, in what was a long lunch conversation and walk up Fifth Avenue, he mentioned, accidentally that same day, that his doctor had told him not to drink until dinnertime. In other words, he broke his doctor's orders to put me at ease. I'm sure he wasn't using that as an excuse; he wasn't that undisciplined. He did put me at ease. He was gracious without being at all condescending. I wasn't that young that I wasn't aware of the possibility. He took me seriously; he responded to my questions. It seemed not right to make it a strictly interview luncheon, so I didn't rattle off a systematic list of questions. I was careful not to waste his time with too much trivia. We both talked some trivia, though. He spoke about coming to New York once in a while so he could get the right handkerchiefs.

---

impressed by his figure, by his bulk, by his self-contained quality. At the same time, he did not read the lecture very well. His head was turned down a great deal of the time, so that one only saw the top of his head. That made it somewhat difficult to follow, so that we didn't get it as well as we might have had he delivered it in a looser way. It was as if he'd written a paper and read the paper. It went over the heads of a great many people there. I spoke of it to my friend Bennett; he hadn't heard it all either, and we decided we would have to wait until it was published and then read it for ourselves." (Taped interview.)

[The following remarks are based on notes of the conversation that Hering-man made either at the time or right after the luncheon. The italicized phrases show the notes as he made them.]

I asked him about *recordings for Library of Congress series. No, don't believe in it.*

I asked if *[William] Van O'Connor was editing [Stevens'] collected essays? No. He wanted to; Norman Pearson also wanted to. Don't want to give any more lectures or write essays and don't think much of ones written.* No, [he wasn't emphatic on this point]; he was being modest there. He didn't know why Allen Tate wanted to publish "The Figure of the Youth as Virile Poet," that beautiful essay!

New book soon or anything? No, but he is publishing poems in various mags. Has promised too many. Wants to do a Hymn to Johannes [sic] *Zeller, not his mother's father but an earlier ancestor—came over in second wave of German immigration—18th C.?—for religious reasons—settled Schoharie, on Hudson—moved to Pennsylvania.*

John Zeller made me think of John Rocket [in "Certain Phenomena of Sound"]. *Arbitrary name. MacCullough also an arbitrary name,* he said. I asked about Major Man. *"Nearest thing to God there is."* I had the feeling that it was something he didn't think particularly appropriate to talk about. He didn't answer in any clear way the relation between MacCullough and Major Man [both in "Notes toward a Supreme Fiction"].

I asked about the possibility of "Peter Quince at the Clavier" being in the *quartet structure. No, but he was thinking in terms of musical movements—sort of libretto,* he said. I'm very much interested in music. He was quite enthusiastic about Bruckner. He raved about the van Beinum recording of Bruckner's Seventh Symphony. He was emphatic enough that I made a note about the specific recording. He told me to be sure and listen to it. He wanted me to share his taste, which is nice, but I didn't do it. I was a snob. I asked if the sets of "variations" like the "Thirteen Ways" and "Man with the Blue Guitar" were on a musical analogy. He confirmed it but in a diffident way. He didn't push or want me to push it, any more than Eliot liked to push the quartet idea of *Four Quartets,* where one time he confirmed Beethoven, another time Bartók.

I also asked about the big change I had seen and written about in my dissertation, the new green symbolism starting with *Notes toward a Supreme Fiction*—that is, not the old green symbolism that represents primal nature, the typical sort of green symbolism, but a green with a synthetic meaning. He said he was *not specifically conscious* of any change. I observed that he was using all the primary colors and asked if he had some kind of color wheel in mind. He said, *maybe, but with the same reservations as above,* regarding musical movements: there was no conscious, systematic intention.

I asked about the man with the blue guitar, "A shearsman of sorts."[25] He said *probably not THE Picasso painting* of the old guitarist was in his mind then, *"hard to remember about many of these things."* He confirmed that the shearsman was a tailor and at the same time sitting in the cross-legged position, like the guitarist in that picture.

I asked about "Farewell to Florida" and its meaning. He said something to the effect that it meant a *farewell to the falseness, sham* of Florida.

I asked him, or he may have brought it up, what he liked about Hi Simons' work [an early critic for whom Stevens had written lengthy answers to queries about the meaning of certain poems]. Maybe this was a tip to me. *Hi got the things (poems, ideas, categories, etc.) in some kind of order—in categories (they aren't so in WS's mind;* he said, *no completely consciously worked out philosophy or other system).* If he praised Simons for doing this, I felt authorized, more or less, to do my own categorizing, which is probably what he intended: to disclaim responsibility but to allow the sensitive reader whatever categorizing made sense. He encouraged that from this and from other indications. The poem, as many poets have said, belongs to the reader. He liked the idea, he took that approach. Here's an approximate quote, *"Simons's much better than you'd expect of a man who'd call himself Hi. He does it deliberately. He's after the Real. Wants to be real."* I put an *R* to reflect his intonation.

He used to think Parts [of a World] *his best book, but lately he thinks it's* Transport [to Summer]! Simple chronology: the newest child is always the favorite.

He mentions Vidal in a poem ["The Latest Freed Man"]. *This is a book-and-art-shop keeper in Paris who used to get paintings for him via correspondence, now the daughter, Mlle. Vidal, does. ("I've never been closer to Europe than Staten Island.") She just sent him a couple (he raves about 'em —quietly) by Eric Detthow—Swedish-French School—contemporary—cheap.* He didn't say why [he bought his books and paintings in Paris]. I'm sure at least once he mentioned that things were cheaper in Paris than in New York. He liked getting things cheap. He mentioned one or two other painters that he liked and at least one or two that I knew slightly and didn't find worth his interest. He was too good a poet and too artistically sensitive. [He had some] established bourgeois taste. His clothes were like that, too. At that point I was more narrow-minded, and the whole idea of his being such a businessman and so devoted to his insurance work bothered me a little.

[There was a] *curious ambivalence about [his] job. He'll be 70 this yr (retirement mandatory at 70—"Unless they make an exception, and I think* *they will for me.")** I remember his tone. He was a little smug. I'm sure I looked disheartened that he wanted to go on working. *Nothing else to do. Can't go live in France (or London or Zurich). Too old and past age when he can devote all his time to poetry—he could have at MY age, he said. All this in spite of remarks and statements he's made about not having time for poetry or reading any more.* And he did speak of that kind of thing in person and in letters, of wishing he had more time to read, of wishing he could keep up with things better.

José Rodríguez Feo was the next person we talked about. *Young Cuban friend. Is going to the University of Madrid next fall—"Madrid is about the only place in the world I don't have the 'feel of.'"*

He also talked about Victor Hammer (typographer). WS likes him, or at least is interested in him—he's mainly a painter and sort of a mystic. We talked about Tom McGreevy and Jack Yeats. *Tom McGreevy—Irish poet, etc. who corresponds with him—knew Yeats—is friend of Jack [Yeats], the painter —lives across the street from him—wrote much TOO enthusiastic (says WS) praise of Jack for show of Jack's paintings. McGreevy wrote to him once to ask for one of his books. WS answered he'd be glad to exchange—provided McG wld. go across the street and get Jack to do a portrait of McG on flyleaf of copy he was sending WS—which was done.* He liked to make deals. After saying that McGreevy was too enthusiastic about Jack Yeats, he still made a deal.

I never managed to get him to correspond about Suzanne Langer. I was much impressed with her at that time and much impressed with him, so I wanted to bring them together, so to speak. I sent him a copy of *Philosophy in a New Key,* a cruddy paperback edition, as a compliment for the luncheon. He talked some about philosophy, about his own amateurish approach to philosophy, but I don't think he ever responded about her. He did somewhat avoid getting into sounding like a philosopher. He didn't want to be taken to be a philosopher, in spite of so many writers since who have insisted on treating him as one. I'm not sure how much of it is from letters any more, but altogether he made it clear to me that he did not think of himself as a philosopher and that he didn't want to be thought of as a philosopher.

I made a note because it flattered me. He *was very pleased that I caught*

---

*The Hartford Accident and Indemnity Company continued to exempt Stevens from retirement until the time of his death. His exemption was not unique; during his years at the Hartford, the company had a rather flexible retirement policy. In May 1954, for example, the board of directors stated that it would not enforce retirement at seventy but instead would require an annual report on all employees over that age which would review their position in the company and their ability to continue in that post. At the time, Stevens was one of fourteen employees over seventy ("Hartford Accident and Indemnity Company, Board of Directors' Records," no. 2, p. 156, HIG).

*his special feeling (frisson—"do you know the word?") for certain lines: e.g.,
"A fictive covering/Weaves [always] glistening from [the] heart and mind."*
("Notes toward a Supreme Fiction.") *WS says definitely to write him—and
he'll look at my poems—probably wants to, but I said, "Maybe I'll send them
in a couple of years."*

When we referred to the concept of poetry for poetry's sake, he said, *"But
it depends on what you mean by poetry!"—approx. quote—"The poet supplies
the whole spiritual life . . . the idea of God is a poetic idea . . . poetry is
everything on 'that' side,"* which is partly a definition of poetry and partly a
recasting of the meaning of the word. You can never be quite sure with him.
He was really very modest and very humble in manner. He didn't talk
oracularly. He said this in a very offhand way. I made notes that come out
sounding oracular when you look at them, but he did not speak, with a capital
P, profoundly. He dropped these things. He wanted me to hear them, and
he knew I would be taking notes, but he didn't pronounce them. That's part
of what I liked about him.

The next note implies the question I asked, which is what I was working
on in my dissertation [imagination and reality in Stevens' work]. *WS said—
there is something to this alternation between imagination and reality (i.e., the
weighing of the two, the attention to them—one against the other, one with
the other, etc.) . . . if a man's mind—he meant himself—happens to work on
those lines there's good reason (WS justifying his own patterns)—WS tries to
get closer and closer to a major statement of or about it—about Imagination
and Reality.* I spoke about going ahead with my dissertation. *"If you want
to go ahead with it, I can guarantee you a careful reading by Knopf."* He died
before I was finished.

*This business of obscurity. WS says his poems aren't obscure. He writes
something he sees or has seen or known clearly. The main thing is to have it
right for yourself. Nobody else ever sees it exactly the same anyway. But you
put it down as it is to you, and it's clear and sharp and simple. You fail
sometimes—(he gave an example I couldn't remember to locate accurately—
I think it was from "Examination of the Hero in a Time of War"—where he
missed—didn't get it clear to himself).*

Lunch lasted a couple of hours. When I realized how long it had been, I'm
sure I said something apologetic, and he reassured me. I remember walking
up Fifth Avenue with him on the way to his next appointment or to shop.
I didn't go all the way; I didn't want to impose on him.

Another time, he was on his way to Bard College.* I had written, hoping

---

*Stevens went to Bard on March 30, 1951, to receive an honorary degree during a literary
weekend at the New York college. Among the speakers that weekend was the writer Glenway

to see him again, and he didn't want me to come to Hartford. Anyway, he said if I liked—he was diffident about it; he didn't want to take it for granted —he said he'd have a couple of hours, and we could take a walk together. We did. We sat at the first [rail] station and talked for quite a while, and then we walked to the other station, talking all the way. I always had mixed feelings about making notes. It didn't seem right to try and be a Boswell. I don't have any notes from that conversation; I felt that we were something like friends then. There was at least one other lunch. We went back to the Passy; it was after I came back from Paris [in 1950, after a Fulbright Fellowship. Finally, in 1952], he actually invited me to Hartford [on Heringman's return to Montana, where he was teaching. Heringman, however, did not go, though they corresponded until the poet's death in 1955].

I've mentioned my favorite memories. It shows more in his letters, but his sense of humor ought to be mentioned. He did have a quite special one. I wrote him a telegram for his seventy-fifth birthday. This was his thank-you note, October 6, 1954: "When Western Union read me your birthday wire and particularly the words—Peace, Pleasure and Promise of Poetry, I asked

Wescott, a last-minute substitute for the ailing William Carlos Williams. "They called on me very suddenly. Williams [had] had his first stroke, and Kenneth Burke and I were on the program. Kenneth had prepared a paper. It came on so suddenly, I did [my talk] without much preparation. I hadn't been told that Stevens was going to be there. And I was deeply moved, sort of scared. When I got done, he stood up and he said, 'I'm sure you've all enjoyed hearing Mr. Wescott's talk, and I have, too. And I want to remind you of something which may not have occurred to you, that what he says to you is the summing up of a lifetime of love of poetry.' I thought it was so kind of him. I didn't expect him to be kind, he was such a curmudgeon to look at. I feel that he felt I had done my best—and it wasn't very good and I knew it— and he wanted to come to my rescue.

"[Years before] I [had] sent Stevens my first little volume of poems, published by Monroe Wheeler. And I inscribed it, 'To my secret master.' The secret was that I wasn't talking about him much: he wasn't really loved by the people around me, and I didn't feel strong enough to fight about it. Everyone around me in Chicago in those days was just mad about poetry, and there was quarreling. The Americans against the Europeans: Ezra Pound in the mess and the locals, Vachel Lindsay. I think that the poem that I liked most in the world in my twenties was 'Sunday Morning.' It was simple and traditional. I think I was ashamed to speak for it because I was tired of being beaten up for it.

"Both Stevens and Williams resented the London connection. Through Harriet [Monroe, editor of Poetry], it reached into our culture more than it deserved to. Yvor Winters made me read the French poems that Pound recommended. When I got to Paris to live, the French simply couldn't believe that I knew Laforgue, Corbière and that I had never read Baudelaire: Ezra, one of the most ignorant men that ever drew breath!

"[After young Wescott had sent Stevens his first book of poetry, Stevens] wrote me a letter: 'Dear Mr. Wescott: It is very difficult to make this sort of poetry fly, but you certainly make it shiver and shake.' " (Taped interview.)

For a full account of the Bard weekend, see Theodore Weiss's "Lunching with Hoon: Wallace Stevens," *The American Poetry Review*, September/October 1978, pp. 42–44.

the girl if you said anything about money. So she read it all over again. And here I am at work as usual."[26] He didn't crack jokes with me, but there was humor like this, very quiet, very low key [when we met]. He was freer in his letters than in person, I suppose.

[He was] courtly, gentle, sensitive—such trite words. Physically massive, spiritually not at all massive. Intellectually massive, yes, but self-effacing, even intellectually. I mean he didn't push his ideas at all. Never pompous, as far as our personal contacts. I'm not just being grateful for his disguised conde-scension. He was plain, and straight, and courteous with me in spite of the vast distance in age and stature. He was a pleasant man, very pleasant.

John Gruen and Jane Wilson

JG: The poetry of Wallace Stevens has always totally captured my imagina-tion, especially my young imagination. What I found so beautiful about this work was that, (a) I couldn't understand it, and (b) it was filled with so many gorgeous colors and images that I was very moved reading them. I thought the man must be so fascinating, and so romantic, and so American; and yet he's so French at the same time. The whole sensibility seemed to be such an odd mixture; that appealed to me immensely.

During those years I was involved in writing songs. One of the reasons why I wanted to write songs was because when I met my wife, Jane, she sang, and so, to induce our love even more, I composed songs that she would sing. That's how it all began, but then I flourished as a young composer of art songs, which I'd always loved. As I was born in Europe, I was very frightened of setting any American poetry. Some of my very early songs are German, or French, or Italian. But then I looked around for works to set and came upon several American poets, notably E. E. Cummings. Then came this mysterious Wallace Stevens figure into our lives. I think Austin Warren introduced us to *Harmonium* and various other volumes. I was tremendously intrigued. Among the poems there was one called "Thirteen Ways of Looking at a Blackbird." I fell instantly in love with it and [later] wrote what is considered my best song cycle. He must have been aware of the fact that his poetry did lend itself to musical setting because it is so musical to begin with. Sometimes very musical poetry does not at all lend itself to musical setting.

JW: Like [Dylan] Thomas.

JG: That's right. Or E. E. Cummings, although he's written many beauti-ful romantic poems, many of which I've set. The poems ["Thirteen Ways of Looking at a Blackbird"] were very short, and that was challenging; and they were filled with this insistent image that kept recurring, the lovely idea of using that one bird to create several worlds. What I was inspired by was the guises of that blackbird, what it all could be. I tried to become very expressive of them in my music. It was one of my first American settings; at the University of Iowa, where I went to school, I had set T. S. Eliot, that was my first American poet.

I must have written [to Stevens] for permission [to set the songs]. I said to him, "I am in the process of composing these songs based on your poem and I would love for you to hear them. So would you please come to our house and listen to me sing them?" I told him, "I certainly don't have a good voice, but it's one of those musical composer's voices. Come and have something to eat." For some reason, God only knows what it could have been, he accepted the invitation and came to where we lived.

JW: 324 Bleecker Street, above a shoe-repair shop.

JG: We were really in deep shock at the fact that he agreed to come. What could he have seen in us that intrigued him enough to come? It must have been just *chutzpah,* insisting on my part.

JW: I suspect that it may have been an interesting, relatively remote relationship with young people who were starting out and who were connected to various parts of the current [scene], since music, art, dance and poetry were all interrelated at that point.

JG: We were unhampered by the weight of life, and he must have sensed that, my composing and Jane's painting. We were very free.

We were expecting a certain romantic figure, someone who spoke poetry. Great poets tend sometimes to even speak poetry. And there enters this man, a kind of solid citizen, who was far from the poetic image. He was a marvelously, impressively handsome-looking man. It struck me as being so funny, to have this man be of such opposites from what his poetry suggests in a way, the lyricism that must have been inside him to have been encased in this stolid frame. Up came this burly gentleman. He was not outgoing in the sense of effusive, but he was friendly and reserved, and had a quiet wit, understated wit. He was not a talker. He stayed for two or three hours.

JW: It must have been in mid-June [1953]; it was a weekday. There was a fancy vegetable and fruit store on Fifty-ninth Street, and he always stopped there and bought on his trips to New York. He may have brought a little fruit for us. My memory, of course, is absolutely visual. What I remember is this late, very sunny afternoon. We had a black, shiny dining-room table, one of those Italian things of the period with dark lacquer on it, and he sat at that table. On the table was a big green glass bowl, which probably had fruit in it. And there was this tall man of tremendously impressive bearing, white-haired, sitting at the table, leaning on it, with the black cats climbing up in his lap. He sat and he listened, made a few remarks. John made conversation nervously; I think Wallace Stevens was quite satisfied [with the silences].

JG: I desperately tried to fill the gaps by making chitchat about something or other—God knows what it was. But, then, there were also pauses. I remember that he spoke very slowly.

JW: With great deliberation. Very low voice.

JG: A kind of monotone and a kind of heaviness, which was his bearing in general. A kind of even, measured speech that was impressive.

I think he did ask me where I was from. I told him I was born in France and raised in Italy. He said he'd never been, and I said I couldn't believe it. He just smiled, gave me a sly look. Now he did say something amusing. "I don't separate my poetry from business. You see, actually I bring my poetry to work and my secretary types them up for me. It's my way of being disloyal."

JW: I remember his talking about how he always walked from the office. Somehow I have an image of terribly cold winter weather associated with that: he must have talked about the ice and snow and trees, and the length of the walk. It's all in a poem ["On the Way to the Bus"].

JG: I asked him what his poetry was really all about. He was very vague. I think he said something to the effect that poetry was such a private matter that it was not possible for him to speak of it. He spoke more about the experience of how it is to make a poem. He told me that he didn't know what his poetry meant at times, that he really had to think hard as to what he meant by that image or that phrase or that word, even. He talked something about submersion, about words being submerged and then rising out, that they seemed to have been hidden and then revealed themselves, if I remember correctly. He then put the word down, and that revelation was then forgotten. There was something rather mysterious about his writing the poetry.

We did not speak of personal matters at all, although it's my wont, having gone into the profession [of] interviewing people and always being very inquisitive about their private lives. But I was awe-struck. He was not a man given to volunteer information. It was interesting to meet his daughter, who came here once [when she was editing *Letters of Wallace Stevens*]. We had a long talk; it centered on her father and the book she was doing.

JW: She talked a great deal more about what their daily life was like. There was a sense of tremendous strangeness and strain [between her and her mother].

JG: I think she may have said something to the effect that she was not very close to her mother and that she was close to her father but only in the last years. She may have said something by which I surmised she didn't know her parents and that they were very strange people, that she was a late child and therefore was, perhaps, stuck with these older people as parents, which I know something about because a fairly similar thing happened to me.

JW: She was almost like an ambulatory orphan, very grieved.

JG: He said to me immediately, "I don't have a good ear, and I don't respond to music very much." One minor things floats into my mind is that he may have told me that he did not think of his poetry as particularly adaptable to music.

JW: All this before [the song setting] was played. Imagine! We had an early dinner [followed by the performance].

JG: I felt very nervous. I sang the songs, but I noticed from out of the corner of my eye that he was distressed over the fact that we had these three cats, and one or two of them fell in love with Wallace Stevens and started leaping on him. I could tell he couldn't bear it, so my feeling is he didn't hear anything—just distressed over [the cats]. When I finished, I think he must have said nice things, of course. He stayed for two or three hours. He was a figure who was remote and also mysterious, someone to be cherished from a distance—not only geographic, but even when he was in the room.

At any rate, when my songs were recorded, I sent him the record. He sent this charming letter, saying, "The record of Thirteen Ways etc. is in Class A. Miss Neway has a voice perfectly adapted to your score. Please hand her a bouquet for me. I should like to have two or three more of these records. There is no address for Contemporary Records, Inc. on the cover. Where shall I write?" Then he said, "They are publishing a book of some of my poems in Italy about now. The translation is by R[enato] Poggioli of Harvard. His translations seem to me to be excellent. When my copies come, I shall send one of them to you. You can then let me know, if you care to, what your own judgment of them is since Italian is your native tongue. I have been to New York only twice since last summer and did not go south of Grand Central," meaning where we lived. "But I look forward to seeing you and your wife before long."[27]

I asked him to come and read in 1953. My wife began her New York career with [the Hansa Gallery]. I enlisted or pushed my way into it, saying, "I will do events, so that I will get people to come to this gallery, and they can look at the wall paintings." I did have four people come to speak, among them Wallace Fowlie—he spoke to us about Proust, of course; and James Johnson Sweeney talked about Gaudí. Among the people I wanted was Wallace Stevens, so I wrote him and asked him if he would be part of the series, that we could not pay anything, except twenty-five dollars. He wrote back: "But there is not the slightest chance of my coming down to read. . . . You are going to have a remarkable roster of speakers. It just shows how eager many people, apparently including old maids, are to get things off their mind."28

[In December 1954] I received a communication from Wallace Stevens informing me that a composer by the name of Vincent Persichetti had set the entire *Harmonium* to music. That was a marathon and beautifully done. "Dear John"—it was now "John"; it used to be "Mr. Gruen"—"Vincent Persichetti's setting of *Harmonium* is going to be sung by Leyna Gabrielli on Wednesday, December 8, at 8:30 P.M. in the Current Music Series at the New School for Social Research at 66 W. 12th Street. I have never heard this and the present performance is taking place at a time when I could not possibly be in New York because of something that has long since been arranged for here at the office in Hartford. If by any chance you go, I shall be glad to have your impressions."29 So I went and indeed wrote him a rather full description.

[A few months earlier] there was a concert of my songs being given by Georgianna Bannister, and she sang the "Thirteen Ways." Naturally I had invited him to come. He wrote, "I wish I could hear Miss Bannister but it is going to be impossible for me to attend. I shall be glad to do what I can for you when the Guggenheim inquiry comes in"—already I was taking advantage of my famous friends, saying would you please recommend me. I never got the grant. "I am horrified to find that you have left Bleecker Street. Best wishes to both of you. Looking forward to seeing you after the reading on November 6."30

It was the only reading [YMHA, 1954] I have ever gone to of his. I will confess that I don't enjoy poetry readings at all; I prefer reading poetry on my own. Some poets are in the habit of intoning in a way that is deeply offensive to me because it is just very unreal. He was so boring that I thought I would fall asleep; in fact, I think I may have. The place was jam-packed. It was a great event, and everybody went. I was really distressed: he mumbled; you couldn't hear him.

JW: He stood on the stage, and his head never came up, always directed down at the lectern. There must have been a microphone.

JG: There was, but the words [were] all muffled. And too, that was rather poignant, the fact that he faltered in his reading, stumbled over words, which naturally diminished the impact of his gorgeous poems. It seemed ironic to us that this man who wrote this extraordinary poetry would then be so unclear about yielding forth the words in his own voice. It was very long; that added to the ennui.

JW: There was some sort of reception in one of the side rooms.

JG: I remember he looked quite flushed.

· V ·

CHICAGO

Late in his career, Wallace Stevens accepted a speaking engagement which took him considerably beyond the corridor between New York and Cambridge where he normally lectured. He had turned down invitations much closer to home because they were not in his orbit, but on November 16, 1951, Stevens came to the University of Chicago as a William Vaughn Moody Lecturer.

Free to choose any subject related to his craft, Stevens had prepared an address on the poetry of philosophy—that is, the poetic nature of certain philosophic concepts. "A Collect of Philosophy," which he subsequently read in New York as well, turned out to be his last major address. It was not particularly well received at the University of Chicago, recalls Elder Olson, a poet on the faculty, who dined with Stevens at the university's Quadrangle Club before the lecture.

Elder Olson

I was on the Moody Committee at the time, and [Morton Dauwen] Zabel ran it all in a rather peremptory fashion—that is, he would make up his mind and ask us whether we approved. Of course, we would approve in the case of such persons as Stevens.

Stevens was here alone, and it was the practice of the university in such circumstances to have an all-male dinner. Zabel was certainly there; George Williamson was there: eight [in all]. Stevens sat at one end of the table, and I sat immediately to his left. We had various odds and ends of conversation. He asked me whether everybody there was an English teacher; I assured him that was probably the case, although there may have been a few "foreigners." I remember in the course of the dinner asking him about the phrase "Rouge-Fatima" [in "Academic Discourse at Havana"]. I said that had always puzzled me. He told me that he had originally intended to put in something like Helen of Troy but decided the poor girl was overworked, especially in poetry, and so he thought of another beautiful woman. I pronounced the word "Fa-TI-ma," by the way. He corrected my pronunciation and said it was "FAT-i-ma." I said, "That's fine, but what about the rouge?" "Oh," he said, "that's just to dress her up a bit."

He then asked me when philosophic ideas became poetic. I told him, when they were handled by poets, and that pure concepts as such had no reference to poetry. Something else had to be done by the poet. He said, "Don't you think there are any ideas which are inherently poetic?" I said I would deny that as I would deny there is any subject which is inherently poetic. I did not know that this was to be one of the topics of his lecture. He didn't argue. He meditated. He struck me all the way through as a very reflective and reticent man. He would hear something, and you could see him think about it; you could practically hear him think about it. He spoke in sentences, not in paragraphs. There was no such thing as a connected argument. What you had instead was a series of intuitive and highly perceptive remarks. When he got on a subject, he would talk with flashes of intuition. That was not a man who thought consecutively. You will find that to be the case with his essays from *The Necessary Angel* and *Opus Posthumous*. His real style was the "Adagia," and that was very much his conversational way.

My own feeling was that he would be very frank with you, that there was a very tough nut underneath, a tough kid of the kind I like. I suppose that's one reason why we struck it off; such people recognize each other. He was a man who was buried under many layers. In the first place, may I say that he was the only poet I ever knew who was a complete gentleman, as I certainly am not, for example. My favorite translation of *"poeta nascitur, non fit"* is Ford Madox Ford's "A poet is a nasty cur even when he isn't having a fit." Dylan Thomas was a schoolboy, very funny. Marianne Moore was very much the spinster schoolteacher. And Edna Millay was the medieval princess, fatigued by too many chivalric romances. But the one who stands out in my mind not only as the best poet I ever met but the most complete gentleman was Stevens. He had a kind of courtesy and interest in the other person. Now he did not, like Thornton Wilder, ask you a whole series of questions about yourself. With Stevens there was a sense that he looked right into the essence of the person, and that odds and ends of facts did not too much matter for him or interest him. At the same time you had the notion of layer after layer. This was a very reticent man who did not speak directly about personal experiences. I think he thought personal experiences were useless except for practical purposes as, let's say, *materia* for poetry. And in that last sense, they would have value only as translated by the imagination into the blue guitar music.

Subsequently he lectured at Leon Mandel Hall, which holds about fifteen hundred people; it was pretty nearly full. It was not as full as it was for Dylan Thomas, for example, when the place was absolutely jammed. Or as full as it was for Eliot and his lectures, when it was impossible to get a seat unless you had a private in. The lecture caused me the same difficulties on reading it when *Opus Posthumous* came out. The fact of the matter is there's no logical coherence. I'm an old teacher of logic; naturally, I look for logical compendency. You had one flash of insight followed by a quotation from Bruno, or Leibnitz, or whomever. He was worried about the philosopher as poet, the poet as philosopher, the question of whether there was an inherent poetry in an idea. I say "worrying" because remember in "The Glass of Water" we had "fat Jocundus, worrying." It was that kind of thing, worrying rather than inquiring, and inquiring rather than proving. There were too many flashes of intuition into problems rather than solutions. [Yet] these were valuable. It was the inquiring mind, not equipped professionally with methods and methodology to work toward a solution. With all this bragging of mine about logic, the truth of the matter is that training in logic would not have helped him because his area was the area of intuition and perception.

[George Williamson, who was sitting next to Olson at the lecture,] said, "The whole damn thing came out of [Arthur Kenyon] Rogers' *A Student's History of Philosophy*. He had a great respect for Stevens as a poet, but he didn't think much of the lecture. As a matter of fact, the lecture did not go over very well. People were very cordial and polite because of the fineness of the poet, but as lectures go, we've heard better ones. He gave his speech, and we went up and thanked him. That was that, and off he went.

A few weeks after Stevens had returned home from Chicago, he sent a copy of "A Collect of Philosophy" to Paul Weiss, then editor of the *Review of Metaphysics*. Weiss had been one of the philosophers Stevens had contacted when he began to work on the lecture in mid-August, asking him to suggest a few major ideas of modern philosophy that were inherently poetic.[31] Weiss obliged and was understandably interested in the outcome of Stevens' speculations. In early December Weiss asked Stevens to submit "A Collect of Philosophy" for possible publication in the *Review of Metaphysics*.[32] After reading the lecture, however, Weiss shared some of the reservations of Olson and others who had heard it earlier at the University of Chicago, and he returned the manuscript to Stevens.

Paul Weiss

It is a very strange mixture. Every once in a while, he edges up to give us an answer to that fundamental question of what philosophy and poetry have in common. But then, when he talks about philosophy itself, he very foolishly was content with referring to an elementary textbook such as Rogers' *A Student's History of Philosophy*. It was the sort of reference that made me think I couldn't possibly publish it in a highly technical magazine. Now the other thing about it is that he actually never tells us, which is what he should have done, *what it is* that philosophy and poetry both see. And that is what I hoped he would do. That there is something in common, of course, I think is correct. I think it's wrong of people like Heidegger to say that poetry knows reality better than philosophy does because how does he, a philosopher, know that it knows it better? And I don't think you can say that necessarily philosophy knows it in a way that poetry cannot, except insofar as the two disciplines are different. But the interesting thing would be in what sense do they catch the same reality with their different tonalities? And this, unfortunately, is what Stevens does not tell us.

He is a phenomenologist—that is, somebody who is alert to what he confronts and gives it its full value, doesn't reduce it by virtue of some preconceived concept, but tries to accept things in their immediacy and their full richness. This is, of course, what one looks to in a poet, somebody who knows what he is looking at, somebody who knows how to accept the phenomena in their full, complete immediacy. I think of him as one who thinks that the world that we see every day is encrusted with all kinds of conventional meanings and that the whole function of the imagination is to penetrate beyond those and catch what the phenomenon really is as it is, there in its nakedness and full phenomenological clarity. That's why he is constantly thrusting in, breaking up the images, challenging the ways, and even, I think, opposing the philosophers because he thinks they're encrusting it. Therefore, I think it's right to say that he's a man of metaphysical insight who then uses the result as an object for phenomenological examination. I always think of Stevens as involved in the immediate, confronted data, which he then sees with a philosophic or even metaphysical depth but interprets in phenomenological terms. That's what we find in what he says about appearance and almost every other thing. I would say from what I've read of Stevens —and I'm not an authority on him or somebody who's worked on it very hard —that his ultimate passion was to try to get to the clean, clear ultimate reality, which required a thrust through everything that we are thinking, naming, using, saying. What I'm not clear about is what he saw when he got there.

As you can see from the quotation I have taken from him in my book *Beyond All Appearances,* I think that he has real philosophic insight. Say "The Emperor of Ice-Cream" is an insight into how some ordinary humdrum occurrence can stand out as a pivotal event in somebody's life. In that sense, he is somebody that a philosopher can read with pleasure and understand, but when he begins to write in prose as if he were talking technically about philosophy, he's rather naïve.

I once published an article by Ted Weiss arguing with a geologist about the nature of poetry and science in the *Review of Metaphysics,* so I was interested in bringing this out. This was the side of philosophy I thought was neglected, and here was a man [Stevens] who could do it. I was embarrassed by the very elementary quotations and references [in "A Collect of Philosophy," however]. I would like to have had such a paper rewritten. Judging from some things that Norman Pearson said to me, Stevens was somewhat hurt by the letter I wrote him, though I never intended to hurt him. He was a very sensitive man.

Weiss sent an extremely tactful rejection letter on December 8, praising the address and suggesting a number of literary quarterlies more suited to publishing it than his philosophy journal.[33] On January 24, as Weiss was preparing to give a talk in Hartford, he again wrote Stevens, hoping to arrange a visit with him when in town. In his note, Weiss also mentioned that he had heard through Norman Holmes Pearson that *The Yale University Library Gazette* was interested in "A Collect of Philosophy," and he encouraged Stevens to send it there.[34] That day, however, Stevens had written Pearson that he now thought so ill of his recent speech he no longer wished to publish it.[35] While Stevens continued to read his poetry and to give brief remarks until his death four years later, "A Collect of Philosophy" turned out to be his last major lecture, his final attempt to make a contribution to the theory of poetry. Given its qualified reception and his own final estimate of it, Stevens' Chicago address had brought the major phase of his career as a public man of letters to a poignant close.

CHAPTER FIVE

The Church Circle

On November 26, 1951, Wallace Stevens read "A Collect of Philosophy" to a lunchtime gathering at the Harlem campus of the City College of New York and then headed to a cocktail party in his honor downtown. As often happened on his frequent trips to New York during the last fifteen years of his life, Stevens ended his day in Manhattan with a few pleasant hours at Barbara Church's *salon* before taking the 8:00 P.M. train back to Hartford. For the first time in years, Stevens had become part of a literary circle, which he had not done since the breakup in the early 1920s of the group of experimental poets and painters, such as William Carlos Williams, Marcel Duchamp and Alfred Kreymborg, who had once gathered at the West Side apartment of the wealthy young connoisseur of modernism, Walter Arensberg. Now, some thirty years later, Stevens was again part of a New York circle, presided over by yet another wealthy collector of modern art and artists. That November afternoon, Mrs. Church had invited a small group of friends from this circle to her Park Avenue apartment to celebrate Stevens' recent lectures.

Stevens' visit to Mrs. Church was an appropriate epilogue to his talk, which he had first given ten days before at the University of Chicago, since she had had a hand in writing "A Collect of Philosophy." The previous July, as Stevens began to mull over the theme of his paper, the poetry of philosophy, he had written to her at her summer house at Ville d'Avray, outside Paris. Would she talk to her philosopher-friend at the Sorbonne, Jean Wahl, and ask for his thoughts on the inherent poetry of many philosophical concepts? Stevens would later open his essay with a summary of the historical survey of such ideas that Wahl eventually provided. But Mrs. Church had gone one step further. "I shall also ask Jean Paulhan, he might have amusing and more original ideas," she wrote back to Stevens at month's end. "He loves new approaches and in his paradoxical way often gets the answers—anyway it will be something we both like to talk about."[1] The question of whether certain ideas are inherently poetic was the kind of thing that Barbara Church and her late husband, Henry, had enjoyed discussing with the group of artists and intellectuals who gathered at Ville d'Avray, either under the poplars on the estate during a summer's afternoon or inside the eighteenth-century château on a winter's evening. Jean Paulhan, editor of *Nouvelle Revue Française* and co-founder of her husband's literary magazine, *Mesures,* had been a happy afterthought of Mrs. Church. His suggestions did, indeed, prove more useful than Wahl's, for Paulhan first called Stevens' attention to the ideas of the physicist Max Planck. Later, Stevens would solve the very real difficulties he had in bringing his argument on the poetry of philosophy to a satisfactory close when he rewrote the ending of "A Collect of Philosophy" for a third time, focusing on Planck as the figure of the modern philosopher-scientist as poet.

Friendship with the Churches had been one of Stevens' fortunes of war. Henry Church, a wealthy American expatriate, had spent much of his life in Europe. Born in 1880 into a wealthy family that manufactured the bicarbonate of soda formulated by an ancestor, Church had lived most of his life abroad, where he had been part of the Parisian avant-garde between the wars. With his Bavarian wife, Barbara, Church had come to America in the summer of 1939, planning to return to Ville d'Avray in November.[2] In September, however, Germany invaded Poland, and the couple did not get back to Europe until 1946. Not surprisingly, Stevens was one of the first writers Church contacted that first fall in exile at the Plaza Hotel. Only a few months before coming to America, Church had been in touch with Stevens from Paris about a matter that was especially pleasing to the Hartford Francophile. Church was at work on a special American number of his magazine "to make known to the french public americans [sic] who have never been published in France."[3] He planned to include three or four Stevens poems in an upcoming issue of *Mesures.* The issue appeared in Paris in July, the month, as it turned out, when Church was actually in Hartford briefly on a vacation tour of New England and Canada. A mix-up prevented him from meeting Stevens, who was himself away on vacation in Maine part of the month. But when Church wrote to Stevens on November 1, hoping to arrange a visit in New York now that he was not returning to Ville d'Avray, Stevens agreed enthusiastically, inviting Church to lunch with him. Stevens was immediately charmed by the fragile man of Parisian letters he met that Thursday as they lingered at the Passy Restaurant in late November 1939. It was the first of many such lunches the two men were to enjoy until Church's death from heart disease in April 1947. Within three years of that first meeting, Stevens indicated just how deep his affinities with Church were when he dedicated his masterpiece, *Notes toward a Supreme Fiction,* to him, one of only two poems Stevens ever dedicated to a friend.

"You have so thoroughly lived the life that I should have been glad to live,"[4] Stevens once confided to Church. Helen Church Minton recalls the debonair and cultivated life her cousin led in prewar Europe. Minton was often at the Churches' Park Avenue gatherings, which Stevens occasionally attended, along with the poet and editor Frederick Morgan, the German painter Kurt Roesch, and the director of the Guggenheim Museum, James Johnson Sweeney, among others.

Frederick Morgan

My first wife and I used to visit the Churches early in the war. I remember first Allen Tate telling me that this very interesting editor was coming over and settling in Princeton. I got to know the Churches in 1942. I had stayed on at Princeton through the summer, taking courses in order to graduate before going into the army. Tate introduced me and a couple of the other students who had become close friends of his. The Churches were extremely gracious and friendly. I remember on many hot July and August afternoons going over to the Churches' pool and swimming and sitting and talking.

Henry Church was a gentle, rather shy man. He wore a Panama hat: he was almost completely bald, and beneath the Panama hat he wore a damp washcloth to keep cool. Without any self-consciousness, he'd take his hat off to meet a lady, and there'd be a little washcloth atop his head. He was a terribly nice man and certainly a very intelligent one, but lacking in energy. I remember him saying to Tate one day that he had read two or three pages of some book of poetry by one of the well-thought-of poets of the day and that he'd gotten so tired he had to lie down and take a nap. Mrs. Church, on the other hand, was extremely energetic.

I was discharged in November 1945, and we picked up our friendship with them soon after I got back to New York. It was a pleasant enough friendship, but we were not intimate. There was a great age gap; they were older than our parents. They led a formal life. They gave more or less the same large cocktail party every year when they came [from Paris in the fall or left for Paris in the spring]. There were French-speaking people, there were German-speaking people, a lot of art people. I was not much into the art world in those days, so it was like a new world to me. And it was at one of Barbara Church's parties, memorable in perhaps no other way, that I first met Stevens. That was in the spring of 1950.

We had already been in correspondence because after World War II Joseph Bennett and I decided to go ahead with plans that we'd had at Princeton and kept alive during the war years of starting our own magazine. After a certain amount of adjusting to civilian life, we got going with *The Hudson Review*. We had an initial list of writers we hoped would contribute to the magazine, which included Allen Tate and R. P. Blackmur and, among the poets, notably Wallace Stevens. Stevens did send us one poem for our first issue, "In a Bad Time."

I can't help but comment on the modesty of his letter. There was no implication when he sent the poem, of "It's very nice of me, famous author that I am, to let you young men have one of my pieces." We did run into that attitude among other writers. "If the enclosed poem is of any interest to you, you are most welcome to it. Since you make a point of being incorporated not for profit, let me say that I don't want to be paid for the poem if you use it."[5] This was generous, the kind of generosity he displayed throughout his dealings with us. My experience with most well-known authors has been pleasant; a few are unpleasant on money matters, but only a handful. At the same time, people who are ready to waive their fee are also a minority. In justice to the majority, they needed the money probably more than Stevens did. The only other case I can remember was a spectacular piece of generosity on Ezra Pound's part when he was in St. Elizabeth's Hospital and we published his version of *The Tra-chiniae.* There had been an earthquake in Greece, and he thought it would be appropriate that the fee for his version of a Greek tragedy should go to the Ithaca Relief Fund. Stevens obviously knew that we were a young magazine that might have a struggle getting established, that we didn't have much money, which was true.

Wallace Stevens was outstanding in the generosity and friendliness of his attitude. I've always had a soft spot for him. His letters to us were formal but extremely encouraging. He was businesslike; there were no long extra-curricular letters of the kind Ezra Pound sent me later, with ideas about everything under the sun. Stevens wasn't that way. Everything was to a point, but he always had a sentence or two that was encouraging. I had heard in 1949 from Barbara Church [for example] that Wallace Stevens had written a short preface to the work of the artist Gromaire. I thought, Let's get that for *The Hudson Review.* He answered:

> The note on Gromaire is merely a word or two of introduction without the least pretense to being anything more. I suppose that in the Hudson Review it would not make much more than a page. It would be interesting to see something about Gromaire in the Hudson Review by someone else, but it would be better to leave me out of it.
>
> I have in mind sending you some poems sooner or later. At the present time I am trying to put a book together before the end of the year and as part of that job is to include in the book things that have not been published elsewhere, at least a few such things, I am not likely to send you anything for a little time to come, but just because I don't do it doesn't mean that I am not going to try to do it. The truth is that I am particularly pleased that my poems should mean anything to you.[6]

Now that last sentence is an example of his generosity because here is a great poet dealing with a magazine that was not yet two years old.

Now, in the meeting with him in the spring of 1950 at Barbara Church's he was formal with me; he was not expansive. He was not the kind of person who immediately gave you the feeling that he'd like to meet you afterward and go for a drink. You had the feeling that he was very friendly, that he was pleasant [but] that he had his own plans, that he had something else he wanted to do after the party. He was like Eliot in that respect. Eliot I also found extremely gracious but by no means the kind of older poet who would open up to a younger literary man and want to know what he was thinking. There was always that reserve. I took it to indicate a certain amount of shyness in Stevens; but I nevertheless liked him very much.

I was a little bit impeded in speaking to him because there were a great many other people at the party who also wanted to talk to this eminent man. And Mrs. Church was somewhat bossy in engineering things so that nobody took his time for too long. I had a pleasant meeting with him. He complimented me on how *The Hudson Review* was doing, said he liked it very much. I told him I would always want to publish his poems any time he had any. We felt confident we could publish anything he'd give us because he was always good. I didn't think Stevens would send out work that was not good. Now he was different in this respect from other poets, who may have been great but whose work embraced a certain amount of material that was not good and that we might not have wanted to accept. We might have been a little more guarded in issuing such an invitation even to so great a poet as William Carlos Williams, who did publish a lot of second-string stuff in other publications, or to a well-known but lesser poet like E. E. Cummings, for example.

I had real conversation with Stevens only that once; 1950 was the point at which my own relations with Barbara Church tapered off. Frankly, it just wasn't a lot of fun. One of the reasons that these parties had a kind of stiffness was that a lot of people were there because of the Churches' money and wanted to add their work to the Churches' collection. Barbara was aware of this, and she used this advantage she had because of her wealth to extract a certain amount of obsequious treatment. Mrs. Church was a little domineering. She could be sharp. She had a side to her personality that wasn't altogether pleasant; one reason that we didn't get to know them better was that I frankly didn't want to have to curry favor with her. She was the kind of person who extracted a certain amount of deference from people, made people feel that if they were her friends they'd have to treat her as a *grande dame*. I don't think it's a very attractive trait anyway, and I'm not sure she was particularly entitled to it. I think Henry might have been entitled, but he didn't require it. He was simple and very nice. He was eccentric but had no airs. Stevens may have felt great warmth toward Henry, who I can see might well have seemed very lovable to a person of his own generation. This affection may have extended itself to Barbara, although from his letters I'd say he genuinely liked her, too. She spoke of him definitely with respect, of a celebrity, someone she was proud to be associated with, an unquestionably superior being. [She spoke of him] without particular intelligence, [but] she certainly had caught on that he was an eminent poet. She was fond of him —I certainly wouldn't accuse her of any cynical manipulation—she was very fond of him. She [also] knew—though she might not have understood his poems—that Henry Church had latched on to a major figure and she was proud of it. She did not have a superior intelligence, but she knew a lot of people. By no means [a deep interest in the arts]; it was chichi, what's à la mode. I think Stevens felt very much at home with them. They shared a whole milieu, this art world, this Paris cultural thing, which Stevens adored and was deep into and knew so much about.

I find him a great landmark, as I find other great poets to whom I don't feel particularly akin as far as what makes me myself write, and yet whose example is something I deeply honor and hope may guide me in some indirect way. Stevens was a very adventurous poet, in my opinion, and his poems are great explorations. Although they are beautifully precise and tight, they are not locked into a predetermined meaning. [They are] an example of consistent elegance in expression and conscientiousness to the inner meaning, letting the poem lead him where it may.

Helen Church Minton

[Henry Church] was my father's first cousin. He was tall, and from what Barbara said, very handsome when he was young. The family viewed him as someone who was very much a dilettante, who wasn't ever going to amount to anything with his extravagant ways. He was very changeable; he'd drift. One time his interest would be music and he'd be studying piano; or the next time it was chemistry; the next time it was something else. Well, of course he lived extravagantly, but at the same time he knew and was interested in all these young artists, so when Harry died he had made more money than his cousins who had stuck to the family business because he had bought these paintings from the artists' studios.*

*When the Church collection was sold posthumously at a New York auction on January 25, 1961, for $610,000, the most valued items were a Utrillo street scene, a Picasso portrait of a woman, and four paintings and four drawings by Paul Klee.

He was married before he married Barbara, to another very beautiful and charming woman. But they quarreled. He wanted to take his music teacher with him [to Europe]; Daisy, his first wife, didn't like it, so she said she wouldn't go. He went ahead on this trip, leaving his wife behind. His daughter was born after they broke up, and he never saw her until she was eighteen.

He met Barbara in Munich, and they fell in love immediately. They were passionately interested in music. She said, "We just went to all the concerts and operas, sometimes two in a night." Then he went to Paris; he had an apartment there. And she followed him. She thought of him as a young student living on very restricted funds. And they did live very simply, off the Left Bank. One time she came in, and she'd seen some dress in a window she thought was lovely. "Harry looked at me," she said. "Would you like to have it?" "Oh," she said, "yes, but it would be much too extravagant." Well of course he went out and bought it; that was the first revelation he was a man of considerable substance. Her father was a farmer in Bavaria. She said from the time she was a little girl, when people would ask her what she wanted to be when she grew up, she would say, "I'm going to marry a rich American and live in Paris." It wasn't a case of his picking up a little Cinderella—except financially they were at opposite ends. I remember Harry saying his brother had married a quite beautiful woman but of very limited intellectual interests; he had married both beauty and intellect.

She was a person who was avid for every new experience, who threw herself into it, someone who loved life. She really was great fun to be with, a very gay person. He was quiet. In fact, it was very seldom that he entered into conversation. You wondered why she wasn't more frustrated, but she never seemed to be. It was quite a romance.

It happened that we all got along very well together, so that whenever we went abroad we would finish our visit at Ville d'Avray, if it were in the summer. It was right on the corner of the village, but of course you weren't at all conscious of the traffic. It had a high wall around it, big high gates. The most beautiful trees were on the property. I don't know the French equivalent of a national monument, but a number of them were so old they couldn't be taken down. Then you went up the hill, and here was [the château]. The original house was quite small; they had Le Corbusier build on an addition and a music room. It had the most beautiful view of Paris. We used to have breakfast with Barbara on a little terrace outside of her bedroom, and you could look over all of Paris.

They were not at all in the American social life of Paris. But they had their coterie of friends, young artists, French people. Rouault [for example] illustrated Harry's book *The Clowns*. I think [*Mesures*, the French little magazine Church edited] was the nucleus of a great many friendships that they had there. They were interested in their garden; they entertained friends; they went to the concerts and operas and plays; they took excursions into the country. Harry, though he was a very mild man, not a sportsman at all, adored cars. They had a couple of Bugattis. One time we went to Deauville; we'd go so fast we'd be rushing through the villages with the inhabitants espaliering themselves against the walls.

When the First World War came, Barbara and he were visiting my parents. I remember the great excitement in their making the decision to go back to Europe, getting leather belts to put gold in to take back because they didn't know what they'd hit over there, but determined to go. The Second World War they were just as determined not to go through a war in Europe again. That's when they lived in Princeton and also rented my sister's house on Long Island; that's when they established their New York roots.

We saw a great deal of her in her apartment in town. It was quite a simple apartment; at the time she got it, apartments were rather scarce. Barbara didn't get a decorator to come in; she'd have some interesting pieces and then some not at all interesting ones, all mixed up. It was very comfortable, but it was not well arranged for parties. It had one big living room along Park Avenue; but it didn't have any proper dining room at all. But she had this marvelous French maid, Suzanne, and she could do anything. She did the parties, which always had magnificent food, so that they were always quite special, not just a caterer coming in.

[The parties] seemed large, large as you could get in there, probably fifty or so. Marianne Moore always was there. I think Marianne Moore's mother promoted this; she saw this as a great haven of security for Marianne, so she encouraged this friendship a great deal, and they became very close friends. And St. John, her secretary [would be there]. She was a character, if ever there was one: English, quite masculine in dress and appearance. She was interested in the metaphysical and wrote at great length. The [Frederick] Morgans were people that Barbara seemed to enjoy very much; they were attractive and used to come to the parties. The [Fernand] Auberjonoises were just charming; he was the son of a quite well known artist in France; she had been some kind of Russian princess. Another friend of Barbara's, Natasha Hesketh, would always be there. Barbara had studied Russian with her [in Paris]. She was a White Russian; she looked like your idea of a Russian princess, very decorative.

At the parties Wallace Stevens was tall and a very handsome presence. I always looked forward to meeting him. Perhaps he was a little shy, but he was the lion; I never thought of him as the shy one. But then, I found celebrities quite often are. I remember driving with Marianne Moore to the Cosmopolitan Club. She said, "I'm not so nervous about the lecture—but meeting all these intellectual women!" He always seemed at ease, [handling himself] very well but quite unobtrusively. I had the feeling Barbara watched out for him to see that the people he was interested in he would surely talk to. But really nothing more than a good hostess would do for someone who was [from] out of town. One thing I remember. Barbara was interested in her dreams and she once told Stevens one dream she had about little men coming down with lawn mowers. He was very intrigued by this; he thought he might put it in a poem.

I do remember her speaking about [Elsie Stevens], and my impression was that she was not very helpful to Wallace Stevens. No particulars; Barbara was very discreet. I was aware that it was a very unhappy situation [at home] and a great burden for him to cope with. Barbara valued his friendship very much; he interested her and she loved him—as a friend. I got no impression it was romantic at all. She was just mad about Henry Church; she grieved for him a long time and wasn't interested [in anyone else].

Kurt Roesch

[The Church] apartment was really very cozy in a French sense, without the French kitsch. First of all, there were remarkably good pictures: good Juan Gris, good Picasso. They were not only the best, but they were livable. There was never that you had to have two efforts by Braque to have a Braque. Mr. Church, whom I only met once, was a man who knew what was fine, what was worthwhile to have. He was a very civilized and cultured man. I was permitted to sit in Henry's chair, and so was Wallace Stevens. Barbara said, "I permit this to you and to Wallace Stevens. No one else sits there." She was sitting on the couch, a little like Madame Récamier. There was a grand piano on which were a few photographs because no one played. This had to be there; Henry [had] had it. She had a fireplace, but there was never a fire. One night—I don't know whether it was Stevens or I—said, "Why don't we have a fire? It's such a chilly day." She said, "Oh, my best wine bottles are there." She had a French cook: the food was marvelous, the champagne was good. Very tiny, unpretentious dining room, a kind of garden furniture from Hammacher Schlemmer, but very nice—with uncomfortable chairs, so people would get up. Big parties would be overflowing in the hall, all over.

Barbara Church was an extremely beautiful old lady, lovely to look at, with this nice Bavarian accent. She was kind of wise and very honest. Not a powder puff, not a person who would admire fringes on carpets or anything. Always very discreet. She was not Teutonic, more Irish. The Bavarians are, anyway,

Celtic. She had imagination; she had sympathies. What she disliked she would say loudly, and very directly, and very clearly. It was never fuzzy. And you couldn't fool her. It was amazing to see that she tried to fool us with her free verse. Once Stevens stayed and she read. I thought, How can he stand it? Because her verse was on the level of Hallmark [greeting cards. He became] kind of inhuman, formidable, absolutely stiff, not saying anything. But she wanted to belong in that sense. And she said once, "I'm alone. And since Henry isn't here, it's really very sad for me." Directly she would say, "I need two kinds of friends. One nearly as old as I am, and that is Stevens. Then one as you are. I like to talk to Stevens; I like to talk to you." She was perfectly honest; it had nothing to do with any kind of flirtation.

She liked to be admired, which we did. He would say, "The color of your dress is something most becoming to you." Or I would say, "Well, Barbara, I see you've got your emeralds out of your safety box." She would say, "They aren't genuine. They're fakes, but nobody would believe I wear fakes." She was very rich. Then there was laughter, and he would agree. "But the color is very beautiful, though they are fakes." She would say, "You know they are very expensive, too, these fakes."

Talking about Stevens' relationships with people, it was easier for him to talk to a charming woman, especially if the woman was, as my late wife, Maria, was, a kind of innocent without pretense. He always picked her to talk to, nothing special, just talk. When we came home from one meeting there, I said to my wife, "I'm not sure that on occasions he doesn't go to bed with a silk hat." She said, "What do you mean?" I said, "I had the feeling that —it's not self-importance, it's not self-indulgence—but he would like to put himself on a pedestal of some kind." My wife said, "I don't think so. I think he finds it just very difficult. He would like to relax very much, but he finds it very difficult. You must forgive him."

There was no real discussion [with Stevens]. There were aphorisms, brief remarks—if possible, witty. With Stevens certainly a bit sharp; here and there not very pleasant. One time we were talking about poetry. I said, "As my friend Horace Gregory would say . . ." He turned to Marianne Moore. "I thought we were talking about poets and poetry." I remember one which was very amusing. A Russian, who had always a chip on his shoulder, had married a French princess—but of the Second Empire, as Barbara would say. One day he appeared with a walking stick, ivory-handled, and limped as he walked. Stevens said, "What's the matter?" He said he had arthritis. So Stevens said, "How fortunate. It makes you look so distinguished—tonight." A series of one-liners.

Here and there the parties were relaxed. Then it was affable. But on the whole it was not really festive, and it was always slightly uncomfortable. Marianne Moore walked around a little like a living oracle, fully aware that she was in the company of people who admired her poetry. What she would have liked best would be for everybody to keep quiet, and for her to read some of her poetry. She was very fond of her whimsical poems. One time she recited "Poetry"—"I, too, dislike it" etc.—an amusing poem, as if she had a sour plum in her mouth. She would look down with her tripod [hat] and not look at people. It was her own amusement. One couldn't tease her. [Stevens and Moore] sat there and talked, not with each other [so much] as they read their lines, fully aware that they were important poets.

Marianne Moore was rather poor, not starving but rather poor. I always had the feeling that she was silently looking for a protector. It was a place where somewhat everybody wanted to have something. One woman was so indelicate, after Barbara's death, she complained, "I didn't get a thing, not even the ring I always admired." I think Stevens was an old friendship; he came for the memory of Mr. Church.

There was an atmosphere that was not quite real. One lady was the kind of woman who would say, all very seriously [to her husband], "Do you remember when Paul said to me . . ." And he would correct her, "I do remember, but you don't mean Paul you mean Pablo." They would call all these artists by their first names, Juan, Pablo, and Oscar and Max. And then our friend Stevens' eyes would wander to a picture or a woman. He was suddenly not there any more when all these guys were mentioned by their first names.

The whole thing was a little bit forced. For instance, Stevens had to go home early because of his wife, couldn't leave her alone very long. I knew from Barabara she was off the beam at that time. Sweeney was always on the run to meet someone. I and Maria would sit a little longer with some Russian friends there. There was a Russian émigré, once head of the secret police under the Czar. There were some very simple country girls, Russian princesses: round, and plump, and warm, and of a very good mood. They could speak English; Russian, of course; German and French—and then their education stopped. They had what I call a flower education. We had a joke in German, then a joke in French; it was amusing. They were pleased. And they loved to eat; the food was really marvelous.

One day I called Fred Morgan, editor of *The Hudson Review*: "Did you get an invitation to come to Church?" He said, "I can't stand it any more; I don't think I'm going. I think all these people go there because the food is excellent and the champagne the best." I said, "Well, it's certainly an attraction." Curt Valentin [owner of a New York gallery Stevens frequented] would come also occasionally and always arrive somewhat drunk because he couldn't stand these parties. He would always bring a great bunch of flowers. One time he arrived, and a little later the police came because he had pulled out a little tree in Central Park and brought it to Barbara. Such things Stevens found unbearable. He didn't say anything; you could read it on his face.

This would sum up these meetings with these people. It wasn't quite human. And one of the least human was Stevens. How did he live, I was always wondering. What are his relationships with people? Here and there there was a glimpse. For example, I remember Holly was departing and I made the remark, "Well, is he tall, dark and handsome?" He said, "Let's hope he isn't existing at all." There was something very funny there, not quite human. I said to my wife that time, "How does the man live? Do you think he is a cold fish?" She said, "How would we know?"

James Johnson Sweeney

I had known Mrs. Church in Ville d'Avray and had heard about Stevens through her before I ever met him. Of course I had known Stevens' poetry long before, and that was a great treat to meet him. It must have been due to Mrs. Church—she must have given me a good reputation—but he would talk to me just as if we were on the same level, and not in any wrong sense. But making me feel comfortable and at home with him. Now that's a side other people probably missed in Wallace Stevens, his graciousness. He had that. [He'd engage in] a pleasant conversation, joking lightly but not noisily, always remembering something that you had mentioned that would interest you. I found he had a very fine sense of humor in a simple way.

I think he was aloof until he found his way, found a sympathetic response. Both Stevens and Marianne Moore were very quiet. I thought that they were really sympathetic. I get a little confused when I think of Marianne Moore and Stevens; I also think of T. S. Eliot and Marianne Moore. Both had such a regard for Marianne Moore and such a sympathy. Stevens and Moore might have been aware [of their importance], but they never rubbed it in on you. Marianne Moore was one of the simplest people in the world; and he was simple, too, in some ways, but very complex in other ways.

Of course it was a little self-conscious [at the Church parties], I suppose, because you were aware of certain people being there. It's rather difficult to be human in a group. Stevens was shy and a little impatient with pretentiousness; and that's what comes out at parties like that [when] people are talking against a background. I think he had the capability to become exasperated. I don't think I ever heard him scold, but that would drive him away from the conversation.

He was a person who was most generous, [at his] best when he was in a group of three or four. He was more human here [at the Sweeney's East End apartment]. He came here three or four times. [On one of these visits Stevens joined Surrealist painter Peter Blume for cocktails.] My wife had made a very good martini. Peter Blume liked it, as most of us did in those days; Wallace Stevens was enjoying it also. I noticed that Peter's hand shook a good deal when he was taking a drink; in fact, he had to place two hands to the glass. I said, "Peter, that's a terrible business. Is there anything wrong?" He said, "Oh, no. That happens all the time. As soon as I have a drink, it will disappear." Wallace Stevens said, "I have the same problem. The drink cures it." I was so surprised Stevens said he suffered that same way. He could have just sat there and not said anything, but no, he entered in. That was a friendly note. Peter Blume admired Stevens, and maybe Stevens had heard of Blume up in that part of the country. [Blume lived in Sherman, Connecticut.] It was just perfectly good fellowship and bonhomie, not a question of meeting the master and the well-known young painter. They were both friends of mine, and we were all friends after the first shaky drink. The conversation moved naturally into the serious, but pleasantly serious, not pedestrian.

[Soon after Sweeney became director of the Guggenheim Museum in 1952, Stevens made the first of a few calls on him there.] When I went to the Guggenheim they had no Braque, no Cézanne, very odd. Finally, I did run across a portrait by Cézanne and brought it to my office, waiting for the trustees, [who] kept putting the meeting off and off [to decide whether or not to purchase it]. Stevens came up and saw it. I remember distinctly the office discussion of *Portrait of a Clockmaker,* laughing about how hard it was to get people to buy a masterpiece.* When he talked to me [about painting], I thought he looked at contemporary painting much as he looked at French poetry, not as something native to him but which attracted him. I found it was always what was interesting to him as a stimulant, not as a document. I don't think he ever went into the discussion of the justification, [only] the enjoyment, the pleasure. Paul Klee was one person he used to speak to me about. He liked Klee. Again, it's the stimulant quality. Didn't he like Kandinsky, too? Yes, he was interested in the musical theory of Kandinsky's painting. It stimulated a good many people in those early days, 1912 and right after. I think that's what appealed to him."7

In most cases [the paintings Stevens owned] belong to a certain period in the early thirties. These are people who are playing it safe, on the inside:

*On April 19, 1954, Stevens wrote to their mutual friend Thomas McGreevy, director of the Irish National Gallery, "I dropped in to Sweeney's museum merely to see a new Cezanne, which looks more like Modigliani than Cezanne," *LWS*, p. 828. "Now why he thought it looked like Modigliani," Sweeney notes, "I can't imagine."

Brianchon, Labasque, Marchand. Tal Coat is a little away from them; maybe at this point he belonged with this group. But they all belonged to a certain type of gallery right down from the Madeleine. Sort of easy-to-like people, the sort of artist who sold well. This is not venturesome at all, rather bourgeois. In a curious way it's related to certain aspects of his poetry: not the great side of his poetry, but the material on which the greater stuff is built. [These painters] were not explorers. They knew how to paint, but they didn't have life. These all have a common line, evidently purchases of a person with one taste, this bourgeois taste. Now whether Stevens was aware it was a comfortable bourgeois taste . . . Maybe he had a certain fondness for the bourgeois comforts. The people in Paris who would have their apartment filled with them would be comfortable, and they would have good dinners, and they'd have interesting conversation—but never to frighten the horses.

He knew how I admired his poetry; we did discuss it. What he wrote about [Ireland] mystified me because I knew that he hadn't been there. I did tease him about writing on a subject he was not immediately in touch with, teasing as I did about "The Irish Cliffs of Moher" and the other poems. Why didn't he come to Ireland and join us there? I was surprised [too], as mostly everyone else was, that he was so interested in the French language, French poetry, and hadn't gone to France. I think he said he was not interested in the representational but the idea it gave him, which was much more important than the real landscape. He told me that he had a feeling through [Thomas] McGreevy [an Irish poet and art critic with whom Stevens corresponded during his last years] and his idea of Ireland, which would be diminished if he had seen the real thing. He had more to lose than to gain.

P·A·R·T III

>>>>>>>>>>>> <<<<<<<<<<<<

THE FAMILY MAN

CHAPTER SIX

Life at Home

In September 1932, the Stevenses moved to 118 Westerly Terrace, the home most closely identified with the couple who spent half their married lives there. The large clapboard and brick residence stands midway down a short block among architecturally more distinctive Georgian and Tudor Revival houses also built in the mid-1920s. Painted white, with dark-green shutters, during the Stevenses' years there, it is located among the houses at the bottom of the terraced street, below the embankment of cherry trees running the length of the avenue that form part of the winter landscape of the late poem "On the Way to the Bus."

Although the Great Depression was at its height when they bought their home, the Stevenses paid approximately $20,000 in cash for it, immune as they were from the financial hardships of the 1930s.* After considering a few others in Hartford, they selected it partly because Elizabeth Park was only a block and a half away. Stevens detoured through some portion of its one hundred acres most mornings on his two-mile walk to work and spent hours there on weekends, composing his poetry.† In 1932, Westerly Terrace was

---

*Stevens' salary during the 1930s reflects the affluence he enjoyed during the Depression: a pay cut during 1932–33 marked his modest experience of its financial effects. Stevens' annual salary, with the date of each raise, is as follows: March 15, 1916, $3,000; April 1, 1917, $3,600; April 1, 1918, $3,900; April 1, 1919, $4,400; January 1, 1920, $4,840; April 1, 1920, $6,000; September 1, 1920, $7,500; February 1, 1922, $8,400; May 1, 1923, $10,000; January 1, 1926, $11,000; January 1, 1927, $13,001; January 1, 1928, $14,000; January 1, 1929, $15,000; July 1, 1932, $13,500; February 1, 1934, $17,500; May 15, 1935, $20,000; November 1, 1945, $22,000; February 1, 1948, $24,000 ("Hartford Accident and Indemnity Company Employee's Record Card," HIG).

†Elizabeth Park was named after the wife of Charles Pond, who, in 1894, bequeathed his

also one of the newest and best addresses in Hartford's fashionable West End, located a block below the governor's mansion.

In front of their new house, the only one they ever owned, the Stevenses placed the small holly tree they had first planted when their daughter was born eight years earlier. Eventually it grew to screen the entrance, an emblem of the privacy the Stevenses cultivated in a neighborhood that valued privacy. Josephine M., who answered a newspaper ad in 1933 and worked at the Stevens house for two years, had an inside view of life at home on Westerly Terrace, where Hazel Vail, Florence Berkman, Robert Halloran and Elizabeth Halloran Chickering were neighbors.

Josephine M.

It was in the newspaper: "Mother's helper. Preferably someone German or German background." Mrs. Stevens didn't want any Irish answering it. She said she had had some Irish maids: she had experience with "dirty Irish"; those were her words. She seemed very nice and agreeable [during the interview]. But she was a very hard person. Very strict. She had her own way. You just had to follow it. She made you nervous if you didn't. I'd help dust and help with the cooking; and when Holly came home, I took care of her. That was my real full-time job: to take her out, to walk with her, read with her. Really like a baby-sitter, though she wasn't a baby. She was about ten or eleven. All summer long she was with me constantly, unless they had to get shoes or clothing. I'm really surprised Holly had a car at sixteen because Mrs. Stevens was quite protective. She was her mother's daughter, as far as I could see, although Mrs. Stevens was very strict. She didn't spoil her.

The house on Westerly Terrace was lovely. It was a great big place.* It

---

estate on Asylum Avenue to the city of Hartford. While Stevens frequented the park from the time he moved to Hartford in 1916, it figures as a setting in his poetry more in later years. "Vacancy in the Park" (1952) concludes with an image of the gazebo, roofed with climbing woodbine, which stands at the center of the park's Rose Garden: "The four winds blow through the rustic arbor, / Under its mattresses of vines" (*CP*, p. 511).

People, often a part of the scenery in this much-used park, were one of its attractions for Stevens, especially on his weekend visits. One group who caught Stevens' eye in 1950 was a cluster of nuns who, setting up their easels on the banks of a lily pond on several occasions, provoked Stevens' commentary on the scene, "Nuns Painting Water-Lilies."

*As one entered the spacious foyer of the Stevens home, to the left was the Rose Room, so called for the color of its silk wallpaper; it was used as a study, first by Holly and then by Elsie Stevens after her daughter left home in the early 1940s. To the right of the entrance was the front-to-back living room. "That was a great big living room," notes Josephine M. "The walls were stucco, sort of off-beige. It was very sparse. He did have paintings. The ones that were in the living room were almost all scenes, very mute. I remember the Venetian blinds; they were just coming out. The fireplace was never used."

At the far end of the living room, to the left, was the dining room, with its bay window overlooking the backyard. The dining-room furniture had been with the Stevenses since their was a cheerful house. It wasn't too heavily furnished. They just bought piece by piece, and what they did buy was good. I remember a couple of chairs coming in when I was there because they really needed more furniture, especially for that long living room. I think he bought most of the things in New York. It would come crated a few days after he'd made a trip to New York.

Annie [Ertel] and I were the only ones there; she was the laundress. She had just come over from Germany because she could just about make the language. She quit a couple of times when I was there, but Mr. Stevens went back and got her. She came Monday and Tuesday and did the washing and ironing; then she came on Thursday or Friday and did all the cleaning from top to bottom, so that all we had to do was just dust and straighten up. But there wasn't much to do because there was never any company. I didn't stay there nights. I came in at nine and left at five-thirty. When I got there he was gone, and then he'd come home just before five. I went half a day on Saturday; I didn't go on Sunday. So I didn't see much of him, though I thought he was an awfully nice person. He had a nice way about him. He wasn't as hard as Mrs. Stevens.

I know on Sundays he never ate, just bland juices. He was always conscious of his figure. Very simple [dinners were what Mrs. Stevens normally served], nothing that would put weight on you. No rich sauces or anything like that, very healthful but very simple. They never made pie or anything like that. He had an incredible sweet tooth. In fact, he would often mention that he had two or three desserts at noon.

Holly was a very sweet girl. She was bigger than I was because I was always thin, but she loved [to sit on Josephine's lap to read]. She just reveled in it. We were very close. She didn't have any friends that I knew of. She had only

---

New York years; the floor was carpeted with an Oriental rug, and Maurice Brianchon's *Still Life* hung, for a time, on the wall. Mrs. Stevens did not care for this painting of a light-blue pottery vase, filled with carnations and other flowers, upon a red-and-blue cloth. After the poet's death, she sold it, along with a few other paintings and some of Stevens' fine bindings, at a 1959 Parke-Bernet auction in New York.

A butler's pantry led from the dining room to the kitchen. At the far end of the living room, to the right, was the sunroom, something of a daytime reading room for Stevens.

A staircase led from the foyer to the second floor, with Stevens' bedroom at the top of the stairs. "All the upstairs rooms were plain," Josephine M. recalls. "His [furniture] was like heavy oak, but I don't remember it being anything special. He used to leave money, brand-new bills, in the top drawer of one of his dressers that if Holly or Mrs. Stevens started to go downtown she could help herself."

On the third floor there were two finished rooms, with a bath, for maids, plus the attic. "They were not typical attic rooms: things were stored there, but everything was neat, and we could play there," notes Hazel Vail, a childhood friend of Holly Stevens.

me, and we got quite attached. In fact, I'll tell a little incident that made her mother quite mad one day. We were trying to show Holly some little kitchen work, cookies or something. Holly said, "I like Josephine. Don't you, Mommy?" She said, "Yes." So Holly said, "If you should happen to die, she can be my mother." She didn't like that one bit. When Holly came home she was with me all the time. I don't know if her mother liked that too much at times, but she always sought me out. I don't remember her ever, in the two years I was there, having any classmates in. She was like her folks; they never had anybody either. As far as I can remember, in those years they had one couple in for dinner one night and four women in for lunch. And that was it.

Mrs. Stevens did belong to a garden club, and she'd go there once a week. And she did putter around that beautiful yard. She did [belong to the Musical Club of Hartford].* She read quite a bit. That's all I remember her doing. She'd go shopping, of course, occasionally. They never had a car while I was there. They always hired one from the Prospect Garage livery whenever they wanted to go anywhere. In fact, Holly went to Oxford [School], and that livery car came every morning and brought her up and back.

I remember Mrs. Stevens telling me she had gone to Vassar. [In 1931, Mrs. Stevens and her daughter attended a summer session of Vassar's Institute in Euthenics.] I just figured she graduated there. She mentioned taking the subject of bringing up children. I don't know if she was trying to apologize for being that stern with Holly.

Mrs. Stevens did put on airs. She acted as if she was born to it. You would never guess it from her appearance that she wasn't all her life that way. She read a lot about etiquette; she knew quite a bit about that. She made sure that Holly had quite a bit of that, too.

She was very stern in her dress; she never dressed to her position. He was very stylish. She was a serious dresser. She was serious really in every way, with Holly and with everything.

Outside of a hello and how are you he just left me to her, more or less. Except the time I was going to quit, and he called up my sister to try to influence me to come back because it was hard for Mrs. Stevens to keep anyone. I came home, and the doctor said it was a nervous breakdown, the

---

*During her Hartford years, Elsie Stevens belonged to two study groups, the Bard and Sage Club and the Charter Oak Study Club, as well as to the Musical Club of Hartford. By the time she moved to Westerly Terrace, however, she was growing less active in local groups. As a result of an interest in genealogy that began in the late 1930s, she also became a member of the Hartford chapter of the Daughters of the American Revolution, the Berks County [Pennsylvania] Historical Society and the Connecticut Historical Society.

tension there. You just felt you couldn't please her. She'd speak her mind out, and then she would act very strange, act very mad. And that didn't help. So after a week my sister called up and told her that I wouldn't be coming back. A couple of days after that Mr. Stevens called and asked me when I got better couldn't I please come back. He said Holly missed me, and they needed me. So after two weeks I went back. She was a little more understanding then, a little softer. It was her attitude, really. She was very hard. She had her own ideas, and she wanted things done exactly as she thought they should be done. It was her house, but she did make it hard on other people.

It was a few years after I left that I had any idea he was a poet. It was in the papers, and I couldn't believe it. She never mentioned it. All I thought was he worked for the two Hartfords. I was there when he was made vice-president. I saw it in the papers. I never [mentioned it]; that would have been too personal.

I never thought there was much relation [between Mr. and Mrs. Stevens]. They just went their separate ways. It was a very cold sort of life outside of their little Holly. She was her life; that was it. He was very formal [with Holly]. He never seemed to have much to do with her, really. He just seemed to leave Mrs. Stevens to take care of Holly.

No two ways about it, Mrs. Stevens was not a happy person. I don't know why, because she had everything she could want to live for. He was awful nice, and Holly was the nicest person. She was just not a happy person, and she didn't try to make other people happy either.

I never heard [Mr. and Mrs. Stevens] snap at each other. I just never heard them talk much to each other. Unless they were afraid of being overheard, all this time I was there I very seldom heard them speak.

Hazel Vail

It was definitely a white Protestant neighborhood. It was definitely a changing neighborhood because of the Depression. You were getting the Irish, you were getting the Jewish in. There were no Italians, no Polish.

There were very few children in the neighborhood at the time [the Stevenses moved to Westerly Terrace]. One of my first recollections of Holly is being invited to a birthday party. Her mother had it in Elizabeth Park. I remember winning a Bo-Peep doll. [Sometimes] the father would get the car from the Hartford and take us to Lake Compounce [a Connecticut amusement park] for swimming and a day, and then out to dinner. Many times it was only Holly and I. That's very true [that Holly was allowed to bring few friends to her home]. Her mother was basically shy, and she kept a perfect house and didn't want it disturbed. I don't remember many toys; I don't remember really playing. We used to put on magic shows, a few of us around here, and Wallace Stevens used to come. My parents were the few invited up the [Stevenses'] house for magic shows. I don't think my parents were ever invited up for a meal.

Among the neighborhood children Holly was always much bigger than the rest of us. A sick child: she had bronchitis that would kick up every winter. She had more money than the rest of us. In the thirties, she liked to go out for lunch and to the movies. Holly and I used to go to the movies all the time, thanks to Mr. Stevens. He used to pay. Holly had unlimited funds, and the rest of us during the Depression were limited as to how much allowance we got.

We were all spoiled in this neighborhood. Holly had an older father like I did, and you got away with so much, then bang-o! He stepped down. I doubt if she was ever hit, but I don't think she was a particularly bad child. She did what was expected of her. She read a great deal. But they were freer with her than most of the parents were. They let her go downtown, that kind of stuff, which the rest of us would have to get permission to do.

You did not raise your voice in the house. You ate what was put in front of you. Mrs. Stevens was a super-duper cook. [She] was very quiet, stayed away from people even more so than Holly's father. She was a small woman who walked very fast. A perfectionist. Everything was done perfectly, everything was done right. Whatever the etiquette book said, it was done that way. Somehow it came out that her mother had not come from a wealthy family. You would not [have known it]. Very modest, because she always wore long-sleeved dresses and relatively long by comparison to the rest of us. She had braids, too; I don't remember if she brought them around or held them in back. Wallace Stevens [on the other hand] wore colored shirts when no one else wore them: pink and blue in the thirties.

I remember being excited to know somebody [Holly Stevens] that had a book dedicated to her [Harmonium]. I don't think she mentioned the poetry much. We were all well aware of the fact that he wrote poetry, but I don't think he was particularly known for his poetry around here. He was known more for being an insurance executive.

Holly was born in '24, and I was born in '26. We were quite close. I don't think we were as close as if we had gone to school [together]. The rest of us would have gone [to Oxford School, which Holly attended] if there had been the money, because the education was better. The answer was there wasn't the money. Remember, most of our fathers were doctors, lawyers, one girl's father was growing tobacco. But all of our fathers' incomes varied and were down, while her father was constantly earning a steady income [$17,500, for example, in 1934]. That was a heck of a salary for an insurance executive in those days. My father was probably earning two thousand dollars as a doctor. She went to Oxford School all her life; she graduated a year before I went. A nice, small girls' school, where everybody behaved like little ladies. They did a good job of educating us. [During Holly's later years at Oxford School, Vachel Lindsay's widow was headmistress.] Scholastic standing under Vachel Lindsay's wife went *choom*. There were probably two reasons: part her, part if you had five hundred dollars you went. I went there in '42; by then people were starting to have money, so they could be selective. Holly graduated either first or second. I know that Holly studied hard and was bright, far brighter than the rest of us in the neighborhood.

Junior year in English we had a survey of English literature, and we did get up to the modern. I remember Vachel Lindsay and Robert Frost. We did not discuss Wallace Stevens. We did something with poetry in my senior year. Again, nothing with Stevens.

Robert Halloran and Elizabeth Halloran Chickering

RH: They were a quiet sort of family. They did not mingle with anybody. They were accepted [in the neighborhood]: this was the norm of the day that there wasn't much friendliness. The neighborhood was aloof. Everyone went their own way. Most of them were older people.

Mrs. Stevens never was very personable. You'd see her out in the garden —her great pride was her garden—you might go by and say hello, and if you got a hello back that was pretty good. I had a grandmother that came up, and she used to like to go for a walk. She saw her out in her garden in the front and admired the flowers. They got to talking and got to be somewhat close. Mrs. Stevens mentioned that she'd rather be gardening than bringing up children. The end result would be my grandmother would come back with flowers, and we'd be aghast as to where she got them. She made it a point to go for a walk if Mrs. Stevens was out, to visit her, but never rang the doorbell or called her up and said, "I'm coming over."

Mr. Stevens was a man you'd say hello to and he would bow his head, sort of nod that he'd heard you. That was his way of greeting you. If he did say hello it was very soft, sober. You felt he was a stately gentleman. He'd sort of acknowledge you one way or another, but there was never any long conversation. You felt maybe you shouldn't have a long conversation because he was in deep thought. I knew he was a poet as a child [growing up in the 1940s]. It didn't strike home until I went to college and his poetry appeared.

EHC: My father and Mr. Stevens would see each other now and then. I remember when he came to the house, which wasn't often, a few times a year, come and talk. It would always be after dinner. I don't remember him staying for too long a period of time. I think they talked generally about poetry. My father was a frustrated actor, went to Yale and had some very famous man that was his drama director: he always went around the house quoting from Shakespeare at the top of his lungs, extremely well-read in literary matters. He would read Mr. Stevens' books because he was a neighbor. Mr. Stevens would give him copies when they were published, so he followed them. What kind of understanding he had, whether they were great favorites . . .

[To the] children Mrs. Stevens was known as the witch in the neighborhood. She had a beaky kind of nose, and that was probably why we thought of her as the witch. But she was odd. In what people would call today a suburban community, mainly professional people, she dressed in an extremely odd way. She looked what I would call a Marian-the-librarian type: always wore a bun, very harsh and ascetic-looking, which was out of character with the neighborhood. Being kids we'd say very politely, "Hello, Mrs. Stevens." [Then after she was out of earshot, they'd whisper] "There's the witch!" She was never nasty, but that was just our feeling about her oddness. She had this strangeness about her, and children pick that up immediately. Like she was closed in with a lot of armor around her. She put up signs saying, "Don't come near me." My reading of that, I think as a child even, would be there must be an awful lot of trouble there that people put up that thick a barrier. I don't remember ever seeing them together; they never walked together as a couple.

She'd never stop and talk, "How are you? How was school today?" Except at Halloween. When we came to the house, she'd kind of check us over and say, "Are you the Halloran children?" She'd invite us in, and there would always be special things for us. Once a year she used to have a conversation with us. We could never piece it together because she was such a cold person passing on the sidewalk, and then there was this special treat. It was like someone gave her permission: okay, on Halloween you can be friendly.

Walking must have been a big thing in that family: everybody walked. It was odd seeing a man walking to work; it just wasn't done in that neighborhood. My father explained that it was his time to think and write poems. Whenever we met him on the street, he always spoke to us by our full name, very formally, Elizabeth Ann or Robert Lewis, never nicknames.

Florence Berkman

Every morning, like clockwork, he used to walk down Terry Road [which connects Westerly Terrace with Asylum Avenue] about nine o'clock, just about the time I was standing by my kitchen sink. I'd always get a thrill. In the afternoon, he'd walk back, this very slow stride of his. Usually, if it was summer or good weather, I'd be outdoors with some of the neighbors' children. I'd make them stop and look at him, and I'd say, "I want you to remember this is a great poet."

I used to walk up and down Terry Road with our cocker spaniel; he wouldn't even look at me, wouldn't even talk to me. But he always talked to my husband: he used to work outdoors on Saturday and Sunday; Stevens would be going to the park. But one morning it was pouring. I drove out to the corner, and here was Wallace Stevens standing, absolutely sopping. I didn't know whether or not to stop because he never acknowledged [my] being on this earth. But I did stop, and I said, "Mr. Stevens, would you like a ride?" He said, "Oh, I'd love it." He got in the car, and I thought I'd be very proper. "Mr. Stevens, I don't believe you know who I am. I'm Florence Berkman." He said, "I know who you are. You live in that little house. I've often thought I'd love to see the inside of your house." This was a carriage house. He talked at length on that trip. He was furious at *The New Statesman*, the English newspaper, which was very anti-American at that time. It would have been '46, '47, '48. I said, "How do you get time to read? You're such a busy man, and you do so much writing." He said, "I get up every morning at six o'clock, and I read for two hours."

As he walked I could almost see him composing in his mind. He had a very interesting walk. It was slow and rather symmetrical. He almost walked in cadences. Every Sunday he used to walk over to the park. Rain, or sometimes it'd be sleeting, he'd walk over. He'd spend an hour; all kinds of weather. We were very aware of him.

It was shocking [the lack of awareness of Stevens in Hartford generally].*

*In 1937, midway through Stevens' years in Hartford, the poetry editor of a local newspaper surveyed his hometown reputation. "One of the most distinguished poets in America has lived for years in Hartford. But to all except a favored few, he has been known here rather as vice president of the Hartford Accident and Indemnity Company. His books have been published in private editions and read by an enthusiastic intelligentsia. Now his *Ideas of Order*, first published last year in a special autographed edition . . . is being put out by Alfred Knopf in a trade edition. . . . It will be read by thousands in Hartford, and Wallace Stevens can no longer remain unrecognized in his home city.

I don't know anybody that knew Wallace Stevens, and when my husband and I talked about him, there was no recognition. We knew a lot of people because my husband was the political writer on the paper. We knew all kinds of people: we knew intellectuals, politicians, people who were leaders in business and industry. When we moved here [to the Westerly Terrace area] we were aware of him because of Odell Shepard [a Trinity College professor of English]. Odell was a poet and a friend of MacLeish; he knew his poetry very well because Odell Shepard was an extraordinary man, a great scholar. Odell got the Pulitzer [for his 1937 biography of Bronson Alcott] long before Stevens. I don't think Wallace Stevens had those kinds of friends; he may have had one or two, but certainly not here. He didn't need it. He made a point of repelling people. There's an awfully good story that Hank Kneeland [tells]. I think it was at the Wadsworth Atheneum. They got into a conversation—Hank Kneeland is a collector—presumably about painters and paintings. Wallace Stevens went into great detail telling Hank about his collection. When he got through he turned to Hank, and he said, "You know why I'm telling you all this?" And Hank said, "No." He said, "Because you'll never see the paintings." Hank got red as a beet, so embarrassed. But he did a worse thing, it seems to me, to the Reverend Rockwell Harmon Potter. He was a very distinguished clergyman who was minister of the Center Church in Hartford. He told the story several times in my presence, about his going to call on Wallace Stevens. He was greeted at the door, not cordially at all. The Reverend Mr. Potter, who was an enchanting man, tried, as best he could, to get over this embarrassing situation. Finally, I don't know what he said to Wallace Stevens. Wallace Stevens said he didn't want him to come there. He might do something that he might think is smart, but that's true rudeness.

Milton Avery was never known in Hartford. He was thirty-two years old when he left Hartford; that was 1925. He used to laugh because his own family never believed he was important until I started to write about him [as art critic for the Hartford *Times*]. It's a strange kind of community, and I

"Paul Claudel, noted French poet, on meeting a visitor from Hartford, exclaimed, 'Ah, then, you know Wallace Stevens!'

"Apparently surprised at the negative reply, he said, 'We think highly of his poetry in France.'

"At that time Paul Claudel was ambassador from France to the United States; in the intervening years, the same question has been asked by many others, and frequently the answer has been the same. . . .

"There are, however, many persons in Hartford who, for years, have read the poetry of Wallace Stevens, although they have respected Mr. Stevens' own wishes for seclusion when he persistently refused all interviews, and constantly eschewed all publicity. . . ." (Martha L. Spencer, "Wallace Stevens Leaves Obscurity," Hartford *Times*, October 30, 1937, p. 32.)

know it intimately. I remember the difficult time my husband and I had with the people here about Chick Austin [avant-garde director of the Wadsworth Atheneum from 1927 to 1945]. Hartford did not understand him. They didn't know what he was doing, and he had a terrible time. Yet he made the Wadsworth Atheneum an international institution. When he left, he was heartbroken. It has the reputation of being a cultural city. Always was an important city for music. Growing up, we had all the best orchestras; we had everybody important in music. And it was supposed to have been a literary city because of Mark Twain and that group. All I know is nobody knew Wallace Stevens, and that always surprised us.

As early as 1928, Hartford was being scolded nationally for ignoring Stevens. That summer Harriet Monroe published the results of a survey on the state of American verse in *Poetry*, the Chicago magazine that had done so much to foster the new poetry since she had founded it in 1912. "No doubt you know that Robert Hillyer, Wilbert Snow, and Odell Shepard live here. . . . The Poetry Club of Hartford meets at Mitchell's [bookstore] and the poetry center here is really at that shop," the poetry editor of the local newspaper had written in reply to Monroe's questionnaire. Monroe was quite irritated, however, to find Stevens' name missing from the roster of Hartford writers. She took special pride in claiming to have discovered him more than a decade earlier, when she published Stevens in a special war number of *Poetry* in 1914. She could not run this reply from Hartford, therefore, without replying to it herself. "Here we must remark parenthetically that in our opinion the poetry center of Hartford is in the residence of Wallace Stevens."[1]

At the time, the Stevenses resided at 735 Farmington Avenue, moving from there to Westerly Terrace in 1932. After the initial summer of country living in Farmington, they spent their first sixteen years in Connecticut in three apartments on or near Farmington Avenue, then the well-to-do thoroughfare leading west out of the city.* Half of that time they occupied the

*A few weeks after moving out of New York and into temporary quarters at a Hartford hotel in late spring, 1916, Stevens wrote to his novelist friend Ferdinand Reyher, ". . . I expect to like Farmington. We are to have a decent house for a few months, which will give us an opportunity to search for something permanent" (letter of June 3, 1916, HL). By the end of August, the Stevenses had found an acceptable apartment in Hartford at 594 Prospect Avenue. The new brick apartment building in which they lived for the next year was in an affluent neighborhood where families such as the Heubleins were part of Hartford society. Stevens had become friendly with the Heubleins a few years before settling in Hartford when he spent a pleasant weekend at their summer home on the Connecticut shore in August 1913. Through the Heubleins and the Strykers Stevens had an entrée to Hartford's social and cultural elite from the outset. Initially, at least, he seems to have enjoyed occasionally being part of that society. "Mrs. Heublein asked me to dinner last night," he wrote to his wife, back home in Reading to care for her ill mother, during their first winter in Connecticut. "Regular blow-out. Everybody dressed like a war-lord except myself—and I looked like old Quaker Oats. Among the people crowding around me was Mélanie Kurt, one of the best singers at the Metropolitan

upstairs apartment in a two-family house at 735 Farmington Avenue, just over the line in the suburb of West Hartford. If the local poetry editor had been reprimanded by Harriet Monroe for ignoring Stevens in the late 1920s, Stevens' landlord during those years, Teresa Curry Gay, was hardly guilty of undervaluing the poet who lived in the apartment above her, salvaging as she did important early manuscripts, such as Stevens' prize-winning play, *Three Travelers Watch a Sunrise*, and his first long poem, "From the Journal of Crispin."

Rev. John Curry Gay and Rev. James Gay

JCG: My mother always felt she was much sorrier that she hadn't looked for more papers. She said, "For God's sake, John, don't say they were found in the trash!" She claimed [however] they were. She said she was throwing something out in the trash, and here was this pile of papers. Now whether this was when [the Stevenses] were moving or when they were still there, I don't know. She looked them over and saw they were his and just decided to hold on to them. [In another version, Mrs. Gay explained to her son James that she had discovered Stevens' manuscripts in a window seat in the poet's apartment after he had moved out.]

JG: For some reason my parents knew he was a great man then. We were always aware that we were privileged to have come that close to a poet. We used to, on Friday evenings, take [the Stevens manuscripts] out and read them. And we would be asked to interpret. I can remember my mother saying, "Mr. Stevens is a poet's poet, and you don't understand that because you're not. But a poet would really appreciate what Mr. Stevens is saying." My father would throw up his hands and say it was beyond him, especially the one of Crispin. I remember them having great difficulty, and I thought,

---

Opera. She is visiting Mrs. Heublein. We must go over after you come back. Young Mrs. Heublein is . . . very friendly, wants to meet you and so on. I think I've almost made the rounds now and I expect to settle down to a peaceful routine" (letter of January 26, 1917, HL). When the Stevenses arrived in Hartford they were, apparently, considerably more sociable than they later became.

In October 1917, the couple moved out of 594 Prospect Avenue and temporarily took rooms at the Highland Court, the hotel where they had first lived when they arrived in town. They remained at the Windsor Street hotel throughout November while their next apartment, much closer to downtown Hartford, was being readied. At the beginning of December, they moved into the St. Nicholas, a large new building located at 210 Farmington Avenue, next to Jewell Court. (Stevens used both street addresses interchangeably during his years at the St. Nicholas, since Jewell Court and 210 Farmington Avenue were contiguous.) It was during the next six years, when apartment D1 was home, that the poet composed the bulk of *Harmonium*, published in September 1923, as his stay there was nearing an end. In the latter part of 1924, the Stevens family, which now included a baby daughter, moved out of the St. Nicholas and into a two-family house at 735 Farmington Avenue.

Well, they're educated people and they can't understand this; I didn't feel so badly. My mother always said they would be of great value someday.

In listening to my mother talk about the different times she talked to him, I think that he told her about his trips, where he'd been and what his impressions were. She always had a great deal of respect for him, that he was always very gentlemanly, very courteous. I guess a bit formal, but very cordial, very friendly. He would have to kind of steal the time to talk, and he would have to be very careful not to cause any disturbance in his own domestic scene. It was kind of surreptitious. No [the Stevenses never came to dinner], only because I think there was a little problem with Mrs. Stevens, that she was a bit different, that she wasn't as friendly as he probably would have been or might have been otherwise.

JCG: We spent all day Sunday with my father. He generally took us for a ride; he always took us to Elizabeth Park because Elizabeth Park was where you went to do anything, if you flew a kite or went ice-skating. We would drive around Elizabeth Park, and very often we saw Mr. Stevens. My father would either just blow his horn and wave to him, or he would stop to talk. That's how I knew Mr. Stevens. He was always dressed in a full suit, with a shirt and tie, and would be walking by himself. And generally in a back part of the park.

They all thought he was very lonely, and they always felt sorry for him, always felt his wife was crazy. He used any kind of excuse in paying the rent to come up and hand them the check. That would be during Prohibition; I have an idea they'd have a drink together. They thought it was awfully sad: he always seemed to be alone.

I remember my parents talking about the famous incident of Holly being naked in the magnolia tree [at 735 Farmington Avenue]. Mrs. Stevens, being into some kind of health kick, let Holly out in the yard without any clothes on. My mother looked out the window, and she was climbing the magnolia tree. She went to tell Mrs. Stevens that she was out there that way. She said, yes, she sent her out that way.

The house on Farmington Avenue was magic. It's a very unusual house: a solid brownstone foundation, thick brick, and it's all oak inside. My parents, in a discreet way, divided the house into apartments. The thing they hated most in life was a wooden sign [they occasionally had to put up]: APARTMENT FOR RENT. INQUIRE WITHIN. It was *the* most elegant neighborhood in West Hartford.

Next to Westerly Terrace, 735 Farmington Avenue deserves special notice on any literary map of Stevens' Connecticut, for here the poet suffered his "lapse from grace,"* as he later described the prolonged silence that began shortly after the Stevenses moved in. If Monroe was indignant to find that the literary editor of a Hartford newspaper had neglected to list Stevens among Hartford's practicing poets in 1928, the omission was somewhat understandable, since Stevens had not appeared in print for some four years. Between late 1924 and 1930, Stevens published no new verse; except for a few scraps, he had ceased to write.

Some have attributed his silence to a crisis of confidence brought on by the lukewarm reaction to his first book, which appeared in the fall of 1923. *Harmonium* did not sell well, nor was it particularly well received by critics. The disappointed reaction of Stevens' friend, the poet Wilbert Snow, was typical of the criticism *Harmonium* met with.

"When Wallace Stevens' poem 'Peter Quince at the Clavier' came out several years ago many of us thought we discovered a new and valuable note in American poetry. . . . Last year the long awaited volume came out . . . and many of us were frankly disappointed. The music of 'Peter Quince' was here, to be sure, in many of the poems, but the thought that should be wedded to music in poetry was conspicuous by its absence. . . . A *Dial* reviewer once called this type of thing 'poetry by subtraction,' that is, poetry with the ideas removed and the sounds retained. Before Mr. Stevens can come into his own he must prove himself to be more than just a music master."[2] As usual, the review cited *The Waste Land,* published some months before *Harmonium,* at the expense of Stevens' work. If Stevens saw himself classified as a disappointment, it was usually in the same breath that praised T. S. Eliot's epochmaking performance. Ironically, when Stevens began writing again in the early 1930s, he would be criticized for having adopted too cerebral an approach to poetry, having gone from being the music master of *Harmonium* to the philosopher fiddling around with *Ideas of Order,* his next book.

Daily life, however, also conspired to silence the poet, as Ezra Pound, among others, found out when in 1927 he asked a mutual friend, William Carlos Williams, to intercede with Stevens for some recent work. Requests to publish new poems from the likes of Pound and Monroe were certainly heartening enough to restore Stevens' confidence in his powers had that been the heart of the matter. But as Williams wrote back to Rapallo, "He says he isn't writing any more. He has a daughter!"[3] Becoming a father at forty-four would have understandably distracted Stevens for a time after his daughter Holly's birth in August 1924. A baby in the family, even after some fifteen years of marriage, however, hardly accounts for Stevens' silence over the next five years, especially since, soon after her birth, the Stevenses moved into a large apartment at 735 Farmington Avenue, where there was ample space for the poet to get away from the distractions of family life, to find a room of

*In the last months of his life, Stevens befriended Stephen Langton, an administrator at Hartt College of Music who had helped to secure the honorary degree Stevens received from that Hartford institution in the late spring of 1955. During one of their talks, Langton recalls Stevens mentioning that "he experienced what he called 'lapses of grace' . . . when he put aside writing poetry entirely. He said nevertheless the desire to write was gnawing at him all the time. He tried to do without it to make life a little more livable personally, with his wife, I think." (Taped interview.)

his own. More to the point, during the latter half of the 1920s the poet in him felt stifled, oppressed by how routine life had become, as he explained to Williams: "believe me, signor, I'm as busy as the proud Mussolini himself. I rise at day-break, shave etc.; at six I start to exercise; at seven I massage and bathe; at eight I dabble with a therapeutic breakfast; from eight-thirty to nine-thirty I walk down-town; work all day; go to bed at nine. How should I write poetry, think it, feel it?"[4] In his mid- to late forties, Stevens the poet was overwhelmed by the quotidian, by the daily round of life at the office and at home.* During the latter part of these difficult years, Stevens' friend and assistant Ralph Mullen, and his wife, Arlene (now Mrs. Philip Van Raalte), were nearby neighbors, privy to some of the difficulties of life at home at 735 Farmington Avenue.

Arlene Van Raalte

There was a lovely brick house just above us, and the Stevenses lived there. But strange to say, I never met Mrs. Stevens. She was antisocial.

Mr. Stevens would tell Ralph, "She's an awful fuss over the baby. She measures every single thing that's eaten. She watches like a hawk every single minute detail of bringing up that baby." To the point that it was an obsession about taking care of it. Mr. Stevens loved to talk to somebody because, from things he said to my husband, there wasn't too much communication at home. I said to my husband, "I don't understand how he happened to marry such a woman, because he was such an outgoing person."

The [first] time I saw her was at the Bushnell Memorial [a Hartford concert hall] one night. They sat in front of us. Those were the days when all the girls were starting to wear short dresses and cut their hair and look very fashionable. She still had her dress down to her ankles; she had her hair pulled back, and she had a little bun. I said to my husband, "It's too bad that she hasn't come up to modern times," because I think he would have appreciated that. We used to have tickets to the symphony there; we'd see them occasion-

---

*Stevens' sense of stifling routine during the later half of the 1920s may owe a good deal to the strict regimen he was living under as a result of health problems. In October 1926, Stevens consulted a New York diagnostician, Dr. William Herrick, to whom his eye doctor had referred him after detecting hemorrhaging and retinal spasms that were causing blurred vision. Dr. Herrick's tests showed high blood pressure and diabetic tendencies; Stevens was immediately put on a strict routine of diet and exercise, and his condition had already improved a month later, when he returned to Herrick. A year later, when he saw Herrick for an annual checkup, the problems were well under control, although Stevens was never able to pass a physical for life insurance because of high blood pressure. Stevens obviously remained concerned about these health problems, for he remained on the regimen, which he alluded to in his letter to Williams, throughout the rest of the 1920s. He was so severe on himself that at one point he was verging on anemia, and Herrick recommended that Stevens relax his routine and gain a few pounds.

ally. I never met her. I think he never knew what her attitude was going to be. I don't think he could trust her.

In the afternoons, after the office, he would love to get away from it all. He never drove a car, and my husband would bring him out [Mullen was Stevens' assistant from 1921 until his death in 1951]. One of the other men would sometimes come, and they'd have cocktails together. I tried to have a few little hors d'oeuvres, and he enjoyed very much visiting here. Not as often [as once a week], but he would come frequently. It was always casual conversation. We'd talk about gardening, flowers. They loved to talk about the games they had been to. Every time they went to the Harvard games, they would always go to Mrs. Jack Gardner's [museum in Boston]. He loved to go in the spring and he loved to go in the fall, because in the spring they have the rose display and in the fall they had chrysanthemums. They'd come back and talk about the tapestries and interesting things. My husband was interested in painting. [They talked about] the trips to New York: Stevens would love to go to the finest restaurants and have a big lunch. When the World's Fair was down there, they went a couple of times.

With me it was more or less general [conversation] because being with my husband so much, anything that was very personal he'd talk about at the office. He'd come in and tell him very personal things about home. The relationship was not very good. When they bought the house [off] Terry Road, he had his own rooms upstairs. He would tell my husband little personal things about how distressing and disturbing the fact that she was so antisocial with everybody. Robert Frost came here for a visit. My husband came home and said, "Stevens is all upset today. Elsie insulted Robert Frost." I know [Carl Sandburg] came, but I don't think he spent much time at the house. Mr. Stevens told my husband, "You know, she insults everybody."

They wanted Holly to have an extensive education. She went to Vassar; she left there [in her sophomore year]. She became interested [in a local theater group]; I think there were a good many young people in that he probably disapproved of thoroughly. And this young man she married [John Hanchak] he disapproved of thoroughly. He said, "I don't want him in the house." Of course she went right ahead and married him anyway. And after that she came to the house only when he was at the office. He was really broken-hearted about it because he felt this man was not her equal in any way, and he was a proud man. He had hoped his daughter would make the kind of match befitting his station. Very upset.

There was also some dissension between him and his [Reading] family. I remember saying to my husband, "How can any family separate and not see

each other for so many years when it was easy to get to them." Mr. Stevens
would tell him everything that he would never tell anybody else.

As antisocial as Mrs. Stevens was, my husband was the only one she invited
there to lunch. She loved to cook. In fact, Mr. Stevens complained about it
to my husband. "She prepares such enormous meals. It's all I can do. She
expects me to eat these tremendous meals every day." She invited him at
different times for lunch, and I always reciprocated. I'll never forget the first
time I asked him. On the way over, my husband stopped at the store. He said,
"Now, Ralph, if you're going in for cold cuts, I don't eat them." And my
husband said, "I'm not going in for cold cuts; I'm going in for a pack of
cigarettes." Really, I had prepared a connoisseur's lunch because I knew he
loved food. I had an elaborate lunch, and he thought it was marvelous. He
loved pecan buns. Occasionally, he would go to Philadelphia on business and
always bring back from some special place a box of them, all gooey and nice.
And if he didn't go, and my husband went, he'd say, "Please, Ralph, go to
such and such a shop, and buy me some pecan buns." So I had started the
day before, because it was a project. He ate six of them. Another thing I made
was a pie: it was quite a preparation to make and really looked quite nice. I
put it on and I said, "Mr. Stevens, this is called Heavenly Pie." He looked
at it and said, "Open up the gates!"

About his association with people at the office, he was very discriminating,
to put it bluntly. He seemed to cling to my husband. He enjoyed his company;
he loved to come here. There'd be many an afternoon he'd drive up. We'd
have these little snacks together and a cocktail or a glass of wine. He'd enjoy
an hour or so, maybe longer. Then my husband would take him home. I would
have loved to have the both of them, but he said, "She doesn't want anybody.
She doesn't have anybody at all." He talked to Ralph about it. He'd say, "I
would like to be able to have visitors. I would like to have company." But
I think he was afraid to bring anybody there because of her attitude. I can't
help but believe it was some kind of mental quirk. It was always very puzzling
to me. I felt very sad about it because my husband enjoyed him so much, and
he enjoyed being with my husband. And to have someone you couldn't
associate with.

When the Stevens family moved from their Farmington Avenue apartment
to a spacious eleven-room residence on Westerly Terrace in the fall of 1932,
their young daughter had asked why three people needed such a large house.
"To be together when we wish," her father explained. Then, more signifi-
cantly, he added, "and to get away when we wish."[5] Naaman Corn chauffeured the Stevenses on those occasions when the family most often did
things together, on their Saturday afternoon drives around the Connecticut

countryside to dine out. Stevens' assistant Manning Heard and Stevens' niece Jane MacFarland Wilson were among the few guests who were asked to Westerly Terrace when the Stevenses chose not to be alone and extended a rare dinner invitation or an even rarer invitation to spend a week.

Naaman Corn

We used to have to work till noon on Saturday [so an outing began in] the afternoon, and it would usually run on into the evening. They would go out and ride, just looking around, and then they would have dinner. Once to twice a month. They'd be back home around seven, eight o'clock. In later years, they didn't go so much. Seemed to me it was from about 1936 to almost 1950. I guess they were slowing down then.

Mr. Stevens was very dominating. Anywhere he wanted to eat, wherever he wanted to go, the whole family went. [One] place was the 1776, going down toward Danbury. There was a place down in Marlborough called Matty's Place. Another place was the Old Hundred, down near Danbury. One place in particular he told me he wanted to go was up near the Rhode Island line called the Russian Samovar. After the dinner was over, he didn't think he was coming back to that place any more; it didn't seem like he enjoyed Russian food. He went several times to the Pettibone Tavern; it's in Simsbury. Oh, he loved that place.

No one dictated anything else but Mr. Stevens. He was the king. Sometimes, he would want to go on some back roads, go up on top of Avon Mountain and take a look. Then, he'd go right down the mountain to Farmington, just dirt roads all the way down there. When we'd go and ride around all afternoon, "Okay, Naaman. Pull in that filling station there. I want to fill up the car with gas and then leave it like I found it." He never would sponge on the company. He would pay for my services. At that time, we didn't have no such thing as overtime; he was very generous, he was very nice like that.

He didn't carry on any conversation with Mrs. Stevens much about something. She wouldn't talk on account of he would snap at her quickly. So she got where she just went in a shell, and she wouldn't say anything. One time I thought she couldn't talk because she never did say nothing, but I found out why. If every time you say something to a person, you're going to snap at them, they quit talking. They go underground. You could hear that, and you figured that's the reason why she clams up.

I used to hear him say a lot of things. It didn't mean much to me: "Well, that's Mr. Stevens, being the way the man was built, and that was his way." There was the Cook's Tavern. He went there once, and so when he came out and got in the car he made the remark to his family, "I don't think I like the place. Too many Jews come in here." Just like that. That's the first time I ever heard him mention the name Jew. I never heard him say it after that time. Another time he'd be going someplace and his daughter wanted to stop to eat someplace. He'd look over. "Too many poor old devils over there." I don't think he meant any of it, just first thing came into his mind. It wasn't no strong feeling, I don't think. He didn't want to go anywhere to eat where he thought poor people came in. If maybe he had a place was five dollars a dinner, he would go to the place where it was ten dollars. Then he figured the poor folks weren't going to be there. He'd make remarks about the poor people, but if the poor would come on his street taking up money for a church or something, he was always willing to help them. He'd be the first to pull out a five- or a ten-dollar bill. That's why I say, it didn't seem to mean nothing. He struck me as somebody just being misunderstood. I never did understand his way. I never could.

We had to take him home one day. He came in [to work] after a little drizzle. The sidewalk was very slippery; it was just a little glaze of ice. He got right to the office, fixing to turn in and come up on the grounds, and he fell. There's a big old bank along there. When he fell, he hit his head there. Some of the officers saw him. He had this bloody handkerchief there, and he went into his office and he sat down. Pretty soon, he rang the bell 'cause he tried to get up to go to the men's room; he had gotten so stiff, he couldn't walk. Two of us had to let him lean on either shoulder to take him around to the men's room. Then he telephoned to Mr. Sigmans to see if he couldn't get somebody to help him get home. We went down to the nurse and put him in this wheelchair. Stevens never did like to be helpless. That was the one thing, he didn't want to see himself coming to an end. When we got him home the problem was we couldn't roll the wheelchair upstairs. We had to carry him upstairs. Oh boy, it was four of us struggling with him to get him upstairs. Mrs. Stevens had a place ready for him, but still, even when he was in that condition, he still was the boss. He didn't want nobody to do anything. He was directing us what to do. "Now don't scratch the paint. Don't do this." It was really kind of funny. My goodness alive, the man can't move and still he's resisting everything. But that was just his way.

Manning Heard

I was very fond of him, and I think he was very fond of me because he helped me every chance he got [to advance at the company, where Heard was Stevens' assistant from 1933 to 1937]. I think my wife and I were the only people, outside of Mr. Kearney and his wife, who had dinner at Mr. Stevens' home. Oh no, not regularly. This was once. He had dinner at our home often, but not Mrs. Stevens. It was in the thirties. We were the only guests. They were perfectly beautiful hosts. We had a wonderful dinner; Mrs. Stevens cooked it and served it. A very fine evening. They had a beautiful home on Westerly Terrace, and he was proud of it. She was terribly meticulous about it; she was one of the most meticulous housekeepers you can possibly imagine. You couldn't smoke in the house. As a matter of fact, one of my friends went there one time to see Mr. Stevens. He reached for a cigar. Stevens said, "No. No smoking is permitted in this house."

[That evening Stevens showed Heard his collection of paintings.] He had this old gentleman in Paris who was his European representative. He died, and subsequently this gentleman's daughter used to pick up paintings for him. He was very proud of them; some of them I wouldn't give house room to, but he enjoyed them all. [Book collecting] was another one of his hobbies. He would go to great lengths to have any particular book he liked bound up; I saw them all at home or when he got them from New York. They'd be sent to the office; he'd call me and show me. He was very proud of those. The original of the sculpture of Mrs. Stevens, whose profile is on the dime, was always on the living room mantelpiece. It was about twelve inches, beautifully done.

Most of our conversation was either at the office [or at Heard's home, a block away from Westerly Terrace]. My mother-in-law is a typical Spanish-French—as they call it, Creole—Frenchy as she can be. Mr. Stevens was very fond of both of them [her and her husband]. They used to visit us [from New Orleans] quite often. Stevens would find out, and he would waddle over. He used to waddle, walking from side to side like a bear. He'd come over, and sit down, and spend several hours, almost two or three times [when] they'd come up here. Just plain conversation. Mrs. Stevens wouldn't come over. It was always [on] business and very seldom [that Heard visited Westerly Terrace, however]. I went over there once with Ralph Mullen, who was then head of fidelity claims [and] who was subordinate to Mr. Stevens, and we walked around the back. Mrs. Stevens was working in her garden. She saw us and ran inside. She was very shy, very shy. I don't think so [that she became shyer over the years], because after Mr. Stevens died I went to see her, and I can't remember meeting a more charming lady, and [we] had such a perfectly normal, interesting conversation. I think he completely subdued her. I think he was a little jealous of her myself, because he was very protective of her, very protective, and he never took her anywhere. As a matter of fact, Mr. Stevens would go to a [company] party but never with Mrs. Stevens. And we'd often wonder why. She told me, after he died, that for some reason or other he just didn't want her exposed. She said, "I would have loved to have come, but Wallace didn't want me to. He didn't want me to go, and I didn't go, naturally." But she was a lovely, lovely person.

I didn't know what their relationship [Holly's and her father's] was at home. But I do know that when she married for the first time, she was working at the Aetna [insurance company]. [Before her marriage to John Hanchak in 1944, the couple went to Stevens' office to tell him of their plans.] I can remember when he found out in the office, and he made a scene that you could hear him all over the place. He was really upset. He let everybody know that he was mad about it. I didn't know what was going on. I heard him with this very high voice raising hell. The only time I saw him mad.

Jane MacFarland Wilson

In 1941, I went up to Hartford to spend a week in August with Holly. I had a delightful week, but every evening that we were home, after dinner everybody went to their own rooms, closed the door, and did whatever they did in their own rooms. This was the private person: [the Stevenses] all had that. I think now my mother [Elizabeth Stevens] and Garrett [Stevens' older brother] were more [alike]: they were very outgoing.

Holly was about sixteen then; I was twenty-one. She had, one time, a whole gang of kids in, and we played Dinah Shore records. I think that was the afternoon I arrived. And I brought her a blue cigarette case. When Wallace came home from work he was quite shocked that I had given her this. He didn't say it, but I felt it. There was no other time she had the young folks in. The family didn't congregate: at the table for dinner, and then afterward up to their cells. Unless Holly and I went to the movies with one of her boyfriends or something, we were closed in our little rooms. [It was] kind of like their castle: that was their own room, their own life, and they could do whatever they wanted. They all felt that way.

I went more with Holly [around Hartford] because she had gotten a red convertible for her sixteenth birthday. She was very proud of it; I was in awe. During that time [Wallace, Holly and Jane] took American Airlines over to [Boston]. I think Holly had been there before, but he knew I was interested in him, and I was his guest [so] he was putting himself out. He showed me around [Harvard]. [Then] we went to a place where it was all handmade jewelry. He said, "Pick out anything you want." So with my poor upbringing, I picked out something [inexpensive]. "Oh, you don't want that. Here, how about this?" It was a beautiful bracelet, silver with tourmalines and lazuli. It cost forty dollars, which was a fortune to me in those days.

That week was the first time I met Elsie. She was remote, just remote. She said very little. I can remember only one thing she said the whole time, which wasn't really like her, I understand. Every morning we had coffee and fresh orange juice. There was a whole set of these beautiful coffee cups—thin, delicate china. I had a different cup every morning. I finally had to tell her how much I thought of this. She said, "Well, now, seeing you two together like this makes me wish I had two daughters." I don't think Elsie and Holly related at all; that's why Elsie's remark stands out, because Holly was just floored by it. [During a recent visit with Holly] I got some feeling that she disliked her mother intensely. And more so toward the end, when she was coming to know her father and get closer to him. I don't think, until the last few years of his life, that they ever came to understand each other. He loved her. I think Holly loved her father finally, but she didn't [earlier]. She had rebelled against him terribly. Her first marriage [to John Hanchak], which was very unsuccessful, was simply done in rebellion. And her father almost disowned her. He could do that sort of thing.

You didn't know the next moment what Elsie was going to say to you or whether she was going to disappear in[to] thin air, because half the time she wasn't there. She loved her garden. Every day there was a fresh rose in my little bedroom. The only thing she had any interest in were her garden and her house. The place was kept immaculate, and [she also did] the garden all herself. It was a comfortable house, the way it was furnished. If Wallace was in it, it was a lovely house, but when Elsie was there, even though everything was light, and airy, and beautiful, it was not.

Sid [Wilson, Jane's husband] and our daughter went back to Hartford in '53. We stayed at a hotel [Stevens had arranged for them in lieu of inviting them to stay at Westerly Terrace]. We visited Holly several times at her apartment, but only one afternoon did we go to the house on Westerly Terrace. Peter [Hanchak], Holly's son, was quite young then. Peter was quite a rambunctious child, but Uncle Wallace could calm Peter down. He'd put him on his knee and tell him little stories that he'd make up. The little boy was just spellbound by his grandfather. I remember out front saying good-by, and Holly saying to her father something to the effect that "That went pretty good, didn't it?" Meaning that Mother must have behaved. Here again, Elsie didn't say anything. He must have felt very strongly about [divorce], because certainly he was no longer in love, yet he never divorced her. Whenever she needed him, he was there, and he took a lot of abuse. I'm sure she could be [sharp], and I will tell you why. After he died, I continued to send Christmas cards and little notes. I addressed the card, "Mrs. Elsie Stevens" because she was a widow, and I would write, "Dear Aunt Elsie." I had my card finally returned to me with a little note. "I am Mrs. Wallace Stevens, and I am not your Aunt Elsie." Cut dead! She could do that. Holly has indicated this. I often wondered whether he told Elsie about the times we met. His letters always came from [the office], and he would say, "Don't write me at home."

CHAPTER SEVEN

Farewell to My Elders

On May 11, 1919, Wallace Stevens arrived in Evanston, Illinois, for a family visit. He had taken a seventy-mile trolley ride from Milwaukee, where a case involving the Hartford Accident and Indemnity Company had gone to trial, to pay a call on a favorite uncle. Harry Carle had recently lost his wife, Anna, the youngest sister of Wallace's mother. The childless couple had been close to the Stevens children when they were growing up, and during Sunday's visit the conversation naturally turned to Stevens' brothers and sisters. Both Uncle Harry and Eleanor Hatch, his housekeeper, knew a good deal more about what was happening in the family than did Wallace. He was stunned to learn that his sister had married a man almost twenty years older than she was, although Elizabeth had been married to George Mac-Farland now for almost two years.[1] While Stevens occasionally went on business to Philadelphia, where the couple were living, he had not visited them. When he had recovered from the news that Elizabeth's husband was a man of fifty with white hair, he also learned that Elizabeth had recently given birth to a daughter. As the conversation turned to his brother John's young family in Reading, Miss Hatch, who was the sister of John's wife, passed around some recent photos. Stevens thought his sister-in-law had put on weight since he had last seen her, but then he couldn't be sure, for he had met his brother's wife only once in the nine years since she had married John and settled in Reading.[2]

The conversation that afternoon tells how far Stevens had drifted from his family by the time he moved to Connecticut in 1916. Clearly, more than a few hundred miles now separated Stevens from his brothers Garrett, an Ohio criminal lawyer, and John, who had a flourishing law practice at home, and from his younger sisters, Elizabeth and Mary Katharine, then a Red Cross volunteer in postwar France.* "That family was close, Uncle John, Aunt Bess and my father," Garrett's daughter, Mary Catharine Sesnick, recalls, and they kept in touch with each other as she was growing up in Cleveland in the 1910s and 1920s. But her thoughts occasionally turned to the uncle in Hartford she had never seen. "What about the other uncle? I would wonder. What happened?"[3] At least part of the answer lay in a crisis that had occurred in the months prior to Stevens' engagement to Elsie Kachel at Christmas in 1908, which alienated him permanently from his father and strained family ties that were not to be knit closely again for some thirty years.

Elsie Stevens later wrote the following discreet account of her courtship as part of a genealogy she composed for her daughter. Elsie was a very guarded woman, however, and never confided even to Holly how much discord her courtship had caused in the Stevens household: a confrontation with his father had forced Wallace to choose between Elsie and his family.

Elsie Stevens

One June evening, in 1904, Mr. John Repplier (then a slight acquaintance of the writer, and a neighbor of the Stevens family) brought Mr. Wallace Stevens to her parents' home, and at this time introduced Mr. Stevens to her, and to three friends who were spending the evening with her; the sisters Misses Alice and Clare Tragle, and Miss Harriet Heller. Mr. Stevens had been away from home a number of years, and was in his 25th year of age when he came to Reading to spend the summer with his parents. On returning to Reading, he found that his friends were either married, or had left Reading, so he made friends with their younger brothers, and Johnny Repplier was one of them. That evening, the six of us had a pleasant time on the front porch, and singing Gilbert and Sullivan songs at the piano. During the remaining summer Mr. Stevens spent many evenings and Sunday afternoons with the Tragle sisters, as well as with the writer, until September, when he returned to New York City to begin the practice of law.

---

*Even as Stevens was being brought up to date on family matters that May afternoon in 1919, his sister Mary Katharine (or Catharine, as she was also known) lay ill in an army hospital in France, where she died ten days later. Born on April 25, 1889, in Reading, Pennsylvania, she was the youngest of the Stevens children. After her mother's death in 1912, she made her home with her brother John and his young family in Reading, where, from 1913 to 1916, she worked as a stenographer. In 1917 she moved to Philadelphia, where her sister, Elizabeth, lived and, following America's entry into World War I, joined the Red Cross and was sent to a training camp in Washington, D.C. As the need for relief workers in France arose, she volunteered her services there, sailing from New York on April 8, 1918. She was stationed for a time at Boulogne, later transferred to the auditing department of the civilian relief section at Saint-Nazaire.

The few extant accounts of her experiences, written while she was in France, show that she had an aptitude for descriptive prose writing. "On Flanders Fields," a Bosch-like account of a day trip through the countryside, typifies her vivid and detailed style (HL).

Mr. Stevens returned to Reading for his holidays and summer vacations, and on his visit to Reading in 1908 for Christmas, he gave the writer a Tiffany engagement ring with a solitaire diamond. On September 21st., 1909, we were married by Rev. William H. Myers, in Grace Lutheran church [sic] in Reading, attended by the bride's parents and two bridesmaids, Miss Anna Rigg, and Miss Mary Stoner.[4]

Stevens' father was not among the well-wishers, if indeed any of the groom's family attended the service. It had been months, in fact, since Garrett Stevens and Wallace had spoken. Years later, over a martini lunch at the Canoe Club, the usually reticent Stevens confided to one of his office assistants some of the details of the family row late in his courtship that had severed the ties between father and son. "He'd rush over to the girl's place, and the family would never see him until it was time for him to leave" for New York again, John Ladish learned that afternoon. "After that had gone on for some time, his father said, 'If you're going to consider our home just a hotel, just a place to bring your laundry, you might as well not come at all.' They had words, and this was the last he saw of his father. He regretted this very much, because the father died [in 1911] without ever having spoken to him. He brooded over that over the years."[5]

While working at Saint-Nazaire, Mary Katharine Stevens took ill and on May 2, 1919, entered the base hospital, complaining of severe head and ear pains. On May 17, she was operated on for mastoiditis; four days later she succumbed, unexpectedly, to meningitis. She was buried in her Red Cross uniform, along with one large red peony from a bouquet that had pleased her so at her hospital bedside. As the friend who was with her at the time of her death wrote, "The boys were all keen about her, she was so friendly and happy with them; they made her sing for them, and I remember how she used to look, with her golden head shining above the mob, for she was taller than a great many of them. Everybody liked her, for who could help liking one so unassuming and kind, as well as remarkably capable and good-looking? And that popularity of the truest and best sort means more over here than it does at home; for people can judge you here only by yourself. . . . I can say with all my heart I never knew a more straightforward and sincere person, or one with a more loveable combination of cheerful human good qualities. . . ." (Copy of an undated letter of Constance M. Hallock to John Stevens, HL.)

The news of Mary Katharine's death deeply affected Stevens. He could think of little else on a train trip back to Wisconsin from Hartford in late May. In midsummer he made it a point to visit Mary Katharine's grave on a trip through Reading, her body having been brought home and interred in the family plot. ". . . on the way to Philadelphia [I] came through Reading where I stopped from 5.50 until 8.39," Stevens wrote to his wife. "I made a pious visit to the cemetery. . . . I went to the Berkshire where I had a piffling dinner and then walked out Fifth Street toward the station. As I passed Huff's house I saw Mr. Huff and stopped to talk for ten minutes. He gave me quite a batch of news about old neighbors. I saw no one else and did not even telephone John, feeling that I had too little time. On the whole, this brief survey of the holy city left on my mind a most afflicting impression." (Letter of July 24, 1919, HL.) While Stevens remained on speaking terms with his brothers and sister during the 1910s and 1920s, he had very little contact with his family until his brother Garrett's lingering illness in the late 1930s and the death of his brother John in 1940.

Garrett Stevens was an unlikely actor in such a family melodrama, a man whom his son once described as "incapable of lifting a hand to attract any of us."[6] And yet Garrett Stevens was not speaking out of character in this scene. He confronted his son not because he felt he was being displaced in Wallace's affection by this young woman but because he felt his son had misplaced his affection on a stenographer from across the tracks.* At the time of this confrontation, in the summer or early fall of 1908, the Stevenses had been a prominent family in Reading's professional class for some thirty years; the elder Stevens' outburst was partly an attempt to bring his son back to his bourgeois senses.

Young Garrett Stevens had arrived in Reading in 1870, ambitious to be more than a farmer like his Bucks County father. In his early twenties at the time, the former schoolteacher had come to town to read law, and two years later was admitted to the bar after clerking in the office of a local attorney.[7] He soon proved a young man to watch, as a local newspaper commented at the time of his marriage, on November 9, 1876, to Margaretha Catharine Zeller, a twenty-eight-year-old schoolteacher from Reading. By then, Garrett Stevens had already narrowly missed nomination to the legislature from this county seat.[8] During the next twenty years, however, as Wallace and his brothers and sisters were growing up in Reading, the elder Stevens made his mark locally principally as a corporate lawyer, counsel to several local banks and director of at least half a dozen corporations.[9] Indeed, by the time Wallace left Harvard in 1900, Garrett Stevens and William Kerper Stevens, who were not related except by friendship, had built up a partnership that ranked as one of the two most respected law firms in town. By then Garrett Stevens also ranked as one of the more prosperous Reading attorneys. With farms in Bucks County and a score of holdings in and around Reading, he estimated his worth at the time somewhere between twenty and thirty thousand dollars,† although he had already begun to suffer a series of financial setbacks that depleted his resources in his later years and helped to bring on a nervous breakdown soon after the turn of the century.

About 1900, Garrett, Jr., was the first of the Stevens children to consider marriage, courting a young woman he had met while studying at Dickinson Law School. Like Elsie Kachel after her, Sarah Shelley Stayman had learned how determined the Stevenses were that their children not marry beneath the class they had worked hard to join. The family crisis during her courtship was one of Sarah Stayman Stevens' favorite stories, one she often repeated to her daughter, Mary Catharine Sesnick, and to her granddaughter Joan Sesnick.

---

*The city directories of Reading list Elsie Moll as a saleslady in 1904, the year she met Wallace Stevens, as a milliner in 1905 and 1906, and as a stenographer from 1907 until her marriage to Stevens in 1909. Though Lehman Moll had not adopted her after marrying her mother, Elsie Kachel used his surname as she was growing up in Reading.

†Garrett Stevens' professional and financial rating appeared in *Martindale's American Law Directory* (New York: J. B. Martindale, 1900), p. 648. Out of the 112 Reading lawyers, Garrett Stevens ranked in the top quarter financially; only the firm of Baer, Snyder and Zieber was as highly recommended.

Mary Catharine Sesnick and Joan Sesnick

MCS: They sent someone to Carlisle [Pennsylvania] to check my mother's parents out to see if my mother was good enough to come into the family. Mamma said her mother and father were indignant over that. "The idea! To look over my family to see if it was good enough for them." She never forgot that.

JS: That almost stopped the marriage.*

MCS: Mother's family didn't like that, because the family was quite prominent in Carlisle. She always bragged about her grandfather being the first county superintendent in Cumberland County.

JS: And her father was a trustee of Dickinson College.

MCS: And they were related to Shelley, the poet, on my grandmother's side. They were very proud of that.

She liked her [mother-in-law, Margaretha Stevens] very much. She said she was quite an austere type of woman and probably wasn't too friendly with a lot of people. But she did take Mamma under her wing and was very good to her. Mrs. Stevens said my mother was like her daughter, but the other two wives were daughters-in-law. And that was that. She was short, sort of pioneer-looking in a way. They would visit there quite often. She liked Grandpa Stevens, too, and he liked her. Well, Mamma was the type that kind of fell over men, and of course he would take to her very much. [Mr. and Mrs. Stevens] were both strong-willed. The household was hers; the other was his. I remember Mamma saying that Grandpa Stevens never set foot in the kitchen, that was woman's work. They had servants.

She always referred to the Stevenses as Blue Book. She always stood a little in awe of the Stevens family: they reacted a little bit differently from a social standpoint, and everything was properly done.

Sarah Stayman proved an acceptable daughter-in-law to the Stevenses, in no small part because of her family background and social standing. By the turn of the century, Margaretha Catharine Stevens—or Kate, as she was known around Reading—had joined the local chapter of the Daughters of the American Revolution and had become too snobbish even for her husband to bear

---

*Crisis seemed to run in the family when the Stevens children contemplated marriage. Elizabeth Stevens, no less than her brothers Garrett and Wallace, found out her parents had definite ideas about a suitable mate. In Elizabeth's case, "there was a young man in Reading, but he was a Catholic and they were strict Presbyterians," Mary Catharine Sesnick recalls. The young couple "just had a terrible time: so she gave him up. I think that, too, alienated her from her family to a certain extent."

at times. As he reminded her, she was, after all, a shoemaker's daughter and he was a farmer's son.[10] If Garrett was more pragmatic about the value of family standing, he hardly discounted it in sizing up a future daughter-in-law, as Wallace well knew. Only a short time before the confrontation over Elsie, Garrett had pointed out to Wallace how useful Garrett, Jr., was finding his wife's connections now that he had moved to Baltimore, where Mrs. Stayman knew "good, strong, plain people: Doctors and Preachers and others of importance" to whom she could introduce him.[11]

The contrast with Elsie's family was only too obvious, although they had not always lived on the other side of the tracks. Indeed, Elsie's mother had spent much of her childhood living in the then-fashionable North Fifth Street area of Reading where Wallace, too, would grow up. Ida Bright Smith was almost six years old in 1869 when her parents, George Washington and Catherine Bright Smith, moved to 537 Elm Street, a block behind the row house at 323 North Fifth, which Garrett Stevens bought nine years later for the family homestead. Ida Smith's family had moved there from the country a year before Garrett Stevens had himself settled in Reading and begun to read law; if anything, the Smiths' prospects had looked far more immediately promising than those of this farmboy-schoolteacher from Bucks County. George Washington Smith, who had been a station agent in a small Pennsylvania town, had come to Reading to run a local coal company. He settled his family into the substantial three-story brick house at 537 Elm Street that his father-in-law, Aaron Bright, a prosperous merchant, had left upon retiring to a large farm in Virginia earlier that year. Almost as soon as the Smiths arrived in town, however, Ida's father's health began to fail, and with it, his business. Indeed, the Smith family fortunes seemed to decline in direct proportion to the rise of the Stevenses' during the next years. When Ida's father died in 1875, his thirty-nine-year-old widow, Catherine, and her nine children were forced to move away from the North Fifth Street neighborhood of doctors, lawyers and prosperous businessmen to a working-class part of town, where, eleven years later, Elsie Kachel was born.[12]

Ida Smith had been some five months pregnant with Elsie when, at twenty-two, she married Howard Kachel, a twenty-year-old spectaclemaker, in February 1886. Too poor to furnish an apartment when they married, the couple were living with Ida's mother when Elsie was born on June 5. A year later Kachel was dead from what was then known as "galloping consumption," and the young widow and baby stayed on as part of Catherine Smith's family for the next seven years until Ida's marriage to Lehman Moll in 1894. Though he had been educated at a Pennsylvania normal school and had taught for two years before coming to Reading, Moll was a stock clerk at the time, and family fortunes hardly improved after the marriage. Indeed, finances became so straitened that Elsie Moll left high school during her first year to take a job in a local department store.

Although Wallace Stevens would later raise some of the same objections to his daughter's choice of a husband in 1944 that his parents were now making to his choice of a wife in 1908, he dismissed such concerns over Elsie's background and social standing at the time as simple snobbery. He tried to reassure his fiancée that, after all, "We both come from respectable families."[13] There were definite degrees of respectability, however, in turn-of-the-century Reading. The Stevenses' objections would not have been unusual in this caste-conscious city. Byron Vazakas, a local poet who wrote one of the earliest biographical sketches of Stevens for a local historical society bulletin in 1938, is a long-time student of Reading mores.

Byron Vazakas

I did a lot of historical research around here. This was a rigid social system, as in London during the Victorian era, they practiced here. Reading was divided into the coal, iron and railroad people and the newcomers, the textile people. Now the Stevenses were no part of this. You had to be very rich, you had to have a big industry [to be in Reading society]. [But] lawyers were respectable, doctors were respectable. In every town you have the business section, then the main street going out. North Fifth Street was one [such street]. Well-to-do burghers lived there. They were attorneys and judges, but they were not society.

[The area at 231 South Thirteenth Street, where Elsie Kachel lived] was not a slum. It was just lower-middle-class. They lived in a porch house, and you'd get in the swing there when you went to see her. It's characteristic of the independence of the Stevenses that he married somebody who was not from a professional family like his own.

Apart from simple snobbery, there was also a more substantial motive for the Stevenses' interest in Elsie Kachel's background. Both Garrett and Kate had once been schoolteachers, and they were rightly concerned about the intellectual and cultural gap between their bookish, Harvard-educated son and a young woman whose family circumstances had permitted only a grammar school education. Years later, sensing this division between her parents as she was growing up, Stevens' daughter shared her grandparents' bemusement and one day asked her father why he had married her mother. Quite simply, she was the prettiest girl in town, he explained.[14] To his family at the time it seemed that Wallace had simply fallen in love with a pretty face, his sister Elizabeth later recalled, "a pretty doll-like creature who never said anything. We couldn't understand Wallace having an interest in somebody like this."[15]

What his family did not fathom was that, among other things, the frustrated young poet had found his muse again in the person of this Reading beauty. At the time of his confrontation with his father over Elsie, Stevens had just completed "A Book of Verses." As slight as most of the twenty lyrics are, they were the first group of poems he had written since leaving Harvard eight years earlier. It had been inspired by his love for Elsie Kachel and was a birthday present for her that summer of 1908. The collection revealed that she was now a source of those poetic feelings that had all but gone out of his life during his trying first years as a lawyer in New York. "In Town" expressed his dissatisfaction with his prosaic daily life and his longing for an alternative.

It's well enough to work there,
When so many do;
It's well enough to walk the street,
When your work is through.

It's night there that kills me,
In a narrow room,
Thinking of a wood I know,
Deep in fragrant gloom.

As "Afield" made clear, it was Elsie who had helped to make the woods sing again, who had brought poetry back into his world.

You give to brooks a tune,
A melody to trees.
You make the dumb field sing aloud
Its hidden harmonies.*

His parents were not so impressed. Sarah Stayman Stevens was visiting her in-laws one afternoon at 323 North Fifth Street when she witnessed a highly emotional scene that dramatized the Stevenses' objections to Wallace's infatuation with Elsie's beauty.

Mary Catharine Sesnick and Joan Sesnick

MCS: I don't think that Elsie went into the house very often, quite a problem there. Uncle Wallace couldn't understand this, he was so enticed with her beauty. Mostly her beauty, that's what [Stevens' brothers and sister said attracted Wallace to Elsie], beauty and style. They never said anything bad or nasty. In fact, my mother was quite enthralled with her style, her type. I think why my mother didn't get more friendly with her was she had to go along with the feelings of the family. My mother had no strong feelings against her at all. She thought she was a little affected, as far as that goes, but Mamma never talked about anyone. She said she was very pretty, and Wallace dressed her in style.

JS: Elsie had won a beauty contest before they were married. It may have been like Gram's mother: she had been named the prettiest girl in Cumberland County for a festival.

*Quoted in Holly Stevens' *Souvenirs and Prophecies* (New York: Alfred A. Knopf, 1976), pp. 195 and 190–91. On the eve of a visit to Reading, Stevens also voiced the poetic role Elsie Kachel now played in his life. "I am no longer a poet. Yet it may be that the sight of Spring waters will restore that faculty, with many others. You must be my poetess and sing me many songs. I shall hear them in strange places and repeat them afterwards as half my own.— Good-night, dear poetess!" (Letter of March 18, 1907, HL.)

MCS: That's when it started, because they didn't accept Elsie. That's when he brought her home. I remember Mamma saying she had on one of those great big hats they wore in those days, and dressed beautifully. All set to make a royal entrance. Mamma said that Wallace was so proud. She came in, so elegant-looking dressed that way. Just didn't work out too well. Wallace said, "I'll never come back. I'll never come back into this house!" That's what Mamma told me, 'cause she was there.

By Thanksgiving, 1908, Garrett Stevens' final confrontation with his son erupted in spite of himself. Not long before it happened, the elder Stevens had wisely resolved not to interfere, for he saw how determined Wallace was to have his way.* By 1908, however, ill health and the financial pressures he had been under since the turn of the century had worn down Garrett's self-control. Around 1901, he had a nervous breakdown, brought on partly by working at the office from 8:00 A.M. to 10:00 P.M. most days and partly by a string of financial reverses that made him feel there was some "Hoodoo" at work in his investments.[16]

In the late 1890s, after going into debt to put his three sons through college simultaneously, Garrett Stevens began suffering setbacks. In April 1898, a fire gutted the Wilhelm Bicycle Works, a company that Stevens had ventured into as a partner only that January. Bicycles were a new craze at the time, with more than a dozen plants manufacturing them in Reading alone. The factory in Hamburg, Pennsylvania, employing two hundred people and worth some $80,000, was a sound investment when Stevens took over the company, hoping to recoup some of the losses he had already sustained in other industrial ventures. The Wilhelm Bicycle Works, for example, had recently developed a chainless bicycle wheel and had orders for ten thousand of them from New York alone when it burned down.[17]

The firm was, apparently, one of a half-dozen corporations Garrett Stevens was directing at the time, and it fell to him to see to the fire insurance claims and to the rebuilding. He was harried by other troubled investments as well, including a steel works that had proved to be a white elephant. Unable to unload either factory during the economic slump of the late 1890s and finding that these holdings were eating up his resources as he waited for the market to improve, Garrett Stevens wondered, at times, if he would be able to get out without declaring bankruptcy.[18]

Under these strains he finally suffered a nervous breakdown and had to take a six-month rest cure in the Adirondack Mountains.† Although he began to

---

*"From the fact that I hear nothing from [you] I may assume that you are absorbed in personal matters—and as you want your own way about them I do not want to butt in" (letter of Garrett Stevens to Wallace Stevens, March 22, 1908, HL). The last extant letter from Garrett Stevens to his son is dated May 13, 1908; between that time and Thanksgiving, when Stevens returned to Reading but did not visit at home, Garrett broke his resolve and "butted in."

†Letter of Wallace Stevens to Jane MacFarland Stone, September 13, 1943, in *L WS,* p. 454. Sarah Stayman Stevens, who married Garrett, Jr., in 1901, later remarked to her children on

practice law again after his return to Reading, he came back something of a broken man who seemed merely to be existing during his last years, according to his former law partner.[19]

Around 1908, Garrett Stevens' long-time partnership with William Kerper Stevens dissolved, and he formed another with his son John. After the financial panic that swept the country during the preceding months, Stevens' bankers were pressing him on notes he had taken out. Years of such strains had worn down Garrett Stevens' self-control. His resolve not to interfere in Wallace's personal affairs, which Garrett had made in March 1908, gave way; by Thanksgiving the confrontation that severed the ties between them had taken place. When Wallace came to Reading to spend the holiday with Elsie, he stayed at a boarding house and did not visit at home.[20] The Christmas spirit did not stir any good will between father and son. When Wallace returned in December with the present of a diamond engagement ring, he again boarded near his fiancée's home.[21] Just how little contact there now was between Stevens and his family was underscored by an incident that took place later that spring. Over Easter weekend, John Stevens, who still lived with his parents, announced his engagement to his family. Although Wallace Stevens visited Reading both at Easter and on the following weekend, he did not learn of John's news until three weeks later, when Elsie sent him a newspaper clipping about his younger brother's engagement to Elizabeth Hatch.[22]

In the months that followed, there was a good deal of interchange between the Stevenses in Pennsylvania and John's fiancée in Illinois, as Elizabeth Stevens' diary makes clear. And yet, though Elizabeth constantly referred to everyone else in her family, her diary does not mention her brother Wallace or his fiancée, not even as their wedding approached in September 1909. At North Fifth Street, the couple had become something akin to nonpersons.

Stevens' father continued to remain estranged, but once the marriage was a *fait accompli*, some conciliatory gestures were made by others in the family.† The following spring, Elizabeth Stevens thought of calling on her brother when visiting in New York, and Mrs. Stevens asked her daughter to convey her love. Both Wallace and Elsie Stevens were out of town that week in April 1910, but when Elizabeth visited her brother Garrett, now also an insurance lawyer in New York with Maryland Casualty Company, she doubtlessly heard how coolly Wallace had received Garrett's overtures of friendship

---

the elder Stevens' illness, which occurred around the time of her marriage. "We never could understand why my father didn't inherit if [the Stevens family] had all this money. My mother said [Garrett Stevens] lost his money, and it caused this mental breakdown. He never quite recovered from it. He really got quite off balance, from what my mother said." (Taped interview with Mary Catharine Sesnick.)

†Garrett's and Wallace's capacity to hold a grudge was apparently a family trait, as an incident during Elizabeth's courtship shows. "Aunt Bess was going with someone her brother John didn't like," John's daughter-in-law later learned. "John came down one night as this guy was kissing Aunt Bess in the vestibule. He told him to 'Get the hell out!' Bess and John sat at the dining-room table for two years after that and didn't speak to each other." (Taped interview with Anna May Stevens.)

toward the newlyweds.* Nonetheless, there was, finally, a family reunion of sorts a year later, when Stevens returned for the funeral of his father in July 1911. Stevens made several visits back to North Fifth Street in the ensuing months to be with his mother, whose health was failing and who died on July 16, 1912, a year and two days after her husband had passed away.

Mary Catharine Sesnick

I do remember [hearing of Stevens' confrontation with his father] before they were married. It hurt my grandmother quite a bit, because Wallace was her favorite. I think my father [Garrett] was the father's favorite. But I know she really doted on Wallace. He was rather sick as a young child; he was rather delicate. And that's why his mother doted so. She had lost I don't know how many babies, and she didn't want to lose any one of those three boys. He was the delicate one; I remember Mamma saying that.

Now my grandmother had a growth; she didn't live long after [her husband] died. Elsie didn't come to the funeral [when Margaretha Stevens died, although she was vacationing only a few miles from Reading]. My mother remarked that it was very strange that she wouldn't come. But then we kept saying, "Well, no wonder she wouldn't come."

He came to the funeral and then left. And that was it.

While these visits had bound mother and son close again, they did little to reunite Stevens with his remaining family: some seven years after his mother's death, as he sat in his uncle's home in Evanston, Illinois, Stevens heard of his sister's husband, whom he knew nothing about, and looked at pictures of his brother's wife, whom he had seen only once. By the time he moved to Connecticut in 1916, and for some twenty years after, Stevens was largely just "a strange person off in the distance"[23] until the illness of his older brother and the death of his younger brother brought him home again, in every sense of the word.

---

*Garrett Stevens, Jr., lived in New York from 1910 to 1912, or so. Years later, his wife, Sarah, confided to a nephew that "she had been offended" during the time both Garrett's and Wallace's families lived there because "Garrett tried to make contact and Wallace was busy." (Taped interview with John Sauer.)

CHAPTER EIGHT

Family Ties

As Wallace Stevens riffled through his morning mail at the office on August 7, 1943, one envelope caught his eye with its unusual code: *S.W.A.K.* In the daily correspondence from field lawyers on bond-claim matters or from editors requesting poems for their little magazines, a letter that came SEALED WITH A KISS stood out. A few nights earlier, four young people had been having a nightcap at a hotel in Reading, Pennsylvania, when the conversation turned to Uncle Wallace in Connecticut. In high spirits, Stevens' nieces and nephew wrote a joint letter to him then and there, filled with family chatter about the new twins and a nephew's promotion to army captain; they also wrote to tell their uncle how often they thought of him and how much they had missed him since his last visit three months earlier, when he had come to Reading for his sister Elizabeth's interment.

"The round-robin has stirred me up considerably," Stevens wrote back immediately. "I am so proud of all of you and so happy to have you think of me that I am not going to allow any dust to gather before I reply." He dictated a long letter, addressing each relative in turn as if they were still seated next to each other in the Berkshire Hotel lounge. When he came to Elizabeth's daughter, Jane, whom he now looked on more as a daughter than a niece, Stevens confided why their note had meant so much to him. "I am a little hepped on family ties. It is one of the sources of strength in life."[1]

Such an ordinary family scene is remarkable when one considers how new such sentiments were to Stevens and how recently he had reestablished ties back home. The funeral of his younger brother John in Reading three years before had been one of the emotional and artistic turning points in Stevens' later life, as he became a member of his family again after having largely stayed apart in Hartford for some twenty years. His older brother Garrett's final illness in the mid-1930s had led to Stevens' first regular contact with any of his family since his move to New England in 1916. But this had merely been a paper tie, a matter of sending money to an ailing and impoverished brother at little personal expense. After years of false starts as a lawyer in Reading, Baltimore and New York, Garrett had begun to enjoy a promising practice in Cleveland when, in the mid-1920s, he was struck with the first of the disabling lung ailments that, along with a heart condition, finally all but forced him to give up his criminal practice by 1936. During the last year or so of his life, his financially secure brothers, Wallace and John, helped to support him, each sending several hundred dollars before Garrett's death on November 3, 1937. "At the time of the funeral, Uncle John came, but not Wallace," Garrett's daughter remembers. "He wrote, though, and said he was sorry, but he just couldn't make it. We thought he would come."[2] If Stevens had reestablished a modicum of family contact with the monthly checks and notes he sent to Garrett during his last months, there was little of the emotional investment or poetic return that came about three years later when he decided to attend the funeral of John Stevens, the prominent ex-judge and Democratic party boss of Berks County, Pennsylvania, who died from ulcer complications on July 9, 1940. His niece Jane MacFarland Wilson recalls the day that Stevens truly came home and how it changed their lives, for a time.

Jane MacFarland Wilson

I didn't meet Uncle Wallace until I was twenty-one, at the funeral of his younger brother in Reading. I lived in Philadelphia at the time with my mother, who was in the hospital for a minor operation, so she couldn't go. I wasn't really close to the Reading folk: Mother and I had to go up to Reading every Christmas and every Easter, and I was bored stiff. They were just family. Now I was going to a funeral. And I met this gorgeous man who wasn't anything like the Reading folk: he was just delightful.

I know it's true of my mother, she hadn't seen Wallace maybe in twenty-five years. He hadn't seen me or my two cousins, who were John's children, and of course there were grandchildren then, too.* All this was just like, "Here's my family again after all these years." It really seemed to delight Uncle Wallace. And I think that's what sparked him into researching the family.

Like as not, when Mother and I would arrive in Reading and John's chauffeur would take us to the house on Douglass Street, there'd be nobody home. Or Bess, John's wife, would be upstairs sleeping. Or, if John was home,

---

*Stevens may have met his brother John's children earlier, for some family members recall him at the Reading funeral of John's wife, Elizabeth, in the mid-1930s. Nonetheless, Jane Wilson is correct that the renewed relationship between Stevens and his Pennsylvania family dates from his pivotal meeting with them when he returned home for John's funeral in 1940.

he'd be reading a book or a legal journal, say, "Hi, Elizabeth. Hi, Jane," and go back to his reading. It was a strange household; there was a mismatch, too. I thought it unfriendly. When I met Wallace in this atmosphere, he was so human, so warm, that it made more of an impression. There was a chord struck between us almost immediately. My mother used to say that the family just wasn't demonstrative, but she was not that way, and when I would meet Uncle Wallace, I would hug and kiss him and he would [hug] me. Mother knew what I felt about the Reading family: "But that's just the way we are, Jane. We've always been that way." And there was a little bit of this in Wallace Stevens, too.

[The day of John's funeral, Stevens] knew my mother was coming home from the hospital to our apartment in Germantown. He said, "Well, I think I'll return home with you. I haven't seen Elizabeth in all this time. I would like to see her."* [Coming] into the apartment, I said, "Mother, guess what? I've brought Uncle Wallace home." So, the first time he's seen her now in twenty-five years, he looks at her and says, "My God, Elizabeth, you've put it on!" My mother was a tremendous person: she was six feet two and weighed two hundred and fifty pounds. But there he was, sticking out like that, too. She was pretty fast on the uptake, so I'm sure she said [something back]. They got on real fine after that. From then on, he replaced what John had been to her. If there were financial difficulties, John [had] helped her out. Then it became Wallace. He was very generous. He helped me more than once, not just financially, after my mother died.

Then I began asking questions of my mother about Wallace. Of course, there were five children, and I don't think they ever wanted for anything. According to my mother, they did have a good family relationship [when they were growing up]. John was the youngest brother, but he and Wallace were very close in age; there was only a year's difference. I gather when Wallace went into high school, he just coasted. Then came John, and there was rivalry

*Holly Stevens has some recollection that, as a child, she met her aunt, perhaps when Elizabeth, working as a dietitian at a Girl Scout camp in Branford, Connecticut, during the summer of 1933, made a day trip to Hartford with friends to see the sights. However, in the long letter that Elizabeth wrote to her daughter, Jane, at the time, detailing the day's experiences, she made no mention of seeing her brother. There seems to have been little contact between Stevens and his sister during the twenty-odd years prior to his spur-of-the-moment visit to her home after their brother's funeral in the summer of 1940. While Stevens apparently wrote to Elizabeth in May 1919, both after her daughter's birth early in the month and their sister Mary Katharine's death at month's end, the only evidence of any contact between them before their reunion in the summer of 1940 is a postcard that Elizabeth sent to Stevens when she was vacationing in Japan in 1931 and a canceled check for seventy-five dollars that Stevens had sent her in the spring of 1940.

all through, so that they were vying for honors. Until John came into the picture, Wallace wasn't really trying too hard.* I think now Garrett [and Wallace] had more [similarities]. Garrett was musical; he could play beautiful piano. He was very gregarious. He never made any money, but he was a good lawyer, and there was a parade of two hundred people down the block to go to his funeral. He was well-loved; his house was open to everyone. Possibly Wallace might have been that type, but he went another route. Wallace went away to Harvard, and he came back after one year with a Harvard accent. The family went "Ugh! Who is this guy?" He got a very bad time. There was another story; it must have been about the same era. He'd stand before a mirror in the kitchen and preen himself: "What a handsome man am I!" His mother couldn't stand it. My mother, frankly, never knew much about Elsie. Apparently, she was the only woman he ever loved, and he went head over heels in love with her when he was young. I can remember Mother telling stories about his taking Elsie for canoe rides, and he'd read poetry to her. She was supposed to have been very blond—pale, childlike skin. Very quiet. Very remote. She was not from the same circle that the Stevens family went in.

They were all kind of loners, when you think about it. The oldest brother went to Cleveland, raised his family, and practiced law. Wallace went to New York and then Hartford. My mother's younger sister went overseas with the Red Cross and died there. My mother graduated from normal school and taught in Philadelphia. John stayed home. [Despite the distances, Garrett, Elizabeth and John kept in touch over the years.] Even the Cleveland folk, we were very close with them. It seems Wallace went away and—this is an impression via my mother's feelings—didn't want to know any more about the family. He was just a strange person off in the distance for a long time. I swear if John hadn't died, I never would have met him.

[After Stevens' reunion with Elizabeth in 1940] they wrote, but I wouldn't say a heavy correspondence. I don't think she ever became interested [in genealogy] but he kept after people because now he was becoming very

*Though John Stevens was a year younger than Wallace, both were classmates for four years at Reading Boys' High School, since Wallace had had to repeat his freshman year. Wallace Stevens once explained that he had "flunked a year because of too many nights out" (Byron A. Vazakas, "Wallace Stevens: Reading Poet," *The Historical Review of Berks County*, July 1938, p. 112). Louis Heizmann, a neighbor and high school acquaintance of Stevens', however, recalled that young Stevens, who was seriously ill one year, had missed a good deal of school and so had not been promoted (Holly Stevens, *Souvenirs and Prophecies* [New York: Alfred A. Knopf, 1976], p. 10). Sometime during his youth, Stevens had, indeed, been seriously ill, having suffered a bout of malaria (letter of Dr. W. W. Herrick to Dr. A. D. Mittendorf, October 15, 1926, HL).

interested and had her look up people like Emma Jobbins [a cousin who knew a good deal about family history] and some other remote cousins in the out-towns of Pennsylvania to see what they might have or who Wallace could contact.

Now I'm not an egghead, but I got so full of myself for thinking I could understand some of *Harmonium,* I talked to him finally about it. In the thirties John [Stevens] received a copy. He said, "What's this? I can't understand this kind of stuff!" They made much about "What's all this?" So I picked up the book and I did understand it. [Later, Jane talked to Stevens about his poetry.] "Is this what you meant?" His answer on one occasion was, "Well, I might have meant that at one time. I don't know what I meant now." I kind of believe that. He may have written things that later on he couldn't interpret. His later poetry I could no longer keep in touch with, and I told him, "I used to understand, but now I don't. Or at least I think I understood. I liked to read it. It does something for me, but now I've lost it." So he stopped sending me books in the fifties. It didn't affect our relationship in any way; our relationship was entirely different. This may be an indication. One time after my divorce [in 1945], I came up to Philadelphia to visit my friends. And Wallace and I planned to meet in New York. He took me to lunch at the Waldorf-Astoria and then to see *Bloomer Girl.* He loved it; I loved it. Ours was a very light thing; we never got into the deep things. This was probably relaxation for him, and he knew I enjoyed it. And he did, too, wholeheartedly.

When my mother died, which was February 1943, he was the one I turned to. I called, and he came down [to Philadelphia]. He made all the arrangements. He stayed with me. [He acted] very warmly. I can remember the day of the funeral. He said, "Now let's get out; it's a beautiful day." [On a winter's afternoon in Philadelphia] you'd think it would be miserable, but the sun was shining, it was warm. We walked along the Parkway and walked along Walnut Street, downtown Philadelphia. We looked in this [bakery] window, and they had a whiskey cake there. He said, "Oh, I bet that's delightful. Now tomorrow you get one and have one sent to me." He loved good-tasting things. He said, "Now you're not alone. You've got me." And I had him. I loved him. I had a father who was never really my father [her parents having divorced when she was a child]. That's what Wallace took on for me, the father image, at that time.

I knew Wallace in the last fifteen years of his life, and it was the best thing that had happened to me up to that point. I swear it was love at first sight at that funeral, because going down on the train to see my mother, he said,

"You seem so much more like a Stevens than any of the Stevenses here." And I thought, That's just great; I really made it now.

Stevens soon grew curious about precisely what it meant to be a Stevens. He began his research casually enough by the summer of 1941, asking the Daughters of the American Revolution, for example, about the ancestral information his mother had submitted when she had joined years earlier. This curiosity about his elders, however, soon turned into the obsession it remained throughout most of the 1940s. A common interest in genealogy, in fact, provided one of the few topics of conversation between Elsie and Wallace Stevens in later years. She had grown interested in her own ancestry even before her husband's search began, when she had become a member of the D.A.R. in the late 1930s. Her interest may have finally piqued his own. Curiously enough, however, Stevens' initial curiosity about the older generations may well owe at least as much to his visits with the younger generation of Stevenses as he was beginning his genealogical inquiries. In the summer following John's funeral, Stevens not only took the trouble to return to Reading for a nephew's wedding but also insisted that John Stevens, Jr., and his bride visit him at Westerly Terrace and invited Jane to spend nothing less than an unheard-of week as a guest at his Hartford home. In the company of this young family, Stevens had come back home as the family patriarch, for now only his sister and Garrett's widow survived from his generation. This role may well have helped turn Stevens' thoughts to the elders who had once occupied the same position. As he later explained, "My grandparents, Benjamin Stevens and Elizabeth Barcalow, were like figures in an idyll to me. When I was a boy my father took me down from Reading to the farm at Feasterville to visit them occasionally. It was my remembrance of them that interested me in finding out about their own parents and grandparents."[3]

No one was more surprised than Stevens, however, at how quickly his thoughts about his ancestors grew into a consuming interest. "Who could ever have imagined that, after three or four years, I should still be at work on this," he wrote to a cousin in 1945, unaware that he would still be at work on the family story by the end of the decade.[4] In the end, over a third of Stevens' voluminous archive testifies to the strength of this passion: some 2,500 genealogical items in the form of letters, documents and the multivolume work-in-progress, as he called his history of his Stevens, Barcalow and Zeller lines. The energy Stevens expended on this enterprise makes one wonder what made him persist in it so intently for much of the decade when either of his other major tasks might well have occupied the full-time attention of a man in his sixties. Stevens not only continued to head the surety and fidelity claims department at the Hartford, where his responsibilities were augmented by the war effort, but he also increased his output as a man of letters, becoming active as a lecturer as well as a poet.

Stevens was not the first member of his family to trace his ancestry, but he was the most thorough. When his mother had become interested years before, young Stevens had sneered at her for putting on airs in seeking to join the newly formed D.A.R.[5] And yet there was certainly a similar element behind his own research, even though in an egalitarian mood he might assert that "after muddling round with American genealogy for several years, I think that a decent sort of carpenter, or a really robust blacksmith, or a woman capable of having eleven sons and of weaving their clothes and the blankets under which they slept, and so on, is certainly no less thrilling" than finding more notable kin.[6] While Stevens claimed he was content that his ancestors were decidedly plebeian, he nonetheless remained intensely disappointed that his lineage did not qualify him, for example, for membership in an exclusive New York society that would have certified his boast of a distinguished Dutch-American pedigree. He very much wanted to belong to the Holland Society of New York, he confided to Lila James Roney, the genealogist who worked full-time for two years on his lines until her death in 1944, because it would bolster his claims to descent from nobility American-style: "when I start to talk about being descended from the first white child born in New Netherland, people who wouldn't believe it otherwise would believe it if I could say that I was a member of the Holland Society."*

At best, his research allowed him to join the less prestigious Saint Nicholas Society. In "Recitation after Dinner," however, the poem he wrote for that society's annual banquet in 1945, the year after he became a member, Stevens described a far more profound impulse than snobbery at the heart of some of his most intense efforts in family history. As he began to read the poem to the fellow Dutchmen who had gathered for a black-tie dinner in New York, he admitted that "A poem about tradition could easily be / A windy thing." He solved this poetic problem, however, by making this partly a poem about what motivated him and the other family historians gathered that evening.

> It [tradition] has a clear, a single, a solid form,
> That of the son who bears upon his back
> The father that he loves, and bears him from

---

*Letter of August 25, 1944, *L WS*, p. 472. The Holland Society of New York is a genealogical organization whose members are descended in the male line from a Dutchman resident in New Netherlands or in the New World prior to 1675, or from a man who either lived in New Netherlands or possessed the right of Dutch citizenship in New Netherlands before that date. Applying for membership in the society, Stevens submitted a genealogy of his paternal line on December 6, 1944; it had been prepared by Roney, a prominent genealogist who had done work on family history for the likes of the Roosevelts. After reviewing Roney's study, however, the Holland Society questioned her findings about Michiel Stevenszen, from whom Stevens was descended. Stevens had applied for membership based on Roney's assertion that Michiel was the son of a Dutchman resident in Albany prior to 1675. On December 11, 1944, the Holland Society wrote to Stevens that its research into church records indicated Michiel was from Danzig when he married in New York in 1699. When a genealogist whom Stevens subsequently hired, Agnes W. Storer, confirmed the Holland Society findings in May 1945, Stevens withdrew his application.

Stevens remained extremely disappointed at this turn of events. After World War II, he tried, unsuccessfully, to have the Danzig records searched in hopes of proving Michiel Stevenszen was the son of a Dutchman residing in Danzig, where there was a sizable colony of Holland merchants in the seventeenth century. As late as February 1953, Stevens inquired at the Holland Society about membership under categories other than direct descent from a male ancestor.

> The ruins of the past, out of nothing left,
> Made noble by the honor he receives,
> As if in a golden cloud. The son restores
> The father. . . .[7]

His romance with the family touched his poetry almost immediately, and one of his earliest family lyrics shows that from the beginning of the 1940s it was as much his sense of filial devotion as family vanity that kept Stevens looking backward for a decade. In March 1942, he published in *Trend* a sequence of poems entitled "Five Grotesque Pieces," one section of which was "Outside of Wedlock." Here, as in later family poems, Stevens did not boast of his pedigree or mystify his ancestors' era in a golden haze. Instead, he commanded the winter wind, that bleakest sound in his work, to sing a dirge, as if it spoke with the voice of two ancestors, his Dutch Adam and Eve, Benjamin and Blandenah.

> Sing . . .
> White February wind,
> Through banks and banks of voices,
> In the cathedral-shanty,
>
> To the sound of the concertina,
> Like the voice of all our ancestors,
> The *père* Benjamin, the *mère* Blandenah,
> Saying we have forgot them, they never lived.[8]

And yet, the poem itself does not, like the wind's song within it, simply mourn the oblivion that was Benjamin's and Blandenah's fate, and by implication the fate of each succeeding generation, including Stevens'. By remembering his ancestors with this filial poem, Stevens alters their fate—on paper at least. Such filial sentiments, of course, were also psychically self-serving. An old man himself at the time, Stevens was Anchises as well as Aeneas. His ancestors were his surrogates. Rescuing them from oblivion, Stevens was reassuring himself. Family ties were life lines that reached in both directions.

Nowhere is Stevens the genealogist more strikingly the Dutch Aeneas of "Recitation after Dinner" than in his dogged efforts to bear his great-grandfather John Zeller, the most prominent family member in his poetry, out of the most profound obscurity. At the same time, "The Bed of Old John Zeller," published as Stevens' three-year search for this ancestor was ending in the fall of 1944, offers a glimpse into the way genealogical research might translate itself into poetry. On April 14, 1943, months after he had begun to inquire about the Zellers, his mother's side of the family, Stevens complained how frustrated he was. Although Mrs. Roney had already uncovered the first of the Stevens line to settle in the New World, Mary Owen Steinmetz, a genealogist working part-time for him on the Zellers, had not even been able to find out the name of his mother's grandfather. "This man's line is the only one in the family on which I cannot even get started,"[9] he wrote in exasperation to a Presbyterian minister in Reading, Dr. Robert Campbell, hoping his church records might offer some clues about his grandfather's parentage. Stevens planned to visit Reading in two weeks when the minister was to officiate at his sister's interment in the family plot, Elizabeth having died in Philadelphia in late winter. It was one of a half-dozen visits home to be with his relatives that Stevens made between 1940 and 1945, the period of his closest ties to the younger generation. He visited Reading infrequently during the war, partly because of the difficulties of travel, but he did come home for family gatherings, weddings, funerals and wartime reunions with furloughed relatives. Once Stevens had become interested in genealogy, however, he also looked forward to these trips to Pennsylvania because they often provided opportunities to seek out information about his ancestors, as on this occasion.

That first weekend in May, Stevens made the breakthrough on his great-grandfather he had been seeking from Dr. Campbell. Arriving in Reading, he learned from the minister's memo that his mother's father had been John Zeller, Jr. In the family parlance, then, John junior's father had been Old John Zeller, as Stevens later referred to him in his poem. By the happy chance that Old John Zeller had christened one of his nine children after himself, Stevens now at least knew his great-grandfather's full name. In every other respect, however, the identity of Old John Zeller remained exasperatingly elusive for another year. But in May 1944, just as Stevens despaired that his Reading genealogist would never find anything more about Zeller, she stumbled upon a reference to his grave as she leafed through church papers listing the tombstone inscriptions in a country cemetery at Amityville, Pennsylvania. Finding Old John Zeller's resting place was the key to the church records that finally unlocked his story.

"Genealogy has become a sort of substitute for the reading of detective stories,"[10] Stevens wrote a nephew that autumn as the puzzle was nearing completion. Born during the Revolutionary War, Zeller had spent his boyhood on a farm in the Tulpehocken area of Berks County, Pennsylvania, where his own great-grandfather, the original Zeller immigrant, had settled in the 1720s, some years after fleeing from his home in the Palatinate to avoid persecution by Catholics. As a young man, John and his wife, Catherine, left the farm for Philadelphia, where he learned the shoemaking trade, which he later taught Stevens' grandfather. (Wallace Stevens' mother, a woman of social pretensions, insisted that her father was not an everyday shoemaker but a maker of fine boots.) John Zeller soon returned home from Philadelphia and bought a small farm in Stevens' beloved Oley Valley, where he lived out his seventy-nine years until his death in 1858.[11] All of these details were important to Stevens the genealogist. They meant little, however, to Stevens the poet.

In "The Bed of Old John Zeller," Stevens reduces his great-grandfather to a certain cast of mind, "the habit of wishing, as if one's grandfather lay / In one's heart and wished as he had always wished."[12] Nothing in Stevens' research had, in fact, uncovered anything specific about Old John Zeller's way of thinking. Rather, Stevens was drawing on his sense of the Zeller line generally. Old John Zeller stands not so much as an individual as he does as a member of the family. For Stevens, the essential feature of the Zeller family was its religious cast of mind, which he judges in this lyric to be a form of wishful thinking. At the time he wrote this poem, most likely in the spring to summer of 1944, Stevens characterized the family in which Old John grew up by its spirituality. The family "seems to have been both poor and pious. But I cannot say that the family was poor because I really know nothing about it."[13] Though he admitted he knew little else about this particular Zeller generation, retracting even his statement that they were poor as soon as he made it, it is not surprising that he did not qualify his assertion that they were pious for a fervent habit of mind was what had struck him most about the Zellers from their beginnings in America. "These people, whatever else they were, were fanatics," he decided about the original immigrants.[14] This particular association of the Zellers with religious fervor contrasts with his view of the original Dutch immigrants on his father's side. "Unlike the Puritans of Massachusetts and the Catholics in Maryland, the Dutch did not come to this country for political and religious freedom. While, of course, they may have had that in mind, the settlement of New Amsterdam was almost wholly a money-making scheme to the Dutch, who came out to better their condition in life. . . . I don't believe they came out for the purpose of being alone with their maker."[15]

Understanding Stevens' close identification of the Zellers with a devoutly pious habit of mind helps to gloss the second half of "The Bed of Old John Zeller."

> This is the habit of wishing, as if one's grandfather lay
> In one's heart and wished as he had always wished, unable
>
> To sleep in that bed for its disorder, talking of ghostly
> Sequences that would be sleep and ting-tang tossing, so that
> He might slowly forget. It is more difficult to evade
>
> That habit of wishing and to accept the structure
> Of things as the structure of ideas. . . .[16]

Here, for example, genealogy provided Stevens with a particularly witty figure to describe the supernatural yearnings that occasionally stirred in his secular heart when he confronted the meaning of the natural world, as if they were the fitful tossings of an insomniac ancestor. By specifying this ancestor as a Zeller in his title, Stevens wryly indicated the strength of these bouts, for a Zeller would be particularly uncomfortable amid such secular disorder and given to a good deal of tossing about.

During the late spring and summer of 1944, Stevens was intent upon finding the actual site in the country churchyard where his great-grandfather lay; that autumn, as "The Bed of Old John Zeller" was being published in *Accent,* he received word that the grave had been located in the old cemetery of St. Paul's Evangelical and Reformed Church at Amityville. Though Zeller had died only twenty-one years before Stevens' birth and had been buried only a few miles from the hometown where Stevens had grown up, Stevens' search for Zeller's grave and the condition in which it was found underscored how quickly one was forgotten by the family, how quickly one suffered the fate of the more remote Benjamin and Blandenah. The marker had fallen to the ground, where it lay untended, the name on the dilapidated stone hidden beneath brambles.[17] The description of complete neglect that the pastor of St. Paul's Church, Dr. Howard Althouse, sent when he located the gravesite in late September spoke eloquently of the fate of Stevens' ancestors, which, as "Outside of Wedlock" shows, touched him deeply from the outset of his research. In early October, Stevens set about having the site restored, the stones reset; his nephew John Sauer agreed to oversee the restoration, helping his uncle-in-law then as he did at other times on the Zeller research.

Stevens himself paid at least two filial visits to the final bed of Old John Zeller, the first of them at Christmastime, 1944, when he returned to Reading for a reunion with his furloughed nephew, John Stevens, Jr. The young army captain and his wife, Anna May, accompanied their uncle to the Amityville grave as one of the genealogical stops the three of them made that weekend as they toured the countryside in pursuit of Stevens' ancestors. The memories of both John Sauer and Anna May Stevens, who had also joined in the round-robin letter that had so pleased their uncle the year before, suggest how some of the strongest ties that bound Wallace Stevens to his young family were woven out of ancestral cloth.

John Sauer

[In 1944] we threw a party for John [Stevens, Jr.]. It was [for] about fifty people; we were at the Berkshire Hotel in the Walnut Room. Mostly, they were our contemporaries; Wallace and a few others were the older people. I'd never known him to be much of a drinking man. Well, I never saw such an exhibition of a guy drinking martinis in all my life. He went all through the night. When we first got there, everybody [acted], kind of, "Oh, Wallace Stevens!" And he was kind of stiff. With three of those martinis, his tongue got a little looser. He was no longer stiff. He was laughing and participating with other people, with all the small talk. Nobody could understand how that guy could stand up—and he didn't even show [the effects of the martinis]. [After] we wound up, one of Eleanor's girl friends and I took Wallace over to the hotel, and we stayed with him. He was reminiscing. He was jovial as hell, and he said, "I [haven't] let my hair down like this in many years. I just had one hell of a good time!"

So that is about the point where he called on me to assist him; he was developing the ancestry of the Zeller side of the family. He, of course, [had] started on the Stevens family first. I'm sure he wasn't particularly bragging that he [had] pumped five thousand dollars in one year to this gal [Lila James Roney] to do a lot of this for him. The one branch he felt was the true branch [was descended from] a bastard from Danzig. He said he found horse thieves and all kinds of people back there, but he had this ancestor in Danzig and couldn't make it [into the Holland Society]. The only thing I got into was when he was going back on the Zeller side. He wrote and said he wanted to go to a cemetery down in Bucks County. It was a pretty cold day, and he was hunting these tombstones. He took pictures of the tombstones. Then he called me or dropped me a note and said could I come to New York? He wanted to chat with me about doing a little bit more, backing up some of his research. He wanted me to go to the courthouse and the cemetery.

I told him I was going to be in New York on business. He said he would be in town: "Call me." [When Sauer arrived, he telephoned Stevens from his serviceable but modest businessman's hotel.] "How about that lunch? Do you want to come to the Hotel Pennsylvania?" "Good lord, no! Meet me . . ." —it was way up in the East Seventies, a very fine little French restaurant. He was just as prim as he could be and had that cute little smile. He was always pretty charming. He needled me that we had twins: "How's that baby manufacturer, your wife?" So we went into this French restaurant that was rather elegant. There weren't too many people around. [Sauer said] "I'm hungry. When are we going to eat?" He chuckled. "Let me order for you." So the waiter came over, and Wallace rattled off a lunch in French. We talked about whatever he wanted me to research. I don't know if I remember that any more, but I do remember a good bit of the conversation was how fond he was of good music, that he had quite a collection of records. I told him that I had some good records, too—the Philadelphia Orchestra and some light operatic music. "Oh, good lord, John, I'm not speaking of that." It was all this heavy stuff. He was very proud of his record collection; it must have been quite something. He said it thoroughly relaxed him. Elsie didn't appreciate the music. Elsie was a good cook. "That's why I've got this obese look about me." Very conscious of his big belly, very conscious. He said Elsie couldn't appreciate the things that he does. "She's a damn good cook and a faithful wife." I never met Elsie. I knew he was in Hershey with her [when Sauer picked up Stevens to visit the Bucks County gravesites]. From what he said, she didn't care to meet the people generally.

The amusing incident that I recall when I met him [at John's funeral, involved his being] a big man. When I took a snap picture of him—I recall this pretty vividly—he said, "Oh, good lord, no! I'm so obese." I never thought he was obese, but he loved to use that word. I can't believe it was chilly [John's funeral was in July], but he covered [his stomach] with his coat and posed with Eleanor, with her brother, and with Jane down on the lawn. Then we came into the house. Uncle Wallace was rather prim and very formal. He talked rather stiff—"Good lord, no," that kind of thing. So we put our son Stephen, he was about a year and a half, in his lap. Stephen proceeded to wet his trousers. Uncle Wallace said, "Eleanor, good God! Take this baby." We had a delightful visit with him.

I became his confidant about Holly's problems. I don't like to talk about it. That was another visit in New York. It was terribly difficult because he wanted answers, and, my God, I didn't think I was in a position to make any answers. He said, "I've just got to talk to someone." Quite bitter. Disappointed in Holly. That was before the divorce. He called [John Hanchak, Holly's husband] a "Polack." He was terribly hurt; he was terribly upset.

When we wound up lunch, he said, "Let's stop at my favorite delicatessen, and I'll buy you a piece of cheese to take back to your brood." He was always kidding about Eleanor and the kids we had. He was very fond of Brie, and I had raved about it, so he took me to that delicatessen and bought me some.

He did talk about the insurance business. He talked about his routine at the insurance company, how he'd walk to work. It was kind of a chore for him, but he knew it was good for his health, something about "My can is getting too big. It's good exercise." He wouldn't talk much about [insurance work]. He enjoyed his work and was quite busy with it. But he liked to put his work down, and go home and relax. He didn't like to carry his work to his home.

[The subject of his poetry never came up] because he knew his brother almost ridiculed him. I'm sure Eleanor and I, and Eleanor's brother, too, we said we just couldn't understand it. We didn't read it. [John, Wallace's brother, would] say, "Good lord, no! Wallace sent me another book of his poems." He was an avid reader, John Stevens was; he read a lot of heavy stuff, but he didn't like poetry, and he rather ridiculed Wallace for being a poet. Maybe "ridicule" isn't the right word, but he'd kind of joke about his brother the poet. I do remember this one [*The Man with the Blue Guitar*] came in the summer, around '36 or '37. John said, "I can't get any of this drivel." We'd always make a joke about it: "This goddamn poetry."

John, who liked to sit with a book, would sit a whole weekend and wouldn't say two words. He was very much of an introvert and [would] just sit there on a weekend and read. Eleanor and I lived with him for a couple of years, and he just didn't have a hell of a lot of conversation. The thing that would be typical of John and Wallace in my opinion is the way neither one seemed to be a great conversationalist and both liked to do a hell of a lot of reading. Wallace told me one time for a vacation he boned up for some symposium in [the French] language [Mount Holyoke's *Entretiens de Pontigny* in 1943]. John had some Greek books, and you'd catch him reading something in Greek. He was nutty about words. You'd come home and catch him not even reading history or a novel, he would be reading a dictionary, just going through it looking at words. He loved new words. He was the Democratic leader in the county, the guy behind the throne. I knew that Wallace was a Republican. He and John didn't share political views. One thing I remember a little about. He was talking about how he and John had helped Garrett, his brother in Cleveland. He called his brother "Garrick," said he was a smart one but he just played pinochle all day. Garrett was a handsome man; he had a Van Dyke beard and reminded you quite a bit of Wallace; more, say, than John. [On one occasion, John and Garrett] were reminiscing a little bit, and they were talking about their brother Wallace, but none of them bothered to go and see him. Just after that was when John had his chauffeur drive him up to Hartford; he visited his brother. That would have been in the late thirties, a year or two before he died. Eleanor and I were so surprised that he was going to take a trip to New England and stop off and see Wallace.

When I was in Wallace's company, I was tremendously impressed with the brilliance of the man. He had a comprehension that just amazed me. I never felt like I could get close to him, but I knew he liked me. He exuded something out of the ordinary.

Anna May Stevens

I just adored Uncle Wallace. 'Course I wasn't afraid of him. I wasn't afraid of John either. Everybody [else] was scared of John Stevens. I'm the only one, including his daughter, who would kiss him in front of Fifth and Penn [Reading's main intersection], if I felt like it, because I'm a kisser-hello and a kisser-good-by. Here was a man everybody was frightened of: an ex-judge, very formidable, very quiet, very well read. An amazing man. The Stevenses don't floor me. I just take them the way they are. I had heard intimidating things about Uncle Wallace, but I didn't find I was intimidated by him. As a matter of fact, I think we got along very well.

He just came down for [John's funeral] and then left. Then John [Jr.] and I were married in June of '41. [Stevens returned to Reading for the wedding. When he learned the young couple were going to Canada on their honeymoon] he said, "On your way up, I *want* you to stop for lunch!" We didn't know whether we would; we went, because we were heading for Lake George, where we were going to stay overnight. If I remember, John called him because we weren't sure what time we'd get there, but we were expected. I'll never forget it, because Aunt Elsie hadn't come to the wedding.[18] I stayed in the car, and John went to the door. This little woman in a brown cardigan kind of thing came to the door. He said, "Is Mr. Stevens in?" She said, "Who's calling for Mr. Stevens?" He said, "It's his nephew," and she said, "I'm Mrs. Stevens." I almost fell out of the car. Here was Aunt Elsie! A church mouse, completely dominated. I can't imagine a sense of humor.

Maybe when she was younger she was a different personality. But knowing women from this area, I think a lot of problems have happened because the women do not grow with their men. I don't even remember a conversation with her. I couldn't believe it, because I think of her in terms of the classic profile on the dime. [Her hair was pulled back] very much so. And this terrible brown long thing, this housedress and nondescript shoes. We talked about it when we got in the car later.

So we stayed and had a divine filet mignon with asparagus hollandaise that she had whipped up. It was a delightful thing, but she was serving us. I'm not really aware that she sat down with us. A wonderful cook. Then we found out about the men's quarters and the women's quarters. Uncle Wallace said, "This side of the house is mine." He had this Spartan bedroom. On the left side of the house were the women's quarters, Aunt Elsie's and Holly's. It was such a shock. But this was their understanding of life. He needed to have his separateness, his privacy, very much so. Very well appointed house, very nice. Everything had its place. *Pristine:* my favorite word when I walk into a house that doesn't show a lot of personality. He didn't share that warmth that he really had inside, I guess.

[One of his last visits with his Reading relatives took place when he returned to his hometown for a party for his nephew, John Stevens, Jr., who was on furlough at Christmastime, 1944.] The famous dinner at the Berkshire Hotel. We were in a private dining room. I teased him about the martinis. When the bill came, we found it was something like thirty-one martinis— well, no [not really that many], but it was unbelievable. It was a good party, a fun thing; it was a relaxed thing. He must have had a good time if he drank all those martinis. Or maybe he drank them so he could have a good time. That's when we did the projects. Uncle Wallace decided he was going to stay a couple of days because he was in this genealogy. And we were to go to Amityville [to see the grave of his grandfather Old John Zeller]. Now this is three o'clock in the morning—we break up and go to bed. At six o'clock John and I are there picking him up, and down to Amityville we go, cross-eyed all of us. We went through the whole cemetery, and we know where the Zeller plot is. It didn't have the stone on it; they were repairing it. I got hysterical, and I said, "You don't even have a tombstone on your plot. And here is my great-great-grandfather buried here—in adjoining plots. I can't believe this. The two families buried side by side." Because my family had been here a long time, too.

We toured. We did cemeteries; he looked up some stuff and talked to some of his old cronies. He had the whole thing planned, and John and I took him. We were with him and we had a ball. He was fun when he had people who weren't asking anything of him, demanding anything of him except just enjoy you. He reminisced on some fun things. Our favorite story was when he was in Cleveland. He saw his brother [Garrett] walking down the street. He looked fine, he looked prosperous. Wallace didn't have anything to say to him, so he crossed over [to the other side of the street] and went right on by.* [He said this with a straight face] but he had a twinkle like Santa Claus. I was used to it with his brother. He talked about [growing up in Reading]. [The Stevens boys] used to go up in the country; sometimes they'd bicycle up [to the] Ephrata area, which was far away. They used to go up there and spend the summer. John [Jr.]'s father darn near killed Wallace one time. They were so close of an age and fought each other all the way through high school. Wallace was held back one year, so they ended up in school together, and they were one and two always. There was an argument and taunting [one time], as boys will do. John was in the back [of the Stevens home on North Fifth Street], chopping wood. Wallace finally got to him, and [John flung] the ax. John went and picked it up and was so darned mad that, to the day he died, he had this gash across his hand. They had tempers. That slow boil, but when it goes—watch out! I could see [Wallace's brother] get red up the back of his neck, and his face would get stern, and his eyes were absolute steel. I'm sure Wallace did exactly the same thing. [Wallace's mother] ruled the roost. She took good care of Grandfather Stevens. He was the originator of what the three [sons] became. Now Garrett [the oldest son] was more phlegmatic. He didn't give a darn, but he had a good wife; she was wonderful. We all adored Aunt Sarah. We never discussed [the breakdown of Stevens' father], except we knew he did have problems and John was the one [son] who stayed around. I don't think John had a desire to go anywhere else. He was the youngest, and his mother never wanted for anything [after her husband's death]. That's why he didn't get married until he was thirty.

I don't think anyone questioned that their way wasn't the right way: when you have a six-foot, big man with a stern countenance, you automatically think of it [his] way. Yet they all had soft spots. His mother was John's soft spot [and] his wife. I think Elsie was very definitely Wallace's soft spot, but

*While on a business trip to Minnesota soon after he joined the Hartford, Stevens related a similar incident to his wife after passing by his uncle James Stevens on a St. Paul street: "As I was coming uptown from the office this evening, I passed my Uncle Jim. I wasn't thinking of him at the time, nor he of me—and I didn't stop him. I think he would be bored stiff—think I wanted money or some such thing. It was very nice to see him and not to be recognized. Let it go at that. Relatives *are* stupid: I'm sure that after we had asked a few questions, there'd be nothing in the world to talk about except Japan [James Stevens having made a trip to the Orient], and I don't feel the need of talking about Japan." (Letter of June 27, 1916, HL.)

in their own way. I can see where he would not have anything to do with anybody in the family who disapproved of something he was doing. It was that disapproval he was not going to tolerate [regarding his marriage to Elsie]. She was not part of the family, from what I gather. The only thing I got from John's father was that when Wallace divorced himself from Reading, he really left and wanted no contact. I never heard John Stevens say anything against Elsie except she was a "sweet little thing." She wasn't equipped to grow with him because of just their objection. Holly was [like] her father, because she was a very independent young lady. Her father was horrified with her first marriage; I'm not too sure that she wasn't horrified with it later, too, because I think it was one of those "Okay, I'll show you." Holly is very strong, very strong. That "Polack-Communist" [Stevens called Holly's first husband]. He was terribly hurt because he was molding Holly, and she was not about to be molded. It broke his heart [that] she didn't finish school [he said]. He was pretty upset about that; we didn't dwell on it, but it was there. When you have strong people, you can't dominate them; you have to let them feel their way.

Every time we were together our association was completely comfortable. I wasn't in awe of him; I guess I didn't understand what it meant to be a Pulitzer or Bollingen Prize winner. [The key to success with Stevens was] be natural with him. I used to tease him about some of his titles. I'd say, "Why a *blue* guitar?" Now I understand it, but not then. Well, he'd just smile. I'd say, "I need Jane [Wilson] to translate this stuff for me." I was completely honest with him. John's father said the only person who understood it in the whole damn family was Jane. She ate it up. I've known John's father since '33; I knew about Uncle Wallace's poetry then. [Wallace Stevens] thought his own father's writing was just trash; he'd just shake his head anytime anybody sent it, saying, "Oh, I've just found something of your father's." [In later years, Garrett Stevens published some poetry and prose under assumed names in area newspapers; after his death, some of his work was published in a local newspaper under his name by friends.][19]

I just plain didn't understand it, but then, I'm not poetry-oriented; I'm musically oriented. Yes [she did talk of music with Stevens]. He used to go to New York to see an opera; he'd always go to the library. Now, he would do this [attend the opera] while he was doing something else. He loved to go see the French movies, the foreign movies. That would be in the forties. But it was just casual conversation about [opera] because we discussed how I was weaned on opera. If he couldn't get a ticket, it wouldn't bother him; he'd go stand. When he wanted to do something, he didn't deviate very much. I remember the remark about Paul Althouse [the Metropolitan tenor who was a personal friend and voice coach of Anna May Stevens]. "He's a fine tenor, but he's not Melchior because of the booze." We didn't get into any depth [about opera]; our times together were too fleeting.

Not more than a half-dozen [times were they together]. [By the mid-forties] I don't think there was much for him down here. He had found what he needed down here, and he really didn't need it any more.

Stevens' visit home at Christmas, 1944, was the last trip he made to Pennsylvania to be with his young relatives. His ties to the next generation had already begun to fray some eight months earlier when he severed all connections with his niece Jane, with whom he had developed the closest bonds among these relatives.

Jane had come to look upon her uncle as the father she had never known, her parents having divorced when she was a child. It was her uncle and not her father that she had wanted to give her away at her wedding in December 1942, a wedding Stevens had made special by sending a gift that allowed Jane to buy a wedding gown she could not otherwise have afforded. "She was positively radiant when she saw the check and hugged me saying, 'Mother he doesn't know what he's done. He's made it all possible now,' "[20] his sister, Elizabeth, had written to Stevens after his gift arrived. When Elizabeth died two months after the wedding, on February 19, 1943, Uncle Wallace was the first person Jane called, minutes after her mother had succumbed to encephalitis. The next morning Stevens was by his niece's side in Philadelphia, staying with her for the next three days to see her through. They exchanged long letters in the months that followed, letters that were uncharacteristically personal for Stevens, as he responded warmly to the niece he encountered on paper. She seemed a young woman coping bravely with the loss of her mother, to whom she had been devoted, and with a wartime separation from her husband, to whom she appeared devoted. Stevens was stunned into silence, however, when Jane wrote in April 1944, after a year of such letters, to say that she was divorcing her G.I. husband.

Jane MacFarland Wilson

He never gave me advice. After all, I was leading my own life, and I was of age. The one time I felt his strong disapproval was silence after my divorce. I got married first during World War II, and it was an unfortunate case. I remember writing to Uncle Wallace that I was going to get a divorce and was leaving [Philadelphia] for Miami. It was very hard to divorce a G.I. He was overseas, and here I was playing the heavy. Uncle Wallace cut me off. Dead silence. And we had written just about every week. I continued to write. I said, "I'm going to continue to write you 'cause I love you, and whether or not you love me doesn't make any difference. But you're going to hear from me." When I got to Miami, I thought I would only be there three months to get the divorce, so I took a bookkeeping job in a tire shop. Finally, I decided I was going to stay there, so I went to Eastern Airlines and became a reservationist. When I wrote him I had done that, he finally broke down. He said, "At least that's better than working in a recap shop!" He never said anything about the divorce. But I never gave up; I wasn't going to let him go.

Stevens' silence in those six months following Jane's announcement of her divorce was understandable, for in her previous letters she had given her uncle no hint of marital problems, much less any suggestion that she had met another man, whom she now told him she intended to marry as soon as she was free. In his research into his ancestors, Stevens had come most to admire the women in his family, precisely for that strength of character and vigor that Jane had displayed in her letters. She became the dearer to him as he saw her, as well as her Reading cousins, carrying on in this tradition. Indeed, feeling part of such a family served as a tonic to him at a time when he was becoming increasingly unhappy with his own daughter's behavior. Receiving Jane's letter that spring of 1944, at the height of his problems with Holly, stunned him the more because it called into question the image of the younger generation at home that he had been fashioning from letters and occasional visits to Pennsylvania. Abruptly, Jane seemed to be not so much his ideal niece as she was Holly's cousin.

Stevens had already suffered the first in a series of bitter disappointments with his daughter when Holly had dropped out of college against his wishes in November 1942. Although Holly later remarked that she had "felt like a perfect ninny sitting by the Hudson River as an English major with a war going on,"[21] at the time, leaving Vassar had more to do with the war of independence she was waging at home. The strain between Holly and her parents was evident in the scene that was played out shortly before she returned to college for the fall term. Her father had purposely avoided seeing her before she left, snubbing her as he felt she had been snubbing him and her mother. Stevens did write to her, however, as soon as she arrived in Poughkeepsie, explaining his pique and adding to her allowance by way of apologizing for not having said good-by. A few days later, as he turned sixty-three, he received a birthday letter from his eighteen-year-old daughter that catalogued her adolescent grievances against her parents and set the stage for her act of defiance in leaving Vassar. "For a long time our situation at home has made me unhappy. . . . When I am at home Mother always bustles around wanting to open windows, turn on lights, etc. I am often occupied and resent these interruptions: I know enough about windows and lights to look after them myself. And you, when I stay at home, usually remark about it in a way that makes me feel I must choose either to stay in every night, or to go out every night. . . . And, will you please tell me the whys and wherefores of the great objection to my staying out overnight with Lotte or Cole? I do not care for the feeling I have that in many cases I am considered but a child incapable of making my own decisions. . . . I am not arguing with you now, but the next time you so outrageously say 'Don't argue with me'

I certainly shall, feeling every right in so doing. . . . This letter, in a nutshell, demands independence and freedom from criticism. . . . I have not felt freedom in being with either of you, and my independence has had to be found elsewhere."[22]

Within two weeks, Holly followed up her letter with a visit home to tell her parents she wished to leave college. Vassar had been her father's idea, an instance of the domination she now found intolerable. After twelve years at an exclusive day school for girls only a few blocks from home, she wanted to attend a large, coeducational institution far from home, such as Stanford or a state university in the Midwest. Vassar had appealed to her father, however, since his weekend visits there in the summer of 1931, when Holly and her mother had enrolled in a progressive program in child-rearing at Vassar's Institute in Euthenics. It had been Stevens' first choice of a college for his daughter, and he allowed Holly to apply only to Sweet Briar, a small women's college in Virginia, as a backup.[23]

By leaving Vassar, Holly was turning her back on the woman her father had hoped she would become: "he had planned my future for me: perhaps the future he'd hoped to have himself. After receiving my degree I would spend a year or so in travel, and then return to either a scholarly or a literary career—as an adolescent I wrote a great deal of poetry, was editor of my high school newspaper, and, I suppose, showed some talent as a writer."[24] At the time, however, Holly insisted to the dean at Vassar that she had no ambitions and did not want to make something of herself. She wanted to leave college and simply find a job that would pay her enough to get by.[25] "None of the great things in life have anything to do with making your living," Stevens argued in urging her to stay on at Vassar, "and I had hoped that little by little, without now being able to say how, you would find the true field for your intelligence and imagination in something that was at least a part of one of the great things of life."[26] Despite Stevens' letters and his last-minute trip to Vassar for a conference with the dean, Holly withdrew from college in November, found a room in a Hartford boardinghouse, and took a clerical job at the Aetna, an insurance company a block or two from her father's office, where she eventually became a fire underwriter. There she met John Hanchak, a serviceman for office equipment, whom she married on August 5, 1944.*

In the midst of these problems with his daughter, Stevens received his niece's completely unexpected letter announcing plans to divorce her G.I. husband. During the months that followed in which Stevens severed all contact with Jane, he began to reevaluate his ties to the younger Stevens

---

*Writing to her half sister soon after Holly's marriage to John Hanchak, Elsie Stevens described her son-in-law. "He is of Russian and German descent. . . . They met about two years ago, in the insurance company [Aetna] when Holly was using an adding machine. He has very black hair and eyes, stocky, but not quite as tall as Holly, and was twenty-seven years old in August, five days after Holly reached her twentieth birthday. His parents have three acres of land . . . where they live and grow their own corn and vegetables and strawberries. They are from in or near the Ukraine, Russia. The father also does war work in a machine company. . . . I am very glad for Holly's happiness." (Letter to Dorothy LaRue Weidner, September 9, 1944, HL.)

generation generally. Eventually he did relent and resumed contact with Jane in October 1944, because "Everyone in the family is precious to me and it is the easiest thing in the world for us to drift apart instead of clinging to each other as we should,"[27] but that drift away from his younger family in Pennsylvania had indeed already started on its irreversible course.

In September 1946 Stevens made his first trip back to Pennsylvania since he had come to Reading for the Christmas reunion with his furloughed nephew near the war's end. He spent a leisurely month at the Hotel Hershey, an hour from Reading, and often crisscrossed the area with a local genealogist who chauffeured him as far as Delaware on research that continued to strengthen his ties to his ancestors if not the younger generation of Stevenses. "We left to go down to Reading, intending to stay for three or four days," he confided to his friend Judge Powell, with whom he had had his last reunion at the posh Hershey resort that September. "But [we] found the place really unbearable and we left almost immediately without seeing a single one of the few relatives of mine who still live there. When one has left home the place naturally changes. What I had not realized is that it keeps changing until a point is reached at which the old familiar life of it is dead and gone."[28]

Though the bonds with his nieces and nephews had grown slack by the late 1940s, Stevens' ties to his daughter began to strengthen. Leaving college and marrying a blue-collar worker had been part of Holly's rebellion against her father. By the end of the 1940s, however, she recognized her marriage had been ill-advised as well and separated from her husband, receiving a divorce from John Hanchak in 1951 on grounds of intolerable cruelty.[29] She had been granted custody of her son, Peter, and during his last years Stevens was their main support, setting them up in an apartment and giving his daughter a monthly allotment so that she did not have to work but was able to stay at home to care for her young son. In the early 1950s, Holly also decided to return to college part-time, attending the University of Connecticut's Hartford branch, where Elias Mengel, a young professor, became a close friend.

After a decade of strained relations, Stevens and his daughter began to enjoy a rapport that was evident to those who saw Holly starting to share the life her father had made for himself away from Westerly Terrace. He introduced her, for instance, into his small Manhattan circle, the group of poets, painters and curators who gathered at the Park Avenue apartment of his friend Barbara Church. After Stevens and his daughter had attended one such fete in 1953, Mrs. Church wrote to Thomas McGreevy, a mutual friend in Dublin, "Wallace Stevens came first for the party from Hartford (4 hours drive) with his daughter Holly, a handsome, intelligent girl. . . . They are both proud of each other, I love to look at them, it was a struggle for both, Holly did not appreciate her father when she was very young and he made no effort to make her. Now she is older and wiser (27, I believe) and there is Peter, the voyant as Wallace Stevens calls him, 7 years old and quite something for both of them. She was married to a Russian, Wallace Stevens said *Roussian* to show his aversion, and is divorced."[30]

Elias Mengel

She was a student of mine at the University of Connecticut. I went there in the fall of 1951; it must have been the next year I taught Holly. I think she intended to get her degree. Of course, she's so bright; she was the best student I had that year.

[After they had become friends, Holly talked to Mengel about her growing-up years] a good deal. She did indicate that she had a very lonely childhood. She was rebelling, of course, in leaving Vassar; very understandably, because her father [had] insisted on her going to Vassar. Then she worked at the Aetna, got married and divorced. That was wonderful to see: the fact that she, after the divorce, was getting to know her father. And I think she was very happy about that. It was very simple. As soon as she got her divorce, all was forgiven. I might be wrong, but from what she said, I inferred that.

I remember wanting to meet Stevens, but also being very apprehensive about it because I'd heard he could be very difficult and sarcastic. I don't know whether this was the first time, but I remember being invited to tea at Westerly Terrace. This was very pleasant. He was extremely kind, even cordial, I thought. He was very courtly. I think I had built him up almost as an ogre. I remember a story about his having written something about a colleague. [When company president Richard Bissell died in 1941, Stevens' brief portrait of him was published as one of a series of anonymous tributes in the memorial issue of *The Hartford Agent.* Wilson Jainsen, a fellow vice-president] popped his head into the office and said, "Very nice piece, Wallace." And Mr. Stevens said, without raising his head, "I hope I can do the same for you someday."[31] But I didn't see any of that in him. He was very stately and pleasant. This tea was rather unusual, I guess, because Mrs. Stevens was something of a recluse. Holly and Peter, her son, were there. Mrs. Stevens made a very good tea with wonderful cakes and cookies.

This was the only time I saw her, except at the funeral of Wallace Stevens. Yes [Holly had talked of her mother beforehand], so I was perfectly prepared for a recluse when I went to tea, although she didn't seem terribly shy then. She was a good hostess. I suddenly think of why Holly told me he married her—now I'm not saying this is *the* reason he married her—because she was the most beautiful girl in Reading. And she still was in the 1950s, as I remember her. Holly thought her mother had psychological problems, and she obviously did. But I don't think she ever saw a psychologist. Holly and her mother were never close at all, and I don't think there was that kind of rapprochement with her mother there was with her father. I think that she thought that her mother was terribly jealous of her father and that she may have destroyed, after Mr. Stevens' death, some things. I got the feeling that Mrs. Stevens felt inferior to him, that she didn't understand his poetry. Holly did tell me that at the beginning [of Wallace and Elsie Stevens' years in Hartford] they did go out to dinner and that Mrs. Stevens would not reciprocate; then they weren't asked. Except that I was prepared to some extent, I would have thought they were a happily married couple. It seemed very pleasant; there weren't any tensions that I detected.

The Stevens home was most attractive and comfortable. I think it was a chintz or cretonne sofa I was sitting on, flowered. I remember paintings on the wall, but nothing that interested me. I thought, Could it be Mlle. Vidal, her taste? [Paule Vidal was Stevens' bookseller in Paris who bought paintings for him.] Could it have been a question of money? I decided not, after he had spent a hundred dollars for silk curtains for his bedroom.

That tea must have been before I went for my year in Europe. I do remember him saying, "Go to Covent Garden for me, and look at the fruits and flowers." I thought that was so characteristic. Holly told me afterward that he had never been to Europe, which amazed me. Mrs. Stevens wouldn't go; she just wouldn't travel. I was very impressed by that, that he would not go on his own. After the tea, we went out in the garden—Mr. Stevens, Holly and I. Mr. Stevens suddenly turned to me and said, "What's your favorite flower, Mr. Mengel?" And I said to myself, Well, I'll say peonies, to be safe—thinking of Keats. He didn't say anything. And I wondered afterward if that was too common a flower. Holly once told me that he sometimes would have a monochromatic lunch, having vichyssoise, for instance, and something else. In a way, I suppose, that's characteristic of his extreme aesthetic sensitivity.

It was in the fall of '54 that we [Mengel, Wallace and Holly Stevens] went down to New York [for Stevens' YMHA reading]. We went to Mrs. Church's for a drink, and Marianne Moore was there. I was fascinated, because Miss Moore and Mr. Stevens were sitting on a sofa together, talking about Robert McAlmon, whom I'd never heard of. There weren't many people there, so it made it all the better. Seeing Mr. Stevens at Mrs. Church's, I thought him very sociable. I don't know if he liked large parties, but he certainly seemed to be enjoying that small one. Then he took Holly and me—I don't think Miss Moore was along—to dinner at an elegant French restaurant. Then the reading. I remember being very impressed and moved by the reading; I thought I wasn't going to be. He never seemed the slightest bit nervous beforehand. A monumental presence, poised. He was rather formidable, but very impressive, "of a port in air." He was almost totally silent on the drive back to Connecticut; he probably was tired. When we arrived at Westerly

Terrace, I offered to help him out of the back seat and he said, "Thank you, but I'm not Robert Frost."

I would never presume to mention anything about his poetry to him. I was twenty-nine or thirty and in awe of him. And I hadn't read much of him. At that time I thought of Eliot and Yeats as the only great poets, and not Wallace Stevens, although of course I thought of him as one of the finest American poets. But I had no idea he would emerge as one of the great. And I found him so difficult when I did start *The Collected Poems*. I remember once—it must have been the summer of '55—when Holly asked me if I could read the poem in which Stevens talks about Peter ["A Child Asleep in Its Own Life"]. She thought I would be able to elucidate it, and I couldn't. We both at that time felt that his poetry was so beyond us. I don't think Holly talked to her father about his poetry. I remember once asking her to ask him something about "The Emperor of Ice-Cream." She did, and he just turned her off. Of course, I would never ask him myself. Probably for the same reason I wouldn't dare [Holly wouldn't ask her father to elucidate his poem on his grandson]. It would be partly that we would feel foolish: why couldn't we understand it?

Holly had him inscribe my copy of *The Collected Poems*. "Dear Elias: When I speak of the poem, or often when I speak of the poem, in this book, I mean not merely a literary form, but the brightest and most harmonious concept, or order, of life; and the references should be read with that in mind." It was quite late [when he inscribed this, on June 6, Stevens dying on August 2, 1955].

There weren't too many people at Stevens' funeral. The casket was open, but I deliberately did not look. We went out to the cemetery. There were very few people there. I just saw Mrs. Stevens at a distance and felt that I should go over. But I'd only met her once, so I didn't.

Last Days

"Oh, hell! Go see a doctor, and he'll blab my business all over town."[1] At first, Wallace Stevens balked at the suggestion after confiding in Anthony Sigmans at work one day that he had not been feeling well recently. Sigmans assured his friend that his family physician was discreet, and he volunteered to make the appointment and accompany Stevens to the doctor's office. Stevens agreed and on March 28, 1955, he paid his first visit to Dr. James Moher, the physician who attended him in what turned out to be his last illness.

That day Stevens explained to the doctor that he had been quite constipated during the past month; for the past few weeks, he had also been experiencing some stomach discomfort, especially after his evening meal, even though he had less appetite lately and had lost a little weight.[2] Noting that his wife had had a stroke in January and was recuperating at home, he ascribed his ailments to the changes her illness had caused in his routine. He had not been getting his daily exercise, for example, walking to and from the Hartford Accident and Indemnity Company.

Dr. Moher's examination at the office turned up nothing out of the ordinary, nor did an x-ray and barium enema on April 1 show anything amiss. On April 19, however, Stevens underwent the G.I. series Dr. Moher had ordered. The tests revealed diverticulitis and a gallstone; more important, the tests showed an extremely bloated stomach. An obstruction of some sort was preventing anything from passing through. Exploratory surgery was called for, and within a week, Stevens was admitted to St. Francis Hospital, the Catholic hospital in Hartford to which Dr. Moher limited his practice. On April 26, Stevens was operated on by Dr. Benedict Landry, the surgeon Dr. Moher had called into the case.

Holly Stevens was in the midst of preparing a birthday party for her son, Peter, who turned eight that day, when she was told the results of her father's operation. Dr. Landry had found a large cancer attached to the back wall of the stomach that was blocking the opening into the intestine. The cancer could not be removed, but Dr. Landry made Stevens more comfortable by performing a gastroenterostomy above the cancer, which would at least allow some food to pass out of the stomach.

When Stevens was released from the hospital on Wednesday, May 11, he returned to Westerly Terrace, planning to spend at home the period of prolonged recuperation he had been told would be necessary. He and his daughter quickly decided, however, that it would be better if he convalesced elsewhere. The following week, Stevens left home, since Elsie had insisted on trying to nurse him even though she, too, was still recuperating from her winter stroke, the first of several she suffered before her death in 1963. He entered the Avery Convalescent Hospital, across town from Westerly Terrace, where he stayed from May 20 to June 20.

Holly had followed the doctor's advice that her father not be told his illness was terminal, and during the weeks that followed at the Avery he began to feel he was making a recovery. Stevens was able to keep down what he ate on his bland diet, though he continued to lose weight, and he began to take some exercise, ambling around the parklike grounds of the comfortable nursing home. By early June, he had grown strong enough to risk an evening out on June 9 to accept an honorary Doctor of Humanities degree from Hartford's Hartt College of Music and to spend a morning in New Haven on June 13, where he received an honorary Doctor of Letters degree from Yale University.

During Stevens' late-spring weeks at Avery Convalescent Hospital, Holly was a daily visitor. Old friends, such as his insurance colleague Anthony Sigmans, also came to see him frequently.

Anthony Sigmans

During his illness, my wife and I and daughter would visit him. He appreciated these visits. I don't recall that he talked too much about his illness, other than the fact that he wasn't feeling too well. He was pretty much of a changed man in a great many ways. This all came on so suddenly, 'cause I'd never heard him being sick before this.

I saw him every week. We'd take him for a ride, my wife and I. He had another good friend [Charles Burns] who we visited on one occasion; he was one of the Canoe Club fellows. I took him around the Passionist Monastery [in West Hartford] one day. My wife wondered whether he wanted to get out. I said no, he didn't want to. I started to leave. He said, "I certainly do. I want to get out. I want to go down and see the church."

Mr. Stevens was not a religious man. I was a practicing Catholic. He never discussed religion, except on a rare occasion he would make a comment that he had an enjoyable afternoon yesterday in New York as he sat in St. Patrick's Cathedral and meditated. During his last illness he became a Catholic. There was no publication of it, and the burial rites were brief, without any Catholic ceremony. [Months after Stevens' death Sigmans learned of this from the chaplain at St. Francis Hospital.] I do recall Mr. Stevens saying to me at one time that he belonged to no church, but if he ever joined a church it would be the Catholic Church.

Elias Mengel

There may have been one or two more visits [with Stevens after first meeting him for tea at Westerly Terrace], but the third, in many ways the most memorable, was the visit to the nursing home with Holly. We went onto the grounds, and I think he was feeling pretty well that day. It was in the summer, toward the end. I remember Holly and I were asking each other whether or not he knew he had cancer. She thought that he probably did know; I don't know if she ever made up her mind about that. But what was fascinating to me, he started to talk about Harvard and Santayana. He obviously was enjoying this, speaking of the past. One thing I noticed. We were in his room either before or after going onto the grounds. I talked to Holly about this recently in connection with his so-called conversion to Catholicism, which we both find very surprising. Now Holly can't remember this, but I *thought* I saw a copy of the New Testament on his bedside table. I was surprised that he would be reading this.

During his weeks at the Avery, Stevens had been worried not only about his health but about his job as well. On June 20, the day he moved back home to Westerly Terrace, he also forced himself to return to work. Though debilitating summer weather soon turned his rooms at home into an oven at night, Stevens persisted in going into the office each day, arriving at around ten and leaving at one-thirty.[3] While he was at his desk only a few hours, he hoped these daily appearances would forestall a conversation with the president he had been dreading for some time. One day, about a year before the onset of his final illness, Manning Heard recalls, Stevens "called me in and said, 'Will you do me a favor? Will you go in and ask Rutherford [the president] to give Daugherty [one of Stevens' assistants] a raise?' I said, 'Why don't you go in yourself?' He said, 'No. I'm afraid he's going to ask me to retire.' Some people just abhor the idea of retirement, and he was one of them."[4]

Though the Hartford Accident and Indemnity Company had set a retirement age of seventy for its employees, it frequently made exceptions, as it had been doing in Stevens' case now for the past five years. Indeed, just a week before the G.I. series showed he had to undergo exploratory surgery, the board of directors had voted, on April 12, to allow Stevens, to stay on at the company for yet another year.[5] Nonetheless, that winter Stevens saw clearly how vulnerable his position at the company was becoming. In January, Stevens had reacted bitterly when the president of the Hartford removed part of his department from his control. Fidelity claims, which had been under Stevens' jurisdiction since he started with the company in 1916, was handed over, along with some of his long-time staff, to the vice-president in charge of general claims, E. A. Cowie. Stevens' separate bond-claims department had begun to seem an anachronism, and soon after his death in August it was absorbed into general claims.

Recuperating from his illness at the Avery that spring, Stevens had good reason to be worried about his job. If he was uncertain about the severity of his illness, he at least knew that any prolonged absence from Hartford Accident and Indemnity would put an end to his long life at the company. Hale Anderson, Jr., Manning Heard and Herbert Schoen were fellow lawyers who saw Stevens frequently during his last weeks at the company in late June and early July.

Hale Anderson, Jr.

I want to make the point that of all the individuals I've seen go through this, he was the most capable in knowing how to die. During his last illness, he would come and sit [in the company's reception room at lunchtime], and put his thumb and forefinger under his chin and just rest, with his eyes closed, and never indicate by word or manner that he didn't feel well. And about the time people began to hustle back to work, he would get up and go back to his office and tackle that pile of files again. He was a true stoic.

Manning Heard

One day he was out of his office, sitting in a chair in a part of the library. I looked at him, and he had a peculiar expression on his face, I thought of severe pain. I said, "Mr. Stevens, are you feeling well?" He said, "Not too well." I said, "Don't you want me to take you home?" He said, "No. I think I'll take care of it later." This is the discipline I was talking about: this was his job, and he'd almost crawl to do a job he was supposed to do. I think during that period he suffered greatly, but he wouldn't tell anyone.

E. A. Cowie

He was mad when they turned [fidelity claims] over to me. I can remember going down to talk to him one day [that winter of 1955], and he was seething. At first he refused to talk to me. Then he got to arguing how they had insulted him by taking his authority away. All of a sudden he got over it. He mellowed, and he talked about what I wanted to talk about, but he was pretty blue about that. He had been practically shaking; he was almost having a tantrum. I was prepared to leave his presence, but finally he softened and he said, "I'm not blaming you."

Mr. Jainsen was president, and he was the one who made the decision: just to consolidate operations and maybe save a little money in the process. I didn't seek it; they turned it over to me. But it offended Stevens. He stayed in charge of [surety claims] until he died; after he died, it came with me. They used to think that he was getting along pretty well in years. I remember Mr. Jainsen was a little bit disgusted with him at times. He was very independent. One time we had some problem in the bond-claims department in Chicago. So I reported what the problem was, when I came back, to Mr. Jainsen. He said, "Let's go in and talk to Wallace." We went in, and Wallace simply tossed it off. "I wouldn't know a thing about it." Jainsen turned on his heels and said, "Let's get out of here." Stevens was a little on the difficult side at times, but he was affable a great deal of the time.

He had several competent men [under him to handle the department's business during his last illness, when Stevens was often away from the office]. Walter Downs was one who did a lot of the work. He worked for Wallace for many years. Stevens had a lot of respect for Downs, but he didn't like him and he mistreated him badly—let's say, salary and things like that. He was tough on him, and Walter Downs hated him with a passion. In fact, he made a remark that he could think of nothing he'd rather do than go to his funeral.

Herbert Schoen

He was very anxious to stay in the office. I saw him the last day he was here. He obviously was in pain. I saw him after that at St. Francis Hospital, in which he was, to my amazement, completely cherubic. He was a jolly Santa Claus to the nurses. I don't know the reason for the transformation, but it was a transformation. I always assumed he knew the end was coming, and he was a changed person—this time for the better. He spoke to the nurses in a very enjoyable, light-hearted way. They obviously had enjoyed him. I do remember that instead of being a sad or strained time, it was light and tripping and gay, which certainly impressed me.

I came back and told Wilson Jainsen. He said, "Unless they told me he had a heart attack, I never would have known he had a heart." It was that bad.

On July 21, Stevens was readmitted to St. Francis Hospital. His condition had been deteriorating since the beginning of the month. By now cancer had spread throughout the liver. It was again difficult for food to pass out of the stomach, and he had been vomiting as often as five times a day. Once in the hospital, where he was fed intravenously, Stevens fared better, for a time.

Rev. Arthur Hanley

I was chaplain at St. Francis Hospital from '46 to '56. We used to try to see all the patients in the hospital, especially Catholic patients. Dr. Ben Landry said, "Well, stop in and see Wallace Stevens." Ben Landry was taking care of him at the time. He received me very well, and he always said, "Be sure and come back, Father. Be sure and come back." [These visits would last] half an hour sometimes. I'd see him every day.

The first time [he was at the hospital] we talked about a lot of things, about his poetry. I had had a course in poetry both at Boston College and also at St. Bernard's Seminary, where we had a good course in Chaucer. He got quite a kick out of me when I gave off about five lines of Chaucer's *Canterbury Tales* in Old English. So that he thought I was a real lover of poetry, but all the time in the back of my mind was, how can I get this man in the Church? He was very fond of Pope Pius X [who had been canonized a year earlier]. He thought he was a very great man. He said that someday he was going to write a poem about the Pope. So I said, "Oh, what are you going to call the poem?" He said, "I was going to call it 'The Tailor,' or 'The Love of Poverty,' or 'The Poor Tailor.' " And during that time I did get some of his poems and I read them so I would have something to talk about when I went into the room.

He really wanted to talk. There was something bothering him all the time. He believed strongly in God. When he went to New York, he told me, he used to spend at least a couple of hours at St. Patrick's Cathedral, meditating. He said he got so much peace and enjoyment that he always, when he went to New York, went to St. Patrick's Cathedral. I think he had such a marvelous idea of what God was. The absolute idea of God. "Everything," he said, "has been created. There is only one uncreated." And that was God.

He was unusual in this respect. He said, "I think I ought to be in the fold, but there's one thing that bothers me. That is that I don't see how a just God could construct a place like hell, because I do think that a merciful God, knowing the weakness of mankind, would not fashion a place like that to punish anyone—not even a dog." So we went through all that business about whereas God is merciful, He is also just. And in His justice, He must recognize that some people, no matter what grace is given them, will repudiate Him. I said, "As far as we know, we don't know that there's anyone specifically in hell except the devil and his cohorts."

I think he was a bit upset by the mysteriousness of the world. That was one thing that bothered him, the evil in the world. And he was always coming back to the goodness of God: how could a good God allow all this evil in the world? So we went into free will and all that business. But he was more of a poet than a Scholastic philosopher.

He gave me the impression he knew quite a bit about the Church. The impression he gave me was there were just a few little things that kept him from being a Catholic, and that was this hell business. I told him hell was mentioned fifty-seven times in the Bible and that our Lord said there was a hell, so we believe what our Lord said. "Well," he said, "that sounds logical."

So we talked along that line quite a bit, and he was thinking and thinking and thinking. One day he had a bit of a spell. He called for me, and he said, "I'd better get in the fold now." And then I baptized him, and the next day I brought him Communion.

He was close [to resolving these conflicts when they had first met in April]. He didn't need an awful lot of urging on my part except to be nice to him. He never mentioned any other priest [he had talked to on these matters]. He did mention having a lot of letter writing between himself and Sister Madeleva [poet and president of St. Mary's College].* She evidently had been working on him, either orally or through letters, to have him consummate his faith in the Church. In fact, she wrote me a letter about Wallace when he died and asked me if he had come into the Church. He told me he admired her greatly, her poetry and so forth.

[Stevens was baptized] the second time he was in. It was just a few days [later that he died]. He seemed very much at peace, and he would say, "Now I'm in the fold." It was not a nervous reaction; it was a real steady reaction. He gave no impression [that he knew he was dying during his first hospital stay in April]. [When he was readmitted in July] he felt there was an urgency about getting in the fold before he went to his Maker. Now during that time, because his wife was not a Catholic and because it might seem that we got people into the hospital to drag them into the Church at the last minute, Archbishop O'Brien told me not to let it be known. Sister Philomena, who was on the floor, knew; she came in for the baptism. I told his daughter,

*Sister Madeleva had been a mentor of Teresa Curry Gay during Mrs. Gay's undergraduate days at St. Mary's College; later, on visits to Hartford, Sister Madeleva stayed at Mrs. Gay's home at 735 Farmington Avenue, where the Stevenses had an apartment from 1924 until 1932. While the two poets may have made contact in this way, no copies of a correspondence between them exist among either Wallace Stevens' papers at the HL or among Sister Madeleva's papers at St. Mary's College, Notre Dame, Indiana.

Holly.[6] I think it never occurred to him [to be buried in a Catholic cemetery].
He had gotten into the fold and that was it.

He and his wife had not gotten along for years. I mean he would live in
one section of the house, and she would live in the other section of the house.
I did bring that up, that after all we must forgive everybody. But he said, "We
don't have to continue relationships when there is too much sharpness, or
criticism or even" he used some word like "acerbity." He was always using
big words. I couldn't get from Holly what exactly happened—or from him
—but for years they lived in different sections of the house. I suppose he was
a man who lived on a higher or a different plane than she did.

During his last stay in the hospital, Stevens was not heavily sedated for he
had grown so weak that he was experiencing little pain. On August 1, he
lapsed into a coma, having been semiconscious for the past day or so. That
evening members of his family visited him for the last time. Holly had to
bring her son, Peter, for treatment in the emergency room at St. Francis
Hospital; before going home, Stevens' daughter and grandson stopped by his
room. He had regained consciousness, and they all wished each other good-
night. That night, however, he fell back into a coma, and his fever intensified.
At eight-thirty on Tuesday morning, August 2, Wallace Stevens died.

John Cleary

At that time, I was obituary editor of the Hartford *Times*. I got a call from
an employee of the James T. Pratt Funeral Home in Hartford, which was the
funeral home most patronized by rich Protestants. He said, "I have an obit
for you." No other introduction. So I put on my headset and started to type
down the information he gave me, which was the man's name, his address,
the place where he died and the date he died. And the fact that the funeral
would be private. I said, "Wait a minute. Wallace Stevens? Is that the poet,
the Pulitzer Prize winner? We can't go on that one with this little information." He said, "Well, that's the way the family wants it!" When there's a
death in the family, especially among families with a strong WASP tradition,
they want privacy.

Margaret Powers

It was a stark funeral parlor. No beautiful music, no beautiful service. There
was some kind of eulogy. I was so horrified. I'd like to have heard what
[Stevens would have] had to say about it. Both Julie [Mrs. Powers' daughter]
and I said, "That isn't like Wallace Stevens." It was just the most mundane
of get-it-over-with [services]. No feeling of an afterlife or anything like that.

[The room] wasn't very big; full of people. I didn't meet Elsie Stevens there. Holly and Elsie were in purdah; they were behind a screen or something like that.

No [Mrs. Powers did not go to the interment]; that was private. Holly wrote to me that Julie's St. Christopher medal had been buried with him. Jim [Powers, her husband, who had visited Stevens at St. Francis Hospital] said that he also had on his pillow a crucifix that his nurse or somebody had given him. He wanted that out there [at the hospital], and he wanted Julie's St. Christopher medal pinned on his pillow right where he could see it.

He and Jim talked an awful lot about religion [over the years]. He knew Jim had a definite faith. Jim had said, "I think Wallace would like to be in a Church but he can't do it." He and Jim sought out these little churches all over Manhattan, mostly Roman [when the Powerses would return to New York over the years]. He loved the feeling of the Church, the atmosphere of churches, according to Jim. I'd never been in St. Patrick's, as a matter of fact, and he insisted that we go. We didn't go to a service. We just went in, and he showed me all around the various chapels and the high altar.

Anthony Sigmans

The only comment I could make about the funeral, and I've thought about it many times, here a world celebrity dies and is buried—and a handful of people are there. Just a handful. The pallbearers were Manning Heard, myself, Ivan Daugherty, John Ladish [William Wallace and John O'Loughlin]: just those around the office, no president of this-or-that, the mayor or the governor.

Very quiet funeral and a very short eulogy. As I say, there weren't many people. Lots of people from the company, people that Stevens would see in the hall thousands of times, didn't bother to come over 'cause a lot of them didn't understand him. They didn't like him. They thought he was abrupt. They thought he was in a class by himself. He wasn't understood. You had to live with Mr. Stevens in a sense, as we did, to know him.

Samuel French Morse

I came back to Hartford to teach the second half of the summer session [at Trinity College]. It was the day I got back that he died. Then there was the funeral, and Jack Sweeney [curator of Harvard's Poetry Room] and Norman Pearson [a Yale professor] and I were [the only literary people] there. I was certainly surprised at the open coffin, and, as I recall, we all walked past the coffin. He had wasted away a good deal, because my memory of him was a big man, not like that last picture in the *Letters*, where the suit is obviously much too big for him.

We did not [go to the interment]. Jack, Norman and I went somewhere and had a drink and talked a little bit. I remember Norman saying that the poetry would take care of itself because there was practically no one there [at the funeral]. 'Course it was a terrible time, and everyone was away on vacation. We agreed that he was one of the remarkable figures of our time.

A few days before Christmas, 1955, Holly Stevens drove to the outskirts of Hartford to lay a few sprigs beside her father's grave at Cedar Hill Cemetery, where Stevens had been interred on August 4 with the same privacy that had characterized his life in Hartford. During his weeks at the Avery, Stevens had told his daughter that he wished to be buried in this cemetery, whose rustic grounds of ponds, streams and tree-lined lanes abutted the convalescent home. Passing the Gothic gatehouse at the cemetery entrance, Holly drove down a half-mile of winding lane until she came to Section 14, a knoll rising gently off the path. Midway up the slope was Stevens' grave, a small tree that grew near the site spare in the winter light. She laid the sprigs of holly in front of the gravestone, which she now saw set in place for the first time. The knee-high slab of Rhode Island granite was simple and discreet. A long-stemmed lily with a drooping flower was carved on either side of Stevens' name, beneath which were inscribed only:

> *Reading, Pennsylvania*
> *October 2, 1879*
> *Hartford, Connecticut*
> *August 2, 1955*
> *His wife*
> Elsie Viola Kachel
> *June 5, 1886*

Stevens had left no epitaph, and the stone bore no line from his work to mark the grave. The poet's monument, the planet on the table, lay elsewhere.

Notes

Abbreviations

Published works by Wallace Stevens:

CP   *The Collected Poems of Wallace Stevens* (New York: Alfred A. Knopf, 1954)

LWS   *Letters of Wallace Stevens*, ed. Holly Stevens (New York: Alfred A. Knopf, 1966)

NA   *The Necessary Angel: Essays on Reality and the Imagination* (New York: Alfred A. Knopf, 1951)

OP   *Opus Posthumous*, ed. Samuel French Morse (New York: Alfred A. Knopf, 1957)

Location of unpublished materials most frequently cited:

Chicago   Special Collections, Joseph Regenstein Library, University of Chicago

Dartmouth   Special Collections, Baker Memorial Library, Dartmouth College

Emory   Judge Arthur Gray Powell Collection, Special Collections, Robert W. Woodruff Library, Emory University

Harvard   Houghton Library, Harvard University

HIG   Hartford Insurance Group

HL   Henry E. Huntington Library

Massachusetts   Special Collections, University of Massachusetts at Amherst Library

Trinity   Manuscript Department, Trinity College, University of Dublin

CHAPTER ONE: *At the Hartford*

1. *The Weekly Underwriter,* February 12, 1916, p. 190.

2. *The Weekly Underwriter,* December 25, 1915, p. 788; *Insurance World,* February 15, 1916, p. 127.

3. As of December 31, 1915, New England Equitable Insurance Company had netted $964,166.21. (*Fifty-first Annual Report of the Insurance Commissioner,* pt. 2 [Hartford: The State of Connecticut, 1916], p. 1023.) Only five out of the thirty-four leading insurance companies in America offering bonds that year had premiums in this line that were larger than New England Equitable's. (*Annual Cyclopedia of Insurance in the United States* [Hartford: R. B. Caverly, 1916], p. 440.)

4. At the start of 1915, New England Casualty issued its report on the previous year's business, which indicated that losses from bond claims totaled 74.9 percent of bond premiums taken in. (*Best's Insurance Reports: Casualty and Miscellaneous* [New York: Alfred M. Best, 1915], p. 193.) After the Aetna Accident and Liability Company took over most of New England Equitable's business in March 1916, it rejected some 6,500 bonds issued by New England Equitable, a number of them no doubt because they ran a high risk of costly claims. (*Insurance Index,* December 10, 1921, p. 531.)

5. *Fifty-first Annual Report of the Insurance Commissioner,* pt. 2, pp. 823 and 819.

6. On April 15, 1916, two months after New England Equitable announced it was divesting itself of all but its line of industrial accident insurance in hopes of remaining in the business, it transferred even those policies to Eastern Casualty Company. By the end of April the insurance departments of Massachusetts and Missouri began their investigation of New England Equitable's home office records. (*Sixty-first Annual Report of the Insurance Commissioner of the Commonwealth of Massachusetts,* pt. 2 [Boston, 1916], pp. v–vi; *The Weekly Underwriter,* March 3, 1917, p. 291.)

7. *Insurance World,* February 15, 1916, p. 119.

8. *The Weekly Underwriter,* January 29, 1916, p. 135.

9. Taped interview with Wilson Taylor.

10. Kearney was one of the first friends Stevens had made after becoming an insurance man. The Maryland lawyer was already working at American Bonding Company's New York office when Stevens started there in January 1908. In March, Kearney was appointed manager of the metropolitan department and, within a year, he was named one of the two vice-presidents in charge of the New York branch. His fellow vice-president was Edward B. Southworth, Jr., who also remained one of the lifelong friends Stevens had made in the insurance business at the outset of his career. (*The Hartford Agent,* May 1939, p. 239; *Trow's General Directory of the Boroughs of Manhattan and Bronx, City of New York* [New York: Trow Directory, Printing and Bookbinding Company, 1910], 123:57.)

11. *Trow's General Directory of the Boroughs of Manhattan and Bronx, City of New York* (New York: Trow Directory, Printing and Bookbinding Company, 1909), 122:1405.

12. *Insurance Advocate*, April 22, 1944, p. 6.

13. Letter of Wallace Stevens to Elsie Stevens, August 6, 1911, *LWS*, p. 169; *Insurance World*, August 29, 1911, p. 644.

14. Letter of Wallace Stevens to Elsie Stevens, August 6, 1911, *LWS*, p. 170.

15. *The Hartford Agent*, March 1916, p. 347.

16. Within a week after Equitable Surety announced that Kearney was resigning as manager of its New York office and that Southworth was succeeding him, it "announced the appointment of Wallace Stevens as resident vice-president at New York. Mr. Stevens is a lawyer and has had seven years' experience in surety underwriting with the American Bonding Company and the Fidelity and Deposit." (*The Weekly Underwriter*, February 21, 1914, p. 151.)

17. Taped interview with Franklin P. Kearney. According to the Hartford telephone directory, in the summer of 1916 the Kearneys lived on High Street, Farmington.

18. *Connecticut and American Impressionism* (Storrs, Conn.: The William Benton Museum of Art, 1980), p. 161.

19. *CP*, p. 533.

20. Letter to Ferdinand Reyher, June 3, 1916, copy at HL.

21. Taped interview with Stephen Langton, an administrator at Hartt College of Music, who was instrumental in securing the honorary degree Stevens received from that Hartford institution in June 1955.

22. Jerald E. Hatfield, "More about Legend," *Trinity Review*, May 1954, p. 30.

23. Letter of June 4, 1900, Massachusetts.

24. For information on Walter Arensberg's career I am indebted to Francis Naumann's "Walter Arensberg: Poet, Patron and Participant in the New York Avant-Garde, 1915–20," *Bulletin, Philadelphia Museum of Art*, Spring 1980, pp. 1–32.

25. Letter of August 3, 1913, *LWS*, p. 185.

26. Letter to Thomas McGreevy, November 2, 1953, Trinity.

27. Letter of Wallace Stevens to Elsie Stevens, August 6, 1911, *LWS*, p. 170.

28. Carl Van Vechten, "Rogue Elephant in Porcelain," *The Yale University Library Gazette*, October 1963, p. 49.

29. Conversation with Holly Stevens.

30. *Geer's Hartford City Directory* (Hartford: Hartford Printing Company, 1916), p. 9. While no similar population estimate for Reading in 1916 is available, U.S. census figures show Hartford was not a great deal larger than Reading during the decade in which the Stevenses moved to Connecticut. In 1910, Reading had 96,071 residents while Hartford had 98,915; in 1920, Reading had 107,784 residents while Hartford had 138,036. (*Statistical Abstract of the United States* [Washington, D.C.: United States Government Printing Office, 1931], pp. 24 and 26.)

31. Letter to Ferdinand Reyher, June 3, 1916, copy at HL.

32. Charles Beach, who joined the army in the early summer of 1916, had heard Stevens was a poet before quitting his job at the Hartford Accident and Indemnity that June.

33. Letter of Wallace Stevens to Harriet Monroe, May 19, 1916, Chicago.

34. Telegram, from R. M. Bissell to Wallace Stevens, April 7, 1916, HIG.

35. The original drafts and final revision of the Declaration and Charter of the Hartford Live Stock Insurance Company, plus the original and 1941 revisions of its bylaws, are among the few extant documents composed by Stevens the lawyer (HIG).

36. Taped interview with John Ladish.

37. Letter of June 22, 1916, HL.

38. Taped interview with John Ladish.

39. Letter to Elsie Stevens, August 15, 1913, HL.

40. Merle Kummer et al., *Hartford Architecture* (Hartford: Hartford Architecture Conservancy, 1980), 3:152.

41. Marguerite Flynn died before I had begun this oral biography of Stevens; her remarks are taken from a memoir found among her papers.

42. "Surety and Fidelity Claims," *The Eastern Underwriter*, March 25, 1938, p. 45.

43. Of the hundreds of cases Stevens dealt with during his thirty-nine years at the Hartford Accident and Indemnity Company, records of fewer than ten are extant today at the home office. James Reik was a company lawyer at the time many of Stevens' later files were "coming up for destruction. The guy was then dead, and we were wondering if we should set these things aside somewhere. I looked at two or three. It seemed to me, and whoever I was looking with, that they would just be incomprehensible if you didn't know everything there was about the whole file: what the problem was, what the insurance coverage was, and to some extent what the law at that time was against which he was reacting—because he didn't mince words. You couldn't just save his letters." (Taped interview with James Reik.)

44. Letter of April 2, 1947, copy at HL.

45. Letter of Arthur Powell to Hi Simons, April 8, 1940, Chicago.

46. Letter of August 7, 1913, *LWS*, p. 180.

47. "Court Bonds—Financial Guaranties," in *General Information Regarding the Undertakings of the Hartford Accident and Indemnity Company* (Hartford: Hartford Accident and Indemnity Company, n.d.), p. 32.

48. *CP*, pp. 286–87.

49. By the end of December 1953, the Dylan Thomas Fund had raised more money than expected; the funds exceeded the needs stated in the appeal, "to meet his medical bills and funeral expenses and, if the response is as generous as we hope, to tide his family over the next difficult months" (letter of November 10, 1953, signed by W. H. Auden, E. E. Cummings, Arthur Miller, Marianne Moore, Wallace Stevens, Tennessee Williams and Thornton Wilder, in a December 31, 1953, memo). Stevens then asked Schoen, in the legal department at Hartford Accident, to research the legal ramifications. Among other things, Schoen recommended that a trust arrangement be submitted for court approval so that the writers who had signed the appeal could not be held personally liable in any way (private coll.: Samuel French Morse).

50. Stevens was on the board of directors of the Hartford Live Stock Insurance Company from 1916 to 1920 and from 1937 to 1955. He was also acting secretary of the annual stockholders' and directors' meetings in New York City in 1917, 1919 and 1920; from 1938 until his death in 1955, Stevens was acting chairman of the annual meeting of stockholders in New York.

51. A memorial exhibition of Walter Gay's seventeenth- and eighteenth-century interiors was held at the Metropolitan Museum in the spring of 1938.

52. *The Third Little Show* was a 1931 revue starring Beatrice Lillie and Ernest Truex, with sketches by Noel Coward, S. J. Perelman and Marc Connelly, among others.

53. *CP*, pp. 160–61.

CHAPTER TWO: *An Affair of People: Judge Arthur Powell and His Friends*

1. "Adagia," *OP*, p. 158.

2. Taped interview with Charles O'Dowd.

3. William Butt, "Georgia's Great Triumvirate of Jurists," Atlanta *Constitution*, August 20, 1951, p. 5.

4. Copy of a letter from Wallace Stevens to Ferdinand Reyher, February 2, 1922, HL.

5. Letter of Wallace Stevens to Philip May, January 27, 1936, Harvard.

6. "A Mythology Reflects Its Region," *OP*, p. 118.

7. Unpublished material omitted from published letter (*LWS*, pp. 232–33) of January 30, 1923, HL.

8. Letter to Arthur Powell, March 22, 1944, Emory.

9. Letter from Arthur Powell to Hi Simons, April 8, 1940, Chicago.

10. "The Comedian as the Letter C" (*CP*, p. 38). For the original lines in "From the Journal of Crispin" see *Wallace Stevens: A Celebration*, ed. Frank Doggett and Robert Buttel (Princeton: Princeton University, 1980), p. 43.

11. Letter of Philip May to Arthur Powell, February 7, 1935, and copy of a letter of Wallace Stevens to Philip May, January 8, 1937, Harvard.

12. Copy of a letter to Wallace Stevens, January 29, 1940, HL.

13. Letter of April 8, 1940, Chicago.

14. Ms., "Wallace S. Meets Robert F.," Emory.

15. "The Irrational Element in Poetry," *OP*, p. 222.

16. Taped interview with Arthur Laws.

17. Ms., "The Stream Lined Train Passes Lake Istakpaga," Emory.

18. Letter of April 15, 1946, Emory.

19. "Esthétique du Mal," *CP*, p. 322.

20. "Democracy in the United States. Before the Ten Club of Atlanta, July, 1937," Emory.

21. "The Dynamic Force of Love," *The Golden Age*, June 25, 1908, p. 7.

22. *OP*, p. 230.

23. Taped interview with Mrs. Arthur Powell, Jr.

24. Letter of January 10, 1922, *LWS*, p. 225.

25. *CP*, pp. 293–94.

26. Letter of January 31, 1940, Harvard.

27. Letter of February 2, 1943, Harvard.

CHAPTER THREE: *Hartford's Writer in Residence*

1. Copy of a letter to Norman Holmes Pearson, April 21, 1952, HL.

2. "Wallace Stevens," *Poetry*, January 1956, p. 235.

3. For a sketch of Hartford's literary circles from the late eighteenth century through the end of the nineteenth century—the Hartford Wits' Friendly Club (1785–1807); the Knights of the Round Table (1819–1833); Lydia Sigourney's salon (1820s) and her literary evenings (1840s–1850s); the Nook Farm group (c. 1860–1900)—see Kenneth R. Andrews, *Nook Farm: Mark Twain's Hartford Circle* (Cambridge, Mass.: Harvard University Press, 1950), pp. 144–215.

4. A poet, playwright and novelist of very modest talents, Annie Eliot Trumbull (1857–1949) published her first short story in *Harper's Bazaar* in 1881. Among the books she published at the turn of the century, when her fiction had some vogue, were *An Hour's Promise* (1889), *White Birches* (1893), *A Christmas Accident* (1897), *Rod's Salvation* (1898), and *Life's Common Way* (1903), her last novel. A collection of her poetry, *Impressions*, appeared in 1927.

5. William Butler Yeats, who had first come to Hartford in 1903 to speak on Celtic literature before the Saturday Morning Club, also returned to the city during Stevens' years there. On December 14, 1932, he spoke at the Center Church House under the auspices of the Poetry Society of Hartford. Yeats was on a six-week speaking tour of the United States, partly to raise money for a series of literary prizes to be awarded through the Irish Academy of Letters. The Hartford church hall was filled, hundreds of people having turned out to hear the poet's talk on Irish history and the Irish literary revival. Yeats was introduced by a local writer far more prominent than Stevens was in his hometown at that time, Odell Shepard. If Stevens and Yeats met, which seems unlikely, there is no mention of the evening in Stevens' papers.

6. Letter of July 7, 1913, *LWS*, p. 179. "The celebrated Miss Trumbull" (so described by Stevens), as it turned out, not only was one of Stevens' hosts on his first visit to Hartford in 1913, but later was also a neighbor for many years after he moved there. Stevens' office at 690 Asylum Avenue was quite close to her home at 734 Asylum Avenue, where Trumbull lived as the *grande dame* of Hartford's literary life, until her death in 1949. Hartford's Poetry Society was only one of the cultural groups in which Trumbull was vigorously involved after helping to organize it in 1921. Robert Frost, Carl Sandburg, Archibald MacLeish and William Butler Yeats were among its guests over the years, but Stevens repeatedly turned down invitations to appear.

7. For an account of the literary life of this bookshop, see Edwin Valentine Mitchell's *Morocco Bound* (New York: Farrar and Rhinehart, 1929).

8. For an account of this friendship with Stevens, see Snow's autobiography, *Codline's Child* (Middletown: Wesleyan University, 1974), pp. 391–98.

9. Mrs. Charles Cunningham, née Eleanor Lamont, was the daughter of the family that established the Lamont Selection of the Academy of American Poets. The award, meant to encourage new talent, is given to a first book of poems by an American author; it guarantees that one thousand copies of the book will be distributed.

10. For an account of this visit, see Alfred A. Knopf's *Sixty Photographs* (New York: Alfred A. Knopf, 1975), p. 25.

11. "Rubbings of Reality," *OP*, p. 258.

12. William Van O'Connor died before I began this oral biography. His remarks are from a copy of a letter to Samuel French Morse, May 10, 1957, Dartmouth.

13. Letter of September 29, 1954, *LWS*, p. 845.

14. Letter of January 4, 1945, *LWS*, p. 481.

15. Wallace Stevens to Elsie Stevens, February 4, 1923, *LWS*, pp. 234–36.

16. While preparing his Italian translation of selected poems by Stevens, *Mattino Domenicale ed altre poesie* (Turin: Giulio Einaudi, 1954), Renato Poggioli put a number of questions to the Hartford poet about aspects of these works.

17. Letter of March 2, 1945, *LWS*, p. 490.

18. Letter of March 19, 1945, *LWS*, p. 490.

19. *Collected Poems, 1930–1960* (New York: Oxford University Press, 1960), p. 217.

20. On December 13, 1940, Stevens replied to Morse's request for a manuscript for the Cummington Press poetry series: "A year or two ago Allen Tate was planning some books to be published at Chapel Hill. I wanted very much to go along with him because I like the idea of small books dealing with single or related subjects, but Mr. Knopf said *no*; and I dare say that he would say *no* again. Moreover, I think that he is right about this. He has always treated me most decently. . . . As it happens, I have just been putting together what I have to see what it would make by way of a new book, and also for the purpose of seeing what else might be needed. . . . The point of all this is that my last contract with Mr. Knopf called for two books; one of them he has already published. If he accepted the manuscript, I would then be free to do a small book . . . this all means that you will have to count me out. . . . Why don't you publish a collection of your own? If you wanted me to do so, I should be glad to do a preface for you. Your poems make one believe in them and have a natural force and abundance. Or, if you like, I should be glad to ask Marianne Moore to do a preface. . . ." (HL.)

21. *The Collected Earlier Poems of William Carlos Williams* (Norfolk, Conn.: New Directions, 1938), p. 100.

22. "Adagia," *OP*, p. 165.

23. Letter of May 5, 1952, *LWS*, pp. 749–50.

24. Ralph Waldo Emerson, "Days," *The Oxford Book of American Verse*, ed. F. O. Matthiessen (New York: Oxford University Press, 1950), p. 107.

25. *CP*, p. 216.

26. For a check list of Stevens' music collection, see Michael O. Stegman's "Wallace Stevens and Music: A Discography of Stevens' Phonograph Collection," *The Wallace Stevens Journal*, Fall 1979, pp. 79–97.

27. "Adagia," *OP*, p. 175.

CHAPTER FOUR: *A Private Poet in Public*

1. "Adagia," *OP*, p. 157.

2. Letter of September 15, 1943, Berg Collection, New York Public Library. Sarton was in charge of a wartime poetry series at the New York Public Library, designed, as she wrote Stevens, to remind people what the war was being fought to save. Even though Sarton had mustered some impressive recruits for her Tuesday evening programs—James Agee, W. H. Auden, Langston Hughes, William Carlos Williams and Marianne Moore—she was unable to enlist Stevens. While citing shyness when he turned down Sarton's invitation to read, about that time Stevens also indicated he disliked poetry readings on principle. He felt there was something vulgar about them, as he quipped to Henry Wells when declining that professor's invitation to read at Columbia University. "I am afraid I don't like the idea. Poets, like millionaires, should be neither seen nor heard. Anyhow, I don't like public appearances except in print" (letter of December 23, 1941, Rare Book and Manuscript Library, Columbia University).

3. Letter to Barbara Church, April 22, 1951, HL.

4. Letter to Robert Hillyer, November 6, 1936, Harvard University Archives.

5. "The Irrational Element in Poetry," *OP*, p. 222.

6. Ibid., p. 225.

7. *NA*, pp. 30–31.

8. For Winfield Townley Scott's account of that Yale evening, see Scott Donaldson's *Poet in America: Winfield Townley Scott* (Austin: University of Texas, 1972), pp. 250–53.

9. Randall Jarrell, "The Collected Poems of Wallace Stevens," *Yale Review*, March 1955, pp. 340–53.

10. Randall Jarrell, "Reflections on Wallace Stevens," *Partisan Review*, May–June, 1951, pp. 335–44.

11. "Introduction," *Sewanee Review*, Autumn 1944, p. 494.

12. Letter to Henry Church, April 16, 1943, *LWS*, p. 447.

13. *NA*, pp. 39, 57–58, 59.

14. Helen E. Patch, Untitled note in *Trinity Review*, May 1954, p. 35.

15. *NA*, p. 43.

16. Letter of April 21, 1948, *LWS*, p. 587.

17. Letter to Henry Church, November 10, 1943, HL.

18. Letter to Barbara Church, June 26, 1952, *LWS*, p. 756.

19. Elided section from published letter of March 25, 1949, copy at Dartmouth.

20. Letter of March 28, 1951, HL.

21. Stevens' audience at the Museum of Modern Art had liked his lecture so much that it was their requests for copies that prompted Wheeler to ask Stevens for permission to publish it. "Your evening here was an immense success with our public," Wheeler wrote five days after the talk. "From old and young we have heard that it was the finest of our series, and many people have asked us to print your paper on the relations between poetry

and painting so that they may reflect upon your brilliant observations at leisure." (Letter of January 20, 1951, HL.)

22. Tape of Wallace Stevens' YMHA poetry reading, November 6, 1954, The Poetry Center.

23. For Winfield Townley Scott's account of that meeting see *"A Dirty Hand": The Literary Notebooks of Winfield Townley Scott* (Austin: University of Texas Press, 1969), pp. 38–40.

24. "Esthétique du Mal," *CP*, p. 325.

25. "The Man with the Blue Guitar," *CP*, p. 165.

26. *LWS*, p. 847.

27. Letter of December 10, 1953 (private coll.: John Gruen).

28. Letter of September 8, 1953 (ibid.).

29. Letter of December 3, 1954 (ibid.).

30. Letter of October 29, 1954, HL.

31. Letter of August 15, 1951, Special Collections, Morris Library, Southern Illinois University.

32. Letter of Wallace Stevens to Paul Weiss, December 7, 1951, Special Collections, Morris Library, Southern Illinois University.

33. Letter to Wallace Stevens, HL.

34. Letter to Wallace Stevens, HL.

35. Letter to Norman Holmes Pearson, *LWS*, p. 736.

CHAPTER FIVE: *The Church Circle*

1. Letter of July 30, 1951, HL.

2. Letter of Barbara Church to Thomas McGreevy, January 4, 1947, Trinity.

3. Letter of March 13, 1939, HL.

4. Letter of January 28, 1942, *LWS*, p. 401.

5. Letter to William Arrowsmith, October 8, 1947, The Hudson Review Archive.

6. Letter to Frederick Morgan, November 23, 1949, The Hudson Review Archive.

7. After seeing an exhibition of works by Wassily Kandinsky, Stevens wrote to Thomas McGreevy on June 26, 1952, "It made Kandinsky for me. I had not seen much of his work up to then and certainly not enough to make it possible to see it as a minor cosmos, which it is. It is the sort of thing that is wholly esthetic and wholly delightful. And from that point of view it seemed valid." (Trinity.)

CHAPTER SIX: *Life at Home*

1. *Poetry*, August 1928, p. 296.

2. "Jazzing American Poetry," *Book Notes*, June–July 1924, pp. 167–68.

3. Letter of October 4, 1927, *Antaeus*, Winter 1980, p. 147. Original in Ezra Pound Archive, Collection of American Literature, Beinecke Rare Book and Manuscript Library, Yale University.

4. Letter of September 7, 1927, ibid., p. 146. Original in ibid.

5. Holly Stevens quoted in George Graves' "Poet/Executive. A Dual Life Reread," "Sunday," Hartford *Courant*, March 25, 1979, p. 5.

CHAPTER SEVEN: *Farewell to My Elders*

1. Elizabeth Stevens' Pennsylvania divorce decree states that she married George MacFarland on September 29, 1917, and divorced him on June 20, 1927, charging desertion.

2. Letter of Wallace Stevens to Elsie Stevens, May 12, 1919, HL.

3. Taped interview.

4. "A Branch of the Bright Family" (1945), pp. 24–25. Elsie Stevens later revised the date she first met her husband, crossing out "One June evening" and adding "July 7th 1903." She was unsure of the year, however, and put a question mark after "1903" and "1904." Stevens' journal indicates he first met Elsie in the summer of 1904.

5. Taped interview.

6. Letter to Jane MacFarland Stone, September 13, 1943, in *L WS*, p. 454.

7. Obituary of Garrett Barcalow Stevens, Reading *Eagle*, July 14, 1911, p. 1.

8. Holly Stevens, *Souvenirs and Prophecies* (New York: Alfred A. Knopf, 1976), p. 6.

9. Letter of Garrett Stevens to Wallace Stevens, November 12, 1897, HL.

10. Letter of Wallace Stevens to Elsie Moll, January 31, 1909, HL.

11. Letter of Garrett Stevens to Wallace Stevens, November 17, 1907, HL.

12. The city directories of Reading list Aaron Bright, in the late 1860s, and George Washington Smith, in the early 1870s, as living at 537 Elm Street, not 521 Elm Street as Elsie Stevens noted in a genealogy she compiled for her daughter in 1945. By 1874, George Washington Smith and his family had moved to 427 Church Street, a house almost directly behind what would later be Stevens' boyhood home on North Fifth Street. After Smith's death in 1875, Catherine Bright Smith moved her large family to a house at 937 Greenwich Street.

13. Letter to Elsie Moll, January 31, 1909, *L WS*, p. 129.

14. Conversation with Holly Stevens.

15. Taped interview with Jane MacFarland Wilson.

16. Letter of Garrett Stevens to Wallace Stevens, April 7, 1898, HL.

17. Reading *Eagle*, April 4, 1898, p. 1.

18. Letter of Garrett Stevens to Wallace Stevens, December 5, 1898, HL.

19. Reading *Eagle*, July 18, 1911, p. 8.

20. Letter of Margaretha Stevens to Elizabeth Stevens, November 22, 1908, HL.

21. Letter of Wallace Stevens to Elsie Moll, December 14, 1908, HL.

22. Letter of Wallace Stevens to Elsie Moll, May 7, 1909, HL.

23. Taped interview with Jane MacFarland Wilson.

CHAPTER EIGHT: *Family Ties*

1. Letter to Eleanor Sauer et al., August 7, 1943, HL.

2. Taped interview with Mary Catharine Sesnick.

3. Undated typescript, HL.

4. Letter to Emma Jobbins, February 19, 1945, HL.

5. Letter to Elsie Moll, January 31, 1909, HL.

6. Letter to W. N. P. Dailey, May 16, 1945, *L WS*, p. 499.

7. *OP*, p. 87.

8. *OP*, p. 77.

9. Memorandum for Dr. Campbell, April 14, 1943, HL.

10. Letter to John Sauer, October 3, 1944, HL.

11. Details of the Zeller family history are based on Stevens' letter to Howard Althouse, August 9, 1944, *L WS*, pp. 469–70; Stevens' unpublished genealogy of the Zellers and his letters to Samuel Bertolet, January 29, 1945, and to William Boone Douglass, July 16, 1945, all at HL.

12. *CP*, p. 327.

13. Letter to Howard Althouse, August 9, 1944, *L WS*, p. 470.

14. Letter to Charles R. Barker, September 30, 1946, *L WS*, p. 534.

15. Letter to Lila James Roney, October 4, 1943, HL.

16. *CP*, p. 327.

17. Letter of Howard Althouse to Wallace Stevens, September 21, 1944, HL.

18. Some family members recall Elsie Stevens accompanying her husband to the wedding. Letter of Eleanor Sauer to Wallace Stevens, June 8, 1947, HL.

19. Poems by Garrett Stevens were published, posthumously, in the Reading *Eagle* on July 30, 1911, August 11, 1911, and July 20, 1924.

20. Letter of October 11, 1942, HL.

21. Holly Stevens, "Bits of Remembered Time," *The Southern Review*, July 1971, p. 656.

22. Letter dated Wednesday [September 30, 1942], HL.

23. Conversation with Holly Stevens.

24. Holly Stevens, "Bits of Remembered Time," p. 656.

25. Letter of C. Mildred Thompson to Wallace Stevens, November 3, 1942, HL.

26. Letter of October 26, 1942, *L WS*, p. 426.

27. Letter to John Sauer, October 25, 1944, HL.

28. Letter of December 12, 1946, Emory.

29. Docket #83302: Holly Stevens Hanchak vs. John Martin Hanchak. Records Center, Hartford Superior Court.

30. Letter of November 1, 1953, Trinity.

31. According to Richard Bissell's son, Stevens contributed the first and perhaps the second paragraph of a tribute to Richard Bissell in *The Hartford Agent*, August 1941, p. 8. (Taped interview with William Bissell.)

CHAPTER NINE: *Last Days*

1. Taped interview with Anthony Sigmans.

2. The medical account of Stevens' last illness is based on a taped interview with Dr. James Moher, who consulted medical notes made at the time he treated Stevens.

3. Letter of Wallace Stevens to Samuel French Morse, July 5, 1955, *L WS*, p. 888.

4. Taped interview.

5. "Hartford Accident and Indemnity Company, Board of Directors' Records," no. 3, p. 177, HIG.

6. Holly Stevens vigorously denies that her father was converted to Catholicism during his last illness. While at St. Francis Hospital, she recalls, Stevens complained of visits by clergy but he said he was too weak to protest.

Log of Interviews Quoted
in Parts of a World

Léonie Adams, October 1976, New Milford, Connecticut

Mary Aiken, January 1978, Savannah, Georgia

Hale Anderson, Jr., December 1975 and June 1978, North Canton, Connecticut

Charles Beach, August 1976, Farmington, Connecticut

Arthur Berger, November 1976, Cambridge, Massachusetts

Florence Berkman, August 1976, Hartford, Connecticut

William Bissell, August 1976, Canton, Connecticut

John Malcolm Brinnin, June 1976, Duxbury, Massachusetts

Marianne Brock, May 1977, South Hadley, Massachusetts

Cleanth Brooks, June 1976, Northford, Connecticut

Clifford Burdge, Jr., September 1976, Hartford, Connecticut

Mrs. Frederick Cason, January 1978, Miami, Florida

Elizabeth Halloran Chickering, August 1976, Amherst, Massachusetts

John Cleary, June 1978, Colchester, Connecticut

William Cole, August 1976, New York, New York

Naaman Corn, March 1977, Bloomfield, Connecticut

E. A. Cowie, September 1976, Bloomfield, Connecticut

Richard Cross, August 1977, Denver, Colorado

Charles Cunningham, March 1977, Williamstown, Massachusetts

Lillian Daugherty, January 1980, West Hartford, Connecticut

Robert De Vore, March 1976 and May 1978, West Hartford, Connecticut

Frank and Dorothy Doggett, January 1978, Atlantic Beach, Florida

Paul and Kitty Dow, August 1976, Dallas, Texas

Richard and Betty Eberhart, April 1976, Hanover, New Hampshire

Donald Engley, July 1976, New Haven, Connecticut

A. J. Fletcher, December 1976, Raleigh, North Carolina

Rev. James Gay, August 1976, Greenwich, Connecticut

Rev. John Curry Gay, September 1976, Old Saybrook, Connecticut

Elliott Goldstein, June 1977, Atlanta, Georgia

Elizabeth Green, May 1977, South Hadley, Massachusetts

John and Jane Wilson Gruen, September 1976, New York, New York

Robert Halloran, August 1976, West Hartford, Connecticut

Rev. Arthur Hanley, January 1976, Cheshire, Connecticut

Manning Heard, December 1975 and September 1976, West Hartford, Connecticut

Bernard Heringman, September 1976, Moorehead, Minnesota

J. Tansley Hohmann, August 1976, West Hartford, Connecticut

Joyce Horner, May 1977, South Hadley, Massachusetts

Mary Jarrell, January 1978, Greensboro, North Carolina

Coy Johnston, June 1977, Atlanta, Georgia

Frank Jones, July 1976, Seattle, Washington

Mary Kennure, March 1976, West Hartford, Connecticut

Hazel Kuhnly, June 1976, Vernon, Connecticut

John Ladish, December 1975, September and November 1976, West Hartford, Connecticut

Stephen Langton, September 1976 and January 1977, Bloomfield, Connecticut

Arthur Laws, June 1977, Atlanta, Georgia

Peter Lee, October 1977, Honolulu, Hawaii

Harry Levin, October 1976, Cambridge, Massachusetts

Josephine M., May 1978, Middletown, Connecticut

Louis Martz, July 1976, New Haven, Connecticut

Elva McCormick, August 1976, Manchester, Connecticut

Alan McGee, May 1977, Granby, Massachusetts

Elias Mengel, January 1978, Washington, D.C.

Helen Church Minton, January 1980, Glen Cove, New York

Frederick Morgan, October 1977, New York, New York

Samuel French Morse, June 1976, Milton, Massachusetts

Dr. Louie Newton, June 1977, Atlanta, Georgia

Charles O'Dowd, June 1976, West Hartford, Connecticut

John O'Loughlin, May 1976, Hartford, Connecticut

Elder Olson, September 1976, Chicago, Illinois

Arthur Park, July 1976 San Francisco, California

Arthur Polley, June 1976, West Hartford, Connecticut

Margaret Powers, July 1976, Portland, Oregon

James Reik, June 1978, Hartford, Connecticut

José Rodríguez Feo, August 1978, Havana, Cuba

Kurt Roesch, March 1976, New Canaan, Connecticut

John Rogers, June 1976, Manchester, Connecticut

Paul and Constance Saintonge, May 1977, South Hadley, Massachusetts

I. L. Salomon, April 1976, New York, New York

John Sauer, March 1977, Reading, Pennsylvania

Herbert Schoen, October 1976, Hartford, Connecticut

Joan Sesnick, December 1976 and January 1977, New York, New York

Mary Catharine Sesnick, January 1977, New York, New York

Anthony Sigmans, January and February 1976, West Hartford, Connecticut

James Thrall Soby, January 1977, New Canaan, Connecticut

Donald Stanford, November 1979, Baton Rouge, Louisiana

Anna May Stevens, August 1979, Reading, Pennsylvania

Richard Sunbury, March and April 1976, West Hartford, Connecticut

James Johnson Sweeney, December 1976, New York, New York

Wilson Taylor, July 1976, Menlo Park, California

Leslie Tucker, February 1977, Lighthouse Point, Florida

Hazel Vail, February 1978, Hartford, Connecticut

Arlene Van Raalte, September 1976, West Hartford, Connecticut

Byron Vazakas, August 1976, Reading, Pennsylvania

Edward Weeks, October 1976, Boston, Massachusetts

Paul Weiss, March 1976 and May 1977, Washington, D.C.

Glenway Wescott, April 1979, New York, New York

Monroe Wheeler, April 1979, New York, New York
Richard Wilbur, October 1976, Middletown, Connecticut
Harry Williams, September 1976, Hartford, Connecticut
Jane MacFarland Wilson, July 1976, Los Osos, California

Index

About the Author

PETER BRAZEAU, who received his Ph.D. in English at the University of Connecticut, is associate professor of English at St. Joseph College in West Hartford, Connecticut. His articles on Stevens have been widely published. Dr. Brazeau received grants from the American Council of Learned Societies, the National Endowment for the Humanities, the Ingram Merrill Foundation and other institutions for his work on this book. He is working on a related book about T. S. Eliot.